Pursuing Idealism through Civil Service

Memories of an Administrator and a Trainer

P.R. Dubhashi

SHIPRA

Price: Rs. 700, US$ 35

ISBN : 81-7541-291-7

First Published in India in 2007

Pursuing Idealism through Civil Service

Published by :
SHIPRA PUBLICATIONS
115-A, Vikas Marg, Shakarpur, Delhi-110092 (India)
Tel. : 91-11-1165277210, 22500954, Fax : 91-11-22458662
Email : info@shiprapublications.com
www.shiprapublications.com

Dedicated to

The Revered Memory of My Mother

Indira

Contents

CHAPTER 1

Prologue

Who should write their autobiographies and memoirs or accounts of their lives and careers? Those whose accounts people would like to read, about whose lives people are curious and interested, those who have been in the lime-light, those who have left their foot prints on the sands of time.

Who would fall in this category? Statesmen and politicians, thinkers and authors, actors and actresses and sports people. Mahatma Gandhi and Jawaharlal Nehru were the most important public figures of India in the twentieth century. Both wrote their autobiographies. They cover the earlier period of their life. Both have become classics. They became a source of inspiration to people of all the countries in the world fighting for freedom. Amongst the statesmen of the Western World were Winston Churchill and Charles De Galle, both intrepid fighters, who became outstanding war leaders of their countries during World War II. Amongst the thinkers was Bertrand Russell whose books nourished the minds of generations of people with his rational thinking on a variety of aspects of life and whose autobiography in several volumes has become an enduring work.

Should Civil Servants write their Accounts?

Compared with such personalities, the lives of civil servants may appear to be almost insignificant. Very few of them are well known public figures. Their professional code of conduct requires them to be anonymous backroom boys and girls. But that does not mean that the accounts of their careers should not be written or read. The statesmen may soar in the sky but the civil servants are firmly planted on the ground. The civil servants are the ones who deal with the knitty gritty of administration, which affects the lives of people.

Legacy of the ICS

The civil servants in India have played a particularly significant role in the life of the nation. The ICS was the creation of the British Colonial rule. It established a name for itself as an outstanding civil service. It came to be known as the "steel frame" of the imperial rule. A handful of ICS officers were able to carry out the administration of a country inhabited by millions of people and gave a sense of solid strength and stability to the colonial rule. In the beginning the ICS officials were British, but in later years, more and more Indian were selected and were able to join the hallowed ranks of the heaven born service.

Free India saw the end of the colonial administration but the ICS was not wound up. Most of the British ICS officers left after India attained independence. Most Muslim ICS officers opted for Pakistan. Those ICS officers who remained in India had to serve the same political leaders whom they had jailed during the freedom struggle. Would they be allowed to continue after freedom? Jawaharlal Nehru, the first Prime Minister of free India, did not have kind things to say about ICS whom he described as "Neither Indian, nor Civil nor Service." Despite this assessment he not only put up with the officers of the ICS but allowed them to hold significant positions in administration. Indian constitution accepted the model of Parliamentary Democracy with a permanent civil service who would continue to serve the Government despite the changes of political party in power. In the first phase of Indian democracy the same party continued in power for several years both at the Centre and in the States. How did the ICS adjust to the new phase in their career in a new environment? Very well indeed. In the traumatic events of partition which accompanied independence, the experience of the ICS officers proved to be of great use to the Indian leaders who were great public figures but had no direct experience of administration. Sardar Patel, the administrator amongst the political leaders was greatly appreciative of the services rendered by the ICS. In making a case for the continuation of the permanent service, particularly the All India and Central Services, in independent India, he stated on the floor of the Constituent Assembly that "in loyalty, patriotism, commitment to the nation and devotion to duty, they (ICS officers) are not inferior to us". They rendered invaluable service to the nation in the critical time of the early years of independence.

The ICS officers thus got the best of both the worlds. They got the perks, perquisites and prestige during the imperial rule and after independence rapid promotions in the vacancies caused in the higher echelons of Indian administration by the exit of British and Muslim officers. Though some ICS officers did have difficulties in dealing with the new "native" rulers, most of them adjusted well to the new relationships and requirements.

The Birth of All India and Central Services

Sardar Patel established the IAS and IPS as successors to ICS and IP. The first All India Competitive examination for IAS and allied services after independence was held in 1948 to produce the first batch of IAS. The early batches were small and therefore more selective. Though the IAS did not have the salaries of the ICS and their perks, they were even more privileged than the ICS—they had the honour of starting their careers as the servants of the Indian Republic, not a colonial power. What could be more inspiring then serving one's fellowmen in administrative positions where their work would make a difference to the lives of the people? The atmosphere in the early years after independence in administration as in the country as a whole was surcharged with the soaring idealism of the Prime Minister Jawaharlal Nehru. The legacy and the moral influence of Mahatma Gandhi and of the great national leaders who preceded him were still a living reality. New plans and programmes were being chalked out for development of the nation. Being a part of the administration which was engaged in these task was indeed an elevating experience. The cynicism of self centred politicians and administration had yet to set in. I belonged to one of the early batches (1953) of IAS.

Memoirs of ICS and IAS Officers

Many ICS officers wrote their memoirs—the senior amongst them with longer experience under the British rule and the younger ones with much less and more under the Indian republic. Amongst the former, the most prominent would be Shri C.D. Deshmukh who had the extraordinary privilege of breaking out of the service limitations and being selected by the British as the first Indian Governor of the Reserve Bank of India and later (for the same reason of his extraordinary ability) by the first Prime Minister of free India Jawaharlal Nehru as the Finance Minister. One would have expected that for generations of administrators Deshmukh's autobiography "The Course of My Life" would be a guiding star. Actually, it turned out to be quite a pedestrian document—dry and insipid. Deshmukh thought it necessary to mention the marks he obtained in every paper in the entrance exam of ICS. One also learns that despite ICS officers like Deshmukh being members of the heaven born service, the Indians were denied membership of clubs exclusively meant for British officers! In C.D. Deshmukh's account one gets little flavour of the change in the ecology of administration after independence.

Another ICS officer who recounted his several years of service during the colonial times was Shri S.K. Kripalani (*Fifty Years with the British*, Oriental Longman 1993). Kripalani joined the ICS in 1922. He thus served the British government for a period of 25 years. His service under the government of independent India was comparatively much shorter. Kripalani belonged to Diwan community in Sind, which acquired the general title *amil*—(i.e., officers because of their flair for administration). His elder brother was also a member of ICS in Bombay cadre and served as Chief Secretary. S.K. Kripalani joined Punjab Cadre. In the first few years of service, he served in several positions in the districts. The English Deputy Commissioner of Lyalpur, his first district, did not leave a pleasant impression on him. He was put up in a dak bungalow and had to wait for two days to meet him in office. He found fault with Kripalani for mixing too much with natives. Fortunately his successor to the post, also an Englishman, was a better person and invited him to stay at his house. Kripalani gives a picture of criminal justice administration of those days when the executive was not separated from the judiciary. The magistrates based their decision on outside knowledge and beating bad characters was considered essential for maintaining law and order. The entire district administration reeked in graft, which was considered customary. The ICS officers were free from bribery and corruption. However villages had to pay for all the clerks and orderlies accompanying high officers on tour. After several years as Assistant Commissioner, he became Deputy Commissioner of the district. He was posted in charge of Revenue Settlement in Lyalpur District to handle land revenue settlement operations. He extensively toured on horse back and introduced an innovation in fixing scales of revenue which went up and down according to rise and fall of agriculture prices. After introduction of dyarehy, nation building activities and rural reconstruction became a part of District Administration. The programmes included vocational education, rural employment and cooperative movement. Kripalani reached the top position of Financial Commissioner in Punjab. He specialized in the task of colonization of newly irrigated districts of Punjab. After independents he moved to Delhi, the seat of government of India, where he was posted as Secretary in the newly created post-partition department of rehabilitation and had to undertake the arduous and even painful task of rehabilitating lakhs of refugees from across the border. A full-fledged programme of rehabilitation of refugees was organized. The members of Kripalani's own family suffered in a tragic way but Kripalani took it in an objective way and did not do anything special for his own kith and kin. Later he severed abroad as Indian High Commissioner in Canada but sought premature retirement from ICS in 1950.

Dharma Vir, is another ICS officer who has written the memoirs (*Reminiscences*, Vikas Publishing House, 1990). The proximity to Jawaharlal Nehru helped him to rise to the position of Cabinet Secretary apart from being earlier the Indian Ambassador in Czechoslovakia. Nehru's daughter Indira Gandhi appointed him as Governor of West Bengal where he clashed with the communists and thereafter as Governor of Karnataka from which post he was unceremoniously removed when he fell foul with the headstrong Prime Minister for making a statement which smacked of some sort of self-assertion on the part of a Governor. Dharma Vir was a representative of ICS officers who easily adjusted to the new rulers of Independent India. He did not carry the hangovers of the imperial rule. He recalls how even during the British rule he had a soft corner for the national leaders. Dharma Vir's account shows little involvement with development work in post independence India. He was placed in charge of the Ministry of Rehabilitation as Secretary of the Department and later appointed as Cabinet Secretary and Governor of two State, *viz.* West Bengal and Karnataka.

Nor does the account of Shri B.K. Nehru "Good Guys Finish Second" shows any involvement in development work at the field level. He worked as Secretary in-charge of the Department of Economic Affairs and later became for several years India's Ambassador to USA during which period he developed a close rapport with American President John F. Kennedy. However, despite his presence in USA the visit of the Prime Minister Jawaharlal Nehru, his uncle, proved to be a disappointment. A notable feature of his career was his closeness to Morarji Desai, the Finance Minister in his uncle's cabinet—so different in his personality from Jawaharlal Nehru, and his animosity to V.K.K. Menon who was his uncle's favourite.

In contrast are the memoirs of Shri B. Sivaraman under the title "Bitter Sweet". It might lack the élan and grace of B.K. Nehru's menoirs but it is rich in his account of deep involvement in development work in post-independence India. Sivaraman became a legend for his work as Development Commissioner, Chief Secretary of Orissa and later as Secretary in the Union Ministry of Agriculture when Shri C. Subramaniam was the Minister of Agriculture who initiated the new agricultural policy which ushered in the green resolution and liberated India from the scourge of food deficiency, hunger and dependence on imports for all time. It shows Sivaraman's innovative approach whether in introducing nutrition programme for school children in Orissa or harnessing commercial banks for agricultural and rural credit. But even such a development-oriented civil servant had his brushes with petty political intrigues in Orissa. That is the reason why in the title of Sivaraman's memoirs the words "bitter, sweet" appear. Those bitter experiences of dealing with self-centred politicians were bound to intensify in later years and create difficulties for IAS officers as they came to occupy higher positions in administration.

Shri B.G. Deshmukh (IAS 1951) has recently published his memoirs (*A Cabinet Secretary Looks Back,* 2004) He had little experience of working on post-independence development programmes in rural areas and yet he rose to the highest positions in Indian Administration, *viz.* Cabinet Secretary and Secretary to the Prime Minister. His real field experience was as Municipal Commissioner, Bombay, besides serving for several years as Secretary to Chief Minister, Shri Vasantrao Naik. This enabled him to develop political contacts and a flair for working with politicians in power which might account for his elevation to the highest administrative positions. However, even in those high positions that he held, he was not able to protect the Prime Minister from the calumny of the Bofors scandal or the misadventure in Sri Lanka which ultimately culminated in the tragic assassination of Rajiv Gandhi at a young age. Obviously, holding high positions does not mean ability to prevent administrative blunders.

Dr. Madhav Godbole's memoires (1959 batch—Maharashtra Cadre; "Unfinished Innings", Oriental Longman, 1996) is a pertinent illustration of the dilemmas of the upright civil servant, the problems he has to face and the ignominy he has suffer at the hands of scheming and over-bearing politicians. He was summarily removed from the position of Chairman of State Electricity Board while on leave for defying the Minister who wanted to have a say in the contracts given by the Board. He was Shri Shankarrao Chavan's favourite. The latter was Home Minister and got Godbole appointed as Home Secretary. Godbole found that his position was by no means a bed of roses. Chavan's junior Shri Rajesh Pilot, the Minister of State indulged in the strange behaviour of one up-manship and humiliated Godbole for neglecting the cobwebs in the corridors of the North Block! But his darkest hour came when the Babri Mosque was demolished on 6th December 1992 and he was blamed when the real fact was that the Prime Minister, Shri P.V. Narasimha Rao wanted to stand still and do nothing. Chavan later denounced Rao for his do-nothing attitude. Godbole says that he had deployed the paramilitary forces who could have prevented the unfortunate demolition and had personally even advised the Prime Minister but though the latter was nice to him he did nothing and Godbole's unfinished innings ended when he prematurely retired.

Clever civil servants could manage to get the blessings of rival politicians as affairs in the memories of Niteesh Sengupta, (IAS 1957, West Bengal Cadre), "Inside the Steel Frame – Reminiscences and Reflections of a Former Civil Servant", Vikas Publishing House, 1995. He was favoured both by Shri Jyoti Basu, the Communist Chief Minister of West Bengal and Shri Rajiv Gandhi, the Prime Minister. His case shows that civil servants, now a days, have to have political savvy; mere professional integrity and competence would not do. With this trait even after retirement Sengupta could get elected to Parliament under the banner of Trinmul Congress. But for the wavering attitude of his patron Mamta Banerji, he could have managed to get a place in the Indian Cabinet.

T.S.R. Subramanian (Uttar Pradesh Cadre, 1961) has (Journey through Babudom and Netaland – Governance India, 2004) given a graphic account of administrative career spanning over thirty-seven years. It shows that in recent years there has been a steep fall in the norms and standards of public administration and idealism has completely disappeared because of the unholy alliance between power hungry politicians and their self-serving pliant bureaucrats. In Subramaniam's words "the innards of the administrative system have crumbled." The politicians are interested only in grabbing and retaining power and have no concern for either development or people's welfare. The ambitious self-serving civil servant are after furthening their on careers and getting cushy and creamy positions in India and abroad by falling at the feet of their political patrons. No wonder sound policy making is scarified at the alter of populism; crores of rupees set apart for development schemes are wasted; subsidies mean for poor people are siphoned off; power of allotment of scarce commodities were systematically misused during the era of "license permit raj" to make private fortunes. Corruption became rampant and so also nepotism. Recruitments, placements and postings are not made on the basis of objective criterion but purely on the basis of subjective considerations. Administrative climate has deteriorated and there is no discipline or commitment to work and performance. Administration has gone beyond redemption and all attempt for administrative reforms fail. Honest and upright civil servants who try to do the right have to bear the risk of confrontation with powerful elements who can get them into trouble—though Subramanian himself was fortunate to rise to the position of chief secretary in Uttar Pradesh and Cabinet Secretary at the Centre. Politicians in power cannot alone be blamed. Sometimes they can be fairer and more considerate than nasty and vindictive superiors in the civil service. No wonder all the generates a sense of cynicism as is exhibited in the "laws" of public administration with which Subramanian concludes his accounts *viz.* (1) administration is conducted for the benefit of administration, (2) in the conflict between private interest and public interest, the former shall prevail, (3) the country belongs to the haves and the have notes do not exist, (4) a public servant's work output and rewards are inversely related.

My Own Account

In my own career in the IAS (which I could complete, without leaving it unfinished), I did came into contact with many politicians but could never get near them and get their patronage because of my insistence on an independent posture as required by the doctrine of political neutrality. But Indian administrative system after independence soon started reflecting the traits of our political culture—the feudal culture of patronage and "chamchagiri" ingrained in our society. Shri B.K. Nehru, in his autobiography, has praised the colonial rulers for leaving behind the legacy of sound administration based on fairness to all. But for us personal loyalties are more important than fairness. No wonder that at the last and the most critical phase of my administrative career, I had to pay the price of my independence by getting marginalized though not actually suffering the ignominy of being punished.

But the accounts of civil servants are not to be read for their contacts with politicians in power and juicy anecdotes about these relationships with them. An administrative career standing on its own can have much to say about the goals of administration, particularly in the context of development, the plans and programmes designed to pursue the goals and objective of development, the organizational set up and human resources development. My career, covering work at all the levels of administration of State and Central level Governments was quite rich in that respect though I do not have many juicy anecdotes to narrate about politicians arising out of close and intimate relationship.

Should I then place on record an account of my administrative career? Would the readers be interested? It is true that we as a nation do not have a flair for administration. In our long history, we have produced many poets, philosophers, craftsmen and musicians but not many administrators, nor many histories chronicling the administrative achievements. Even our great sculptors have remained anonymous. In our long history, we have had few administrators and have little information about their administrative work. We have Ashoka's edicts but do not know much about his administrative system. Chanakya's "Arthshastra" is perhaps the only work on administration and statecraft. Among the few administrators in India's long history may be mentioned Sher Shah Suri, Akbar and his Revenue Minister Raja Todarmal and Shivaji, the founder of Maratha kingdom in the teeth of opposition of Delhi rulers and local Muslim sultanates. But in our history, more attention is paid to battles fought and won by them rather then their administrative work.

We should make up for our shortcomings and take greater interest in administration. The standard of governance in India is steeply falling but we pay greater attention to politics than administration. We should, therefore, welcome all narrations of administrative work for what it is worth. I have no doubt that in the perspective of history of post-independence India, such narratives would have a place.

Throughout my career, I was continuously writing and publishing papers on various aspects of administration. These made many of my colleges debunk me as an "academician" though I could claim that as an administrator the "academic" aspect was a help rather then a hindrance. I firmly believe that thought should be preliminary to action and my approach of reading about the subject I was called upon to handle and writing on administration based on reflection and experience was meant to set up a new administrative tradition. I realize that my efforts were too meager to set up a new trend of "thinking administration."

After I took over as Director of Indian Institute of Public Administration in 1981. I thought of beginning to write my memoirs. I wrote the first page and stopped at that. The idea of working on a Ph.D. thesis came to my mind and that engaged me. By the time, I completed and got Ph.D., my tenure was over. I joined as Secretary (Co-ordination) in the Cabinet Secretariat and continued to write papers but did not touch the project of writing memoirs. I retired from IAS but soon took over as Vice-Chancellor, Goa University. I was immersed in that work for five years. After laying down that office, I wrote an account of my five years tenure and brought it out in the form of a book "Building of a New University" (Allied Publishers).

When I was working as VC, Goa University, Shri Prakash Tandon, who was Chairing the Board of Management of a business establishment in Goa called on me and suggested that I should write my memoirs not as dry as dust account of administrative events but against the larger background of Socio-political picture as he had done while writing his own account. That was certainly a very stimulating advice. But I could not immediately take to writing my memoirs. It was only after completing my account of work as VC, Goa University, that I took to writing about my administrative career.

This has no doubt delayed the account. My juniors in IAS like Godbole and Sengupta have already come out with their readable accounts. But better late than never. I am, therefore, placing before the readers an account of my service in IAS for what it is worth.

I kept brief diaries in my service years but when it came to writing, I relied on memory rather than the script. I was more interested in giving a broad account than specific details, which may not be of any interest to the readers.

I have given the title to my autobiography "Pursuing Idealism through Civil Service-Memoirs of an Administrator and Trainer." Cynically minded people may debunk the title as pretension but for me it is a genuine description of my sincere career in the Indian Administrative Service.

CHAPTER 2

Choice of the Administrative Career

I did not become an administrator by choice.

The choice of a person's career is governed by many facts – by the accident of birth (i.e., circumstances of the family in which he is born), the opportunities available to him, the course of his education and the ideals, if any, that inspire him and the dreams of future life that he has. Most of the time, in an environment of limited choice, the career is simply forced on an individual by his circumstances.

I was born in a middle class family in our sense of the term. My father was a graduate in Agriculture and had his education in the College of Agriculture, Poona. He joined the Department of Agriculture of the Government of Bombay. He was deeply frustrated in service where he found that no amount of sincere service and dedicated work would bring any advancement of career. There was complete stagnation. He had several achievements to his credit, e.g., he was the first Superintendent of Modibag gardens and ran it as a profitable project. As superintendent of the vegetable extension scheme during the years of world war II, he pioneered the growth of cabbage, cauliflower and other "western" vegetables on a large scale. However, all these were of no avail and he was deeply frustrated in service.

However, he wanted his sons to achieve what he could not, and he was prepared to make any sacrifices to make this possible. He was blessed by four sons; my elder brother Ratnakar born on 29th March 1926, myself on 7th March 1930 and my younger brother Arvind on 3rd August 1932. His fourth son Prakash was born much later on 2nd October 1944 three sons he used to say with pride and hope, were his greatest assets, and he had dreams for their future life. His first son he wanted to be Collector (he turned out to be an Engineer), his second son he wanted to be Barrister and his third a Doctor.

He thought of me for the barrister's career because of my proclivity, which he noticed from early days, to be argumentative. Even my grandfather – my mother's father, noticed this and during the happy days that we spent in summer holidays in Karwar at his newly constructed house, he would fondly address me as "Barrister Saheb."

There was no reason why these expectations could not have been fulfilled. I was a keen and ambitious student. I took part in essay and elocution contests and won many prizes. And I stood first in the matriculation examination of the Bombay University in 1946 to the lasting pride of myself and my father.

I was in Karwar for the summer holidays when the results of my matriculation examination were announced. For the entire day, I did not know my fate since a telegram expected from my father had not reached us. I was confident about my performance. However, it was only two days later that when the full mark sheet reached the Head Master of the Government School, Karwar, by post that to his and every body else's amazement (but not to my surprise), it was seen that I was probably topping the list of the entire Bombay Province. Soon this was confirmed with my father's arrival from Poona the same night.

The event created great enthusiasm in the people of Karwar. I had never studied there, I was not a student from Karwar. But I belonged to Karwar and that was enough. Some leading people from the town took the initiative and arranged a function to offer felicitations. Replying to them, I thought, I should say a few words about the future career I had in view. Already under the influence of my father's expectation and my grand father's mode of address to me, I said that I wanted to be another Bhulabhai Desai, a foremost lawyer of the country.

But man proposes and God disposes, and so the events and the course of my life took a different turn. I took the arts course and after the Intermediate Examination, I took Economics and Political Science because I thought that the subjects interested me. After a year in the arts course my father started having second thought since everybody told him that the future lies with science and a good student like me should have jointed the science course. But I was interested in history and human affairs and so I did not agree to change the horse in the midstream.

There was an interesting event in relation to this. My father's anxiety regarding my joining the Arts course could not keep him quiet. He made me write to Mahatma Gandhi and Jawaharlal Nehru seeking their advice. I was somewhat reluctant because I felt that these great persons would hardly be expected to find time to give advice in such a matter to a student even though he might have topped the list of the matriculation examination of a leading University like Bombay. However, he himself dictated the letter which I wrote in my hand and signed. It is rightly said that it is the biggest persons who find time for everything. It is the one with little to do, who find it difficult to find time for anything. A reply came in Hindi form Raj Kumari Amrit Kaur which curtly told me that "this is not a matter in which you should seek Bapu's advice." But the prompt reply which came from Jawaharlal Nehru was very positive. Nehru was already the head of the interim Government at the Center and was obviously very busy. But he found time to give a very positive and decisive advice which was "Once you set your hand to the plough, do not look back". So this was the advice which I really followed.

I chose Politics and Economics for my degree, which I obtained from Bombay University. For my M.A. from Poona University I took all the eight papers in Economic. I had the good fortune of being the student of Prof. D.R. Gadgil for my postgraduate course. He taught the theory of Value and Production Economics. But what most fascinated me was Kaynesion Economics. His "General Theory of Employment, Interest and Money" completely changed the character and content of Economics. His theory was in response to the Great Depression of 1929 which was a great setback to capitalism and laiser faire. His theory provided the basis of positive action by an interventionist state to promote employment through public investment. Compared with the somewhat humdrum micro-economics dealing with the choice of the "Economic Man", his macro-economics opened up a vast area of public policy. In my usual style, I read in original the important books written by Keynes—"Tract on Monetary Reform", Treatise of Money" and the "General Theory", as well as enormous literature that grew round his new theory.

I stood first in first class in my M.A. examination of Poona University in 1952. It was a crowning point in my academic career. The next logical step was to appear for All India Competitive Examination for selection to the Indian Administrative Service. The IAS was set up as a successor to the ICS which was called a heaven-born service. The IAS, though in the mould of the ICS but without the high salary and perquisites of the ICS and the authority and prestige in a colonial state, had never the less great attraction because it was the best opportunity then offered by the newly Independent India to young people to serve the nation and translate the long felt hopes and aspirations of people into reality.

I myself did not feel very enthusiastic about the service. Left to myself, I would have liked to be an economist. Indeed as I was completing my degree, I had written to the Cambridge University for Tripos in three subjects – Political Economy, Political Science and Philosophy. I was admitted at the prestigious Trinity College where no less a person than Jawaharlal Nehru had studied. After my admission, telegrams after telegrams came from the Indian High Commission in London asking me to join since admission to the Trinity College was a rare opportunity. But ultimately, I did not join. Father suggested that I complete my M.A. examination first. He must have reasons – not the least being monetary. In those days scholarships were not readily available. The British Council had not started its scholarship programme. The entire expenditure including on travel, stay and fees would have to be borne by the candidate. If I had joined Trinity, the course of my life would have been different.

As soon as I passed my M.A. with flying colours, I applied to the UPSC to appear for the IAS and other All India and Central Service examinations. My M.A. results were declared in June and the examinations were in August. There was hardly any time left for preparation. Nowadays students are asked to prepared for these examinations even while studying for their degree but I had made no such advance preparation. There was no idea in my mind at all to join the civil service; so the question of preparing in advance did not arise. In those days, there were no coaching classes in Pune for the purpose and I had to be on my own.

The structure of examination in those days was different from what it is now as a sequel to the recommendations of the Kothari Committee. A candidate had to offer papers in three subjects in addition to Essay and General Knowledge. Moreover for candidate aspiring for the IAS and the IFS, two advanced papers had to be given – thereby indicating the higher standard set for these two services. With my academic background, I took the basic examinations in Economics, Political Science and World History while for the two advanced papers, I took Economics and Political Theory. With my recent success in M.A., I had not much to do by way of preparation to make for Economics Theory though as I realized later, for problems of Indian economy, I could have prepared myself better. I had read extensively in Politics for my degree examination. I had read all the books by Harold Laski. But looking at the nature of the syllabus, I had to do additional reading and read the books suggested by my teacher Prof. Kogekar. World History was a subject, which I had never studied at the college. I had studied Economic History for my degree but not general history. I had left study of history after the school –level which was hardly an adequate preparation or background for a paper in world history in a competitive examination. But I was fascinated by the subject and wanted to read it in any case. Prof. Dixit, teacher of history at the Fergussion College whom I had known as a student, suggested half a dozen books, which I thoroughly read with great interest. Thus, the preparation for IAS rather than an imposition or an exercise was for me an interesting academic pursuit. For General Knowledge, I bought a copy of huge Mohan's encyclopaedia readily available in the market and diligently went through it. For the essay, my regular reading of the Times of India could be helpful in addition to the general reading.

The examination had to be given at Bombay since Pune had no center. Fortunately, my brother was serving in Bombay and had a flat in Santa Cruz. The examination was in C.J. Hall. So I had to commute a long distance to appear for the examination. Fortunately, locals in those days were not overcrowded. Moreover, my brother escorted me to examination hall, which was a great help because I was not familiar with the big city. Catching the local on right time was important. Otherwise, I could be late. Actually, on one occasion I was just in time. The invigilator had already started distributing the paper.

The examinations generally passed off well and I was happy to receive the invitation from UPSC to appear for the viva on December 24, 1952. I was new to Delhi though I had visited it once as a student on my way to Banaras Hindu University where I had gone to participate in an All India Elocution competition. In Delhi too, I had a local host. My maternal aunt was staying there and her husband was good enough to leave me at the Dholpur House where the office of UPSC was located. I was not particularly well prepared for the viva which had an important place in the selection process. Unlike at present, when marks in viva are only for minimum qualification, the marks 300 in all counted for determining the rank. In Pune, Wrangler Paranjapye and other senior persons like Justice B. S. Dhavle and scientist Principal Agharkar met aspiring students once a week and carried on conversations in English. Prof. Paranjapye would bring a copy of the "New Statesman and Nation" and make us read an article. Any mistake in pronunciation would be promptly corrected. A discussion in English would be held on the content of the article. Apart from the help this could have given for the appearance at viva, this company of benign elders was always a blessing.

Delhi, like the whole of North India, is very cold for Southern people. My father had got stitched for me a light woollen suit to appear for the viva but in Delhi's cold it was hardly an adequate preparation and I was almost shivering when I arrived at Dholpur House. A respectable looking elderly clerk with a huge white turban received me, checked my particulars and made me seated along with other five candidates who were to be interviewed that morning.

A candidate appearing for an interview is advised to go meticulously through the morning paper since the interviewers having gone through the same paper are inclined to ask questions relating to important news appearing in the papers. That day's morning paper carried on interesting news—the marriage of the Finance Minister C.D. Deshmukh, with Smt. Durgabai (a member of the Planning Commission) with their photos side by side. For us, not in the know of their relationship building over sometime, this was a big surprise. The handsome face of C.D. Deshmukh did not seem to match not so handsome a face of Durgabai. But their's was, as one realized later, an affinity based on common interest.

Any way, no question was asked on this important news of that morning. The Chairman of the UPSC was R.N. Banerji. He was assisted by eight other senior persons of which one face looked familiar—that of Prof. G.S. Mahajani, formerly Principal of Fergussion College, Prof. N.K. Siddhant and Shri S.B. Bapat, ICS were among the members of the panel. How should the interviewers behave with the young people that appear before them? They should put them at ease and gently draw them out. But Banerji did not believe in this theory. He appeared to be quite aggressive in his approach. His first question was why I wanted to join the IAS. My answer was quite straight forward—"to serve the nation". He felt that could not be true. Persons joined the IAS to earn a good salary, perquisites and prestige of the office. But I could not agree with him. I was brought up in the idealistic atmosphere of Poona in the days of 1942 struggle for independence. Then, the interview turned to other non-personal matters. What is a "Welfare State"? I said that the concept was that of Labour Government in UK which was providing comprehensive social security to its people as recommended by the Beveridge report. Is it right for India to be a member of the Commonwealth—especially against the background of British Imperialism against which we fought? Yes, I said, there might be advantages—economic and otherwise in joining the Commonwealth. The interview lasted about half an hour. It was followed by a group discussion—an innovation that was introduced that year. I thought I had not done too badly at the interview.

In the meanwhile, I had also applied for a job of a Research Officer in the Reserve Bank. There, I was interviewed by a panel headed by Shri B. Ramarao, ICS, Governor of the Reserve Bank. Interviews over, I waited for results.

The results for IAS and allied services came in February. They were announced on the All India Radio and published in newspapers. My name appeared high in the list of 32 candidates selected. I was selected both for the IAS and the IFS. But while applying I had given my preference for the IAS, and so the offer came to me to join the IAS. I was in two minds. IFS in those days held a glamour which, for many reasons, it has now lost—to such an extent that top ranking candidates do not even mention it as a first or second choice. Even Revenue Service appears to them to be more attractive.

About the same time, I also got the offer of the Reserve Bank to join as Research Officer. Here also I was in two minds. I thought in the Reserve Bank I could use my knowledge of Economics in a specialised manner. But here again the advice of my father and elders was categorical. There was no comparison. For IAS, sky is the limit. Such advice was the result of optimism generated in the early years after independence. The British officers in the ICS having left and Muslim Officers (except one) having migrated to Pakistan, the remaining Indian officers could rapidly rise in service and occupy high positions in early life. The names of officers like H. M. Patil, C.C. Desai, HVR Iyengar often figured prominently.

I expressed my hesitation in joining the IAS to elders like Principal R.P. Paranjpye and Prof. D.G. Karve, I told them that I would prefer an academic career. Paranjpye said that after joining the IAS, I would find it quite interesting. D.G. Karve said that S.G. Barve, one of his students who was in the ICS had also expressed his reluctance but was now doing very well.

So without much enthusiasm with which young people celebrated their selection for the IAS, I decided to joint it. I cannot say that I had full understanding of the implications of a life long career in the service.

Soon after my selection, I received a letter asking me to join the IAS Training School at Metcalfe House in Delhi, as a probationer for one year initial training. I joined it on April 14, 1953. Thus started a new phase in my life at the age of 23.

CHAPTER 3

Training at Metcalfe House

Grooming of an Administrator

Training—Then and Now

On 14th July 1953, I joined the IAS Training School at Metcalfe House situated in Old Delhi on the banks of the Yamuna. The school was later transformed into the National Academy of Administration and shifted to Charlville, Mussorie. This was not just a change in location but transformation of an institution. On the recommendations of the Kothari committee report, the Institution started providing an integrated initial programme of training not just to new recruits of the IAS but also, at the same time, to the probationers of all other All India and Central Services. The idea was to break the exclusiveness of the IAS at the time of an initial induction and promote inter-service understanding. The character of training course also changed. A sandwich pattern of training was introduced which meant that after field training, the candidates would come back for a final top up. Consequently the period of probation was extended from one year in our time to two years now. How far these changes have proved to be beneficial should be assessed.

One result of the change was obvious. The institution and the numerical strength of the participants became much bigger. In our time, the intake for every IAS batch was small. Ours was perhaps one of the smallest of batches. There were just twenty-seven of us in the IAS and five for the IFS. Later, the number of recruits became much larger. For all the services put together; the number could be several hundreds. Making physical arrangements for all of them and handling a common training programme for all of them, itself became a task of large proportions. Class training was turned into mass training. Having later become a life-long trainer, I could not help feeling that training requires an atmosphere of intimacy and closeness and not of distance and remoteness which is inevitable when the number of participants is very large.

Another basic change has been the relaxation of age limit for the candidates appearing for the IAS. The case for relaxation of the age limit was that for the candidates from rural areas and belonging to backward classes, the process of education began late and might even be prolonged. The age limit of 23, in our time could be all right for candidates from middle class families in urban areas, but not for other categories mentioned above and for them, the age limit was extended from time to time, specially for those from SC & ST. This was quite contrary to the earlier theory of "catch them young" Also, earlier only three chances were allowed for appearing the entrance examination. Now more chances are given. As a result now one comes across many more mature candidates who are not just out of the college and the University but already have some experience of service. The habits and attitudes of such candidates have already formed and to that extent training could have lesser impact on them. There could be a case for reducing the age limit and reducing the number of chances. But this would prove difficult because it is our experience that relaxation once given cannot be withdrawn.

A Small Batch

In a small batch knowing each other can be an easy process. More particularly, the IFS batch consisted of just five candidates. A.K. Damodaram, Sham Sunder Nath, Alexander, Ashok Sen Chib, N.K. Jain and K. Natwar Singh. Of them Natwar Singh later became more well known. He systematically built up his proximity to Nehru family, resigned from the service, when he was Secretary in the Ministry of External Affairs and joined the Congress party to become Minister of State in Indira Gandhi Government and later in Rajiv Gandhi Government. In the UPA government which came to power in 2004, he became a Cabinet rank Minister for external affairs but had to resign when he was mentioned in the Volker report as non-contractual beneficiary of award of oil contract by Saddam Hussain regime. Damaodaram also became well known as a diplomat. He was our ambassador to Italy (I remember to have enjoyed his hospitality at that time) and in USSR; After retirement he joined the JNU as Professor of International Relations and was a frequent participant in the discussion circuit of New Delhi. He was more advanced in age than the rest of us because as a freedom fighter he was given some age concession. Like most Keralites in those days, he had a leftist background.

The IAS batch of 27 candidates was topped by S. Venkitaraman from Trivandrum University. He later became Finance Secretary, Governor of the Reserve Bank and a well known columnist on economic affairs. He was a student of mathematics but developed into an economist and finance expert.

The School Campus

The school was actually located in barracks attached to the Metcalfe House built for the air force personnel during war time. The accommodation was quite adequate for running a small school. There were one room hutments joined together in two rows. Each hutment had an independent room with a *verandah* in front and a bathroom at the back. The bathroom did not have a modern sanitary latrine but the old type commode which the sweeper cleared every day and for whom the backdoor was kept open. It is to our lasting shame that we did not protest against such arrangement and did not insist on modernization of the latrine. Perhaps even if we had protested, the change would have been difficult, needing some investment. But we did not even feel for such a change, which at this distance of time appears to me to be inexplicable. Perhaps we betrayed our smug status quo mentality of a bureaucrat even in those early days.

Beyond the residential hutments but in close proximity to them was the main building with a classroom, a lounge and a dinning hall. The mess was common and was run on a sharing basis, with both vegetarian and non-vegetarian food. The arrangements on the whole were quite simple and by no means elitistic.

Shri S.B. Bapat, ICS (West Bengal Cadre of 1930 seniority) was the Principal of the IAS school. As he often used to say, he wore three hats—Joint Secretary in the Ministry of Home Affairs, Establishment Officer and Ex-officio Principal. The day-to-day working of the school was looked after by the Vice-Principal Shri J.D. Shukla, ICS (U.P. Cadre of 1939 seniority). The full time teaching staff consisted of Barrister Munir who taught law and Bhattacharya who taught Economics and an Ex-Army person supervised physical drill.

Content of the Training Course

The limited teaching staff reflected the limited character of the content of the training course. But it must be realized that during the British days, there was no such institutional training for the ICS recruits. The recruits selected in England were placed with a British University or Institution like the School of Oriental and African Studies. The IAS training school was an innovation introduced after independence. That the recruits to administrative and other services should undergo initial and in-service training was a new concept and today such institutions have proliferated. Each service has its own school. For example the Police Service has its training institute in Hyderabad, the Revenue Services in Nagpur, the Audit and Account Services in Shimla, the Railway Services in Baroda (Vadodara) and the Secretarial Services in New Delhi. Besides, almost every state has by now set up its own Administrative Service Training Institutes, with their own buildings and establishments. To what extent such institutional training has contributed to the betterment of the quality of administration is a subject that needs investigation. The fact remains that the gap between the expectations of the people from administration and the actual performance has widened over years and training has been unable to fill up the gap

In our days the training programme was somewhat informal. The classes were held every day in the morning hours. Munir taught the Indian Penal Code, and the Criminal Procedure Code. He went clause by clause. Ratan Lal's commentary was recommended for case studies relating to each clause. Munir was a good natured old man but not particularly effective in delivery. Bhattacharya hopped from one topic to another relating to Indian economics. He did not seem to have any strict and formalised structure of teaching. He was an amiable and a shy person and not quite confident in teaching the recruits to IAS, but he stayed for long as a teacher in the school and later in the Academy and might have improved over years. The Vice-Principal Shukla taught administration by which he chiefly meant District Administration. He was a student of History and taught his subject with great relish, drawing on his experience in UP administration. His formula to describe the working of the District officer was RME – Revenue, Magisterial and Executive. His main point was that the administrator was not there to do something big or spectacular. He was there to discharge the day-to-day functions of administration effectively and without much fan fare and solve the problem of the common people. He had not much to do with the grandiose academic theories of Public Administration. In the early summer months, when we joined, he used to come to the class in white shirt and trousers without a necktie and his youthful personality was quite impressive.

Shri Bapat worked in his Government office at the Home Ministry but paid frequent visits and took classes. He had his standard gray pant and khadi bushshirt quite appropriate for the summer months. His classes were informal in nature. He invited questions and used them for extensive analysis of the various aspects of administration related to it. He had a sharp and analytical mind and was obviously an intellectual in administration. He was enthusiastic about reforms needed in the administrative system in the wake of independence and interacted with Dr. Paul Appleby, the American expert, who was then in India at the invitation of Prime Minister Jawaharlal Nehru to give his report on Indian Administration.

But more important and stimulating than the regular lectures were guest lectures and interaction with leading personalities like Dr. Paul Appleby, the American expert on Public Administration who was on a visit to Delhi. Delhi was the national capital and the hub of administration. The location of the school at Delhi facilitated these frequent interactions which is hardly possible in Masonrie which in its splendid isolation cannot be visited without long and time consuming journey. We used to hold dinners once a month where also such informal interactions could take place. I remember Penderel Moon, a British ICS officer, who chose to serve India even after Independence—he was then adviser in the Planning Commission—joining us for dinner and eliciting our views regarding the abolition of the jury system in Indian judiciary. Practicing civil servants were available to give lectures on various aspects of administration. I remember excellent talks given by Shri K.B. Lall, the then Deputy Secretary, Ministry of Commerce, specking on the export promotion programme. These lectures were much more useful than purely academic talks on public administration which is not just an academic discipline but a practising art.

Dr. B.R. Ambedkar's Visit

We had also associational activities. Once, I happened to be the secretary of the association and invited Dr. Babasaheb Ambedkar to address one evening. I remember to have gone to his house on the Alipur Road not far from the school. It was a cold evening of Delhi. Dr. Ambedkar had recently resigned from the post of Union Minister and there was no paraphernalia of office (in any case such paraphernalia was much less ostentatious in those days. There were no black cats and even Jawaharlal Nehru the Prime Minister would travel in a single white ambassador without a fleet of cars accompanying to disguise identity.) Dressed in a white shirt and pajama Ambedkar was sitting by the side of an electric heater. His wife Mai Ambedkar was sitting by his side. My friend Bapu Chowgule had accompanied me. We had the pleasure of talking with him in Marathi. He appeared like a wounded lion, frustrated and especially bitter about Nehru which somewhat upset me. He referred to Nehru's grandchildren Rajeev and Sanjay as sons of a Parsee father! observation of his, which I distinctly remember, was about changes in social equations. He predicted an alliance between the Brahmins and the depressed classes against the dominant intermediate classes, who had assumed power. Dr. Ambedkar readily accepted our invitation. I remembered to have said while welcoming him that "it was an event when Dr. Ambedkar spoke and the event was now taking place in our school". It is unfortunate that I don't distinctly remember what Dr. Ambedkar said but he talked about the Hindu code and the judicial system.

Placement with Army

Other interesting items of our training was placement with the Army on the Uri border in Kashmir, stay with IPS probationers in the Police Academy which was then located at the hill station Mount Abu, which was then in Gujarat, stay at the Forest Research Institute in Dehradun and Bharat Darshan. The Army placement was for about a fortnight. After visiting Army Command Centre at Baramullah where we had tea and briefing from Lt. Colonel Hazarika, the Commanding officer, we stayed in bunkers with an Army Subedar and his Jawans at the border post 6092 from where we could readily see the Pakistani soldiers and Pakistani Army position beyond the border. What I distinctly remember was the bitterness the army people felt that a wrong decision was taken to abandon our advance positions when the Pakistani army was on the run. We could have vacated the Pakistani aggression from the rest of Jammu and Kashmir; instead we left an unfinished business. The tendency to leave things halfway was betrayed later too in 1965 when India entered into Tashkent Pact, vacating the hard won Haji Pir Pass and in 1971 when the whole army of 93000 Pakistani soldiers was allowed to go scot-free as per the Shimla agreement without getting anything concrete in return. The stay with the jawans created in my mind an abiding link with the army which was renewed on several occasions later especially when I became Divisional Commissioner Belgaum, which was a station for the Army and the Air Force.

With the Police Academy

The visit to Abu gave a glimpse of the police training. The IPS officers have to work closely with the IAS officers for the maintenance of law and order in the district where the IAS officer is the District Magistrate and the IPS officer, the District Superintendent of Police. The District Magistrate is supposed to be in over all charge of law and order. There was no ambiguity about it in the British days. But after independence when the police started having direct links with the politicians in power they started resenting the superior position of the District Magistrate and occasions for tension between the D.M. and the S.P. started becoming frequent, sometimes creating ugly scenes. The police officers wanted law and order to be their exclusive preserve and resented any "interference" of the IAS officer. In the British days the Collector and District Magistrate could inspect the police stations, a practice totally stopped after independence. The District Magistrate even now writes the confidential report of the SP but the DIG the superior police officer could nullify the comment of the collector. The police officers have become reluctant to appear in police uniform and salute the IAS District Magistrate or the Divisional Commissioner which they readily did in the earlier days. The police successfully introduced the system of Commissionership in major cities where the IAS District Magistrate have no place in law and order administration. The tendency of IPS officers to assume "stand off" position *vis-à-vis* IAS officer and develop close, direct links with the politicians has not been conducive to good law and order administration. On one side it has deprived the police of the benefit of a wider understanding of the situation with bearing on law and order and on the other, it has led to politicisation of the police both of which have contributed to the deteriorating law and order situation. But this aspect has not received the attention that is due to it. The Police Commission recommended greater autonomy to the police but the politicians are reluctant to give up their grip. They use the police machinery to put down their political opponents. With the criminalisation of politics, this has had disastrous effect on the law and order situation in the country.

Forest Research Institute

The visit to the Forest Research Institute introduced us to the treasure of Indian forests and an abiding love for the flora and fauna of the country. In later years preservation of environment has become a major goal not only in India but all over the world.

Visit to Bulandshahar

Once, Shukla, the Vice-Principal, took us to Bulandshahar, the district HQ in UP, not far away from Delhi to introduce us to district administration and show us the system of village revenue records like Khasra and Khatauni. The system of revenue records is intended to be records of rights of the landlords, tenants or actual cultivators, the crops grown, the extent of holding and revenue fixed for them. Though broadly on the same lines, the system of records differs from state to state. While the system was well established in Rayotwari areas like Bombay and Madras provinces, it was inadequate in Zamindari areas like Bihar and West Bangal where maintenance of such records became a matter of land reform.

Bharat Darshan

The Bharat Darshan programme was intended to open our minds to the beauty and diversity of India. We were divided into two batches one of which went to Assam and another to Rajasthan. I went to the pictursque state of Rajasthan. The visits to the lake city of Udaipur and the Pilgrim centre of Ajmer left a lasting impression on my mind. Another memorable travel was to the city of Chandigarh, the new capital of Punjab which was still under construction. Punjab had lost its pre-partitioned capital Lahore, and Chandigarh at the foot of Shivalik range was selected for the establishment of the new capital. Instead of building an old style city, an imaginative new type of city was contemplated and the work was entrusted to the famous French architect, Le Carbousier. Nehru himself took this imaginative initiative. The city was divided into twenty-seven sectors, each with its own purpose and connected with a system of wide roads and boulevards. The major structures, *viz.* High Court and the State Assembly were still under construction. We visited some of the residential buildings. A special feature of these buildings was the sun-breakers. The North Indian summer is often unbearable. The direct rays of the sun-hitting the walls makes the inside temperature unbearable. The sun breakers were a device to prevent this. Chandigarh certainly looked like the city of the future. Unfortunately Punjab was divided into three states and the capital city became a bone of contention between Punjab and Haryana. Punjab is supposed to get a central grant for building its own capital. But this is still to happen and in the meanwhile both the states are using Chandigarh as their capital. To make this possible, the city has become a central territory. The haphazard growth on the periphery has also adversely affected the unique architechural personality of Chandigarh. Such are the quirks of history. The visit to Chandigarh opened our minds to various aspects of city architecture and planning. The visit to Punjab was not possible without going to the temple of modern India – the Bhakra – Nangal project which was still under construction. A check dam was constructed to divert water to enable the construction of the main dam which was the tallest among the dams being constructed in India to exploit waters of rivers for irrigation, hydro-electric power and water supply to cities. I was really impressed by its immense proportions. Driving by road from Delhi to Punjab was a thrilling experience. On either side were vast stretches of mustard crop and its yellow tops spread like carpets of nature to welcome us. Makkki roti and sarson ka sag are the favourite dishes of Punjabis. I repeated the journey from Delhi to Chandigarh and back several times later but the first journey remains permanently etched on my mind.

Horse-Riding and Motor Mechanics

Included in the programme were two special items, *viz.*, horse riding and motor mechanics. The horse riding activity was conducted by the Delhi Police on their grounds. They introduced us to trotting and cantering, keeping the horse under control was itself very important. The wayward horse could run amuck and dethrone the rider if the rider was not firm in his seat. This often happened to the discomfiture of the rider. Once a horse bolted and took the rider straight to the stables! Horse riding, despite such mishaps, was most invigorating and enjoyable in the codmorning cod. It was expected that horse riding might be required later in the district assignment. But the times had changed and touring on the horse back had long gone out of fashion. No body kept a horse when mechanical vehicles – jeeps and cars with power of several horses had become available. However, horse training had a metaphorical significance. If one who could control a wayward horse one could control an awkward situation! I am not sure whether the metaphorical logic has any validity.

Motor mechanics training was conducted by one Mr. Basrurkar. For the training we had to go to Scindia garrage in the Connaught Place. Basrurkar introduced us to important parts and systems of the car engine – the electrical system and the fuel system. Car may stop working if the spark plugs are not clean or petrol is not flowing due to some foreign material. He showed how these problems could be handled. However since one did not actually handle the parts, one was not confident about actually conducting the operations. For a non-mechanical person like me tinkering with the car even for minor repairs was an anathema. Basrurkar did not teach car driving while introducing us to motor mechanics. Without the experience of car driving it looked very unnatural. For car driving the probationers used the services of Hari who was an institution by himself. He was given one hutment to run a general-purpose shop, which supplied all the needs of probationers. In addition, he had an old car, with which he used to teach car driving on payment of a moderate fee. Many learnt car driving in Hari's informal driving school. I was not one of them. I learnt car driving later on my father's car.

One skill which we ought to have acquired was typing. Since throughout my career, I had the services of a typist or a stenographer. I never acquired the skill which I greatly regret. On retirement, without a steno at my disposal I feel handicapped.

Another personality on the campus was the tailor—a Muslim with a small black beard. As soon as we joined we were asked to have stitched a sherwani and churhidar pajama or a Jodhpur suit. The sherwani had to be of cotton for summer and woollen for winter. They had to be worn at dinner time and on ceremonial occasions. I got stitched the sherwanis and wore them on all ceremonial occasions not only at the school but later as well. This was the dress Nehru wore which looked very impressive. But neither Sardar Patel nor Rajaji ever wore it. They went in native dhoti. At that time Nehru's attire looked right and that of Patel and Rajaji's looked odd. Now I realize it was not quite so. Churhidar pajama was not easy to wear. Moreover Sherwani was essentially a North Indian (U.P.) dress and was not in usage in Southern States. In the early years after independence we were very meticulous about dress stipulation. All civil servants and even ministers and politicians made it a point to appear in the formal dress on all ceremonial occasions like the Republic Day Parade and at homes at Rashtrapati Bhavan. This lent great dignity to the occasion. I regret that no such dress code is followed now and people come dressed any way they like, greatly detracting from the dignity and decorum of such occasions. The lackadaisical attitude about the dress code is but a part of general fall in the standards of our public functions. As probationers we were privileged to be invited to the Rashtrapati Bhavan parties on the Independence Day and the Republic Day. Mingling with the gathering of distinguished people including President Rajendra Prasad, Prime Minister Nehru, his colleagues like C.D. Deshmukh and T. Krishnamachari and ambassadors of different countries was a thrilling experience. In later life I had many occasions to attend these receptions but the thrill of those days never returned.

Visit to Teen Murti Marg

The most memorable occasion of our one year training was the visit to the Teen Murti Marg residence of Prime Minister Pandit Jawaharlal Nehru. This used to be the residence of the Commander-in-Chief during the British days. After independence, it became the residence of the Prime Minister. It was a majestic, impressive building and the person residing in the house according to our feeling was fit to occupy it, though Mahatma Gandhi whose disciple he was might have preferred him to live in a much humbler place. Actually it was Mahatma who had suggested that the Viceroy's palace should be converted into a public hospital. But after independence it was Nehru and not Gandhiji who was leading the government and independent India had no use of him in running the administration. After all King Ashoka was ruling the nation.

On the day we had our engagement with the PM in the evening. Earlier in the day we had gone to Tilpath range to witness the show of the Indian Air Force on the occasion of its twenty first anniversary marking it as a day on which IAF had come of age. The air show was most impressive. But such was the rush of vehicles on the return journey that we were late for the PM's engagement. He was seated on a sofa with Principal Bapat and was impatiently waiting for our arrival. Some of the early arrivals amongst us were sitting on the carpet in the large hall excitedly waiting for the address of the PM. PM began asking us whether we had read the book Asia and the Western Domination" by K.M. Panikkar which had just come out. PM had finished reading it and the book was in his mind. PM's address, as I realized on several future occasions when I had the benefit of listening to him, took the nature of loud thinking on whatever was uppermost in his mind. And this time it was K.M. Panikkar's historical survey of the Western domination of Asia. Taking off from that, PM made a broad survey of the contemporary scene in Asia and gave a rationale of the new policy of Non-alignment which was emerging under his leadership. PM should have spoken at least in a later part of his address on the role of administration in India, as he often did, but that subject he did not touch in his address. This was disappointing. But the very fact that we had listened to the great man at his residence was itself a matter of much gratification.

Reading on Administration

During the year at Metcalfe House there was some limited reading as well. The ICS officers had written on administration and their rare books were recommended reading. Omelley's book gave a good picture of British administration. More specifically Blunt's book on District Administration describing the role of the District Collector/Magistrate as the pivot of district administration was very instructive. But a book edited by Prof. Robson on Civil Service in Britain and France particularly impressed me. It brought out a clear difference between amateurish tradition of civil service in Britain and the professional tradition in France and I found the latter more relevant to India. Also because the administration of departments and prefects in France looked more like our district administration and the prefectoral officers more like our district officers. In later years Mitterand's reform for decentralization looked more relevant to our own Panchayati Raj system. The initial training of civil servants in France was consistent with their professional approach. They were first selected for admission to Ecole National de Public Administration and after training in scientific administration and management were sent to the field to departments or big enterprises and then brought back to the school to relate practice with theory. This was called sandwich pattern of training which after the recommendations of the Kothari Committee was introduced in India—with what effectiveness one does not know. These matters, unfortunately, are not professionally pursued in India. However I always felt impressed by the French approach and advocated it in one of my first published articles in *Modern Review* then published in Calcutta and was reported in *Asian Survey*.

Overall Impact

What was the overall impact of training at the Metcalfe house? As I have mentioned above it was the interaction with several leading figures in our administration culminating in meeting with the PM which left an abiding impact. One of the visitors to the school was Y.N. Sukhtankar, the Cabinet Secretary, who is also the "head" of the civil service. The role of the head is somewhat ambiguous and as I realized later the civil service has hardly any sense of unity and cohesion or *espri de corps* to be led by a single "head". In any case the interaction with the people at the highest echelons in administration gave a sense of confidence at the very beginning of the administrative career.

The atmosphere of the time was also very stimulating. Under Nehru's leadership, the nation looked forward with a great deal of hope and confidence. There was none of the cynicism, which developed in later years. There was absolutely no doubt that free India was destined to reach great heights and in doing that administration had to play a crucial role. Talk of planning and welfare state gave a constructive orientation to our thinking. We had to leave behind the tradition of colonial administration and develop new traditions of Indian Public Administration. IAS was not to be just a carbon copy of the ICS. It had a new role to play.

Looking at the present situation, it is sad to reflect that the early optimism and idealism was not vindicated during fifty years of Independence. And this is a subject on which those in administration should give a deep thought. But people engaged in acquisition and perpetuation of power and worried about the survival of their government have hardly any time for thought. People like Rajaji and Sardar Patel who understood the importance of good administration are no longer around. But this is skipping a span of half a century. I must go back almost fifty years.

Alloted to Mysore Cadre

The IAS is divided into cadres and I was allotted to Mysore. It was a part B State and did not belong to the tradition of British colonial administration. The Maharaja of Mysore, particularly Krishnraj Wadiyer III was known as a progressive ruler. Mysore was fortunate in having as its Dewans people like Sir M. Visveshariah and Mirza Ismail. The one gave Mysore great assets like the Krishnaraj Sagar Dam, Mysore University, Bhadravati Iron & steel and Mysore Sandal soap (examples of public sector enterprises before independence) while the other gave the Brindravan Gardens and the city planning in Mysore and Bangalore with their broad roads and parks and gardens. The first gave the functional and the other the aesthetic dimensions to administration – both important.

Allotment to Mysore meant losing the opportunity to serve in Bombay province which was my first preference. But I was not much disturbed. Mysore was a neighbouring state. The British ICS officers had come all the way leaving their home 6000 miles away and why should we of the IAS grumble to go anywhere in India – I thought.

Having learnt of my allotment to Mysore cadre, I had two things to do. First to pick up Kannada to which I was a total stranger and second know something about the state. The school had appointed part time tutors to teach probationer's languages of "their" states. I had one Prabhu working in the Central Secretariat to do the job. Since I was the only one required to study Kannada, it was one to one relationship. He came to my room after dinner and started with Zeigler's practical phrase book for learning Kannada. It was intended for foreign missionaries coming to Kannada territory for their work. The book included usages prevalent in three Kannada speaking regions, *viz.* old Mysore, Bombay Karnataka and Mangalore. It was as well I learnt this way because later Mysore was integrated with the rest of the Kannada area and acquaintance with vocabulary of different regions became very relevant. I also read Minoo Masani's "Our India" translated in to Kannada. This proved very useful later because it gave vocabulary needed for rural development administration.

I read the gazetteers to know about Mysore. I came to know that Mysore had nine districts divided into two broad regions *Maidan* (Plateau) and *Malnad* (Ghat area) – Chitradurga, Tumkur, Bangalore, Mysore and Mandya, Kolar, belonged to the *Maidan* area while Shimoga, Chikmaglar Hassan and Coorg belonged to *malnad* Coorg was a centrally administered territory merged in Mysore. While the *Malnad* area was covered with forest, and had heavy rains, *Maiden* area was a plateau but at a height of 3000 feet above sea level. Because of this altitude the Mysore State has equable climate throughout the year without extreme heat or cold Mysore had some 30000 tanks built over years which provided wide-spread facilities for irrigated agriculture. The topography of the state had ups and downs, hills and valleys and the water running into valleys was collected into a series of tanks, each with a waste weir allowing surplus water to flow down the valley to be bunded down stream. The villages were supposed to maintain these tanks through voluntary labour. It was called *Somwarad Kelsa* (Monday labour) Later I was to learn that with the weakening of the traditions, this social obligation had fallen into disuse. As local administrators would keep on saying *Somavared Kelasa* got sacrificed at the alter of *Somaritana* (laziness). I was new to Mysore and to Kannada. I had never visited either Bangalore or Mysore. My elder brother, an engineer, had once been to Bangalore as a part of his course and told me that Bangalore was like Poona where I had my up-bringing With this acquaintance, I was ready to go to my "Cadre" state.

At the end of one year of training, there was a general assessment based on examinations and general performance. I was able to improve my ranking from seventh to fourth, which meant I had done well.

What was the benefit of the one year spent at the IAS at Metcalfe House, Delhi? The training there was important not so much for the training given in law or administration as for abiding feeling that it created in our minds that India is one country and IAS officers have to serve the country as whole, not just a particular part of the country no matter to what cadre they belonged.

CHAPTER 4

Joining the Cadre – Practical Training at Bangalore

One day, I received a letter in a brown envelope just before leaving Metcalfe House. It was from K.M. Ramkrishnayya, Under Secretary, Government Secretariat, (Atara Kucheri) Bangalore asking me to report for joining the Mysore Cadre. It mentioned nothing about arrangements for my stay in Bangalore. I was a total stranger to the city and would not know where to stay. So I wrote to him asking to make arrangements. I thought there would be some government arrangement for me. I had read about the ICS officers treating the new recruit as a personal guest. But there was no such personal touch. Arrangements were made not in some Government guest house but in Modern Hindu Hotel at Anandrao Circle, Bangalore.

I took a direct train from Pune (where I had returned from Delhi on completion of stay at Metcalfe House) to Bangalore which was a long 36 hour journey on a meter gauge train via Hubli. There was no need to change the train at Miraj which has become necessary now because Pune-Miraj sector has been changed into broad gauge. This partial broad gauging has made it necessary to change the train at Miraj. I did not take the route via Gunthakal which though less time consuming, involved a change from a broad gauge to meter gauge train at Guntakal.

The "Reception" at Bangalore Station

The train arrived at Bangalore station early morning. I looked for some one to receive me. But none was to be seen. At long last an old man twitching his face all the time, clad in a lungi and a white shirt asked me for my name and said he had come from Modern Hindu Hotel to receive me.

He made me seated in a "jutka" at the station to take me to the hotel. It was a horse drawn carriage but different from a "tonga" to which I was used. In a "tonga" you could sit as on a chair but in a "jutka" you had to squat which was a strange experience. The Hotel was very near the station and even with a reluctant horse drawing the jutka, it did not take much time to reach the hotel.

Arrangements at Modern Hindu Hotel

A single room was booked for me on a monthly charge of Rs. 180 (Rs. 6 a day). The room had no attached bath-room which was a great inconvenience. The food was served in a dining hall below. The breakfast consisted of Idli and Dosa while the meals consisted of rice with sambar, Rice with Rasam and rice with curd, a three-course meal no doubt but entirely based on rice. Vegetables of two or three types, chutney, pickles and potato chips were the accompanying fare. The hotel was purely vegetarian, in fact the first purely vegetarian hotel established in Bangalore, as Ramakrishnayya told me later, at the initiative of no less a person than Diwan Visheshwaryya. A vegetarian hotel was no inconvenience to me as I was basically vegetarian in food habits but the meal served on banana leaf was something I was not used to. The liquid Rasam would often flow out of the leaf, but food on a fresh banana leaf was clearly a cleaner way of serving food than on used and washed dishes. Bath and breakfast over, I had to get ready to go to "atara Kacheri". I had no transport of my own. I inquired at the hotel as to how to go to the place. They asked me to walk to the nearby "Majestic Circle". Which was the hub of he market area from where buses left in different directions. I took the bus and reached the red building known as "Atara Kacheri", where the Mysore Government secretarial was located.

The First Sight of CM-Hanmanthiah

On arrival, I had a strange sight. Just at the entrance of the lift to the first floor two liveried peons with a mace in hand ushered in a person obviously carrying with him a lot of authority to the lift in which none else was welcome. This was K. Hanumanthiah, the "*Mukhyamartri Galu*" a plural word for a single person – the Chief Minister of Mysore. In his laced turban accompanied by two mace bearers also in local turbans, he looked more like a royalty than a democratically elected Chief Minster! It appeared that after the end of the hereditary monarchy and ushering in of democracy, the mantle of royalty had descended on the Chief Minister. The Maharaja Chamarajendra Wadiar had no doubt become the Rajpramukh, and later Governor but it was said that the Chief

Minister Hanumaniah would not hesitate to make the Rajpramukh know where in lies the real authority.

Anyway I did not take the lift but climbed up the staircase to report on time, i.e., 11 am. to the under secretary in GAD Shri KM. Ramakrishnayya, who too was wearing a laced turban but clad in a suit. But the laced turban had by no means made him overbearing. He was an elderly, kindly person with all the benignness and the calmness of a Mysore city dweller.

IAS – A New Institution in Mysore State

In these days Bangalore was an extremely quiet place – not the swanky, bustling place it had become now. The city's residential area consisted of mostly one story structures and not multi-stored buildings as in Bombay. The Atara Kacheri (eighteen offices) was itself located in the large Cubbon Park, named after Sir Mark Cubbon, the British Commissioner in Maharaja days. Mysore had a well established administrative and secretarial system but the IAS was still a newly introduced service. Before the merger of Mysore in the Indian Union it had State Civil Service and initially the members of the state service were opposed to the incursion of the IAS. But when it was decided to induct the officers of the State Civil Service in the IAS, there was the rush to get inducted in the IAS. The Union Home Minister worked a scheme for such induction and according to that scheme three lists were prepared – first, second and third according to the merit suitability and experience of officers. Those considered by the selection panel as most suitable were in the first list, less suitable in the second and even still less suitable in the third. The Civil List indicated all these gradations. Those excluded tried to get in later and this struggle to get in was an on-going process. Mysore had Mandalisation type reservation years before it was thrust on the national scene by V.P. Singh. Only a few candidates were selected on the basis of merit – the bulk on the basis of backwardness of caste. Mysore had two major non-Brahmin castes, *viz*. Vokkaligas (Peasants) and Lingayets but even the latter were divided into two groups – the urban, trading group and the rural, farmer group. The rest included several "lower" castes like the Kurubas (i.e., Shepherds) and the Dalits divided into *Yedagai* and *Balagai* (Left hand and the right hand), the *Adi Dravids* and the *Adi Karnatakas*. Every one was identified on the basis of caste and the officer caste was known even before his arrival at any post and people's attitudes to him were adjusted accordingly.

All this I came to know gradually and felt uncomfortable about it. In my upbringing in Pune. I had hardly come across such intensively caste surcharged atmosphere but as in Mysore in rest of the country too caste was a dominating consideration in politics and administration.

An Outsider

I was an outsider, indeed the first "outsider" directly recruited to IAS on the basis of competitive examination. The first direct recruit was Shri T.R. Satish Chandran, a brahmin whose father too belonged to the civil service of Mysore. He had at the end of his training, joined as Assistant Commissioner Sager in Shimog District. He was the only one of my "kind" and no wonder I took the first opportunity to write to him. His reply was prompt and warm and I could feel the "kindred spirit" in him. But he was a native of Bangalore, a "son of the soil" with a bungalow built by his father, and relatives and friends. I was an utter stranger and could feel it. I had to find my own lodging and boarding and make my own arrangements. I had rudimentary knowledge of Kannada and started using it. I could talk in Kannada without much difficulty when I realized that its vocabulary was mainly derived from Sanskrit with which I was familiar. Only the verbs were different. Kannada like the other southern languages, has its own script. Vinoba Bhave had suggested that all Indian languages may adopt *devnagari* as the common script. That would have facilitated the study of Indian languages by the other language groups but his suggestion was naver accepted.

Any way Ramkrishnayya welcomed me with friendly *Namaskara* and I reciprocated. Whenever possible I made it a point to talk to him in Kannada and he would encourage saying *Matadutta, matadutta Band Bidutte*, i.e., practice speaking in Kannada and you get it.

One-Year Practical Training Programme

Ramakrishayya give me a typed statement of the training programme chalked out for one year. It consisted of three parts, *viz.* first month long programme of visits to various secretarial departments for getting acquainted with their work, later placement with the district office—in my case Bangalore district including the Bangalore subdivision taluka and survey office and later work as magistrate in the judiciary. A visit to the Reserve Bank office in Bangalore and Madras was added later on, probably at my request.

The recollection of my training programme brings back to my mind Upamanyu Chatterji's novel "English August" which gives a fictionalized account of such training programme of newly selected IAS officer *Agasti* anglicized as "August" in a remote mofussil district. It depicts how a product of an elite college in Delhi finds himself utterly maladjusted in the suffocatingly narrow atmosphere of life of the local official, who is least interested in his training and finds a solace in sexual fantasies and indulgence. I was not a product of such an elite institution in Delhi. I was brought up in a more conservative atmosphere in Poona and conditioned to exercise moral restraint in all ways. I once felt utterly scandlised when while staying at Melcalfe House, once past midnight while fast asleep in my room with window wide open as it was summer I was rudely woken up by noisy disturbances. It was Natwar Singh a product of Cambridge who never stopped boasting his "Friendship" with E.M. Forster, the author of "Passage to India" asking me as to what I was doing with my "cock" alone in the bed. Such talk was for me shockingly indecent and I said so to which Natwar Singh response was "Would you have come into existence without your father's cock?" Such is the behaviour of people like "English August" and K. Natwar Singh products of elite institutions who suffer from a peculiar "superiority complex" to which they feel entitled as products of elite institutions. Throughout their career they tend to maintain such attitudes. They could hardly be expected to be at home with the humdrum life of the ordinary people.

Uncomfortable in Bangalore

But though I was not "English August" I cannot recall with pleasure the one-year training programme in Bangalore. I felt by and large neglected and lonely and living in Bangalore was uncomfortable despite the appellation of so called "Air conditioned" city of Bangalore in which I was living for the first time.

The single small room on the hotel without a fan was no comfort. Bangalore does become quite hot for a few days in summer. The talk of the local people that Bangalore can be a fan-less place because it was air conditioned by Nature was, I found, quite a myth. The sun in summer could burn. Rice diet for lunch and dinner all the time could also be monotonous. Above all the impersonal atmosphere of a hotel could be galling to a person brought up always in the warmth of a home. I also did not like waiting for bus and wanted to have a vehicle at my command. I soon solved the problem by buying a bicycle. I also started looking for an alternative accommodation. Here Shri S.N. Kalabhairavam, Superintendent GAD was helpful. He suggested getting a room in YMCA hostel in which I succeeded. While the change appeared for a while better (the hostel was in a quieter cantonment area) it still left me lonely and uncomfortable. For some time I stayed in the guest house of the Century Club but found it far too expensive. But let me keep aside the problem of finding comfortable lodging and boarding and return to the training programme.

Visits to Secretariat Department

I started visiting various Secretarial Departments as programmed by Ramakrishnayya. I would first meet him in his room and he would get his head out of the pile of files on his table to arrange for the day's visit. His next in command Shri Kalabhairavan, the Section Superintendent, was also on hand to help. He was quite a sophisticated person for his positron in the administrative hierarchy. He gave me an official compilation containing articles on the Secretarial method of functioning—pompous and slow moving.

My days spent in the Secretarial department were mostly uninspiring—dull and boring. Secretaries and even deputy Secretaries were always very busy and left training of the new IAS recruit to an Under Secretary. They hardly had any awareness of the background of their visitor and the purpose of training. To my great resentment they and even Ramakrishnayya referred to me as a "probationer". That hurt my "status" since I had already been declared to have successfully completed my "probation" at the end of my Training in IAS school and was a full-fledged officer. The probation period has changed now and the probation has been extended to two years, i.e., till the end of the "Sandwich" type-training programme which includes the District training. The Under Secretaries had a feeling that I was sent by centre for training to Mysore because it was a "model state". They did not realize that I had come to stay, to be an officer of the IAS Cadre of Mysore state. No wonder their attitude was quite lackadasical. They would give some general information about their department without much interest because they themselves were little interested in their own work and discharged it as a matter of routine duty. No doubt there were some exceptions like Shri N.S. Bharat in Finance Department. Bharat was a bachelor and devoted all his time to his work. In budget preparation days, he said, he would live in the Secretarial itself to attend to the work of budget preparation.

Though secretaries did not find any time for me, there was an exception—Shri G.V.K. Rao. He was youngest amongst the secretaries and held a dual charge Secretary to Local Self Government Department and Secretary to the chief minister. The latter must have been a demanding task what with the megalomania of Shri Hanumanthiah But Rao, as I saw over many years of association in later life, had a flair for human relationship, especially with politicians. Amongst all the state officers working as secretaries, he was the one who was an exception and made me feel comfortable as a member of the IAS cadre of Mysore state. He had a great sense of belongingness to his state and when I told him that I came from Karwar he at once made me a member of Kannada fraternity though Karwar was yet to be a part of Karnataka. G.V.K. Rao later rose to be Chief Secretary, Karnataka, Secretary, Agriculture of the Union Government and a Member of the Planning Commission. He had a great deal of self—confidence and told me with a sense of certainty that one could always decide one's next posting—something which he could achieve in his career but which I could not figure out throughout my own! Two other secretaries who impressed me were Shri D.K. Shrinivsachar who was Secretary, Public works and Shri K. Balasumbramanyam, Revenue Secretary, always attired in laced turban with a mark of "*Gandh*" on his forehead. The former was known as a very efficient officer but he was somewhat taciturn while the latter was known as an expert in revenue matters.

Dispite the somewhat lackadaisical nature of the attitude of officers at the level of under secretary regarding my training, I was diligent and kept an account of what I learnt about the work of every department as also the method of working in the secretariat to learn how the files are dealt with I want through the secretariat manual and rules of business of Government.

An appointment was fixed for me with the Chief Secretary and the Chief Minister. The Chief Secretary, Shri N. Puttaranagaswamy was not the seniormost officer but the Chief Secretary was a selection post and in Mysore state tradition it was not necessary for the occupant of the post to be seniormost. Later, I realized that there was caste angle to it. Shri Puttarangaswamy was a Vakkaliga, the ruling caste of Mysore. The chief Minister, K. Hanumanthaih also belonged to the same caste. When I called on Puttarangaswamy, he appeared to be immersed in his work and apparently had no time for me. He looked at me with his squint-eyed face which conveyed no feeling. This cold reception had, no wonder, a disconcerting effect on the new recruit to the IAS cadre of Mysore state.

Meeting with CM

Then came the event of meeting with the Chief Minister. As soon as I entered into his chamber, he got up and walked into the corridor attached to it and started moving to and fro expecting me to follow him. I had no option. His first question – "whether I was a Muslim." My name appeared to him very unfamiliar. No "appa" or "aiah" in Mysore style. Perhaps he felt "Dubhashi" was like Qureshi! My name "Dubhashi", meaning a person talking two languages or an interpreter, misspelt as "Dubashi" throughout my career in Mysore and I had to put up with it. To the CM's query, I replied in the negative but did not disclose the religion to which I belonged. Then he asked me what I was doing. I told him that I was "studying" the working of the secretariat. He immediately took objection to the usage of the word "studying" and corrected it as "learning". Even at this distance of time, I can find no fault with my usage of the term 'Studying' which was what I was doing. Hanumanthaih had apparently a feeling that art and craft of "Secretariat" work had to be learnt but that required "Practice", actual handling of cases which I never did. Neither the Chief Minister nor the Chief Secretary made me feel at home. While the former was brusque in the arrogance of authority of the Chief Minister for which he was well known, the latter was cool and distant – not a good reception to a young person entering into civil service career. It had a demoralizing effect. The experience was an illustration of the general atmosphere of government where concepts like human resource development or inter – personal relationship had no particular place. If there were exception, they were personal in nature and not attributes of the system. For example, Shri Kadidal Manjappa, Minister, Revenue, whom I had to meet because the positions like Assistant and Deputy Commissioner which IAS officers occupied in the early years of their career were supposed to belong to Revenue Department, was much warmer and with a human face. When he asked me why I, an outsider, had been allotted to Mysore State, I told him that this was because outsiders had "no vested interest" and could give an objective administration. I told what I considered to be true and was indeed the theory behind the policy of allotting 50 per cent of the cadre's new recruits from outside the State. The Minister did not like my reply and sharply remarked – "No body had any vested interest" though in the heart of his heart he must have known that every officer in the state was identified as belonging to a caste and expected to work accordingly. Now this feeling has become so wide spread that IAS which was supposed to transcend all such caste and other such narrow considerations has become fully mired in them. The IAS officers are grouped according to castes and attach themselves to ruling politicians of their castes. This is a good example of institutions changing their character according to the genius of the people. Fifty year after the working of our democracy and constitution, every single institution borrowed from the West Minister model has been "Indiansed". The "Bureaucracy" envisaged as a rational-legal instuition of the twentieth century by the great sociologist Max Weber has been unable to remain so because administration entirely on rational and legal basis is alien to our traditions of caste consideration as the dominating influence on our behaviour. Over the years the influence of caste on Indian politics and administration seems only to have grown and it is not clear whether the Weberian model would ever flourish in the country. What is important is not the model per se but the impact which deviation from that model has had on the character of our administration.

As a part of the Secretarial training, I had a day with Shri C. Narasimhamurthy, Secretary, Mysore State Insurance Department. Mysore was probably unique in having state insurance whereas in other parts of India, before the insurance business was nationalized, there were only private insurance companies. All Mysore government officers took policies with the Government Insurance Department. Narasimhamurty was persuasive enough to make me also take an insurance policy with Mysore Insurance, a link attaching me to the State.

District Training

At the end of the Secretarial "training" I was attached to the Bangalore District. This was an urbanised district, not the typical moffussil district in rural area whose drab life in the District HQ has been the subject matter of Upamanu Chatterjee's "English August". I had to continue living in Bangalore. The head of the district, the District Deputy Commissioner was one Shri Rangamallah. He was supposed to be a senior Deputy Commissioner but I hardly came to see much of him because he was always out of HQ and busy with his work. I was left to his HQ assistant Shri R. Anandkrishna, a young bright looking handsome officer who handled the never ending file work of the District Office.

He was quite friendly but was confined to his office work and I never come to see the "field work" which is the essence of district administration. Here was an officer like any Secretarial officer immersed in files. As a part of the District Office attachment, I was also "attached" for some time to the SDO, Shri Channaraj Urs who was a typical mild mannered officer of the Mysore Government service. I studied the District and Sub-division Office Manuals but could hardly get the "feel" of District Administration.

The real feel of the field I got when I spent my time with the survey office. The whole land area is mapped and divided into survey numbers. The map precisely indicates the boundaries of survey numbers and important features like nullahs and hills. The maps are prepared on the basis of a cadastral survey. The survey supervisor took me to the field and made me take measurements and check them with those indicated on the map. This I found very interesting. The precise surveys and maps of the rural area and indication of survey Nos. with their "pot-hissas" or sub-survey numbers is indeed a great achievement. It also gave the owners of survey numbers a definite understanding of the boundaries of their holding and helped in settling boundaries disputes or cases of encroachment as I discovered later.

Judicial Training

The last part of my training was in judiciary. I was made third-class and later second-class magistrate with limited powers of punishment. I was working under the guidance of the city magistrate. I actually had to sit in Court, hear cases and record evidence. In a short period of fifteen days, I heard and disposed off a case in which a small girl Jayalashmi had been accused of theft. I had to ask questions and record evidence in Kannada. Since the girl actually confessed to have committed the small theft, I had no alternative but to give her simple imprisonment of fifteen days.

With the AG

At the end of my training in the District and the judiciary I spent some time with Assistant Accountant General Shri Sethumadhavan. This was a Central Government Office with a different flavour. The AG in those days maintained the account of expenditure of the state Government (a work which has since been bifurcated) and also audited them. Shri Sethuraman was a young officer of the IAAS, an intelligent nimble headed Tamil with whom I felt quite easy. Dealing with Audit objections is an unpleasant task which all administrative officers have to undertake but as I learnt later if all expenditure is regular, i.e., incurred according to rules, there should be no scope for irregularities. However now a days with several cases of deliberate misuse of public money and wanton public expenditure which does not bring intended results, the audit function has assumed great importance as a bulwark against mal-administration. But in those days it was felt audit officers often raised purely "technical" objections against some procedural irregularities which on receipt of objections had to be set right. Another such unpleasant work was "reconciliation of accounts". Often there were some variations between Departmental Accounts & A. G accounts and until the they were reconciled, the AG's officers would continue to raise objections. The one thing for which the officer assumed the greatest importance was the issue of the "pay slip". Till it was received from the A. G. office and presented to the treasury, the officer could not draw his salary! Often the "slip" was delayed for some odd reason (it was a real "slip") and the officer would suffer anxiously because without the slip the officer could not draw his salary. And on the delayed payment, no interest of course is payable. The odds were all weighed against the officer in this complex system.

With the RBI

My last part of work was with the Reserve Bank office in Bangalore and Madras. This part was included at the instance of Bharat. The RBI had to issue cash to the Govt. treasuries where all dues to government were credited and from which all amount were drawn. With the transfer of treasury work to bank officers, the old type of treasury system does not exist. The treasuries were under the supervision of the RBI. The treasuries had also to be inspected periodically by the District officers. Despite such supervision and inspection system, huge amount were drawn and misused recently in the "fodder scam" in Bihar. This only goes to show the extent to which the inspection system has fallen into disuse allowing huge corruption to go on with impurity.

Fed up with living in a single room and eating restaurant food, I had, near the end of my stay, hired a three room flat and employed a cook. The arrangement made me feel much more comfortable.

Departmental Examinations

While completing my training I had to give departmental examinations in Criminal Law, Civil Law, Revenue Accounts and

Kannada. With Criminal Law I was familiar thanks to Munir's lectures at Metcalfe House but Civil Law I was not familiar with and had to study Civil Procedure Code and Transfer of Property Act. For Revenue examination I had to study Revenue Law & Code. For Kannada. I was required to read petitions written in Kannad – often in *modi*, i.e., running script. The written examinations in four subjects I passed without much difficulty. Oral Kannada examination required reading of a petition. Passing of examination was important because it meant an advance increment raising my salary from Rs. 400/- directly to Rs. 500/- p.m. It was good I crossed the milestone during the training period itself as some officers who failed to do so had to break their work as officers and take leave only to complete the departmental examinations.

My First Posting

At the end of my training in the year 1954-55, I was posted as Assistant Commissioner/SDO Chikmaglur subdivision, the place made known all over the country because later it became Indira Gandhi's constituency. However in a few days the posting was changed to Davangere a subdivision of Chitradurg (then wrongly spelt as Chitaldrug) district. I was glad about the change because I seemed to be familiar with Davangere on the main rail and road route from Bangalore to Pune and "nearest" to my home!

CHAPTER 5

Subdivision Officer – Davangere – My First Charge: Igniting the Spark of Community Development

One late night I embarked on the rail the journey from Bangalore to Davangere. To my great discomfiture just when I was about to leave for the station, my cook Vishnu suddenly vanished from the flat. I had to leave for the station without him. While the train was about to leave he hurriedly made his appearance! He had gone to take leave of his "friend". Such is the waywardness of personal servants. One just does not know what comes in their minds. I realized that he showed the ability to reach the station on his own and locate the train and me travelling in the first class compartment.

The train arrived at Davangere station next morning. As advised by Shri Narasimha Murthi, an officer of Mysore Administrative service, working in the Insurance Department as secretary, I had written to the head clerk of SDO's office and he, one Sastri, received me at the station. My predecessor Shrinivasulu Naidu had retired from service and I a fresh recruit, was to take his place on my first appointment. The age difference between the two of us was noticeable. The SDO had a bungalow but if was occupied by Shri Naidu and I had to stay in the room booked for me in the Traveller's Bungalow.

Since I was alone, this could not be much of an inconvenience. In addition to the staff of the traveller's bungalow, Vishnu, my personal servant was there to look after my requirements of food and other services.

The "Rahukalam"

Shri Naidu, like the most government servants in Mysore was a very religions person and believed in taking or giving charge of official position at an auspicious time avoiding *rahukalam* I realized that this was almost a universal practice in the South. I, on my part, found this practice strange and believed in taking charge whenever it was found most convenient. I might have exposed my self sometime to the ill effect of *rahukalam*!

The Jurisdiction

As SDO Davangere, I had the charge of five northern talukas (tahsils) of Chitradurge District. Davangere, the HQ town was 167 miles to the north west of Bangalore. It was a textile city of some 1 lakh population with three major factories. The biggest textile tycoon was Ramsetty with his palace like bungalow at the outskirts of the city. The other two were Gundi Mahadevappa and Chigteri Murgappa. Their presence in the city was felt but I had not much to do with them. Davangere was a Municipality, and a Municipal Commissioner was in charge of city's civic administration.

The SDO (Subdivision officer), also known as Assistant Commissioner was in charge of the rural areas comprising of five talukas—Davangere, Hariher, Jaglur, Holalkare and Hasadurga. Harihar and Holalkere were on the main railway line joining Pune and Bangalore. Each taluka consisted of about 100 villages. So I was in charge of about 500 villages communities.

SDO was a field officer hierarchically between the Deputy Commission in charge of the District and Amildar renamed a tehsildar in charge of tehsil or taluka. The District and tehsil offices were much bigger than the small office of the SDO consisting of head clerk, two regular clerks, one additional clerk on a temporary position and two peons—one in the office and another at SDO's residence. Neelkantappa and Pralhadacher were the clerks on the two permanent positions and Shivanna on the temporary position. Durgappa was the peon in office and Ujappa at the residence.

The Role of The SDO

It was then often said that the position of SDO between the Dy. Commissioner and Tahsildar did not serve much purpose; it was just a post office and could be conveniently abolished. But this never happened. It was no doubt true that sandwiched between the two much large offices of the Tahsildar and the Deputy Commissioner, the small office of the SDO appeared insignificant. But the SDO had a district role to play. Firstly, he was the Land Acquisition Officer and only he could acquire land for public purpose under the Land Acquisition Act. This was an important role because public projects like water supply and roads inevitably involved acquisition of private land. Only acquisition of land under the Act give indefeasible right to Government. over the private land under the Act. Secondly, the SDO had powers under the Revenue Act to deal with cases for grant of land (Darkhast) or encroachment on common lands like *Gomal,* i.e., meadoes (known as Takrar cases) which was quite frequent. In those days there was still uncultivated Government land available for disposal. The landless SC and ST had a priority in the allotment of these lands. Thirdly, the SDO could also sanction small amounts of relief in cases where houses were consumed by fire. Fourthly, SDO was given the special power of Agricultural Income Tax Officer to levy tax on Agricultural income under the new act. The income tax was in addition to the land revenue and was on large land holdings. This could have been a growing source of income to the state but was unfortunately abolished – a case of populist policy measures which became more and more frequent in later years. Fifthly, the SDO was a Returning Officer for Assembly elections and also the electoral officer in charge of preparation of voters' list. Sixthly, the SDO was a Muzrai Officer – a peculiar charge in Mysore State where administration of temples was supervised by Revenue officers. The SDO had to approve the budget of the temples with their small incomes out of charges on *sevas* and expenditure on remuneration for the *Archaks.* Seventhly, the SDO was a Magistrate and dealt with "Chapter Cases" under S.107 and S 109 under the Criminal Procedure code under which criminal elements were required to give bonds for refraining from crime. Eighthly, as a Revenue officer, the SDO was to conduct annual *Zamabandi* fixing land Revenue assessment for a year in revenue village. In olden days the officer could go from village to village for the purpose but in my times it involved no more than signing the statements prepared by village *shanbhogs* (accountants) and submitted to Tashil Officer. Ninthly, the SDO had to here revenue cases relating to land disputes and claims to revenue offices like the hereditary Patel, the village headman.

Like all revenue officers SDO was supposed to be a touring officer. The prescribed touring was for about 15 days a month. He had to prepare an advance monthly tour programme and also keep a daily diary and send both to the District officer for information.

Coming to Terms with Duties

It was not easy for me to adjust to the new environment and deal effectively with the responsibilities of officer for the first time in my life—despite the "theoretical" training in the IAS school and the "practical training" in Bangalore. It is rightly said that administration, like swimming, has to be learnt by actual practice.

Residense and Transport

After staying for about a fortnight in a single room in the Traveller's Bungalow, I was able to shift to the SDO's official Bungalow after Naidu vacated it. The Bungalow was a small, compact one on a fairly large size plot with a garage attached. It had a varandah, two bed-rooms on either side, a hall, and separate kitchen and dining hall. With my personnel cook Vishnu and Ujappa, the official peon at the residence my creature comforts ware met. I had to acquire a vehicle for touring since unlike the present day no car or vehicle was provided to the SDO. I went to Bangalore and with the help of a loan from Mysore Bank arranged by Dy. Commissioner, Shri T.V. Reddy whose father-in-law was the Manager of the Mysore Bank, I bought a second hand Austin for a sum of Rs. 3300/-.

As revenue officer I had no vehicle but I wore a second hat as a Project Executive Officer of the community development blocks. In that capacity I could avail of the jeeps placed at the disposal of the block development officer. The community development blocks were established in a phased manner all over the country from 1952 onwards. Of the 5 taluks in my subdivision, there were CD blocks in two—Davangere and Hollkere. One more was established in Harihar during my tenure.

Community Development Work

The work of Community Development attracted me more than the revenue work. The latter was of a routine character dealing with humdram cases, while the community development work was of a creative nature. The idea of community development itself was new to Indian administration. The idea and programme was introduced by Shri S.K. Dey, who migrated from Lahore after the partition and took charge of the work of rehabilitation of refugees at Nilokheri near Ambala. Instead of merely depending on Government help all the time, the refugees were organized and motivated to help themselves by establishing their own enterprises. Jawaharlal Nehru, who visited the refugee camp, was greatly impressed and asked S.K. Dey to develop similar community development projects all over the country. The idea was to be extended all over the country through the community development programme. The concept was that the rural community itself was to be organized to identify its "felt needs" and meet them through its own effort and initiative. The CD programme and administration was expected to help the local community in this effort. The idea was very exciting and appealed to my sense of idealism. The content of the programme underwent charges but the basic idea was the same. The concept of "Extension" was combined with that of community development. The concept of extension came from the enterprise of Land Grant colleges in USA. There The "County Agents" under the technical guidance of the colleges were to extend supplies, services and technical knowhow to the very door of the farmers. Here in the Indian community development blocks the work was to be done by eight extension officers at the block level and the village level workers at the village level. The block consisted of above 100 villages while the VLW was to be in charge of ten villages. The eight extension officers were in charge of (1) Agriculture, (2) Animal Husbandry, (3) Co-operation, (4) Panchayats, (5) Rural Engineering, (6) Rural Industry, (7) Social Education for men, and (8) Social Education for women. The first six were from the departments while the last two were newly recruited since no department of social education existed.

Rhythm of Work

It took quite sometime for me to get in the rhythm of work. Since the rules laid down a minimum touring of 15 days, a tour programme had to be prepared accordingly. The tashil offices had to be inspected in course of the year and the *dafter* of revenue inspectors had to be checked. The head clerk took the liberty of submitting a draft tour programme. He also fixed dates for hearing cases both on revenue and magistracy side. The two seldom matched. The HC (Head Clerk) did not care to see that I would be in office when the cases were fixed for hearing. I also realized that I was not the master of my time and had to keep my work aside to attend to VIP duties – whenever some Ministers and Senior officers like Deputy Commissioner or Divisional Commissioner came on visit. On the top of this there was the file work. The files had to be attended daily whether I was at HQ or on tour. The file would come in bundles. In the beginning I would not know how to attend to all this work simultaneously.

The files, were shabbily kept and contained ill assorted papers relating to a case including trivial correspondence and reminders on matters pending for sometime because reports from Tashil officer or RI wore not received. The clerks put up the files seeking orders.

In took sometime for me to realize that it is not necessary to go though every paper in the file from beginning till end. What was required was to see the papers related to the point under immediate consideration, the rules and procedures related to it and indicate action to be taken

After fumbling at the beginning regarding the arrangement of my tour programme I started making it more systematic and ensuring that I would be in office when cases were to be heard. A week could be divided into two parts – touring days and "hearing" days and the rhythm would as far as possible be maintained. With experience, I could ensure smooth arrangement of my work. This helped in proper hearing of cases. The Revenue officers are notorious for not hearing cases and keep them pending for years. Cases hanging on for years without timely disposal was a rule rather than an exception. This was because of the unsystematic way of working. Pendencies were noticed in the course of Inspection by senior officers and reminders were routinely issued from the district office regarding 'pending case' but improvement in system of work was necessary which could not be effected in the routine of attending to the visits of higher officers. With regular hearings, the 'court work' could be disposed off early. I remember that a case relating to a holder of the office of village Patel was pending for ten years and the one relating to compensation for land acquired for water works for Harihar town was pending for 20 years. If took me some time but after continuous hearing, I disposed off both the cases.

Visits of VIPs

I got the experience of a VIP visit soon after I took charge. Shri Hanumanthiah the Chief Minister was to visit Hosadurga, the HQ of one of the taluks in my jurisdiction. I did not realize what was involved in the visit of CM. He came with the entourage of several MLAs and many other local politicians – in all forty in number for whom arrangements had to be made by the Revenue Officers. The arrangement for his stay was made at the government TB (Traveller's Bungalow) which underwent a metamorphosis thanks to the hectic efforts of the officers of the PWD who otherwise had no time or money for the purpose. I never knew how the Tashildar arranged for the meals of the entire CM's entourage. Mercifully I remained free from the burden. But surely this could not have been done without resorting to questionable means of raising money. How can then he be free from "corruption?" The meals were by no means simple and supply of sumptuous meat dishes was a must. Why should any body charge a tahsildar or any other officer with corruption when people in authority do not bother to find out of how expenses are met for their ostentatious touring and do not make it a habit of paying their bills? But we have a feudal mindset and "living off the land" is a feudal habit ingrained in us.

The example of the Chief Minister was followed by several senior officers in administration as well. The Kirloskars had a factory in Harihar. It had a guest house where the Deputy Commissioner invariably stayed free of cost. As his junior I had also to stay in the same guest-house but it always bothered me. Wherever I camped in Harihar on my own, I always stayed at the TB (Traveller's Bungalow) on the banks of the Tugabhadra and paid for my stay at rates which were quite moderate. In fact having been filled up by revulsion against the practice of living on the expenses on the subordinate officers, I took my cook and provisions including fuel in the dicky of my car so that I had not to depend on the Tashildar and the revenue inspector for looking after my requirement of a vegetarian meal.

During one of the visits of the Deputy Commissioner, Shri T.V. Reddy, I was accompanying him in his official vehicle on a journey from Davangere to Harihar. On the way there was a tank in which some black ducks swam. It was a nice sight to see. Suddenly Shri Reddy took out his gun and shot at the birds. The shot hit the bird which died with a shriek. It was a heart rending experience for me. The bird was cooked at the Kirloskar Guest House at Harihar for delicious meal for the Deputy Commissioner but the painful incident rankled in my heart and reminded me of poet Valmiki who stopped the hunter from killing the *Kraunch* bird.

Despite my incorruptible ways which remained with me throughout my career in public service lasting over forty years, I was involved in a corruption case which originated in my very first visit to Hosadurga Teshil office a few days after I took over as the SDO (Sub division officer). A petition written in Kannada was handed over to me. Though I had managed to read a handwritten Kannda petition for my examination, I was not quite at ease in reading one and so handed over the petition to the Tahsildar little realizing that it would open up an accusation of corruption against me. That petition was an accusation of petty corruption against a local revenue official. Several years later the Anti-Corruption Bureau asked for my comments on the allegation. Since I had no papers in my possession, not realizing the turn the case was taking. I replied in some-what casual manner that I had received a petition which I passed on to the Tehsildar and had no comments to offer. But the matter persisted for several years with repeated reminders from the Anti-Corruption Bureau. Ultimately, I was horrified to know that the Bureau recommended to the Revenue Secretary that action should be taken against me for involvement in a corruption case in which the Revenue Inspector had asked for and taken some money for showing a favour. The Revenue Secretary fortunately turned down the recommendation. He took the view that my action was due to "inexperience" and no action need be taken. I remembered the case of Surendranath Bannerji of the ICS who was dismissed by the British Government on a petty case. He later became the President of the Indian National Congress. The moral of the experience was that a Government Officer had to be ever careful lest by sheer inadvertence he gets involved. He should not neglect even a petty matter. In this case as soon as I got a communication from the Anti-Corruption Bureau I should have insisted on getting all the papers and should have given a detailed refutation. Better still when a non-descript handwritten petition was given to me I should have insisted that it be read out or taken it with me to the office and got it read by the Head Clerk of my office and then got started an enquiry. But with just a fortnight in office and on only a familiarity visit to the tahesil office all this hardly occurred to me. "Government swallows the camel but strains at the gnat."

Visit of PM Jawaharlal Nehru

One of the memorable visits of a VIP during my stay was an overnight visit by Prime Minister Pandit Jawaharlal Nehru accompanied by his daughter Indira Gandhi. Nehru was parsing through Harihar on his way to Shimoga. He was to get down from the train in the evening and after an overnight stay and a civil reception he was to leave by road to Shimoga. It fell to me to supervise erection of buntings on the rood and prepare the address to be given by the President of Hariher Municipality in his honour.

The Chief Minister Hanumanthiah had arrived in advance of the arrival of the Prime Minister in order to receive him at the station. But even nearer the time of arrival of the Prime Minister, he would not come out of the room in which he had been ensconced and the Deputy Commissioner, Shri T.V. Reddy started getting extremely nervous. Shri Hanumanthiah was given to show off the aura of his authority and perhaps wanted to keep his officer on tenterhooks to show that in his state, the Chief Minister is no less then the Prime Minister of the country. Ultimately, the Prime Minister arrived, was received on the platform and taken to the Kirloskar guest house with hardly any pomp.

The next day the Prime Minister with his daughter Indira Gandhi moved in an open jeep to the ground where the "reception" function was arranged. Impeccably dressed as always, Jawaharlal was in a cheerful mood and threw garlands at the audience to everybody's great delight. Those were different days and Nehru always moved about not as a person in authority but as a popular leader. But an incident occurred which gave an inkling of things to come. When the crowds surged forward towards the jeep, the police with their *dandas* started pushing them back. They were only doing their "duty" of ensuring orderly progress of the jeep and there was no particular incident of indulgence in excessive use of the force but the Prime Minister's daughter started suddenly shouting at the top of her voice that "police are beating the people", stamping her foot on the floor of the jeep. Nehru took it casually and nothing happened but this experience showed the temper of the Prime Minister's daughter arising out of arrogance of authority of which the civil servants could be victims and who have to bear it as a price of their service.

Visits of the VIPs could be a big menace. In old Mysore, there was the system of receiving the VIP at the border of the district. Once the Union Minister of State for Home Affairs, Shri B.N. Datar was to arrive by road. The Deputy Commissioner, Shri D.J. Balraj and myself went to the border and waited for him. The VIP who was to arrive in the morning at 10 AM arrived only in the evening at 5 PM! We wasted our time waiting for him for hours! Such time was precious and should have bee spent on doing our work. But since waiting for VIP was part of the duty, it was reckoned as time spent on duty. Such is the tragedy of work of the public servants. I had to experience it on several occasions and in various forms throughout my career.

One of the frequently visiting VIP was the local MLA from Harihar who was no less than the Home Minister of Mysore State — Shri Hanagwadi Siddaverappa. A stocky short rotund figure, he was considered a powerful Minister of Mysore Cabinet, next in authority only to the Chief Minister, Shri K. Hanumanthiah. If KH was the leader of the Vokkaliga, Siddeverappa was leader of one of the two sects (peasant sect as against the trader sect to which another great Lingayat leader Shri Nijalingappa belonged). When I had just joined the State his name carried headline in the newspapers for suspending the powerful Inspector General of Police, Shri Babu Reddy. I had little understanding of the event but could realise the power of the Minister.

Shri Siddaveerappa made it a habit to frequently visit Harihar-Davangere and review the work done in his constituency. Many local people would meet him and make complaints against local officials of one department or another. It was then the occasion for the Minister to flare up and take officials to task in the presence of the people complaining. His favourite target was the Executive Engineer who was not an official of his department but as the local Minister he could ask him "to stop dilly dallying and shilly shallying" The elderly officer had to bear the rebuke crest-fallen. Lokmanya Tilak had once said that half the salary of the civil servant is for meekly bearing the insults and reprimands of the superiors. Fortunately I was never the target of the ministers' fury. Perhaps he spared me and treated me with indulgence because of my young age. Siddaveerappa made himself comfortable in the Kirloskar Guest House as a matter of right and the question of payment of his expenses never arose. In return Kirloskar enterprise could expect favourable treatment whenever the need arose.

Dealing with Ordinary People

While public servants have all the time for the VIPs, they have none for the ordinary people. They come to the public office and wait for hours to meet the officer for getting their work done. But the officer is busy otherwise and the poor visitor has to go to the "clerk concerned" who then demands his price. That is how petty corruption thrives. From the beginning of my service, I realized that this was a great injustice to the common man for whom the administration exists. I, therefore, always made it a point to meet the visitors, accept their petitions and promptly attend to their work. I never insisted on their coming only during the visiting hours. In a district, the visitors come from far off villages and to insist that they should come only during the visiting hours was not fair. First, they could not always be expected to know the "visiting hours" and secondly, it would not be easy to travel in the bus and reach the office on time and then get transport to go back. I received visitors at all times and even at my official residence. I remember once a visitor coming at 7 AM at my bungalow. He was a poor old farmer had some problem of his land being snatched from him. He had come all the way to seek help at that early hour at my house. I met him and tried to help him. I always believed that *nirbal ke BalaRam* should be the motto of every civil servant. It is the poorest whom the administrator should give the strength. But what happens is just the opposite. The civil servants are available to the affluent and the powerful who being influential could also help him in his career development but the poor have no voice.

Intensive Touring

I did fairly intensive touring. During the first year, I was a bachelor and could tour at will. I often used the train to visit one of the taluka headquarter, *viz.*, Holalkere which was on the rail route to Bangalore. On the other hand, another taluka headquarter, Jagalur could be only reached by road. During the tour, I made spot inspections related to revenue cases which were necessary to deal with them. They were cases either before me or referred to me by higher authorities, *viz.* the Deputy Commissioner, the Divisional Commissioner or even the State government. But during tours I gave more importance to the work connected with community development. I did it with the missionary zeel like that of F.L.Brayne whose book "Socrates in Indian village" I had read at Metcalfe House. The villagers often received me with a basket of fruits or at least a lemon and often flattered me with a *binnavettale* or laudatory welcome address. This was the costomary practice from the days of the princely state. Whether formally presented with an address or not, I received petitions or oral representations and always tried to go to the bottom of the case and wherever possible gave prompt relief in the shape of a decision. Under the community development budget a number of small works were taken up in villages such as approach roads, simple drainage works, school buildings, dispensary buildings etc. These were taken up by the villagers or on their behalf by some local contractors with an element of *shramadan* equivalent to 25 per cent of cost. The payment could be made after an inspection by the project excutive officer. I verified the measurements with reference to actual work done and in the process learnt the elements of constructions and their costs. Local officers would say that this experience would be useful when I would build my own house. It was a dream of every Mysore civil service officer to acquire a plot and build his house at the earliest in Bangalore. I found I had no such urge. I was more interested in inspiring villagers to take up local development works with *shramadan*.

Community Development Work

Community Development work gave full scope for my evangelical fervour for development work. I thoroughly enjoyed being with the village people, sharing their aspirations and problems and solving the problems and fulfilling their aspirations through community development effort. I liked spending time with the village level workers and Block Extention officers and participating in village meetings. I had the opportunity of setting up new community development block in Davangere and Jaglore talukas. The cooperative credit programme was then in an incipient stage. We set up village level primary cooperative credit societies and started a substantial cooperative credit programme through them. This was in consonance with the crop loan credit programme as recommended by the Rural Survey and Credit Committee set up by the Reserve Bank of India. This was one of the most promising development in post-independence India.

Shri S.K. Dey, Union Minister for Community Development had great enthusiasm for seminars as a tool for bringing together officers of various levels and sharing their experience through exchange of ideas. One such seminar was held at Kanyakumari which was then in Kerala. The participants in the seminar included Development Commissioners of the Southern States and several collectors. I belonged to the junior most category of Project Executive Officers with just a years experience. As a young participant I enjoyed talking on equal terms with senior officers in free discussion at the seminar. I had the temerity of telling Shri S.K. Dey quite bluntly that he introduced community development programme though no homogeneious community existed. It was quite a radical statement to make though quite in accordance with fact. The village society did consist of rich land owners as well as land-less, high-caste leaders as well as low-caste and untouchable dependents. But these divisions were overlooked and the programme was revised as though a homogenious community existed. After the euphoria in the initial years of community development was over, programmes had to be devised for the weaker sections of the community such as anti-poverty and employment programmes to raise the people above the poverty line.

The seminar was one of the many innovations introduced by Shri Dey which brought fresh breath in the administrative climate. They were very different from the administrative conferences of the official type which provided no scope for exchange of ideas and experiences but were confined to review of government orders and directions and their compliances in a strifling hierarchial and authoritarian atmosphere. Yet there were some who thought that the seminars were paid holidays for government servants at public cost. Even if they were holidays they could not be faulted if they could rejuvenate the fixed minds of the civil servants. Certainly for me my participation in Kanyakumari seminar was an exhilarationg experience. Meeting collegues and senior officers from other states also gave me a feel of what was happening in other states.

At the seminar senior officers were comfortably lodged in the circuit house while junior officers like me had to make do with meagure accommodations provided by the *choultries* of *dewaswan* (trust) However as young people we did not mind the inconvenience. I greatly enjoyed the stay on the sea-shore at the confluence of the Arabian Sea, the Bay of Bengal and the Indian Ocean where the sun rose and set on the sea-shore. In those days the sea-shore had the pristine purity of white sands and was not spoiled by crowded cement buildings and hotels which now disfigure this once wonderful sea-shore.

Marriage and After

After a year in Davangere, I went to Bombay (now Mumbai) and got married. Back to Davangere, I was back to my routine of touring and office work. Once when I was about to leave for Jagalru, my wife started crying. I asked the reason. She said she just did not want to be left alone at home. I told her that on the tour she would have to bear the discomfort of traveling on dusty roads and living in the TB. I would be busy at work and may not have the time for her. She said she would not mind and I started taking her with me on tour. So there would be four of us in my black Austin – the driver and the cook in (both my private servants) front and we two at the back. The old Austin car was faithful and never failed.

Head of Cooperative Institutions

An SDO carries some subsidiary responsibilities as well, two of which I should mention. I was the Chairman for three cooperative farming societies in Holelkere taluka. Two of these were of the extent of 600 acres and the third of over 1200 acres. A cooperative inspector of the department was the secretary of these cooperatives. They were set up out of some idealism to provide livelihood to landless families. I felt excited about the venture but when I visited the farms I found that they were not in good shape and the families appeared poor despite the considerable extent of land at their disposal. The instructor complained of lack of animals and tools. The families divided the land among themselves and did whatever they could with their meagure resourses. There was nothing "cooperative" about the farm. I asked the inspector to prepare "a plan" for cooperative farming with joint operations. But the inspector had neither the vision nor the idealism which he could convey to the wretched families. He just carried on his work in a routine manner. When in my next visit I tried to verify the progress, if any, made in the direction of joint cooperative farming operations I was sorely disappointed. There was no progress made. The families used to their own little pockets on the farm were not prepared to undertake cooperative farming. I had heard of *moshavs* in Israel but any dream of replicating them was destined to fail without the necessary fervour. I myself found little time to make repeated visits which were necessary to meet the families and make them appreciate the idea and benefits of cooperative farming. I myself lacked the skill and the experience needed to make the idea of cooperative farming a success. Once a minister Shri Channabasappa was on a visit to the taluka and I told him of the cooperative farms and the difficulty that I was facing. He turned round to me and said " how can these farms be run on a cooperative basis? Farming is an operation for individual families". That put paid to any further discussion on the subject. Later on I tearnt that 3200 cooperative farms were set up in different parts of the country. Nehru supported the idea but the experience of cooperative farm was not good. Several expert committees reviewed their working but ultimately the entire experiment of cooperative farming was given up as unworkable. The pioneering spirit of the *moshav* farmers in Israel was lacking in the Indian landless families.

Another hat that I wore was that of a Chairman of land mortgage banks. They disbursed loans to farmers against mortgage of lands for redemption of their old debts. They had yet to graduate into land development banks giving loans for investment in irrigation works like wells and lift irrigation projects. The SDO had no business to chair these cooperative banks but in those early days such arrangements existed. The secretary of the society – a lawyer used to meet me periodically for clearing several cases of loan applications. I sanctioned them after convinsing myself that the value of land mortgaged was an adequate cover for the loan.

Improving Communication in Kannada

During my tours in the villages I spent a great deal of time talking to the villagers about their problems. I also had to address village meetings. This gave ample practice to improve my communication skill; in Kannada. I might be committing mistakes but the villagers greatly appreciated my talking to them in their own language. Kannada contains a great deal of vocabulary of Sanskrit words. And my Sanskrit background made it easy for me to talk in kannada. What was particularly remarkable was the fact that even the village people were quite at home with Sanskrit words. I always found that though I was from an urban background and was brought up in another language area, there was absolutely no cultural gap between me and the village people of Karnataka. This personal experience convinced me of the essential unity of the Indian people.

A Spiritual Center

Even in remote areas of our land one comes across centres of high spiritual and cultural excellence. One such centre existed in the village Mlladihalli in Holelkere taluka. In this interior village a Swamiji (he was known as Malladihalli Swamiji—I never knew his real name but only knew that he was from distant Mangalore) had set up his *ashram* where he did *yogsadhana* and social work. He had a *goshala* and a *kalyana mantapam* (a marriage hall) His yogic exercises with deep inhaling and exhaling were a wonderful experience to watch. I always liked to spend time with him whenever I visited Holelekere. His ashram had a civilizing influence on the surrounding rural area.

The Second General Election

The scond General Election took place in 1957. I was the Returning officer of two assembly constituencies and one parliamentary constituency. The preparations for conducting elections started several months before the actual dates of election. The Chief Election Officer of the state Shri M.K. Varadrajan issued detailed instructions in the form of a manual. This was followed by a series of circulars. The objective was to make the elections free and fair as required by the Constitution. I was solely responsible for the smooth and efficient conduct of elections in the constituencies of which I was the Returnung Officer. I felt it both a challenge and an exhilarating experience. I was just 26. but the responsibility of Indian Democracy at least in a small part of the country fell on my young shoulders.I was quite aware of the importance of the work and took it quite diligently. I carefully studied every clause of the manual and circular issued by the CEO. The first step was the appointments of Polling Officers drawn from amongst the government employees who included teachers of government schools and colleges as well as employees of the government offices. After the appointment of the Polling Officers, the next job was of their training so that they meticulously followed the election procedure without commiting a single mistake which could render them null and void. There was a training manual to be followed for the purpose. The training included a demonstration of the handling of the ballot boxes while opening them, locking them and sealing them. The training was given more than once so as to insure infallibility. I greatly liked my role as a practical teacher. My students, i.e., the government employees were also quite earnest. Then there was the job of selecting the building for locating the polling station and ensuring that they had proper facilities for secret voting. All the while, the work of preparing and updating voters' list was going on. Simultaneously the work of checking the condition of ballot boxes was going on to make sure that they were in good working condition. Finally came the day for voting. The Returning Officer had to ensure that there were no mal-prctices. One of them was providing vehicles for carrying voters. While I was moving to see that this was not happening, I found that a vehicle was indeed carrying rural voters. I stopped it and made the occupants get down. It would have been more appropriete for me to proceed against the candidates for indulgence in corrupt practice but I stopped short of doing so feeling that establishing the guilt with all the evidence might not be very easy and might have distracted from my general duty of conducting and supervising the election. At the end of the day, after all the votes were cast, the sealed ballot boxes had to be safely lodged in the strong room of the treasury. I slept well past mid-night after ensuring that the last box was received and the strong room securely locked and sealed. Siddavirappa raised the objection that the ballot boxes might be tempered with. I convinced him that this was simply impossible. It was the same minister who had collected a number of cars for election propoganda, more than prescribed.

Then came the day of counting the votes. I had to supervise counting for two assembly constituencies as well as the parliamentary constituency. For the latter the number of voters was large and a number of counting clerks had to simultaneously do the work. The agents of the candidates were there to keep a watch to ensure that no vote was miscounted. At the end of counting and tabulation, I had to declare the results wich I did. The results came as a shock because the strong incumbent candidate of the ruling party (Congress) was defeated while a new comer of Praja Socialist Party was successful.

My experience as a Returning Officer was indeed memorable. It taught me at a young age as to how to take up a responsible job and do it successfully, how to press into service a large number of employees and make them do teamwork and how to conduct far the flung operations. I had definitely matured in the process.

Outcome of Two Years

At the end of two years I felt quite selttled in Davangere. I gained confidence and developed interest in village work. Prominent villagers in several villages came to know me personally. I could understand the problems of the rural people and took it as my personal responsibility to solve them. I also gained control of routine office work and files. I had hardly any personal or social life since my work always kept me busy and left little time for the lighter aspects of life. On the other hand, I started reflecting on my administrative work and wrote my first paper on "coordination" which was published in the Indian Journal of Public Administration. The article dealt with the problems of coordination in development work at the field level—especially between the settled departments of government and the new machinery of block administration in reaching the common goals of development.

Transfer

As it always happenes in the government, a sudden transfer order broke my sense of settling down in Davangere. I had just completed two years and in the official merry-go-round, I was due for transfer. I was transferred as SDO, Pandavpura in Mandya district in southern part of Mysore state.

Every transfer disturbs the even tenor of the personal life of an officer as well as the rhythm of administrative work. The former aspect becomes more serious as a family grows. I had just married and children had yet to make their appearance; and so for me at that stage the aspect of family inconvenience had not assumed importance. I had accumulated little personal baggage but whatever I had, I packed and loaded in a truck and sent to my next destination.

But the personal aspect apart, I felt that my development work was disturbed. I had just started the activity in a new community development block and had planned a number of small projects which I wanted to be completed. I had to leave all that behind. Later on I was to learn that in one's administrative career there is no such thing as personal attachment to work. One simply does the work attached to the post as long as one holds a post. Continuity is provided by the post and not the person. That is why an officer can leave a personal stamp only if he stays in a post long enough. Most of the time the work of an administrator tends to be a routine continuation of faceless office work. Men may come and men may go, but the work of government administration goes on in an impersonal manner to which an individual civil servant can make only a marginal contribution. Bound by official framework of procedures and limited time of which any office can be held, it is hardly possible for a civil servant to think of leaving "the foot prints on the sands of time"

However, the local people do remember the work of a good officer. Long after I had left Davangere, indeed even after I retired from the IAS, I was amazed at a seminar held in Bangalore to meet the son of the *Sarpanch* of Anagodu, a village near Davangere who fondly recalled the work I had done there. And there might be many others who would have remembered my contribution to the work of rural development.

CHAPTER 6

SDO Pandavpura (1957-58) Giving Relief to Tenants

Giving Relief to Tenents

Pandavpura was a sub-division of Mandya district carved out of Mysore district. The whole of Mandya area was drought prone till Visveswariah Canal taking off from the Krishnaraj Sagar Dam brought precious waters of Kavery and irrigated the parched area. Irrigation facilitated the growth of sugar cane crop and establishment of a sugar factory which brought prosperity to the farmers who were till then drought-stricken and poor.

But the whole of the Pandavpura sub-division was not irrigated. It consisted of four talukas of which only Shrirangapattan was intensively irrigated but not the other three talukas, i.e., Pandavpura, K,R.Pet and Nagamangala. It was an area inhabited by the Vakkaliga community, the dominant caste of old Mysore.

Shrirangpattana was irrigated and prosperous with intensive cultivation of paddy. It was a historic city, the capital of Tipu Sultan. Tipu petronised the temple of Ranganathswami. In some parts of Kerala he was called a tyrant who killed the Hindus but in Mysore he was known as a benign ruler who generously donated to the Shringeri temple and *Math*, introduced silk manufacturing which became a major enterprise for which Mysore became famous, gave good administration and was a supreme patriot who fought the British. He was in touch with Nepolean for halting the advance of the British Empire. While personally leading his forces against the British troops he died fighting in the battle of Shrirangapattana.

The town of Shrirangapattana was just fifteen miles from Mysore on the road from Mysore to Bangalore. A moat encircled the town and one had to enter through a big gate to reach it. Pandavpaura, the headquarters of the sub-division was just a village tucked in the interior. A small road from Bangalore-Mysore highway led to the town. It consisted of no more than a few roads at right angles on one of which was the small office of the SDO and on another the beautiful small bungalow of SDO.I was reluctant to move from the city of Davangere to the small town of Pandavpura. But the sub-division was considered to be a good posting and was even coveted because of its proximity to Mysore city and to Krishnaraj Sagar Dam.

I soon started enjoying the locational advantage and on the weekends slipped into the Mysore city (though strictly speaking the city was outside the sub-division and going there required prior permission) We bought vegetables in the Mysore market (Mysore *badnekai* brinjalwhich were famous for their butterlike quality and Nanjangud *balehannu,* bananas delicious in taste) I conveniently held my Saturday court in the Harris bangalow on the bank of Kavery and then after the day's work visited Mysore city.

Tenancy Cases

There was enough reason to hold the weekend court at Shrirangapattana. Soon after I look over I discovered that on the court files of the SDO were a number of tenancy disputes under the tenancy act and there were regular new accretions. That was because the rich paddy lands of Shrirangpattana were owned by landlords who lived in Mysore while the tenants were the local peasants.Either of the two parties would appear in the SDO's court for fixing the fair rent. The landlords expected more while the tenants wanted to pay less. Some cases were pending for several months. I went through the tenancy law and found that there were definite guiding principles for fixing rent and there was no particular problem of arriving at fair rent based on those principles. I therefore held regular hearings and asked the lawyers on either side to place their arguments in one or two hearings. I rarely gave adjournments. After hearing the lawyers I promptly passed the orders. The disposal of the cases was so quick that the pendency of tenancy cases in my court rapidly fell. I was told that this became the talk of the town in Shrirangpattanm. Both the litigants landlords as well as tenants were happy because the disposals were quick with uncertainlty ended and rent ordered to be paid was reasonably satisfactory and considered to be just. The quick disposed of tenancy cases could be considered a positive achievement of my short stay of six months in Pandapura.

With my experience at Davangere, I could get a better grip on work in my second sub-division. I could quickly dispose of routine work and files. I could see villagers approaching clerks regarding the pending matters. I asked them to come to my room so that I could attend to their problems. I did not want ordinary villagers to pay small bribes to clerks for getting their work done. My method of dealing directly with the needy village people coming to the sub-division office had also a beneficial effect.

Community Block Development Work

I missed the intensive community development work that I did at Davangere. The CD block was sanctioned only for one block in the KR Pet taluka. The main crop was paddy and I found that productivity could go up with the use of improved seeds. There was the government scheme of growing "foundation seed" on government farms, which was to be supplied to "seed farms" to be established in block areas which in turn was to be supplied to farmers for wide-spread use. Once the Chief Secretary Shri PVR Rao visited the KR Pet block. I asked him for the supply of foundation seed from government farmers. He turned round and asked me—"Why don't you yourself set up a seed farm in the block?" I turned around the idea in my mind but found that the block had neither the technical nor the financial resources to set up such a farm.

A new block was sanctioned for Pandavpura taluka. I decided to arrange a programme for the inauguration of the Block. I invited the Deputy Commissionor Mandya, Shri Rehmtulla for the function as also the Divisional Commissioner, Shri Sheshgiri Rao. Shri Rehmtulla was under the impression that he would be only Chief Guest at the function. But when he found that his "boss" would also be the there, he was greatly upset and told me in no uncertain terms of his extreme unhappiness. Obviously I should have told him when I invited him that I would be inviting the Divisional Commissioner as well. On the other hand Shri Rehmtulla need not have made heavy weather of the presence of the Divisional Commissioner at the function. But that was a case of petty pride, which often overtakes an individual. However despite the hitch, the function went off smoothly. Perhaps for starting work in a new block, I need not have arranged any function and invited the wrath of the Deputy Commissioner, my immediate boss.

Visit of Vinoba Bhave

A memorable event during my short stay at Pandavpura was the *Padayatra* of Acharya Vinoba Bhave. He was to walk from Mysore to Pandavrpura where he was to make a night halt. I went to the border to receive him but he hardly took any notice. He was to stay in the school building. I felt like meeting him but he was surrounded by his workers who were in search of cow's milk and ghee for his consumption. I did not like this kind of insistence on special food for him and did not feel like imposing myself on the saint and disturb his work. Nor did he express his desire to meet with local officers. He did not seem to be keen on meeting with any body. Later I regretted that I missed the opportunity of having a personal meeting with the saint who became a legend in his life-time.

"In Charge" Deputy Commissionor

While I was still an SDO, I got the opportunity to be the "in charge D.C." of Mandya District. Shri Rehmtulla was transferred to Bangalore as Secretary. He left handing over the charge to me. I was just 27 and was mighty happy to be elevated to the position of D.C. though as an in-charge arrangement. I took up the additional work with great gusto. I continued to stay at Pandavpura and did not shift to the impressive residence of the DC, Mandya. Whenever I was at Mandya Shri Pandit who was a very senior officer but still working as Superintendent of Police of the District and his wife would invite us to have a meal with them. My wife and I availed of their hospitality on more then one occasion.

I remember a memorable cultural function at Mandya where Shri Nijalingappa, the Chief Minister came as the Chief Guest. He was very friendly and affectionate. The more influential politician in Mandya District was Shri H.K Veeranna Gowda. He would often come on tour and courtmarshall local officers in front of villagers for deficiencies in their work. He obviously took pleasure in insulting the local officers before the village people forgetting that this may reduce their effectiveness or adversely affects their motivation. But how could he show his authority as a minister without insulting the local officers? Fortunately I had no personal unpleasant experience with him.

The Bunglow and the Cook

My house at Pandavpura was quite comfortable. There was a garden around. There was a cook attached to the house—old Ramaswami who had been there since the days when Shri K. Balasubramanyam was the SDO He produced excellent thick *averekayi* (beans) sambar which we remember to this day. *Averekai,* a kind of beans, are very popular in the diet of Mysore people and are abundantly used for preparing a variety of dishes like sambar and semulina snack known locally as *Khara Bhat* and in Maharashtra as *Rovyacha Tikhat Sanja*.

Posting as D.C. Raichur

My stay at Pandavpura was short—just about six months. I was promoted to the position of DC and posted to the remote district of Raichur in the Hyderabad Karnataka area. I was happy that the promotion order came before completing five years of service of which one year was on probation as an IAS officer under training in the IAS school, Delhi and another as officer under practical training at Bangalore. Two and half years as SDO Davangere and half a year at Pandarpura of which a month as in charge DC Mandya constituted the totality of my experience. In some other states promotion to my batch mates was given just after four years. It all depended on the vacant positions in the states and there was no mechanism or arrangement to maintain inter-state parity though this was supposed to be an All India Service.

But there was a slip between the cup and the lip. My promotion order was withheld because Shri Venugopal Naidu and other officers of the Mysore Administrative Service (not yet absorbed in the IAS) complained that they had served longer as Assistant Commissioner and their claims should be considered first. Their case was taken up by Shri T. Mariyappa, the influential Home Minister and number two in the Cabinet. It was argued that the IAS officers should not be preferred to local officers. I felt distressed and did not know where to turn and what to do. I went to Bangalore and met the Chief Secretary Shri K.P. Ramanathiah who himself originally belonged to the Mysore Administrative Service. I told him that other officers of my batch have been promoted in other states and I should not suffer just because I do not happen to be the "son of the soil" of the old Mysore state". He looked at me severely and asked me not to be emotional. Then I decided to go and see Shri T. Mariyappa himself. He was more sympathetic and asked me not to consider myself an outsider now that I was in the service of Mysore State. His assuarence assauged my worry. He was true to his word and soon my orders were cleared.

This was my first experience of civil service manipulation in postings. I also realized that politicians are more effective then even the seniormost civil servants in coming to the rescue.

CHAPTER 7

Deputy Commissioner, Raichur 1958-59 – Administering a backward, droughtprone area

Administrative Struggle in a Backward Area

From Pandavpura to Raichur was a long journey. We went by car to Bangalore and had a night's halt. Next day I took to Bangalore – Bellery road via Chitradurg and reached Munirabad across the Tungabhadra river and had lunch at Indraprastha guest house. After lunch we soon left for Raichur – a distance of some hundred twenty miles, hoping to reach by early evening at about 6 p.m. expecting to cover the distance in four hours.

Munirabad was the place where a huge dam had been built across the Tungabhadra River. A huge area of 560,000 acres of Raichur District had come under irrigation under the project. It was one of the major irrigation projects in post-independence India about which Henry Hart has written a very informative and interesting book "Rivers of Modern India". The project was expected to change the face of Raichur – a drought affected district turning it into a granary of Karnataka State. I would write more of this later. But the stop at Munirabad gave us the first beautiful view of the huge lake under the Dam. On one side of the Dam was the Indraprasth Guest House and on the other was the Vaikunth Guest House of the Andhra pradesh government which also benefited from the project. K.C. Canal (Kadappa Carnool Canal) took the precious water to the parched areas of the Rayalseama of Andhra consisting of Kadappa and Carnool Districts. The Tungabhadra Board also had its office on the Andhra side.

Hard Road to Munirabad

But we did not know what was in store for us in our journey from Munirabad to Raichur. Up to Munirabad the road was tarred, but from Munirabad onwards to Raichur, there was not the slightest bit of a tarred road. It was a dirt road all the way full of pits and ruts. For my tiny Austin it became difficult to negotiate. The car bumped every few yards and the speed went down. We kept on driving, hoping to see a better stretch but there was no luck for us. Mysore area had made me used to better terrain with tar roads, friendly road side villages and towns with tiny restaurants offering coffee and dosa. But here nothing was in sight. Villages appeared to be deserted with nothing to offer. I asked for a place to stop for a cup of tea and was told that I could get it at the next town Gangavati. It was some forty miles from Munirabad. But Gangawati was not on the main road and we had to take an approach road crowded with rustic people to enter the town. It was supposed to be a taluka HQ but had nothing to offer by way of rest and refreshment and so we decided to press on to the next main town, Sindhnoor, some thirty miles away which turned out to be even more backward and without even what Gangawati had to offer. Disappointed we pressed on to the next tahsil town of Manavi with increased disappointment. All that these Tehsil towns had in common were huge rocks at the bottom of which the towns were situated. Towns elsewhere are located on the banks of river. Here they were at the bottom of rocks! Tired and hungry we had a sense of relief when we saw the board signaling branching off from the main road to Raichur town. Some ten miles journey brought us to the District HQ—Raichur with its cement road. We were to go to residence of the D.C. which was not a government building but a huge two storied private house earlier belonging to a contractor which was acquired by the government for the collector's residence. A meal was waiting for us and we had a sense of relief.

D.C.'s Residence

The Bungalow which was a private property and acquired as DC's residence was a vast sprawling two story building with a large bed room on the first floor. The ground floor had a large deep verandah covered with plants and creepers, which provided relief from the torrid heat during the day. A large garden surrounded the bungalow which was regularly watered by a *mali* who I later came to know was a municipal employee. Though the two-storied building was huge, it was old and not at all well maintained. There were crevices in the stone-walls which provided secure quarters for snakes which slithered on the roof. Only a few days after we started living there, once while I was standing on the verandah, a black snake fell from the roof missing my head by whiskers. This did create some unease if not fright; fortunately, the experience did not get repeated.

Backward Nizam Area

The long journey from Munirabad on the East to Raichur on the west had given me a full idea of how backward were the mofussil areas of the old Hyderabad state under the Nizam's rule. Everything was concentrated in Hyderabad-Secundarabad twin city and the palaces and harems of the Nizam and his jewellery. The mofussil areas were deprived of even the basic facilities like good roads and electricity.

The old Hyderabad state was trifurcated as part of the process of state reorganization. The areas of Telengana were joined to Rayalseema and the sarkars of the earstwhile Madras province to constitute the state of Andhra Pradesh. The Marathwada area consisting of Nanded, Parbhani, Beed, Osmanabad and Aurangabad Districts were joined to Maharashtra while the Districts of Gulbarga. Bidar and Raichur, were joined to Karnataka state. Raichur district itself lost two talukas—Gadhwal and Alampur to neighbouring Mehboobnagar district of Andhra Pradesh. The three Hyderabad Karnataka districts, *viz.*, Raichur, Bidar and Gulbarga constituted an independent division of Gulbarga.

The backwardness of the area and its distance from the capital Bangalore, made the officers of the old Mysore state extremely reluctant to accept postings to any of these districts. They were "reserved" for people like me who were not counted as the "sons of the soil". The discomfort caused by distance from Bangalore and the backwardness of the infrastructure were compounded by hot, harsh weather which was in sharp contrast to the invariably pleasant wheather in all seasons in most part of the old Mysore state. Raichur, even after losing two talukas, was indeed a huge district of long distances. It stretched from west to east and was a *doab* between the two rivers—Tungabhadra in the south and Krishna in the North. The former was a tributary to Krishna and met her at Mantralaya which being a confluence of two rivers was considered to be a holy place. Raichur had one advantage. It was on the main broadguage railway route from Bombay-Pune to Madras. Since my parents were in Pune, this was a plus point for me.

Mughal *tehzeeb*

The day following my arrival, I was to take charge of my office as D.C. As I was getting ready, I was greeted by Mehboob Khan, the head peon of the Bungalow, with a deep bow, salaaming with words *Adabarz* He was not the Jawan of old Mysore but a dignified functionary dressed in Sherwani—Pyjama with a turban with Mugal *tehzeeb.* I returned his *Adabarz.* The DC's household had five servants who served by turn—Mahboob Khan and Ziauddin for office, Madar and Hari for cleaning furniture and Hannumantharao as vegetarian cook.

I had to get myself acquainted with the huge district and its administrative and legal system which was different, since it carried the legacy of the old Hyderabad state.

Saath Kacheri

My office was located in a magnificent building on the top of an elevated place and was known *Sath Kacheri* or seven offices. The Bangalore secretariat was known as *Athara Kacheri* or 18 offices and here I was in charge of seven offices. Which exactly they were I never came to know. I had some senior officers to help—a Revenue Assistant and a Development Assistant both of the rank of Assistant Commissioner, the former held by Shri Abdul Jabbar a Muslim officer belonging to Curnool who went to Haj during my tenure and the latter by Shri Giridhari Pershad a *Kayasth* officer *(Kayasth* officers were prominent in Nizam's service as they were in the service of the Mughal administration in Delhi). The former was somewhat aloof and stern but competent. At the less senior level were two other officers—Shri P.G. Paranik, the District Panchayat officer and the District social welfare Officer Shri Kumar—both belonging to Hyderabad Civil Service. The former was quite bright and was later on promoted from the state quota to the Indian Administrative Service. The latter was good at sports—particularly tennis. Yet another officer was an engineer Shrinath of the PHE—Public Health Engineering department. He executed all local development works—drinking water projects, sanitation, roads etc. The public health engineering dept did not exist in old Mysore area and the Deputy Commissioner had to depend on the regular PWD for the execution of these works. That created problems of co-ordination between the office of the Deputy Commissioner and the PWD—both blaming each other for delay in execution of projects and the utilization of grants made available to the district for small local development works, which were essential for meeting the local needs of the village people. Yet another officer directly interacting with me was the District Excise Officer, a Muslim officer. From all the six officers I got papers and files on a daily basis. They also frequently met me for disposal of matters after personal discussion. There was clerical staff working under the six officers—some of whom were used to working in Urdu rather than English. Day's work meant dealing with a mad variety of matters—revenue, development, municipalities, panchayats, welfare of SC & ST, local development programme and development under the Tungabhadra Project.

As though these diverse official responsibilities were not enough, I had several other hats to wear. As Deputy Commissioner, I was Chairman of the Regulated Market and District Cooperative Central Bank. Shri Amarappa Petal, a non official was the Vice-President of the Bank, who frequently came to me with proposals for sanction of loans. The regulated market was constructed on spacious land on the outskirts of the city. It had area for parking of bullock carts and sale yard for produce of farmers. The regulated market functioned under its special Act. The purpose of the market was to provide infrastructure for the sale of agricultural produce and protect the farmers from malpractias by ensuring correct weights and measurements and disallowing unwarranted cuts from the sale price. An officer of the weights and measure department served as Secretary of the Committee.

I found that Hyderabad state had passed some very progressive legislatons, among them the Panchayat Law and the Tenancy Law. Slowly I got acquainted myself with the work of the District office. In my judicial capacity I had many cases to hear under the Revenue, Tenancy, Panchayat and Municipal laws but more distinct were the cases under the Workmen's Compensation Act. Most of these cases were related to workers who had died or had been incapacitated in the Hatti gold mines located in Raichur District.

Huge Sprawl of Raichur District

The District officer's work is not confined to his office. It spreads over the entire district which was so huge. It comprised of three sub-divisions—Raichur, Lingsagur and Koppal—each consisting of three Talukas. The Raichur sub-division comprised of Raichur, Manvi and Devdurg takukas, the Langsugar comprised of Lingasugar, Sindhnoor and Kustagi talukas and the Koppal subdivision of Koppal, Yelbarga and Gangawati talukas. The former two talukas belonged to the Salarjung estate and were even mere backward than the rest of the district. Each sub-division was in charge of a Sub-Divisional Officer (SDO) all belonging to the State Civil Service. The SDO Raichur was an officer of the old Hyderabad

Civil Service. Clad in sherwani, pyjama he called on me after I took charge, *salaaming* me with a deep bow in the Muslim style. He was polished in the Mughal way but I found later that he was not quite competent or reliable.

In order to acquaint myself with the District, I got hold of the gazetteer and started reading. I came to know that Raichur District now drought prone and barren of trees was once in the 15th and 16th century full of forests and had heavy rain of 40". But the depredations of oppressive rulers and their neglect of nature had led to denudation of natural resources. What happened in Raichur over centuries has happened elsewhere in the country and reforestation was necessary to restore the denuded vegetation.

There were two outstanding places in the otherwise nondescript Raichur. One was Hatti gold mines – still in operation and the other was Maski where lay an Ashokan Edict. I visited the Hatti gold mines, which were run by a British Company. The English Manager showed me round I was fascinated to see its operations. The English Manager was later replaced by an Indian Manager. I stayed in the Guest-House of the Company, the only comfortable resting place in the entire district apart from of course the guest house of Tungbhadra project. To my lasting regret I could never visit Maski to see the Askhokan Edict with my own eyes though I was keen to do so. Distance and bad roads somehow thwarted my wishes.

Touring

To personally get acquainted with the District I had to visit every Taluka. I had a landrover at my disposal for touring. But the vehicle was uncomfortable and I found that to cover the distant talukas I had to traverse long distances over bad roads. Journeys to distant places like Yelbarga left me thoroughly exhausted. At the end of long dusty hot journies there was no comfortable place to stay. The traveller's bungalows in Taluka HQ were far from comfortable and attending to files at night coming from my office in gas light (there was no electricity) was an unpleasant experience. The most backward of all Tehsil places was Yelbarga. It was deep in the interior and did not have even a TB. No DC ever camped there but I was determined to break the tradition. I considered it a matter of duty to halt there at least once. So despite attempt by my personal staff and local office to dissuade, I made a tour programme to camp there. Arrangements were made for my stay in a small room in the local school. The arrangement was most inconvenient. But I had the satisfaction of having camped at the Tehsil HQ where no previous DC had halted.

The objective of DC camping at HQ Taluka or visiting villages was to review the performance of local administration and meet with the local people. But the latter objective was hardly fulfilled. In old Mysore, I had the experience of local people meeting me at the TB at Taluka HQ and the Panchayat office in the villages. They would come with their problems or representations. But in Raichur district, I found no body would meet me. There simply was no practice of local people meeting the DC on arrival. It was the measure of alienation of the people from administration in the old Nizam area. The people-oriented administration of the Maharja of Mysore and his progressive Dewans had made people meeting the DC or other local officers a long established practice. On the other hand, the Nizam administration, focused entirely on the privileges of the court officers, had a tradition of alienation from the people who probably wished to keep away from administration which was authoritarian and oppressive rather than friendly and responsive.

Visiting the Tahsil or villages was therefore a very frustrating experience. There was simply no contact with the people and no feed-back. I had to be content with formal inspections of offices or conduct of formal official meetings. I could see the need for change to make the administrative people oriented. But the change was not easy to come about. The whole tradition and atmosphere had to change and that could be accomplished only in the long run.

My predecessor Shri R.R. Walvekar had retired more than a month earlier. As I had succeeded a retired officer as SDO Davangere, so had I succeeded another retired officer as DC I should have taken charge from him but for the last minute postponement of orders owing to the objections raised by the state civil service officers as mentioned earlier. He had handed over charge to Shri P.R. Nayak an IAS officer of 1954 batch (a year junior to me) who was serving in the district at Munirabad. As Deputy Administrator of the Tungabhadra project he was responsible for the development of the *ayacut* under Tungabhadra Dam. Newspapers had reported that Nayak had taken the salute at the Republic Day parade on Jan 26 at Raichur which should have been my privilege which I had missed. I took charge from him at the District office whereafter he left for Munirabad.

Meeting Officials and Non-Officials

A new officer has official and non-official visitors. Amongst the former was Shri Kagal, the S.P. He was a senior officer of the IPS. He came in uniform and saluted me – a much more junior officer. But he was brought up in administration of the eastwhile Bombay state and followed the protocol unlike some other IPS officers with whom I came in contact later who had resented saluting the IAS officers and did not like to appear in uniform before them. This may appear to be a symbolic change but had its impact on the functioning of the law and order machinery, which was dependent on the acceptance of the supremacy of the District Magistrate. Another senior officer was the Civil Surgeon Dr. Dharamraj. Both he and his wife (as S.P.Kagal and his wife) were gracious personalities whom it was nice to meet at the club and on the social occasions. Dharamraj were Tamil and Mrs. Dharamraj was proud to mention their Brahmin origin before they were converted to Christianity. The District Judge Ahmed Ali was a senior judge who could not be expected to call on me. He and his wife had gracious Hyderabadi *tehzeeb*. I met them at the club. There were two clubs, one general and another *Zenana* enclosed by a high wall. I went to both the clubs at the former to play billiards and at the latter to play Tennis.

Amongst the prominent non-officials who called on me soon after taking charge were Raghvendrarao Jahagirdar and Bhimachari Ahobali, President and Secretary of the District Congress Committee respectively. Both of them were Brahmins (apparently Brahmins were yet to lose their position in politics to the backward castes in the Hyderabad-Karnataka area) and appeared to be decent enough. They mentioned that since they all belonged to the Congress party, the ruling party in Karnataka, I had nothing to bother about. This was a red rag to my conviction of political neutrality of the civil servants and I curtly responded by saying that this should make no difference to the work of the civil servant who should be independent in the discharge of the duties. Later I felt that I need not have been so candid in my response and kept my conviction to myself rather than give open expression to it. but I was callow and had yet to develop discretion which is better part of the valour. Perhaps one cannot change one's nature. Shri B.V. Desai was the local MLA who was pleasant enough a person and did not throw his weight about. That he did not join the DCC President and Secretary in meeting me showed him as an independent, self-confident person. Another MLA was Smt. Basweshwari, smiling and pleasant, who mentioned that she, belonged to some minor royalty. She was glib and talkative but quite ambitious and later rose in politics to becomes a minister in the state and at the centre.

There was one non-official whom I particularly remember—Pestonji, a Parsee gentlemen, and his two sons—Minu and Russi. This was a lone Parsee family with all the characteristics of the community to which it belonged—friendly and generous. The family had apparently come as Railway contractors and caterers and had settled down there. He never asked for official patronage or favour but was always helpful particularly in organising social events for the club. Long after I left I was agreeably surprised when once while travelling from Pune to Bangalore, he came to know I was travelling and came with a big thermos full of excellent vegetarian meal. I was touched by this. The hot clean meal was a boon to a railway traveller.

On the other hand I was always wary of undue intimacy with the non-officials fearing that they may have an axe to grind. Soon after I came a basket of fresh vegetables was delivered at my house. On enquiry I was told that it was sent by a neighbour—who had his big bungalow by the side of the DC's residence. He had made his money in excise contracts. I returned the basket of vegetables.

One outstanding individual with whom I came into contract was Shri R.B. Magal, Principal of the local Laxmi Venkatesh College. That in the intellectually barren area of Raichur, one should come across a sophisticated person like him was a pleasant surprise. He had recently been for studies to USA on a Rotary Fellowship and spoke with American accent but without pretension. It was always a pleasure to spend time with him. I readily accepted the invitation to visit his college.

Excise Sale

Soon after I assumed charge I had to hold the excise sales—sales of contracts for exclusive right to sell liquor both *desi (arrack)* and foreign (Indian made) liquor. The District Excise officer told me that this was an occasion for money to flow. But I was only interested in conducting sale in the interest of maximum revenue for government. I was suspicious of contractors excersising undue influence to fix sales in their own interest rather than in the interest of government. I therefore kept them at an arm's length. The sale was conducted in an open auction—held throughout the day in my large court-room and brought hefty rise in the revenue some Rs. Sixty lakhs accruing to government. I was quite happy at the outcome. It was a clean operation without the slightest hint of any underhand dealing. Looking at my stern attitude, neither money nor any small gift came to me from any of the contractors – big or small. Though clean excise sale bringing higher revenue to government was an achievement by itselt there was none to appreciate it!

Irrigation Development

As always I was interested in the development side of the administration.Raichur was an extremely underdeveloped district. It was drought prone as it was in the rain-shadow area. Successive droughts and backward agriculture had made Raichur district, a case of "Low – level equilibrium" It had been trapped in the vicious circle of poverty. It needed a dynamic impulse to break out of the vicious circle. That was provided by the Tungabhadra project. An area of 560,000 acres of Raichur district covering talukas of Gangavati, Sindhanur and Manvi stretching from east to west came under the *ayacat* (irrigated area) of the project. The dam was built accumulating a huge reservoir of water but that water was waiting to reach the parched land which was not easy as I soon realized. As I got acquainted with the problem; firstly, a network of canal distribution and water courses taking water right down to the fields had to be in place. Here while the dam was ready, the network was not in position. Without such a network, the irrigation potential could not be utilized and the huge investment in the construction of the dam remained infructuous. That was what happened under the Tungabhadra project. The idea of simultaneous construction of the dam and distribution network was not visualized at the outset itself. On the other hand it was conceived as a two-phase operation – first, the construction of the dam and then the construction of the distribution network. The latter was a much more difficult operation. The dam construction though a big and impressive work could be carried out under central supervision. All it needed was big investment, machinery and a huge labour force. The engineers were used to it. But the distribution network was a dispersed operation. Here again the engineers were comfortable with the construction of huge canals and distributories, but not with the small field channels and water courses. But without them there, the dam and the huge canal were infructuouss. The engineers had decided that water-courses with less then 3 cusec capacity should be done by the farmers themselves. And it is here that the difficult problem arose. The farmers were either reluctant or unable to construct the water channels.

While the engineers were responsible for the construction work, the task of development of the *ayacat* (irrigation potential) was entrusted to the Deputy Administrator (who was also designated as additional Collector). The latter post was held by Shri P.R. Nayak, a brilliant IAS officer of 1954 batch. He was helped by a number of officer at Tahial level. The engineering organisation was headed by a Superintending Engineers by the name Shri Subhan Khan.To coordinate the work of construction and *ayacat* development, a coordination committee was set up headed by the Divisional Commissioner, Gulbarga, who was also designated as Administrator of the project. Dy. Administrator provided the secretariat for the coordination committee. The Deputy Commissioner was designated as Director and was a member of the Committee.

The meetings of the committee were a constant battlefield—tussle between the Superintending Engineer and the Deputy Administrator. The former claimed that a high potential of irrigation was created and it was for the Deputy Administrator to develop the potential which was the objective in view. The latter pointed out that the former's claims regarding irrigation potential created were exaggerated and premature even before the distribution network was in place. The engineers claimed that the potential was actually there. A lot of such disputed claims came to be discussed at the meeting.

The farmers' reluctance to construct the field channels became the Achilles heel of the project. Ultimately it was decided that even the field channels would have to be provided by government, a task which the engineers were most reluctant to undertake. It meant doing work deep in the interior. Moreover it was a low investment work where not much money was involved and engineers were not attracted.

But even where water courses and field channels were constructed, irrigation development was not automatic. Farmers who were for centuries growing only dry crops had now to shift to irrigated crops. That required more work and knowledge regarding irrigation techniques for growing crops like paddy, sugarcane, irrigated cotton and fruits and vegetables. This was a huge cultural change and not just an agriculture transformation. This was a case of water being taken to the horse but the horse reluctant to drink it.

Long years of rain-fed agriculture constantly affected adversely by bad seasons had made farmers fatalistic and static in their outlook. They were lazy and reluctant to be active, while irrigated agriculture badly needed dynamic entrepreneurs. How to infuse dynamism in the farming community? That was a million dollar question.

That could be done, it was felt, through "demonstration plots" where the technology of irrigated agriculture could be convincingly demonstrated to the farmers. A number of such demonstrations were arranged by the officials of the department of agriculture. Shri Nayak thought of the idea of "commercial" demonstration plots which not only demonstrated the technology but also viable economics of the irrigated crops. But apparently mere demonstration was not enough. A more comprehensive and intensive extension work was needed but the extension machinery was weak. Institutional arrangements for the supply of seeds, fertilizer and credit had to be set up, rural roads and transport were needed for transporting agricultural inputs and produce. All this was a big challenge.

To get over the problem of a reluctant community of local farmers, an ambitious programme of importing farmers from other districts was conceived. There were the land less *lambdas* from the neighbouring district of Bijapur. They were to be settled in the underdeveloped irrigation area. I was somewhat doubtful about the project of govt. engineered transplantation of farmers. Ultimately, the magic of irrigation development was accomplished not by government imported *lambada* families but by waves of immigrant farmers from the sarkar area of in Andhra Pradesh. These farmers from delta area were quite canversant with irrigated agriculture and brought with them the skill and dynamism needed for developing irrigated agriculture. They also had the capital needed for small pieces of developed irrigated agriculture. They sold away their valued land in sarkar area at high prices and bought huge tracts in the *ayacat* area in Raichur at throw away prices which were readily sold by the lazy farmers of Raichur district. Nearly two decades later when I was Divisional Commissioner Belgaum I travelled by road from Belgaum to Hyderabad through Raichur district, I was thrilled to travel though flourishing irrigated Varalaxmi cotton and paddy crops on either side developed by the Andhra farmers. When I stopped at either houses I could see the symbols of prosperity—furniture and TV.

But I must go back 20 years to my job as D.C. Raichur. I was excited by the challenge of irrigation development but I found I had only a limited role to play. The Collector was Director of the Tungabhadra Project, but this was only a paper designation. The entire work of "Director" was taken over by the Deputy Administrator who had a specialised administrative machinery at his disposal. The Collector Director was only a member of the coordination committee and there was only an "Assistant" – Upadhyay by name who handled the files relating to the project in the Collector's office. The Deputy Administrator had direct communication with the Administrator – Divisional, Commissioner Gulberga. The Deputy Administrator sent progress reports and I dutifully sent my comments to the Dy. Administrator. Sometimes they might not have been to the liking of Shri Nayak. But I had a feeling that he took little notice of those comments. The position of Collector as "Director" was of undefined responsibility and such a position can seldom be effective. But I need not have bothered because Nayak was an officer of great commitment and intelligence. Through my contribution to the challenging task of *ayacat* development was minimal, the first hand experience of the problems of *ayacat* development stood me in good stead some sixteen years later when I worked as the first Administrator of Malaprabha and Ghataprabha projects.

District Development Plans

My enthusiasm for development work found a new expression when the government asked all Deputy Commissioners to produce District development plans. This was a part of the approach of decentralized planning. It was advocated by some people in the government and outside that democratic planning as against totalitarian planning in Soviet Russia should be "planning from below". The approach should not be "top down" but "bottom up" Planning should begin at village and district level and go upwards, to the state level and then on to national level. In centralized planning schemes would be formulated at the top and passed on to the state and the district. In the decentralised planning process it would be the other way round. Planning from the top would reflect the planner's choice while planning from below would reflect the people's choice.

As soon as instructions came from Bangalore, I went about enthusiastically preparing the District Plan. There was hardly any district machinery for planning. But I held a series of meetings of District Officers to prepare the District Plan. I worked out a general outline of chapters and entrusted the work of preparing sector-wise chapters to the Departmental officer concerned – agriculture, *Ayacat* Development, Industry, Roads, Transportation, common facilities like drinking water, welfare etc. Each chapter had to contain basic statistics, and information and charts and schemes and proposals with financial implications.

Soon the chapters were ready. I as the coordinator put them together, prepared three copies of the plan and sent one to the Planning Department to Bangalore. I was hopeful that the state plan would be prepared on the basis of these district plans. But I was in for disappointment. Firstly, while I and few others had sent the District Plans, others had not. In the meanwhile the state plans had already been prepared reflecting the plan prepared by the Planning Commission. The State-Planning department, which was pressing for preparation of the District plan appeared to have lost interest. All our work for District Plan seemed to have been wasted. But I had to learn that in government this happened and one should do work with Geeta's approach of *Nishkama karma*. After all work is its own reward! The preparation of district plan did help us to go about the development work in a systematic manner.

Small Savings

While formulation of development programme and their implementation was one aspect of planning another was the mobilization of small savings. Targets were prepared for each district and the Deputy Commissioner had the responsibility to meet the target. I went about with the job in all earnestness. One day I was happy to receive a letter of commendation from the Finance Department that Raichur district was chosen as one of the best in the task of mobilization of small savings.

Choosing The Best Village-Level Worker

As D. C. with multifarious responsibilities I could not be in as close a touch with the block development programmes and its teams of extension and village-level workers as I could as SDO. However one opportunity came when the Ministry of Community Development wanted the best village-level worker to be chosen. Each district had to look into the work of village-level workers and chose the best. This could have been done on the basis of reports but I thought that field-work should also be seen. A Committee of three was to be appointed to make the recommendation in which the MLAs and representatives of the political parties had also to represented. I prepared a programme for field visits. This was an arduous task – going to villages and seeing the development work of VLWS. I then realized that the politicians were little interested in this type of work. They only talked of development schemes with votes in view. After some initial show of association, they all absented themselves on some pretext and I was left to myself to complete the field-work and make my recommendation.

A Course At Mussorie

I had a break from my demanding responsibilities of the work of the Deputy Commissioner in the torrid atmosphere of Raichur when I was selected to participate in the month long course of training at the National Institute of Community Development, Mussorie. It was newly set up by the enthusiastic Minister of Community Development, Shri S.K. Dey. Among all the ministers in government then and since then, he was the only one who attached great importance to training. In private business as in military great importance is attached to in-service training. But it was non-existent then for governmental-functionaries and nowadays though extensive facilities do exist for in-service training for civil servants it is not taken seriously and is not linked to professional development of the civil servants. That is because of the non-professional mindset pervasively prevalent in the civil service and lack of real concern and earnestness among the politicians for the development of professional civil service. The latter are interested most of the time in political power and do not see the connection between that and good administration and professional civil services. Dey had come from the private sector and attached importance to systematic training of all the personel working in the field of community development at all levels. Thus he set up 100 villages level workers training centres, some 14 social education' organizers training centres, one orientation and study centre in each state for the block development officers, panchayat training centres, one in each district and at the apex the National Institute of Community Development at Mussorie. The idea of one-month course at Mussorie was to bring together civil servants at the higher level like Collectors, Commissioners and heads of Departments and politicians like MLAs, MPs and even ministers. Politicians who later in their careers reached great heights like P.V.Narasimha Rao and Ramakrishna Hedge had participated in the course. Bringing together civil servants and politicians was a novel idea – but a necessary idea. The two have to work together in administration in a democracy but often they work apart living in their own world and distrusting each other and working at cross purposes. The politicians in power feel that the civil servants have no feel for the needs of the people and are engaged in red tape and delay while the civil servants feel that politicians are interested only in power and cheap popularity and have no real interest in the long term development of the country. The mindset of both had to be changed and hence the idea of bringing them together in a course, in an atmosphere uninhibited by hierarchical differences. Even amongst the civil servants there is often a distance between the general administrators and the officers of technical departments like agriculture and engineering. All the distances had to be bridged and barriers removed. All this was sought to be done through the training course.

For me, the course was indeed a welcome break. The Institute was located at Radha Bhavan at the end of a hill overlooking the valley around. We were housed at the nearby Chaman Estate. To reach the property one had to walk from the library point on a winding road past the famous Savoy Hotel. From Chaman Estate to Radha Bhavan there was one furlong walk which every participant had to take up to and fro every day. That itself was an exhilerating experience. My walking companions were Dr. H.R. Arkeri then Director Agriculture, Karnataka and Shri Shinde, Collector Satara, Maharashtra. We would converse in Marathi. Arkeri though a Kannedga was from Bijapur and educated in Pune and was quite familiar with Marathi. We became friends. The Institute was headed by S. Chankrarathi, ICS (an Andhrite often mistaken because of the name as a Bengalee) who was Joint Secretary in the ministry and doubled as principal. A. Prakash, Deputy Secretary, an officer originally from the army but inducted in IAS was the Vice-Principal. The classes were held in the morning. There was considerable flexibility in the organisation of the course. There was no permanent faculty but guest lectures. This was a good idea because it gave the opportunity to listen to outstanding people who were invited as guest lecturers. Amongst them was Acharya Kripalani who talked of the importance of creating employment opportunities in rural areas. He held forth on the Gandhian approach of creating these opportunities through *Gramudyog*—khadi and village industries. Without these productive capacities in rural area would remain unutilized. He also expected us the civil servants to work in an independent manner without compromising on principles: "Always go with a resignation letter in your pocket", he exhorted. "Do not remain in the civil service if you have to sacrifice your principles". How many civil servants could follow his advice? Some distinguished academicians also came as guest lecturers; amongst them Prof. S. C. Dube the Professor of sociology from Sagar University. His book on the Indian village had made a mark and was much discussed. The community development programme, borrowed from USA opened out and stimulated research in Indian Sociology.

Dube was an eloquent speaker and spoke on the thought ways and the work ways of the village people but his sociological outpouring seldom came near the nitty gritty of development administration. Another academician was Prof Paul Leagns, Professor of Extension of Cornell University USA. Extension was again an American idea connected with the work of county agents of Land Grant Colleges. In American phraseology, extension was education. Leagans taught typically in the American style with audio-visual aids. Now they have become common in India—so much that now a days no lecture is given without such aids whether they are needed or not. But in those days they were rare. Leagans brought a picture of Man with his body organs. Pointing at heart, he said " the heart feels", pointing at head he said "the head thinks", pointing out at hands, he said "the hands work". I thought it was all elementary. In later life I seldom felt enthusiastic about such use of audio-visual aids for delivering a lecture. Apart from these guest lectures, there were seminars with group participation. Minister Dey came on the last day and said that he hoped we all would leave with shining cheecks and rejuvenated for work in our field of activities. How true he was! It was indeed a stimulating interlude. On return I prepared an article on my participation and published it in *Kurukshetra,* the mouthpiece magazine of the Ministry of Community Development.

Cases Under Workmen's Compensation Act

While development work was my first love, quick disposed of cases coming before me, was my professional commitment. In Pandvarpura I had the satisfaction of quickly deciding tenancy cases. In Raichur what gave satisfaction to me was the disposal of cases under the Workmen's Compensation Act. Widows or dependents of workers who had died or incapacitated while working in Hatti Gold Mines were entitled to compensation. But they had to file claims with the District Deputy commissioner' office. It was only after hearing the claims and the orders of Deputy Commissioner thereon that the claimants could receive the compensation legitimately due to them. I found many such claims – some very long standing were pending with the District office. The claimants had long left Hatti to live with their families in distant Hyderabad, Aurangabad or elsewhere. In some cases even their addresses were not known. I took up all such pending cases, made repeated attempts to trace the claimants, fixed hearing and passed orders on the basis of the norms laid down in the Act itself. There was one norm in the case of death, another for full incapacitation and still another for partial incapacitation. When these claimants came to receive their compensation, some old and living in indigent conditions I felt God's work was done.

Pressurization by Minister

There were revenue cases as well. One case left a very bad taste in my mouth. There was a dispute about a land claim between two parties. The case came for hearing before me. The lawyer of one party said that the opposite party was bringing political pressure by the ruling party. I said that he had nothing to fear and I would be deciding the case entirely on merit. But perhaps I need not have said so in the open court. My bravado about my ability to give judgement in an independent manner need not have been expressed in the open court because there are people to carry tales as I soon realized. The judgement went in favour of the person belonging to a local party of Koppal and against the person belonging to the ruling Congress party. That same night I got a long distance phone call from Minister H.M. Chanabasappa from Bangalore. I never expected such a call and was not ready for it. From the word go, the Minister started having a go at me. He bluntly charged me of playing politics in deciding the case. I was flustered and did not know what to say. Till that time I had no idea of the political forces at play in the case. I tried to tell him that it was a court case, implying that a Minister could not interfere with it. But the Minister would have none of it and felt that he had every right to interfere or pull up an erring Deputy Commissioner. The Minister belonged to Mysore and I could not understood what personal interest he could have in Koppal. Perhaps it was Lingayat connection. I felt very unhappy that I was at the receiving end of such a virulent phone call for no fault of mine.

The Minister did not stop after banging the phone at the end of this unpleasant conversation. He complained against me to Kadilda Manjappa, Revenue Minister. The latter was known as an upright person. Besides he belonged to the *Vokkaligar* caste which ways in rivalry with the *Lingayat* caste. So there was an automatic corrective. Manjappa told Chanabasappa that he knew the officer and he could not be accused of any caste bias. Moreover the Minister could not have interfered in a court case, which has to be decided in a legal manner. Manjappa was a lawyer and could easily understand the sanctity of a decision in a court case. Chanabasappa was not a lawyer and could not understand the sanctity of court cases which have to be beyond the pale of Ministerial interference. Chanabasappa could not get me transferred forthwith. My transfer had to await some other incident.

President Rajendra Prasad's Train Journey

The humdrum mofussil life of a district officer is suddenly lifted up above the ordinary by the visit of a VIP. While I was posted at Davangere, it was Prime Minister Jawaharlal Nehru with his daughter Indira making an overnight stay at Harihar; at Pandavpura, it was Vinoba Bhave on his padyatra staying overnight at a school; at Raichur it was no less than the first President of India, Rajendra Prasad passing through Raichur in course of his train journey. The train from Mumbai to Madras halts for a few minutes at the station. It was not known whether the President would come out of his compartment. It was midnight hour. He could be expected to be a sleep at that hour. As a local officer I was officially informed. I went to the station in a mood of uncertainty.

I was surprised that the President did appear out of the compartment to give *Darshan*. I introduced myself as the Deputy Commissioner but it hardly registered. He was himself in sleepy mood. The station was not properly lit up and people were not there in large number to give him a rousing reception. After a few minutes standing at the door Rajen Babu, clad in simply *baniyan* and *dhoti* went back to his compartment. It turned out to be a non-event.

Another visitor whom I remember was Dr. TMA Pai of Manipal. He and his wife came to my Bungalow one morning without prior intimation. Sindhu had gone to Pune and I was alone. I pressed them to stay for lunch which they did. They were very affectionate. Dr. TMA Pai's mission was probably to mobilize funds for his pioneering educational institutions which were still in an incipient stage.

A distinguished visitor though not to Raichur, whom I had privilege to meet was Vice-President, Philosopher Statesman, S. Radhakrishnan. He had come to Gulbarga to inaugurate an educational institution. I was invited by Divisional Commissioner, G.N. Nagraj Rao and K. Prabhakar Rao Deputy Commissioner, Gulbarga, to receive him and be introduced to him. A photo of mine in his presence along with Nagraj Rao and Prabhakar Rao became my prize possession. The tall figure of Radhakrishnan clad in long white coat and white turban was indeed very imposing as was his eloquence. One incident relating to the visit I still remember. He was to be housed in the comfortable residence of an opulent businessman who had generously donated to the educational institution which Radhakrishnan was to inaugurate. But Radhakrishnan refused to stay there and preferred to stay in his railway saloon parked in the station yard. The local organizers should have ascertained his wishes before they made arrangement. They would have escaped the rebuff and consequent ambarrassment.

Shooting at Raichur Station

Administration is not always smooth sailing. Suddenly some untoward incident occurs creating an awkward situation. Such an event occurrerd one day while I was in my office engaged in work. It was suddenly reported to me that a soldier had run amuck at the Raichur station who had started shooting indiscriminately. I did not know what to do. I asked for the District Superintendent of Police but he was on tour. I did not know what I could do as Deputy Commissioner. I had nothing to do with the police force and none was at my disposal. I sent for the SDO – Assistant Commissioner. He was a more experienced officer and his advice could help. But he started saying that Railway area was not in our jurisdiction and we were not concerned. I checked up the Criminal procedure code which mentioned some role for a District Magistrate. That designation was reserved for a judicial officer who was next to the District Judge. I phoned up Noronha who was holding the position but being a judicial officer he said he could do nothing as he could only deal with a case if it came to his court. So I decided to go with the reluctant Assistant Commissioner to the station. By the time I reached the station, the train had left. The shooting had not led to any casualty. I went back to my office in an uncertain state of mind.

In the evening I got a phone call from the Chief Secretary Shri PVR Rao enquiring about the incident. I told him what had happened. The reason for his phone was that the matter was being raised on the floor of the Legislature Assembly. He told me to send a detailed report.

I needed a detailed police report about the occurrence. But it could not be secured immediately. The SP took his own time to return and more time to send his report. It was only after that was received that I could send my own report. The CS was obviously not happy with the delay and wrote me a stinking letter passing the stricture saying that the manner in which I had dealt with the matter was not satisfactory. I felt very unhappy. The CS had given no guideline but was quick to pass stricture. The incident was unusual. Though nothing actually had happened, the incident could have taken an ugly turn if death or even serious injury to passengers or others on the station had occurred. But there were no clearcut rule's to deal with the military personnel. Secondly what is the role of the Deputy Commissioner? He is supposed to be the head of law and order administration. But the police force is neither at his disposal nor is it accountable to him, orders were passed to downgrade the Deputy Commissioner to the level of Additional District Magistrate giving the District Magistrate designation to a judicial officer but he was reluctant to accept any executive responsibility. While changing the designation, the Government did not find it necessary to clearly outline the respective responsibilities of officers. It is the kind of vagueness of position in dealing with law and order matters which created awkward situations leading to dilatory judicial enquiries which find faults with executive officers without leading to any improvement of the situation. After some months when P.V.R. Rao was on a visit to Munirabad I tried to broach the subject but he was reluctant to talk about it and brusquely said that the letter of displeasure had to be sent. Perhaps with more experience I could have passed on the buck to others but in terms of concretely dealing with such a situation it was the government whose responsibility it was to issue clear instructions for handling such cases which now a days are on the increase with military personnel often taking law in their hands. Such situations are dealt with in an adhoc manner.

Shifting Trade to Regulated Market and Its Aftermath

The incidence had no further consequence but another had that related to the regulated market of Raichur. Government was been that trade carried on in the crowded area within the town should be shifted to the spacious premises of the new regulated market, which provided facilities for trade in agricultural commodities Raichur town was quite congested. Round the town was a moat which limited its spatial expansion. The only road outside the town was the one leading to the station along which the clubs and Dy. Commissioner's acquired bungalow were situated. At the end of the road it took a turn towards the traveller's bungalow. Under written communications of the marketing department in the Secretariat, I issued a notice to traders to shift their business to the new regulated market within stipulated time. They came in a delegation to press upon me to withdraw the order and give them more time. But I could not comply with the request. Their shift was long overdue and I was under the instructions of government to effect the shift. Disappointed with my response, the traders left the same day by train to Bangalore as I learnt later.

A couple of days after the meeting, I left for Bombay to stay with my father for a few days stay at his newly built house. A few days later I received a telegram from Bangalore apprising me of my new posting as Deputy Commissioner, South Kanara with Mangalore as HQ. It was a much more advanced district as compared with backward Raichur which was indeed a hard posting. But when I returned to Raichur expecting to shift to Mangalore. I was in for another surprise. My posting to SK was cancelled. Instead, I was posted as Director (youth) and Deputy Development Commissioner Bangalore. It was Deputy Secretary level posting. The enthusiastic and progressive G.V.K Rao who was Additional Development Commissioner had specially selected me as his number two. While I was happy about the new posting I felt bad that the shift was ordered under the pressure of the trader's lobby. The chief minister Jatti was an upright administrator but he must have had his own reasons to succumb to the pressure of trader's lobby. But what message would it carry? The traders could with impunity flout the law regarding regulation of trade in agricultural commodities. This did not auger well for good administration which under much lesser persons than B. D. Jatti went from bad to worse in the years to come.

I stayed as DC Raichur for a period of sixteen months. That was too short a period to leave any impact on so large and backward a district as Raichur. I had just completed one round of visits to all the taluka HQs and while preparing a District Plan had outlined priorities for the district. Giving effect to the plan required sustained effort. But the vicissitudes of transfer never allow the civil servants to implement the plan and politicians hardly have much commitment to hard work of development. Though my transfer from Raichur was premature, for me personally it was a welcome escape from the heat and dust of Raichur.

Birth of My Daughter

It was during Raichur that we had our first child – a daughter. While pregnant my wife needed medical advice. There was a lady doctor in the civil hospital who provided it. Once when I took Sindhu to her for some specifies advice she needed, we found that the lady doctor was just recovering from jaundice. A pregnant lady is very much sensitive and should keep away from contact with such infectious disease as jaundice. We made a mistake and had to pay for it. Sindhu contacted jaundice and the child was born prematurely. Fortunately the expert care of Banu Koyaji of Pune where Sindhu had gone for delivery (my parents lived in Pune) helped the child's growth in the incubator.

Travails of Transfers

From Raichur to Bangalore was my third transfer – first was from Davangere (North of Mysore) to Pandavpura (south), the second from Pandavpura to Raichur (from south to north) and now the third from Raichur to Bangalore (North to South). By this time a child had been added to our household – Every transfer meant packing up household articles and transferring them. The task became more difficult as more household articles accumulated. And more serious became the problem of children's education as they grew. But at Raichur there was no such problem. Medha, the daughter, was only one year old. I decided to dispose of my old Austin which I did not use for touring in Raichur district as I had a land rover at my disposal. But getting a customer in Raichur for old Austin was not easy. The driver got a customer from Hydrabad who offered Rs. 2900/-. He was a Pathan who gave a small advance. But I remembered that as per service rules. I had to get prior permission for a transaction involving a durable article. I asked for permission – wrote a letter to the Chief Secretary. This took its own time and in the meanwhile the Pathan started pressurising and I had quite an embarrassment. I found the rule for prior permission was quite irksome. Later on I realized that such rules create problems for honest civil servants. The more dishonest for whom they are meant get around quite easily.

CHAPTER 8

Deputy Development Commissioner and Director (Youth): Combining Sacreteriat Work and Field Supervision

The posting as Deputy Development Commissioner and Director of Youth was to my liking. The post of Director Youth was funded by the Ford Foundation. Prof. Douglas Ensminger was then the Representative of the Ford Foundation in India. He was a sociologist and was a personal friend of S.K. Dey, the Minister. He was greatly interested in promoting the cause of Community Development in India. He had authored a book on community development in India which served as an excellent manual on the subject. It was greatly appreciated by officers working in the field of community development. Shri C.S. Seshadri was the first incumbent of the post of Director (Youth) and I was the second. The designation of Dy Development Commissioner was added to the designation of Director (Youth). This enabled the Additional Development Commissioner and Secretary Development to have one more deputy to him in addition to a Deputy Secretary. The Chief Secretary was designated as Development Commissioner. The "designations" Deputy Development Commissioner, Additional Development Commissioner and Development Commissioner were all executive designations appropriate to the heads of field administration who generally had their offices outside the secretariat. But these officers were very much officers of the secretariat itself. This combination of secretariat post and field post was an innovation. They combined the responsibilities of secretariat work and executive work. The former is mainly concerned with policy making and the latter with field supervision. The combination of the two responsibilities in the some post broke the barrier between the secretariat and the field. This had its advantages. The secretariat could be field oriented and the field-work could be more policy oriented. Could this distinction not have been obliterated in respect of other departments? But it never happened although combining Secretariat and executive responsibilities was sometimes mentioned as a possible administrative reform. The British had set up the dual system of Secretary and Head of Department and it continued.

Pleasure of Working in *Vidhan Soudha*

As Deputy Development Commissioner and Director of Youth I had my office in the secretariat which was recently shifted from the red *Athara Kacheri* building situated on the fringe of the Cubbon Park to the new *Vidhan Soudha* built by the Chief Minister Hanumanthiah. The magnificent ornate three-story building made of the famous granite stone of Bangalore (Ramnagar nearby had huge granite quarries) was more like a palace rather than the usual lack lustre official building. Hanumanthiah had treated the construction of *Vidhan Soudha* as his dream project and a major achievement as Chief Minister. It embodied all his megalomania. *Vidhan Soudha* overshadowed everything else and became a great tourist attraction. The cabinet room on the third floor had sandal wood door. Sandalwood and granite were the wonderful material of Mysore and both went into the making of *Vidhan Soudha.* To give a central pride of place to the majestic building, the entire road system was redone and changed beyond recognition. The entire layout underwent a metamorphosis.

The building cost Rs. 4 crores – a high sum in those days and Hanmanthiyya was accused of gross extravagance and criticised on the floor of the assembly. Nijlingappa, the senior leader, described *Vidhan Soudha* as *Vishad Soudha.* The building housed the Legislative Assembly as well as the Legislative Council (the Upper House) as well as the cabinet room with sandal wood door, the imposing room of the Chief Minister as well as Ministers' rooms as also the rooms of the Chief Secretary, other Secretaries and their supporting staff. The entrance to the Legislative Assembly was at the end of imposing flight of steps which gave it an aura or grandeur. Later events were to show how utterly misplaced the criticism was. The building came at the right time to house the assembly and the Secretariat of the larger state of Karnataka in which were incorporated the old Mysore State, four districts of Bombay Karnataka, three districts of Hyderabad Karnataka, and one district of South Kanara from old Madras province. As new departments were set-up and more ministers appointed even the large *Vidhan Soudha* building was founds inadequate and new buildings had to be built. But no other building could have the grandeur of *Vidhan Soudha*. Perhaps no other state in India has the privilege to have its assembly and government located in as magnificent a building as *Vidhan Soudha*, which has become the pride of Bangalore and Karnataka.

It is in such a magnificent building that I had the privilege to have my office on the first floor where the Additional Development Commissioner and the rest of the staff of the department were located. I had a large room with an attached bathroom all for myself, a privilege which even secretaries would not have elsewhere.

The new posting gave me two privileges. First, I could participate in the Secretarial work at the highest level in State government and second, I could tour the entire state to visit the CD blocks in several districts of the state. There was a pool of vans in the Department which could be requisitioned for touring.

The file work in the Secretariat is at a much higher level then the file work in the mofussil offices. In the latter files are submitted by clerks and signed by officers in a routine manner mostly handwritten. In the Secretarial files the note sheets are separate from the correspondence papers. In the note sheets, the officers make their contributions, give their inputs on the basis of analysis. Some files relating to important matters and involving policy decisions go to Minister and even the Chief Minister, or if the rules of business require they go to the cabinet.

Close Centre – State Relationship

One special feature of the Community Development Department was that the central ministry of community development was not only active but was also the fountain-head of thinking and policy making. Detailed guidelines would continuously flow from the ministry to the state. Working in community development department brought the state officers in a constant touch with Union government and administration. In an article under the caption "Unitary Trends in a Federal System" published in the Indian Journal of Public Administrations and later included in a book on federalism edited by S.P. Ayer and Usha Mehta of Bombay University I described and analyzed this joint state – union system of administration. The meeting of minds of officers in the state and the centre was facilitated by the annual conference of Development Commissioners convened by the Union ministry.

When I joined at *Vidhan Soudha* to take up my new assignment, I found that such an annual conference was taking place at Mysore. Every body in the department including the Chief Secretary and Development Commissioner PVR Rao, and the Additional Development Commissioner G.V.K. Rao had left for Mysore to participate in the conference. A word was left for me that I too should join, so I too left for Mysore. My friend Anant Datar was Deputy Commissioner, Mysore. He kindly invited me and my family to be his guests. The conference exposed me to my first All India Conference with participants from different states and the Union Ministry. I remember stalwarts like M.R. Bhide and Tandon; Union Secretaries, HVR Iyerger, Governer, RBI, Tarlok Singh of the Planning Commission, all of ICS, actively joining discussion along with some senior development commissioners and chief secretaries from the states. I remember some excited discussion regarding the new co-operative policy. While people like Tarlok Singh stood for autonomy of the cooperatives, M.R. Bhide, who was Union Secretary for cooperation, minced no words to assert that whatever be the ideology, in reality cooperatives were creatures of the state.

Residential Accommodation

Back to Bangalore from the conference, my first worry was to get suitable residential accommodation. Unlike some other state HQ, Bangalore did not provide official accommodation. An officer on transfer had to be on his own. There was reason for this. Most officers in old Mysore had their own houses in Bangalore. In fact, there was a tradition for a person newly recruited to civil service to lose no time to acquire a plot and build a home. The City Improvement Trust was in charge of development of sites and civil servants had a priority in allotment of sites. In fact to get a good plot was the ambition of every civil servant. Housing loans from Government were available, so a loan was taken and a house built. Civil servants of all levels from peons and clerks upwards to secretaries to Government were all engaged in this activity. That was also the subject of conversation at all times. Everybody considered Bangalore to be the most beautiful place on the face of the earth and there could be no greater ambition than having a house of your own in Bangalore.

But I had no house of my own and had to go about in search for accommodation. The first step was to consult the list of accommodations available on rent displayed on the notice board of the rent controller's office. I had an experience of this when I first stayed in Bangalore during my training year in 1954-55. Now in 1959 things were not very different.

Another problem was to get household help. A maid for sweeping and washing was hired but an all time servant was needed. My office peon arranged for a boy from his village—one Javariah who lived and ate at the house and did odd jobs.

Mobilising Rural Youth

I soon started getting acquainted with my new responsibilities and indeed plunged head long into them. I was fascinated by first designation, *viz.* Director (Youth). I had to promote the rural youth movement in Karnataka. The idea was that the youth had to play a crucial role in rural transformation, in assimilating new technology and ways of life. Every village must have a Yuvak Mandal and Mahila Mandal in addition to a Panchyat, a cooperative and school. There was of course no field department for promoting the rural youth movement. It had to be done through the community block's village level workers and extension agents.

In order to develop my knowledge about the literature on rural youth movement, I started reading books on the subject. I found the books on the 4 H clubs in USA quite interesting. The 4 H stood for Heart for better feeling, Head for better thinking, Hands for better service and, Health for better living. I started spreading the 4 H gospel in the rural youth clubs set up in the community development blocks in Karnataka. The significance of the rural youth movement was that youth could more readily absorb innovation and change, both technological and social.

Taradevi Youth Camp

The Union Ministry of Community Development and Agriculture were also interested in the promotion of the rural youth movement. The Department of Agriculture in the Union Ministry had an extension wing. Yasmin Morenas a Parsee lady was in charge of youth work there and Nirmalendu Basu was actively doing work for theYoung Farmers Organisation, a voluntary body supported by the Ministry. There were other voluntary organizations like YMCA which were engaged in youth activities, though in their own way. I got an opportunity to meet representatives of youth organizations and officers of state governments working in the field when I got invited to participate in a seven-day youth camp at

Taradevi near Shimla. Shimla was known but not Taradevi which had excellent camp facilities. It was some 7 km down the road from Shimla. One morning I landed there away from office and city life. The seven days spent in that camp was an enjoyable experience. I could also build up on my knowledge about youth organizations. Following the National Youth camp at Taradevi we were expected to organize a similar youth camp at the state level for youth workers in the state. I decided to organize the youth camp at Dharwad Village Level Workers' Training Centre which was a good success Shri Patil the Principal of the centre made good arrangements for organization of the camp, which generated a lot of enthusiasm

On the basis of the knowledge gained on the subject I prepared a rural youth manual which could be of use for rural youth workers in the community development blocks. I wished to get it published but it never saw the light of the day.

Visits to Community Development Blocks

My position as Deputy Development Commissioner gave me an excellent opportunity to visit community development blocks all over the state. I vividly remember my first visit to Coorg (Kodagu in Karnataka) and South Canara districts. I had never visited these areas before. Going over the beautiful picturesque Western Ghats down the steep slope on the west leading to the benign coastal areas and ending into the vast spread of the sea was a thrilling experience.

The natural and social landscape of Coorg had distinguishing characteristics of its own. People of Coorg had a martial tradition and given to India generals like K.M. Cariappa the first commander in Chief of the Indian army after independence and K.S. Thimmeryya who made a name for themselves. I remember visiting Cariappa at his spacious house in Madkeri (Mercara) and having tea with him. The people of South Canara were different. They were more enlightened and on the move.

At all these visits to community development blocks I would hold meetings with the BDOs and the extension offices and review the implementation of various development programme and also ascertain their problems. I would produce tour notes on the visits to these blocks. These visits served many purposes. First they were a source of stimulus to the local development staff—a break from their daily routine. Ideas from HQ needed to be communicated to the field staff to create better understanding of the programme. This purpose was served by my meetings with field staff, Second, they made the HQ familiar with field problems. Pending matters or difficulties at local level could be taken up at HQ and necessary orders or clearness could be issued. In those early years of development work, there was still a considerable amount of idealism and enthusiasm for development work amongst the officials as well as non-officials. The non-officials were associated through the block development committees.

Panchayati Raj

Following the recommendations of the Balwantrai Mehta Committee, (1956) three tier Panchayet Raj Institutions were set up and the block administration was made answerable to the elected representatives of the people. But it was not as though these institutions were set up for the first time. The Panchayats already existed at the village level and local boards at the higher level. But they were rejuvenated and entrusted with the programme covered by the block-development budget as well as other local development schemes.

Karnataka framed its own law on these Panchayat Raj institutions. The Zilla Parishad was called the District Development Council and was headed, to start with, by the Deputy Commissioner. The Panchayat Samithis and Panchayats were elected institutions. While I was working as Deputy Development Commissioner, the work of framing rules under the law was on hand. The work was entrusted to an experienced Under Secretary, Shri B. Venketramiah. While he was competent he was carrying with him a secretariat mentality. He had never visited the field nor worked at the grassroot level and had no feel for the rural community. No wonder the draft rules that he framed, mostly on the basis of past formulations, did not reflect the impulses needed for development and the need for freedom and dynamism. Such an imaginative approach could not be expected from him. The dynamism of community development could not fit with the dry as dust approach of a secretariat functionary. The latter always has a suspicious outlook on conferring autonomy on the local government institutions and wanted to retain maximum control, covert and overt, on them. When the draft rules came to me couched in the traditional control syndrome, I tried to modify them to suit developmental requirements and free, flexible and autonomous functioning of Panchayati Raj Institutions.

Essays on Development

I got frequent opportunities to deliver lectures at the courses conducted for the Block Development Officers at the newly established Orientation and Study Centre at the Mysore. It was located at the beautiful spacious premises known as Jocky's quarters facing the Chamudi Hills. They provided me opportunities for study, reading and reflection. I sent essay for the competition held by the Union Ministry on the topic "The second front". It was awarded the first prize. Chief Secretary Hirannayya on getting intimation from the Ministry wrote a warm letter of congratulation to me. I also sent essays for the Annual Essay Competition held by the Indian Institute of Public Administration. They got prizes for two successive years – 1959 and 1960. I had the previlege of receiving these prizes at the hands of Pandit Jawaharlal Nehru, the PM, who as the President of IIPA presided over the annual general meetings at which prizes were delivered. On the latter occasion, the photographer took my picture receiving prize from Nehru's hands. On return to Bangalore, I thought of sending the picture to PM requesting him to send it back with his autograph. The PM was about to leave for Yugoslavia and I wondered whether he would find time to give his autograph. But as is rightly said it is the busiest person who finds time. I was pleasantly surprised to have the picture back with Nehru's autograph. I was greatly disappointed that exposed to the glare of the evening sun, the autograph faded in course of time. However the photo with Nehru has ever remained my prize possession.

My two essays in IIPA competition were on "Scope and Implementation of Democratic Decentralization" and " Training of Public Servants in a Developing Economy" The former was published in *IJPA*. The article on the "Second front" was published in the *Kurukshetra* journal. I felt happy that in addition to my normal work, I was able to write these award winning essays. Later I included them in my book "Essays on Rural Development".

My participation in All India Conference broadened my horizon. I remember the conferences held at Ootacmand (Ooty), Hyderabad and Srinagar. But what I remember is not what transpired at the conferences but the image of actor Rajendra Kumar running around the bush after Vaijayanthimala in the famous Botanical Garden at Ootacmand while shooting was going on for a Hindi picture (was it Arzoo?) and Yamini Krishnmoorty giving her pioneering displays of Kuchipudi Dancing which she introduced to the Indian audience. I and my wife also enjoyed the ride in Shikara on the placid surface of the Dal lake, whose enchanting beauty brought me back to it several times later till the militancy there made it impossible to visit.

National Development Council

But the conference which I particularly remember was the National Development Council conference presided over by Prime Minister Nehru on the subject of measures to control inflation. As Deputy Development Commissioner in charge of community development, the subject did not fall in my province. But Dr. Iyengar, the Planning Secretary had referred the file to me and I had recorded a note on the subject. The Chief Minister, Shri Jatti appreciated the note and recorded on the file itself that as "Dubhashi has the information, he should be the official in attendence at NDC conference". It was Chief Minister Jatti's way of encouraging a young officer. It was also Dr. Iyengar's goodness that though as Secretary Planning it was his privilege to assist the Chief Minister, he did not object and allowed me the opportunity to attend the NDC. Only Secretary level officers assisted the Chief Minister at NDC. I had the rare privilege at a young age. The National Development Council is perhaps the highest official body in the Indian administrative system. Under the Indian Constitution such an inter-state council was constituted for tackling All India problems. The NDC comprised of all the Chief Ministers and some prominent Central Ministers who were ex-officio members of the Planning Commission and presided over by the Prime Minister. While the PM and his colleagues sat at the head of the table in the conference Hall in Vigyan Bhavan, the Chief Ministers sat round the tables. The officers sat in the row of chairs behind the Ministers and their respective Chief Ministers. It was educative to see the meeting held at the highest level. Several Chief Ministers simply read the speeches written by their officers. Inflation being a technical subject was not the one on which politician Chief Ministers could speak on their own. Nehru often closed his eyes while listening to these speeches monotonously read by the Chief Ministers. Nehru did not read the speeches but delivered them and often intervened.

I watched Nehru walking his steps on the staircase through the corridor to the conference hall. His face full of energy, he walked into the conference room exactly on time. There was a feeling of earnestness as the conference went on—not a trace of cynicism. But there was a habitual late comer as well—no less a person than Gobind Ballabh Pant, the Home Minister and Nehru's senior most colleague. Shaking his head due to Parkinson disease or old age, he came late. He was too senior and respected colleague to be scolded by the PM. A Chief Minister who could not be overwhelmed by Nehru's august presence was Dr. Bidhan Chandra Roy of West Bangol. He could have his say and PM had to listen.

MPs' Camp at Nandihalli

One event I vividly remember was the MPs, camp at Nandihill, a hill station near Bangalore. It was held at the instance of Minister S.K. Dey. The objective was to get the MPs involved in thinking on Community Development. It was a pioneering venture. The Chief Secretary P.V.R. Rao, and G.V.K. Rao, the Additional Development Commissioner and Secretary took an active part in arranging the camp. As Deputy Development Commissioner, I also took an active part. It was a well-attended camp and there was animated discussion on all aspects of the community development programme.

But my participation had a bad fall out. During my stay at Nandihill I used to walk in the morning mist from my cottage at the base where I stayed to the hill top building where discussion used to take place. When I returned from Nandihill to Bangalore, I started wheezing and coughing and that went on for days. I was susceptible to cold and cough from my childhood and thought it was one of those ailments. But days went on and the trouble was not over. I felt weak and tired. At night I could not sleep properly because of coughing bouts. I went on long leave to Bombay. My brother Arvind was a doctor. He took the blood test and discovered that my eosinophilic blood count which in a normal person should be less than six had shot up to hundred and more. He advised a prolonged course of hetrazen tablets, which slowly brought the count down. Eosinophilia is an allergy and is attributed to environmental pollution, caused by pollens of pantheism weed. Also Bangalore has considerable humidity in the atmosphere almost all the year round. Clouds hang low and diurnal changes in temperature are high. It may be warm while going to office but a heavy down pour in the evening, known as "Secretariat rain" would bring the temperature down causing chill. The body does not find it easy to adjust to these changes. I could understand only later why in Bangalore officers generally came in woollen suits which were a good protection from cold caused by evening rains. Sneezing and asthma are quite common in Bangalore though Bangalore is known for its good weather. For me the good weather of Bangalore became an anathema after the first attack of eosinophilia which recurred during my next stay in Bangalore as well. This had an effect on my relation to Bangalore. I could not decide on a permanent stay in Bangalore and was the only IAS officer who did not build his house there, though every one else did. That even led to a state of uncertainty and impermanence and lack of confidence. I started looking at myself as an impractical person who could not take timely decision on building his own house though I acquired a reasonably good plot in HAL extension which developed well as flourishing Indira Nagar.. It was because of my adversarial relation to Bangalore weather that I could not have the desire of sticking to Bangalore.

My Colleagues

There were three officers at the middle level below the secretary – Deputy Secretary, Deputy Development Commissioner and Director of Youth and Director (In-service Training). The last post was held by B. Rudramoorthy who was an officer from the Dept. of Agriculture. He was greatly interested in the Extension approach of USA because of his stay in USA where he had acquired an M.Sc. After he took over as the first Principal of Orientation and Study Centre in Mysore, Dr. Dwarkinath, also of the Agricultural Department, took over. The latter later acquired a Ph.D. from Cornell in Extension and became Director (Agriculture) and Vice-Chancellor Agricultural University. I had good professional relationship with both the officers, Shri K.M. Mirani, another IAS officer of 1951 batch, my senior by two years, was Deputy Secretary. He had worked in the field of O & M. G.V.K. Rao thought of using his expertise for allocation of work between the Deputy Secretary and the Deputy Development Commissioner. He suggested a re-allocation of duties on the basis of the principle that the Dy. Secretary should handle all matters relating to policy while the Deputy Development Commissioner should handle matters relating to supervision and operation of programmes – a logical division between the secretariat and Head of a Department. As a result of his scheme, the Deputy Development Commissioner lost many important items of work. I was not informed in advance about the revised allocation of work and felt hurt. I raised my objections on paper pointing out that since the Secretary was called Additional Development Commissioner, and the Deputy Development Commissioner worked in the Secretariat itself, the organizational principle was that the work of the Secretariat and the Head of the Dept. should not be bifurcated but be merged. This made for policy making which reflected feedback from the field and programme operation and supervision which was guided by broader policy considerations. But the die had already been cast and my objections made no impression.

Soon the people in-charge themselves were to change their positions. G.V.K. Rao moved as Secretary PWD while Mirani moved to Finance. Dr. Iyengar came as the new Additional Development Commissioner and Secretary Planning. He relied a great deal on me. He was a kind and affable person. Once S.K. Dey came on a tour. I went with Iyengar to keep company with Dey. Dey was very fond of good non-vegetarian meal, particularly chicken which was served with lunch. We both took vegetarian meal. Dey felt bad and turned to us asking, "what crime had you committed in your previous birth that you have to deny the pleasure of eating chicken in your present birth?" I should have said, "Perhaps the same crime you are committing now".

Deputation to Centre

I had just completed two years as Deputy Development Commissioner when I suddenly got orders of my deputation to centre to the post of Under Secretary in Ministry of Defence. I was taken aback though I had agreed to my deputation to the centre, I did not like to go to Defence and work with Colonels and Generals (as I understood I would have to do). I preferred to work in the field of Development. My Secretary thought that I should not go at the junior most level of Under Secretary. I should go at the level of Deputy Secretary. But the orders were issued and Chief Secretary Rebello was not willing to help. So I met Chief Minister Jatti and he immediately agreed to keep me on with the state. He did not want to force on me a posting at Delhi which was not to my liking. The new Development Commissioner Shri SAL Razvi who had come from Hyderabad was also very helpful and put in a word with Jatti. I also spoke on phone to our previous Chief Secretary PVR Rao who had gone to centre as Secretary in the Department of Community Development. I told him I would like to go to a like Ministry He heard it as "light" and I had to correct him. He agreed to help and advised me to take some leave.

I was in a state of uncertainly, not sure of avoiding a posting at Delhi. I had got packed my personal effects. This time I had no peons to help as in my pervious field posting. Packing up personal effects every few years had started taking its toll. I remained in such state for a month or so with considerable personal in-convince. I did not know whether I was right in not going to Defence. I would have gone to a quintessential Central Ministry like Defence and worked in prestigious South Block. But I could have got entangled in some thing like Bofors, which of course was several years away. But the jeep scandal was there even in Nehru years!

Soon the uncertainty ended. A special post was created for me as OSD in the department of development. I started practically doing the same work as Deputy Development Commissioner. Shri H. Maharudrppa was posted Deputy Development Commissioner but Razvi reposed his trust in me and referred many files to me. I did not feel like an odd man out because of my designation of OSD. But I had lost my precious chambers and had to make do with a room specially fitted for me in a corridor space.

As my uncertain stay at OSD continued, I got an offer from the Centre. Shri S. Chakravarthi who was Joint Secretary in the Ministry Community Development and ex-officio Principal of National Institute of Community Development on a visit to Bangalore told me that the Minister S.K. Dey would like me to join as Director (Studies) and Vice-Principal of the National Institute of Community Development Mussorie. I was happy about thc offer but in the meanwhile another development had taken place. I was selected as a British Council Scholar to enable me to complete a post-graduate course at the London School of Economics in economic and social administration which was funded by the Ford Foundation. I told Chkravarthi that my acceptance of the ministry's post should not come in the way of my joining the LSE in September. That meant that I could be in Mussorie for a short period of only two and a half months.

I had applied for the British Council Scholarship following the example of my senior colleague in IAS Shri Satish Chandra. He was selected for the year 1961-62 and I was following his foot-steps in 1962-63. My academic carrier was bright. I had stood first in M.A. with Economics as my subject. I was interviewed by a panel of the British Council (of which M.A. Khusro of the Institute of Economic Growth in Delhi was a member) and was duly selected and was preparing for my departure to join the course in September and now the offer from the Ministry had come.

The offer from the union ministry duly came and I was relived by the state Government to join the Institute at Mussorie. I had to wind up my establishment in Bangalore. I sold away my car and even some pieces of my furniture and left the rest packed at my father's house in Bombay. I did not need them at Mussorie since I was provided furnished accommodation at Chaman Estate of the Institute.

CHAPTER 9

Brief Interlude at Mussorie

The Role of a Trainer

Mussorie has been my favourite hill station. I had been there before and liked the walk on the Camel's Back Hill, the road from the library point to Kulri and Landor Bazar and the shimmering lights in the Dehradun valley at night, which could be viewed from several points. This time I was going to Mussorie on my regular posting but since it was to be for a short period, I had a feeling of having yet another holiday at the hill station.

But this time of course I had a job to do; moreover, the time I was there in July—August was not the peak holiday period. At that time there used to be heavy down pours not conducive to holiday activities.

Faculty and Staff of the Institute

After I joined, I found that two one-month long orientation courses were scheduled and I had to be in charge of them. The Director (studies), the post I held was in charge of the conduct of the training courses. Earlier the Institute did not have a large permanent faculty and depended upon the invited guest faculty to deliver the lectures. That was the position when I was there as a participant (as Deputy Commissioner Raichur. I was sent to the course to which I had referred to earlier). But now there was some faculty in position which consisted of three academicians—Prof. S.C. Dubey, the sociologist, Sugota Dasgupta, qualified in social work and Rajani Kothari, a political scientist. Dubey with his two books on Indian village had already made a name; Kothari, yet at the threshold of his academic career had completed his M. Sc in Government from the London School of Economics. He later become India's leading political scientist and even became a member of the Planning Commission. Sugata Dusgupta later became the Director of Gandhi

Institute of Social Studies at Varanasi and still later went to Australia. There was another academician, Prof. Henry Maddick the Ford Foundation consultant at the institute. He was on deputation from Birmingham University where he taught politics and administration. He lived in Savoy Hotel and was hardly seen at the Institute. Obviously he was collecting material for his forthcoming book on Panchayati Raj in India. I read some of his papers on local government, which laid emphasis on great measure of decentralization—what can be decentralized must be decentralized, he said.

What was striking about these academicians was their minimum institutional commitment. They were there for pursuing their own academic ambitions and treated their posting as some kind of stand-by arrangement before they could reach greater heights or greener pasteurs. Not for them the humdrum activities connected with the conduct of courses. That was left to M.L. Sudan, the Research officer, who took up matters with the Director (Studies) for the conduct of courses. The administrative matters were looked after by the Registrar, a post held by another IAS officer Shri T. Balakrishnan of A.P. cadre. In the system, the academicians were not answerable to any body. The consultant Prof. Meddick never showed himself at the Institute. But even the three academicians holding regular posts and drawing regular salaries never believed in regular working hours. They stayed at their residences provided by the Institute. Dubey was fond of drinks of which he had a good stock at his residence. The Principal, Shri Chakravarthi ICS, was also a Joint Secretary and was looking for a posting in the Ministry. He soon succeeded in his ambitions and took over as Additional Secretary in the Ministry in the Department of Community Development when PVR Rao who held the post moved as Secretary in charge of Defence.

After Chakravathi left I thought I would be in charge as Principal of the Institute. After all I held the position of Vice-Principal. But that was not to be; it was Prof. Dubey who was appointed to the post. I felt over-looked. But the authorities felt that Dubey was a senior academician who would not like to work under a youngster in charge of the post of Principal. I did not stake my claim or register any protest realizing that I myself was about to go to LSE under the British Council Scholarship. I busied myself with the conduct of the two courses which were scheduled during my stay at Mussorie.

Two Training Courses

In the absence of the Principal, I welcomed the participants, got them introduced to each other, formed syndicate groups and supervised syndicate discussions. I also delivered some lectures myself. The participants were surprised that I could address them by name after just one introducing session., I could remember all their names. That was because I kept the list of names of participants before me and fixed in my head the connection between names and faces and the images remained indelible. One of the qualities a trainer must possess. is capacity to have a personal engagement with the trainee and not a generalized communication. This trait of a personal approach of a trainer remained with me in my further career as a trainer.

After the day's work was over we took walks to the Kulri Bazar. Balakrishnan and his wife often joined us. Sudan had his residence in Kulri, so he could sometimes join. On walks we could meet some of the participants as well.

Preparing for LSE

While my course involvement was going in, I was making arrangements for leaving for London. The British Council official in charge of scholarships, Miss Tunks, was sending communications after communications. I had also to make arrangements for obtaining formal clearance from the Ministry for joining the course and accepting British Council scholarship. My study leave was sanctioned only on half pay. I was disappointed that full pay study leave was denied to me. I got in touch in with Shri G.V.K. Rao who had moved to the Ministry of Community Development in Delhi as Training Commissioner. He frightened me saying that the committee of Secretaries had sanctioned my study leave and if I wanted it on full pay leave, they may withdraw the sanction. Those were days when going for training abroad was looked upon as a privilege granted to a civil servant. This retrograde policy was changed later when training abroad was encouraged and full pay leave for 24 months was incorporated in rules as a matter of policy. Pioneers often have to suffer.

Miss Tunks sent me a booklet "How to live in Britain". It contained excellent tips regarding living in Britain—the weather, British culture and practices and shopping facilities etc. I was going on my first visit abroad and the booklet came very handy. I also wrote to Satish Chandran for his advice. He told me that I need not take much clothings and could buy them there – the Burtons could supply ready made woollen suits and Marks & Spencer shirts. He also advised that if I were to take wife and family additional resources could be needed. The scholarship may not be adequate. Since in those days Reserve Bank of India was extremely stingy in releasing foreign exchange, I decided to go alone leaving, Sindhu with child Medha at her parents.

Originally the British Council had arranged my journey by sea on the ship Silecia. But since my formalities regarding sanction of leave took time, they arranged flight to London – which saved time.

Flight to London

So I left for London – my first trip abroad and a landmark in my personal life.

A memorable part of the flight on Air India was that Rajaji, the elder statesman was on it. He was on his first flight abroad in his life to New York via London to meet John F Kennedy, the American President. His mission was to persuade him to renounce atomic weapons and save humanity from the scourge such as that suffered by the citizens of Nagasaki and Hiroshima. The elder Indian statesman was to meet the young American President – an interaction between ancient Indian wisdom and young American ebullience. The President was greatly impressed by Rajaji's sharp intellect and logical arguments. But America did no destroy the stockpile of atomic weapons or give up its search for perfection in developing the technology of annihilation of humanity and the world suffered in later years.

CHAPTER 10

At London School of Economics (1962-63)

Return to Student Days

The plane landed at London's Heathrow airport at about 11 am after a halt at Geneva airport where I bought a ballpoint pen. Since the British Council was aware of my programme I expected to be received. There was a British Council representative at the airport and I introduced myself to him. He had a list of British Council scholars whom he had expected to meet but I was not one of them! There were three or four scholars from the African countries. Any way along with them I was also escorted to a hostel near Knight's Bridge for temporary accommodation. By the time I reached the hostel, and had settled down after a meal, it was already late in the evening. I was keen to send a telegram to my father in Bombay about my safe arrival but it could not be sent from the hostel. I had to go to the post office. But where is the post-office? On inquiry, I learnt that it was not far away—I could go by 'tube'. But I was not familiar with tube or the underground railway. Going down the lift at the entry point to catch the right train on the right route was an undertaking I was hesitant to take up. So I decided to go by bus. A pedestrian asked me to hop in a moving bus—which I did. The conductor told me that was not the right thing to do but gave me the ticket and also helped me to get down at the bus stop near the post office. At the post office I gave the message to be sent by wire and waited for the "receipt". The clerk at the counter told me that no such receipt was necessary and the message would reach. This was the first experience of business being done without needles paper work as was being done in India.

At the International Hall

The hostel was full of dark people—students from Africa and I was not comfortable. Next day I went to the British Council office at 65 Davies Street and met Miss Clive, the Scholarship Officer. She was an old lady quite used to dealing with students from India. She gave me some advance and gave the address of the hostel where I had to live during my stay in London. The hostel was known as the International Hall. The LSE students traditionally stayed at the Passfield Hall (named after Sydney Web, the founder of LSE who was later to be Lord Passfield). But my arrangements were made in the newly built International Hall which only a few months ago was inaugurated by the Indian High Commissioner Smt.Vijaya Laxmi Pandit. Being a modern Hall, it was centrally heated unlike the Passfield Hall. Central heating gave excellent protection from cold. It was a distinct advantage. The winter of the year 1962 turned out to be the worst since 1841. Everybody started talking of artic cold. Central heating saved me from extreme cold which I shuddered to deal with. The Passfield Hall had oil heaters in the room and coins had to be inserted from time to time to make them work. The room in the International Hall was also bigger than the room in the Passfield Hall and was well appointed with modern furniture. My room was on the first floor of the Hall while the dining room was on the ground floor where self-service arrangements were made. One had to stand in the queue, take the tray and the plate and get served. Two German girls were providing the service and were given rooms to stay in the hostel itself. The breakfast and meals were served at fixed timings. Tatersall was the hostel superintendent. One advantage of International Hall was that it was at a walking distance to LSE. One walked passed the underground station Holburn to reach LSE in ten minutes. As I walked on the pavement to LSE I was rapidly overtaken by other pedestrians who I found were given to fast walking—as though always in a hurry.

I went to Burtons as advised and bought a couple of woollen suits available for as little as Pound 5 under "sale". They served my purpose very well. I also bought a felt hat and an overcoat which also served as a raincoat.

The LSE

LSE was easy to locate. It was near the Indian High Commissioner's office at Aldwych. Three solid massive buildings away from the main road housed the LSE. The hallowed centre of academic learning was established originally by Sydney and Beatrice Webb, the famous couple and leading lights of the Labour Party, to provide education for the working people through evening classes. This was what distinguished the LSE from the traditional Universities, Cambridge and Oxford. Ofcourse over years LSE grew as a fullfledged academic institution providing education in a wide range of subjects like Economics, Sociology, Social Work and Political Science and conferring degrees – both graduate and post-graduate. Distinguished persons like Harold Laski, J.M. Keynes, Hugh Dalton had taught at LSE. Generations of Indians who later distinguished themselves in public life had passed through the portals of the LSE. It was my dream to study at the Institution after having missed the opportunity of studying at Trinity College Cambridge where I had secured admission after my graduation

The Ford Course

I was to join the one-year "Ford Course" leading to post-graduate diploma in Economic and Social Administration. It was a multi-disciplinary course specially designed for overseas administrators. Three faculty members Prof. Peter Self teaching a course in administration, Peter Hodge teaching social work and Cassen teaching Economics constituted the Trinity of this multi-disciplinary course. They were supplemented by large number of other courses taken by academicians who had distinguished themselves in their respective subjects. Of them one was Prof. Richard Titmas whose lectures on social work were attended by a large body of students. He was eloquent as well as learned. On the other hand Prof. Lucy Mair who had also a big name simply read her lectures which were nothing but case studies from different countries of Asia and Africa. Also reading lectures was Prof. Walter di Smith who was an expert on constitutional law and served as consultant to several African countries in designing their constitutions. Knox took lectures on economic development. Later he joined as Vice President in World Bank. So did Robert Cassen who made a name in the population studies. Prof. Yamey also took a course on economics of development. Along with P.T. Bauer. he had written a book on Economics of Development which together with Prof. W. Arthur Lewis's Theory of Economic Growth and those of Kindleberger and many others were standard text books on economics of development. The course provided an excellent opportunity to study a wide range of subjects specially Economics of development of underdeveloped countries, politics in countries emerging from colonization and social transformation connected with technological change. These were the great contemporary themes of the latter half of the twentieth century. The course also opened out acquaintance with several African countries like Nigeria, Ghana and Tanzania with which I was not quite familiar. The course really broadened my horizon. It also deepened my knowledge. A long list of books was recommended and I read many of them. I was back to my student days. Indeed the desire to keep track of up-to-date thinking by reading books never left me. In other words I remained a student throughout my life. My stay at LSE was merely an intensive phase of that way of life.

LSE turns Rightist

But in a fundamental way LSE was a disappointment. We in India had thought that it was a centre of liberal and leftist thinking . What I found was an intellectual centre completely taken over by rightist thinking. Laski was almost forgotten. None of his books appeared in the recommended list of books. There was a room named after Graham Wallace but there was no memorial for Laski. Michael Oakshott., Professor of Political Science was the leading light and guru of rightist thought. The samc was true in Economics as well. Prof. Bauer's influence was felt and later it grew. He became the inspiration of Margaret Thateher who elevated him to lordship. Bauer was totally opposed to any kind of central planning, a position taken by the Austrian economist Ludwig Von Mises and Fredrick Von Hayek. The latter's "Constitution of Liberty" became the bible of those opposed to planning. Bauer used to take tutorial discussions for small groups. He was a critic of planning in India and uncompromisingly asserted that all aid to India should be stopped till India gives up planning. In his book he had commended on the role of the moneylender in the Indian rural economy, who according to Bauer was discharging an essential function. If he charged a high rate of interest it was because of scarcity of capital and the risks involved. It was therefore wrong either to abolish him or control his activities. He stood for the untrammeled functioning of the market economy without the least regulation or interference in the market except for the removal of hindrances to its working. In spite of his strident and pugnacious writing he was an unimpressive puny little guy. When my turn came to write a paper I attempted one on Indian Planning Because of shortage of time and lack of ready availability of up-to-date material I could not do justice to my assignment and was myself dissatisfied. But Bauer expressed his deep disappointment because I, like all good Indians at that time was supportive of a planned economy. It was thirty years before India took a U turn in the macro-economic policy abandoning a planned and controlled economy in favour of a free market economy.

While in the course of my College and University education, I had studied Economics and Political Science, I had not done systematic reading in Sociology and social work except later in the context of community development. At LSE I studied Sociology more systemically beginning with standard text books on the subject, I always felt that knowledge of social sciences was not complete without the knowledge of Sociology and an administrator dealing with development programmes should be familiar with the subject. In the seminars held by our Trinity, Self, Hodge and Cassen this was prominently brought out. On any subject taken up for discussion, Self would pinpoint the political and administrative aspects, Cassen would mumble on economic aspects, (but his sharp intellect gavc edge to his argument) and Hodge was gently persuasive in emphasizing that socialological aspects should not be overlooked. These group discussions were held in a small room exclusively available for the Ford group which had also a small library of its own.

Our small Ford group consisted of less than twenty participants from different countries—Canada, Jamaica, Spain, Nigeria, Southern Rhodesia (now called Zimbabwe—the participant was a white man), Nepal, Sri Lanka and India. In a way it was a disappointing group because I felt that other participants were not academically of a high level or claiming high educational qualifications. Those in charge of Ford Foundation felt that administrators from developing countries participating in the course would advance their career with an academic qualification from LSE. I thought this was hardly true in my case. A mere post-graduate diploma even from LSE could hardly make a difference in my official career. On the other hand, the opportunity to catch up with intensive study was itself an advantage apart from being exposed to a variety of new subjects.

LSE was a large institution with a wide variety of subjects and courses. It was known as a "functioning anarchy". It was headed by Director Sydney Caine—a position later held by our own I.G. Patel. We hardly had an opportunity to be in direct touch with the Director. I some times saw him dragging his feet on the stair case—apparently he did not use the lift. He met us only once when he gave us tea. I remember to have met on that occasion the grand old lady Vera Anstey whose book on the Indian economy became a celebrated textbook.

Celebrated Academicians

Two celebrated academicians who had retired from regular academic posts were Prof. Robson of Public Administration and Prof. Lionel Robbins. The former was giving a course on Public Administration. I remember to have consulted him regarding my dissertation on Decentralization. I did not find him very helpful. On two occasions I attended the weekly seminar taken by Prof. Lionel Robbins. Like every student of Economics I had read his book on "Scope and Significance of Economics" and was acquainted with his definition of Economics as study of means which are limited for fulfillment of ends which are unlimited. At that time the report on educational reform by the committee which was headed by Robbins was a subject matter for discussion.

Week-end Visits

LSE had a large library situated at various places. I often used to borrow books from that library. My reading was sustained and continuous. That came in the way of moving about in London or attending concerts. I did attend tea get-togethers arranged by the British Council and also participated in various weak-end courses arranged for visiting holiday resorts and places of historical interest. I remember two or three such visits – to Brighton where there was an Indian palace, to the Lake District, on whose enchanting natural beauty Wordsworth wrote his poetry and Swansea in Wales which I found very charming. The fortlike building where I stayed was the same which I visited years later while attending commonwealth conference as Vice-Chancellor, Goa University. The British Council held classes to familiarize overseas students with ball-room dancing. I now regret that I did not take advantage of that opportunity. I thought that as a married person with my wife away in India, I should not dance with another girl – a typical middleclass conservative attitude. I also thought dancing skill would not be of any use to me since I would not dance once I go back to India. Opportunity never came again to learn dancing.

British Politicians

During the time I was in London, Britain's entry in the common market was a hot subject for discussion. I remember once attending a lecture attended by no less a person than Clement Attlee, the former Labour Prime Minister who succeeded Winston Churchill who was defeated despite his triumph as Britain's leader during World War II.

Attlee came unobtrusively and sat on the third row. I was impressed by the simplicity and honesty of the great man. I also once had the opportunity to listen to the then leading lights of British politics—Sir Reginald Maudling, Edward Heath, Enoch Powell who was later ostracized from British political life after his notorious "rivers of blood will flow" speech, and James Callaghan who later became the Labour Prime Minister (I heard him again at Swansea Conference—by then a politician long retired). I found all of them were excellent public speakers—particularly Enoch Powell who ruined his political future by one thoughtless speech. Maudling too lost his career because of his involvement in some doubtful financial deal. Heath rose to become British Prime Minister till he was ousted by Margeret Thatcher, the "dark horse" at that time.

The British government of the Conservative Party was headed by Harold Macmillan. Of aristocratic lineage, he was a mature politician who led the government and the party in a grand style. The slogan of the Conservative party in those days was "Britain never had it so good". After a long and tortuous effort Britain at long last had overcome the ravages of World War II and reconstructed the shattered economy and standard of life had started visibly rising after the long aftermath of war-time scarcity. But Macmillan received a big jolt when one of his ministerial colleagues Profumo was found indulging with a call girl in a swimming pool. Pakistan's General Ayub Khan was also found to be giving company. The scandal made head lines in the British Press and Macmillan was hard put to it defending his party from the scandal in which his colleague was found involved. The criticism was in line with the British tradition that a person's private life was his own concern—even of one in public life. But the matter for concern was that as Minister for Defence, Profunio was privy to official secrets which could easily leak from a Minister involved in peccadillo with a prostitute. Profumo had to resign. His wife bravely stood by him. Eventually even Macmillen had to resign giving opportunity to Edward Heath to head the government. The day following Macmillan's resignation, he was found at the bus stand waiting for the bus. In Britain a person had to give up all privileges of public office hours after his relinquishing public position. Such are the standards of British democracy.

British Society

Britain and British society on the whole left a favourable impact on me. We in India had seen the face of British colonization—

overbearing and contemptuous towards the Indians with a stiff upper lip. On the other hand the British in their own country appeared to be highly civilized and courteous. I was never at the receiving end of any manifestation of racism. That was perhaps because of the fact that the Indian immigrants was yet small in number and clashes between "skinheads" – young white rowdies and the Indians or Asians and Africans and the West Indians had not grown. Moreover I was not staying with a land-lady but in the International Hall. It was only when a photo was being taken of all the residents in the hall that one of the lady staff members talked of the "coloured" inmates of the hostel and I felt uneasy.

The country-side in England, Wales and Scotland I found enchanting. The image in my mind indelibly left was of vast green meadows with cows full of milk in their udders lazily grazing. As Prof. Maddick, Ford Foundation consultant at Mussorie remarked to me, the whole of England was like Kashmir. I visited Meddick's house in Birmingham. While at Birmingham I went round a "new town" one of the innovative projects undertaken as a part of post-war reconstruction. While visiting a workers' housing colony, I soiled my shoes in mud. The head of the worker's household cleaned my shoes and made them look as bright as they were before I soiled them . I was touched by that gesture of kindness. Maddick and his wife were also very hospitable in welcoming me to their house. I was greatly impressed by the picturesque beauty of Edinborough, the capital of Scotland. There I participated in group-dance in the open, a speciality of the folk dance of the Scottish people dressed in their kilts.

London is a vast city of innumerable places to see. What Johnson, the great literary figure said of London is very true – the one who is tired of London is tired of life. There is nothing that London does not have to offer – historic as well as modern. Yet London and its roads are not as imposing as those of Paris, Paris, thanks to Napolion has well laid out planned roads, boulevards and avenues at right angles to each other. London's roads are not as systematic. Yet it was a smooth and orderly place and homely as well. Indians felt completely at home what with the absence of the language barrier. London's glory was its attractive large parks – the Hyde Park, the St James Park, the Regent Park etc. To wander in these parks was a great delight. It had many well known landmarks like the Picadally Circus, Horatio Nelson's statue, and Oxford Street its excellent shopping centres, the Harrods and the Selfridges and the network of Marks and Spencer Super Markets.

London was much cheaper than Paris as I realized after visiting Paris for three days. Britain had not joined the Common Market and the high European prices had not yet invaded Britain. For half a shilling (6 d) one could go by tube to all the nearby localities. For the same price one could have a cup of tea at Lyons outlets. That was also the minimum tip for a nearby trip by the taxi. London taxis large, black with their own design, were distinguished vehicles in which one could move about. The taxi drivers were well informed about the London roads.

Every locality had its own little park. There was one such park in front of my Hall. The Hall porter had a key to the park, as did other residents around the park so that they could have its private use.

The International Hall also was very reasonably priced for pounds 5 & 10 shilling per week I had breakfast, lunch, afternoon tea and dinner in addition to lodging. During weekdays I would generally have my lunch at the LSE refectory; for as little as two and half shillings, one could have soup and bread and sometimes nice curry. I often went to the basement of the Indian High Commission right opposite the LSE and have rice, dal, and vegetables or fish curry for as little as 2 shillings. Now all these rates have long become obsolete and prices of needs have gone through the roofs. Hotel accommodation has also become very expensive.

End of the Course

Soon my course was over and stay in London was coming to a close. There was end of the course, written examination as well as submission of a dissertation. My dissertation was on "Decentralization". In my dissertation I tried to co-relate the concept of decentralization in Public Administration and in Economics. The administrative concepts of decentralization included delegation, administrative deconcentration and political decentralization through the local government institutions. The economic concepts included the market economy, decentralized planning and dispersal of economic activities. Later on I prepared a paper on "Decentralization, Planning and Public Administration" which was published in the *Indian Journal of Public Administration* and included in my book of collected papers under the caption. "Economics, Planning & Public Administration". I did well in the examination as usual and my name stood at the top of the successful candidates; I indeed did not have any stiff competition. But my purpose was not to give any examination or acquire any qualification but have the opportunity to have a wide exposure. My teacher Prof Kogekar had, before I left, suggested that I do my Ph.D. but though I did explore the possibility I found that it was not practicable because that would have meant a longer stay which was not possible because I was bound by service and family obligations.

A lower level functionary in the Planning Commissioner, Shri Chabra, one of the participants and the only other Indian, became my good friend and I often used to go to his room near the Regent's Park. He used to cook his own food. Hot Basmati rice and vegetables curry was a delightful dish to savour with him. Once we were going from Russel Square tube station where I purchased two tickets to Regent's park tube station one for me and one for him. Chabra said he did not need one as he had a pass. I went back to the window clerk and asked for refund. He asked me to collect it at the other end. I thought he was passing on the buck. But when I asked for refund at the other end, I did get it without any hesitation. One could rely on the lower level functionaries for a responsible and civil behavior based on trust. Once I left my overcoat in the Ford room and realized it only on going back to my Hall. It was already late in the evening. But I went back. The LSE was closed and all the rooms were locked. The only one person available was the porter at the reception desk. I had taken my overcoat as lost but still enquired with the porter. Without any hesitation he took it out from his desk and asked me whether it was mine. When I said "yes", he handed it over without any hesitation. Such as civil behavior based on trust which is taken for granted is a thing rarely experienced in our own country.

Winter and Spring

The academic year was coming to close. The winter was over. Lovely spring had made its appearance. In winter I had my first experience of snowing. One morning I woke up and was enchanted to see through the window the snow flakes slowly falling on the earth. But the days were small and sun rarely appeared—only at midday through shroud of clouds. Days were dark and dismal and even during the day the lights were on. But as spring made its appearance and life started totally changing as though undergoing a metamorphosis. Day lengthened and became bright. The sun shone and to make full use of the lost opportunity, men and women in light dress started bathing in the sun in the parks. This was a magical change. I remembered poet Shelly's lines—"if winter comes can spring be far behind?" I had no experience of seeing sun setting nearly at 9.30 pm. Long bright days became exhilarating.

Good-bye to London

But that was the time for me to say good-bye to London.

The British Council arranged a farewell function for all the British Council scholars. The British Minister for overseas Development Mr.Donald Carr was invited as the Chief guest. I was given the honour of responding on behalf of the scholars. In my speech I said that in ancient India scholars from all over the Eastern world used to congregate at our ancient seats of learning Naland and Taxashila. Now they are congregating at the British Centres of learning in search of knowledge. They would surely use the knowledge for the betterment of their own societies and serve as links between Britain and their countries. The speeches were followed by dinner.

I felt my stay in London and Britain was too short to sea and experience all that I wished for. Much time was spent in reading and studies leaving little time to stand and stare. But that I did not waste time and withstood the cold winter without once falling ill was itself a great solace. I saw a bit of England, Wells and Scotland and visited France (Paris), Italy (Rome), Switzerland (Zurich) and Liechtenstein.

My return trip was arranged on board the ship Circasia. I had to catch the boat from Liverpool. The journey by ship was expected to take a couple of weeks. This was my first long sea voyage.

With the little saving from my scholarship I bought a refrigerator and a mixer to take home. Both served quite a few years.

The rail journey from London to Liverpool was non-stop and led straight to the port. The ship was full of British passengers. There was one Prof. Cornish who was to join IIT Delhi. Another Prof. Ilrich from Oxford was to visit Banaras—he had translated Tulsidas in English. Crossing the turbulent Bay of Biscay the ship passed through Casablancha into the placid blue waters of the Madiderrenean. It stopped for a while at Port Sayed. I got down and stepped on the Egyptian soil and walked through the streets of the Port City. I had a similar walk on the streets of Karachi, when the ship stopped there. The journey through the Red Sea was another unforgettable experience. And then the ship reached the destination after a long sea voyage—perhaps too long for my liking.

Throughout my stay at London I used to send regular letters to my father in Bombay. He was forever anxious and would get worried if my letter got delayed. He kept a set of my letters which collectively was a good account of my stay and activities in London.

CHAPTER 11

New Delhi – In the Central Ministry (1963-67)

Working as Training Administrator

When I reported back to the Ministry, I found that I did not have to go back to Mussorie. The post of Director (Study) was filled up after I left for London by the appointment of my friend Satischandran who had returned from London. I did not regret it. On the other hand I welcomed the opportunity to work in the Central Ministry – the Ministry of Community Development. Shri NES Ragherachari an ICS officer of Madras was the Secretary in charge of the department. S.K. Dey continued to be the Minister.

There was no debriefing. Nobody tried to find out what I had done at LSE nor how whatever I learnt during my study leave there could be of use in Public Administration in our country. That was a reflection of the impersonal and indifferent attitude of our public administrative system towards human resource development. There was no realization that training should be meaningfully linked to career development of an individual civil servant as well as for qualitative development of the performance of the civil service officer. But perhaps my appointment as Deputy Secretary in charge of training was a reflection of such an attempt.

The Ministry of Community Development was located in Krishi Bhavan. The Ministry of Agriculture was the senior Ministry occupying larger portion of the building. Ministry of Community Development and Co-operation was the poor relative. The room of Minister S.K. Dey and B.S. Murthy, Deputy Secretary were located on the ground floor. My room was on the first floor. The post of Commissioner (Training) held by G.V.K. Rao was replaced by the post of Joint Secretary (Training) – a higher post to which G.V.K. Rao could not be appointed due to seniority consideration and Rao returned to the state without completing his tenure at the centre.

Accommodation

Before settling down as Dy Secretary, I had to settle down in New Delhi. Unlike Bangalore, Delhi had a good number of flats for housing the civil servants. They were located in different colonies in the city. Civil servants were entitled to different types of accommodations according to their status in the hierarchy. I was entitled to type V accommodation. One had to apply to the Estate officer for allotment of a flat. But that took time and in the meanwhile I had to locate some private accommodation. For a few days we stayed at my aunt's place. Soon I located and hired a flat in Green Park which was a newly developed colony beyond Hauz Khas. In those days getting accommodation in a far off colony like Green Park was not difficult. I got it at a reasonable rent. The colony was airy and not crowded as today. It was a good two bed room spacious flat. The owner Mehta was friendly and his wife gave generous Punjabi hospitably on the first day.

Also I had to acquire a car for moving around – going to office and coming back. I bought a green new standard car from the Sikands for Rs. 15,000/- I had to take delivery and wanted to leave office early but a session with Joint Secreaary Shri IDN Sahi held me in office and it was only late in the evening that I could take delivery and drive back with great difficulty on an unfamiliar road to my flat in the Green Park.

We stayed in Green Park for about a month and a half when I got a type V flat allotted to me on Vinay Marg near Diplomatic Enclave. It was a D-I two bed room flat on the first floor, with servants quarters and a garage attached to it. I thought it was a comfortable spacious accommodation with a large lawn in front and Sarojini Market nearby for all the household requirements including fruits and vegetables.

But as winter advanced and cold winds started blowing, we soon realized that the flat could be quite uncomfortable. For going to the bed-room we had to pass from the living room through an open *varandah* which could be punishingly cold. I had just returned from London and its coldest winter since 1841 but never did I feel the cold as much as in Delhi because being centrally heated the International Hall including my room and dinning hall were always warm. But here the heaters could provide relief only while sitting nearby otherwise the large living-cum-dinning room could be very cold. Nor was there the hot water running in the tap. The ice cold water could freeze the hands. While I had experienced Delhi cold before, my wife was new to it and was facing it for the first time. However the rays of the sun could provide warmth during the day.

Atmosphere in The Ministry

The heaters in the office room could provide warmth. But the atmosphere in the office was far from warm. Though S. K. Dey spread warmth through his eloquence at the conference of community development officers all over the country, in his Ministry he could create an atmosphere of unease and tension. He was a volatile, restless and self-centered personality with temporary favourites. It was said that for the first few days an officer newly joining the ministry could be made to feel welcome. But after the honeymoon period was over, he could be in the docks. Dey described the relationship between the minister and his officers as between a husband and wife. And Dey had many wives! I always abhored such similes as others like the civil servant being a horse and the minister a rider, or the bureaucracy being a car and the minister the driver. All these similes were not only misleading but symptomatic of a feudal tendency deeply rooted in our psyche. I resented such similes and rejected the sycophantic attitudes on the part of officers. Krishnan who later became Chief Secretary, West Bengal, and was then serving as Deputy Secretary talked of the ministry as all "activity without action". Though the minister made quite a splash in the states, he did not carry much weight at the centre with other dominant ministries like Home, Finance, Defence and External Affairs housed in North and South Blocks carrying more weight and in charge of senior ministers. Dey was only a Minister of State.

The Minister

Dey often asked draft letters to be prepared in reply to letters received by him. He expected not routine replies couched in the usual official style and language but with some distinction and substance. It often fell on me to prepare draft replies. I was delighted when they came with Minister's approval and appreciation congratulating me on good drafts. I wondered whether any in other Ministry the Minister could be expressing his appreciation of a draft on file but that was like S.K. Dey.

Once he phoned me on the internal circuit "Dey speaking" he announced. Not expecting Minister himself taking the phone to talk to a mere Deputy Secretary, I asked "Who Dey?" Minister said "*Are bhai mai Dey Bol Raha Hun*" I felt flustered that I could not identity him immediately. That was Dey's style of personal communication. He spoke to me about some not very significant matter.

Training Centres

A Deputy Secretary I had to deal with matters connected with training in community development Shri IDN Sahi often referred to as "Training Programme". In my view a programme referred to schemes of community development while training referred to courses to develop personnel engaged in the programme. Dey had set up about a dozen "Orientation Training and Study Centres" (OTSC), one in each important state to provide institutional training for CD personnel at intermediate level – BDO's and the like, with the National Institute of CD providing courses for senior personnel. Dey had gone to great length in setting up these intuitions when Government administration had yet to recognize the importance of training. It was my job to deal with files connected with training activities and also visit the training centers. We also held training conferences. Shri Nanavaty was working as advisor on social education in the training division. He was supposed to advise specially at Social Education training centers Social. Education was an altogether new concept then and dealt with promotion of awareness in the rural societies about problems and programmes of development.

Dealing with Difficult Bosses

All this activity did not give any particular joy mainly because of difficulties of working in the Ministry. Shri IDS Sahi was known as " I do nothing Sahi" He did not believe in doing any thing himself. He wanted to get things done. His complex Kayastha mind, though brilliant in flashes of verbal repartees, worked in a tortuous manner. For every thing he wanted to "pick-up" other people's brains as though there was nothing in his own brain. He wanted me to prepare draft notes on every matter that came up but once I prepared the drafts he would send for me and sit over them for hours going over them "dotting i's and crossing t's". Some times he would search for an alternative word or phrase or another time he would feel that a sentence was "weak" and ought to be made stronger. While his meticulousness appeared praise worthy, it was always excessive and futile and resulted in big loss of time and energy disproportionate to the result accomplished. Though interested in preparing good notes and drafts and providing intellectual inputs I did not find these long sessions of going over and correcting my own drafts a very interesting exercise. In fact I found them a drain on my time and energy. The exercise became all the more frustrating when the meticulous minister wanted to show his sadistic tendencies by rejecting the elaborately prepared drafts and asking for fresh draft and notes.

There is a sense of proportion about things and I felt that this draft producing exercise took time and energy disproportionate to what would come out of these drafts. There was lack of substance, achievement and result as a consequence of what we were doing in the Ministry. Administration is a creative activity which must achieve results and not simply be a paper producing activity. That is what the ministry became. It did not have the place of prestige in Government and remained a minor outpost in spite of Dey's struggle. He often tore his hair that there were no "cabinet paper" emanating from his Ministry. But for a paper to be qualified for cabinet consideration it had to be concerned with high policy matters, which the Ministry hardly handled. In fact the ministry came to be looked upon, more and more, as meddlesome interloper in activities legitimately belonging to other substantive Ministries like Agriculture, Health and Education or in matters belonging to the states. I could sense what was coming.

The Ministry of Community Development was slowly moving to extinction. It was the creation of Dey and ended with his exit. With the departure of his patron Nehru its days were numbered. The ministry under Dey had its own character which reflects Dey's volatile personality. Dey, though originally a Bangalee from Sylhet in Aasam, was a refugee from Punjab where he was a business executive in an electricity firm. On migrating to India after partition he took the task of rehabilitating the refugees and set up a camp at Nilokheri. Nehru visited the camp and was so impressed with his work of community development amongst the Punjab refugees that he asked him to undertake the task of community development in rural areas. He undertook the task first as Administrator on a salary of one rupee per month. But as the work of community development spread, the Ministry was brought into existence and Dey became its first and effectively the last minister in charge of Community Development.

Dey was an epicurean and liked the good things of life including good officers. He would like to take more of them and then reject them and look for others. He was also given to tantrums I experienced all these facets of his personality. He would take a junior officer newly joining the Ministry as his aide on tours. I was asked to join his tour to Bihar. I do remember his meeting with Krishna Vallabh Sahay the Chief Minister of Bihar to discuss the state of community development and Panchayati Raj in Bihar. K.B. Sahay appeared to be some kind of feudal chieftain and law unto himself. Such Chief Ministers planted the traditions of feudalism in Indian government and administration Dey also toured in the state. I remember the visit to Rajgrih which is famous for hot springs. There Dey remembered *khaja,* a local sweet and got a stock for himself. And when we stopped at Patna to catch the train for Delhi, Dey was worried about ensuring that the sackful of potatoes which he had collected for his household was not missing from his baggage! Obviously there was, for Dey, something special about Bihar potatoes. On another occasion he left for a tour to Gujrat and suddenly a word came from him that I should accompany him on the tour. I was hard put to it in procuring a ticket at short notice, missed the plane and could not get money refunded by the Ministry because, Kaul, Deputy Secretary (admin.) would not oblige! I wondered whether Dey appreciated my services as an aide on tour. He needed probably a sycophant and perhaps, I lacked the qualities needed to play the role.

Dey's deputy B.S. Murty, a harijan from A.P. was the opposite. If Dey was ever restless, Murthy was placid and happy go lucky with a sense of humor. He was enjoying his position as Deputy Minister with hardly any responsibility. At official meetings he would make humorous interventions taking the sting away from Dey's tantrums. But once it was even beyond Murthy. Dey was discussing official briefs on his Ministry's demand for grants; he was thoroughly dissatisfied with briefs given to him and started having a go at the hapless Secretary Raghavchari an ICS officer, intelligent, experienced but mild in disposition. He could not face Dey's onslaught. Dey's temper rose rapidly. It was an almost midnight meeting and officers were held up away from their homes for no reason. The meeting could have been held early morning next day. Even Murthy could not pacify him. Dey dramatically tore to pieces the papers given to him and threw the pieces at Raghavchari, asking for a fresh brief. It was given to him the next day. Gentlemen that he was, Raghavachari did not protest but suffered silently. Nor did anybody walk out. The incident left poor taste in everybody's mouth. Soon Raghvachari left the Ministry.

But with all this 'homework', Dey's performance on the floor of Parliament proved pathetic. Dey's eloquence fell flat. He could not respond to M.P's interventions with political savvy Dey was a political lightweight. Though an imposing personality at officers' meeting, he fell flat in Parliamentary performance which requires political skill and sensitively which Dey was found lacking.

Visit to Andaman and Nicobar

One advantage of posting at the Centre is to have opportunities of tours in remote parts of India and also to go abroad,. an opportunity lacking in those days for officers working in the states. Once B.S.Murthy, the Deputy Minister, undertook the tour in Andaman and Nicobar islands and I was asked to accompany him I was excited to have that assignment. We left by air stopping at Calcutta. and Rangoon enroute. Admiral Katari was India's ambassador at Rangoon. After another hop, we landed at Port Blair. Maheshwari the Chief Commissioner received us at the airport. We were his guests during our stay at Port Blair at the Chief Commissioner's bungalow overlooking the sea. There were two great memories of Andaman—first its notorious Cellular Jail where India's freedom fighters specially Vinayak Damodar Sawarkar were interned and secondly, it was under the occupation of Netaji Subhash Bose's Azad Hind Force albeit for a while during World War II. The Chief Commissioner arranged for our visits to the Cellular Jail as well as the timber factory, the handicrafts store, the co-operative consumer store etc. He gave us a marble wood swagger stick as a present which is still in my possession and gives me company on my morning walks.

Andaman islands had human beings belonging to Negroid tribes, *jarwas, Andamanies* and *sentineles.* The *Jarwas* lived deep in the jungle and were practically naked. They were hostile and defied all attempts to civilize them. One *Jarwa* boy had strayed away and had become an exhibit. Anthroplogists stayed for days in the island to attract the *Jarwas* by giving them presents. The total number of people belonging to these tribes did not exceed a few hundred and attempts were being made to see that tribes did not become extinct. We also visied the Car Nicobar island, a self-contained place inhabited by a polynesian tribe called *Car Nicobares*. They were probably cast off from Malaysia. We had to make an overnight boat journey to reach the place. During the journey I completed reading the Marathi book '*Mazi Janmathep*' by Swatantyravir Sawarkar. I had borrowed it from the library of the Cellular Jail.

As I read the book, tears came to my eyes. How much did the great freedom fighter suffer at the hands of the merciless Irish Jailor!

The Car Nicobaries were all Christians. They were converted under the influence of father Richardson who had gone to mainland and we could not meet him. The Car Nicobaries had their own life style. They had stilted houses and the ground portion was used for keeping pigs which were nurtured to provide pork which was their staple food along with bananas. The Car Nicobaries were well educated. The volleyball team of Nicobarie girls had won in all India matches. The girls had a beautiful hairstyle and wore flowers.

We were impressed by the consumer co-operative stores both in Andaman and Nicobar islands. They served a very important purpose of supplying essential consumer goods for communities removed far away from the mainland.

Maheshwari served us excellent vegetarian food but it became a little difficult to swallow and digest on learning that it was served by the hands of murderers who had joined as waiters at the bungalow of the commissioner after serving their term in the Cellular Jail.

The main purpose of our visit appeared to be to go round and see things somewhat in the style of tourists. But we had to do our job too and so a meeting had to be held of the staff engaged in the work of community development. At the meeting, présided over by the Deputy Minister, I as on officer of the ministry started taking on active role, but I was shocked with what suddenly happened! The Deputy Minister rudely interrupted me and called me to halt. The ego of the otherwise mild mannered Dy. Minister had got the better of him. He did not tolerate a meeting presided over by him conducted by an officer. Once again I learnt the lesson that the ego of a Minister should never be hurt because the Minister always feels that the officer should play a subordinate role. I kept mum during the rest of the meeting.

AARRO Conference at Kuala Lampur

I got the first opportunity to represent India at an international meeting when the Ministry (in my honey moon period) deputed me to participate in the first conference of the Afro Asian Rural Reconstruction Organisation. (AARRO) held at Kuala Lumpur, capital of Malaysia. The live spirit behind the organisation was an Indian, one Sharma, one of the early go-getters who could muster support of the Minister to set up a high profile organisation. There were participants from a number of Asian and African countries.

Indonesia under Sukarno had set up a well talked off programme called '*Royang Gotang*' or "get together" for rural areas. Philippines also had a very articulate person to address the conference on its programme on rural construction. I made a presentation on India's community development which was well received. The leader of the Indian delegation was Minister of State for Agriculture. Shri Ram Subhag Singh. He was a Bihari, speaking English with markedly rustic Bihar accents . He came late by a day. A suite was reserved for him at Hotel Merlin, the only modern hotel at that time in Kuala Lampur which had yet to become a modern swanky capital it has now become with the tallest towers in the world. Ram Subhag, I found to be a benign person who dealt with me as a colleague in a friendly manner. The essential goodness of a person, I realized, was far more important than the trapping of good accents or power of authority.

The inaugural address at the Conference was delivered by the host Prime Minister of Malaysia, Tunku Abdul Rahmanputra. He came clad in the black cap and Malaysian national dress. He read his address looking up at the audience from time to time. Used to spontaneous extempore addresses by our leaders like Nehru and Minister like Dey, it was for me a strange experience. But soon I realized that reading formal address at such international conferences had became a rule rather than exception. Ram Subhag Singh being not good in English also read out his address.

What left greater impact than discussions and addresses at the conference, was a presentation made by Tun Abdul Razak, the Deputy Prime Minister of Malaysia at his office. He had introduced a "Red Book" for every village in Malaysia which gave all information regarding the development work needed there that became the basis of planning rural development programme in Malaysia.

I could see the Hindu influence on Malaysia. Lord Hanuman was warshipped in rural Malaysia. The cultural programme arranged for the participants in the conference displayed that influence. The women did not wear *burkha* but blouses and *sarong*. But all that changed as under the Arab influence Muslim consciousness grew and women started covering themselves from top to bottom. Sanskrit words like Duta, (ambassador) Putra (son), and Nagara (city) had entered into Malayan vocabulary.

There was a racial mix in the Malaysian population—the majority were Malayans, the progressive Chinese dominated in business, and the Indians mainly Tamils who had come to work in rubber plantations had become prominent as teachers and officers in police force. Sindhis were prosperous shopkeepers. South Indian food like Idli and garments like sarees were plentifully available in Selanghor Street in Tamil locality. On the outskirt of Kuala Lumpur in Batu caves there was a Tamil temple devoted to Lord Ayyappan.

Before leaving for Kuala Lumpur I had met Dey who asked me to bring Old Spice, (after shaving lotion) and shaving brush; and Chakravarthy, the Secretary asked for blades. I brought these article for both of them. In those days such ordinary articles were greatly prized since ther were not locally available. There was a craze for foreign goods.

A Change in Assignment

After two years of working as Deputy Secretary in the Department of Community Development I had a change. I was shifted to the Dept. of Cooperation in the Ministry as Director (Coopertive Training) to fill up the vacancy caused by retirement of Shri Vora, who was holding the post. It was the same field of training but for another programme, *viz.* cooperation. Dey considered Cooperation—(*Sahakari Samaj*), Community Development (*Samuhik Vikas*) and Panchayati Raj as trinity of rural development. The new posting was a promotion for me—promotion to the "Selection grade" between the senior scale and the pay of the joint secretary. I thought it was change for the better both because of the higher pay and relief from Sahi's tortuous 'draft correcting' sessions, which were a punishment and waste of time and energy.

Committee for Cooperative Training

Though Director (Cooperative Training) was a post in the Ministry, I had no office in the Krishi Bhavan. That was because that post was combined with another, i.e., Member Secretary, Committee for cooperative training which was a non-official committee under the auspices of the Ministry. For long the work of cooperative training was handled by the Reserve Bank of India, which had set up a committee to look after the programme. But Dey fought and got the subject transferred from RBI to the Ministry. And so the committee was being set up by the Ministry. When I joined the committee, it was headed by Chaudhari Brahm Prakash who after being the first Chief Minister of Delhi had entered into the cooperative field and was the president of the National Cooperative Union of India. The other members of committee included representative of some state cooperative unions and representatives of other related Ministries. The Committee was to look after the programme of cooperative training at three levels—The National Cooperative college located at Pune for senior cooperative personnel (i.e., Assistant Registrars and above), cooperative centers for each state for cooperative personnel at intermediate level and cooperative schools for junior personnel looked after by the state governments. The office of the committee was in a hired accommodation at Patel Nagar. I had my regular office there, but when needed I had to go to the Ministry to dispose off pending files at the government level. I had to commute in my own car and was given a princely car allowance of Rs. 90 per month for doing so. The files in the ministry were handled by the Deputy Director, Shri Chakku who had a small room in the Ministry. I had to make do, sitting in his room and disposing of files ready for my consideration. Many a time I felt like asking for a separate room for myself in Krishi Bhavan but I did not make a case and adjusted to the situation. In the committee office, however, I had a large room for me and being the head of that office with no body to oversee me, I felt free and without strings. I felt it was much better to be left to myself to run my office than being a cog in the wheel in the ministry.

The office of the committee had a team of excellent workers. I had two Joint Directors—one Shri G.P. Bhave who was on deputation from the R.B.I. and another Shri R.D. Bedi who had to his credit a well known text book on history, principles and practices of cooperation. Shri M.D. Joshi on deputation from the Ministry of cooperative was Deputy Director. The office was headed by an officer from the central Secretarial service Shri M.C. Jayaraman. He was also a competent officer. With such knowledgeable staff I could run the committee's office very well.

The committee met once in a quarter. In the agenda of the committee was invariably a review of the work of all training centres in addition to specific matters. The Chairman Shri Braham Prakash, though a politician, behaved in an exemplary manner with me and never once interfered in my work, by making '*sifarish*' of any sort. There were meetings of the selection committee to recruit training faculty. Here too selection was made in an objective manner on the basis of qualifications and experience.

Some matters regarding the Committee specially budgetary approval had to go to the ministry. All funds handled by the committee for running the training centre came from Government. The committee had no independent resources of its own. These proposals had to be cleared by the Ministry. Here I came in the picture wearing another hat, *viz.* that of Director in the Ministry. The Deputy Director J.N. Chakku was a Kashmiri Saraswat Brahman with the sharp Pandit mind. He would go meticulously through the proposals and come with comments or opinion of his own and sometimes proposals coming from the committee could be modified. But with my dual position, I always maintained a balance in the relationship between the committee's office and the Ministry. It was a special kind of organizational arrangement and gave me a special experience of being in the government and yet outside. I did not find he experience incompatible but indeed comfortable.

Cooperative Training Centres

The position also gave me the opportunity to visit the training centres spread over the country. The National Cooperative College was located at 5 B.J. Road, Pune in an old bungalow with country tiles and broad verandah. Many bungalows of this sort existed in the Poona Camp area. There were some centres like the one at Anand and Kalyani on the University premises, the former at Vallabh Vidyanagar University and the latter at Kalyani Agricultural University. While visiting Anand centre I came into contact with V.S. Vyas, the agricultural economist who was heading the agro-economic research centre at Vallabh Vidya Nagar I also met Ishwar Bhai Patel the Vice-Chancellor who had a rustic bearing to suit a university located in a rural area. Not far away was Kurien's Amul-Anand Milk Union, a cooperative which in the years to come was to grow into a well known set up steering milk revolution in the country. The centre at Hyderabad was in the institutional area at Rajendranagar. I had some hand in finding new locations for the centre at Pune (where the premises approved by me are still in use) and Dehradun centre on Rajapur road. The latter was in the ascent to Mussorie covered by thick spread of trees. It was my favourite spot where I liked to stay.

Each centre was a small self-contained entity headed by a principal with a faculty of less then a dozen dealing with various subjects like principles of cooperation, cooperative audit, finance, and cooperative practice in different sectors of cooperation like credit and marketing. During my visit I would meet with the faculty and try to make an academic review of their activities. While the Pune college provided a long course leading to higher diploma in cooperation, the centres conducted a course for lower diploma. The participants were in-service personnel from the departments and institutions of cooperation. I convened annual conferences of principals of training institutions to review all aspects of the conduct of the training courses so as to make them more effective.

Establishment of VMNICM

But perhaps the most important single effort during my tenure as Director Cooperative Training was the formulation of a project for the establishment of the apex institute of cooperative management. As cooperative activities in various sectors like agricultural credit and banking, supply of inputs, marketing and processing, dairy fishery and rural industry, consumer cooperative and housing proliferated and grew in size and complexity it became obvious that a high degree of professional management was needed for running the cooperative enterprises in on efficient manner. But can professional management be combined with cooperative ideas and principles? A person like the late Vaikunth Mehta who was dedicated to cooperative ideology was also a competent manager of the estate Cooperative Bank. The late Prof. D.R. Gadgil who was an economist trained in Cambridge was also a cooperative idealist. Both of them keenly felt that the time had come to set up an institute of management for senior executives working in cooperative enterprises. "Management" as a discipline was established at the beginning of the 20th centaury in USA and slowly grew in prestige and influence. In India too a prestigious Institute of Management was set up at Ahmedabad at the initiative of Vikram Sarabhai a scientist with multidimensional personality.

It was tribute to their foresightedness that Vaikunth Mehta and D. R. Gadgil within two years of establishment of the Indian Institute of Management for private enterprise thought of establishing a similar institute for cooperative enterprise. The first step was taken when a committee under the chairmanship of Vaikunth Mehta recommended that such an institute be set up. It was like blazing a new trail in the cooperative movement in India. Traditionally, cooperation in India was a part of social work. Cooperative managers were social idealists. They were part time social workers. But as cooperative enterprise grew, these concepts became obsolete. Cooperative managers could no longer be part time social workers. They had to be full time professionals. Such persons had to be properly recruited and trained. Hence the idea of cooperative management institute put forward by Vaikuntha Mehta, D.R. Gadgil and others was very timely. Once the idea was accepted in principle by Government of India, the next step was taken when another committee under the chairmanship of D.R. Gadgil worked out the outline of a long term course in cooperative management for cooperative personnel. The idea got a further boost when two Ford Foundation experts Hedlund and Birkley submitted yet another report that a strong dose of professional management needed to be injected in cooperative business in the country.

As the ideas gathered force, time had come to give them a practical shape and the task fell to me as Director, Cooperative Training in Govt. of India. I prepared a project report on a National Institute of Cooperative Management incorporating all the ideas of the three committee. The report was submitted to the Secretary and the Minister who approved of it but that was not enough. It was a new item of expenditure and a new financial commitment had to be approved by the Ministry of Finance. The Ministry had a mechanism of expenditure finance committee to approve new projects. I had to prepare a financial memorandum for the new project of National Cooperative Management Institute. The Committee approved the project after exercising their privilege of scaling down some portion of expenditure. The approval of the project was for me a great achievement.

Gadgil was happy and now the time had come to take steps to implement the project report. But the project was to be in the cooperative sector. In the project report I had suggested that the existing institutions, *viz.* the National Cooperative College and The Central Institute of Management of Consumer Business (CIMCOB) would be incorporated in the new Institute of Management. CIMCOB had come into existence in the wake of the boost given to consumer cooperatives to check the price rise in the wake of devaluation of the Indian rupee in 1966. The Swedish experts were invited to set up consumer department stores on modern basis. They introduced techniques like prepacking, open shelf display, cash register machines and ABC analysis for inventory management. To train senior personnel in charge of these modern consumer department stores, they had helped set up the Institute of Management of Consumer Business at Bandra, Bombay. The Institute was looked after by the consumer section of the Ministry and financed by National Cooperative Development Corporation. Both were unwilling to part with CIMCOB and resisted its incorporation in the new National Institute. However since the project was approved at the highest level, their resistance was overcome.

But there was another slip between the cup and the lip. Dr.Ravi Mathai, Director Indian Institute of Management got the idea that this new Institute of Cooperative Management should be part of their newly set up branch for agriculture and rural management. This last minute intervention put up a question mark to all I had done. The challenge was not easy to overcome. C. Subramaniam, the Cabinet Minister was apparently not well disposed towards cooperation. He had no good opinion of S.K. Dey and deprived the latter with the help of his Secretary B. Sivaraman of the portfolio of agricultural credit. And now Dr. Ravi Mathai had approached him to deprive the cooperative department of the Institute of Management. C. Subramaniam invited a meeting with Dr. Ravi Mathai and the Cooperative Dept. to consider the proposal. On behalf of the cooperative department D.R. Gadgil who was working as president NCUI and Chairman of the Committee on cooperatives training and myself attended the meeting which was held at the residence of C. Subramaniam. I was nervous about the outcome of the meeting with a headstrong Minister. As the meeting commenced Minister first asked Ravi Mathai to present his proposal. His point was that when already a well established Institute of Management existed and it was prepared to take the responsibility for cooperative management why set up a new Institute? D.R. Gadgil was called upon to respond. He patiently explained the background of the effort to set up the institute of cooperative management and subtly suggested in his unimitable scholarly manner that Institute of Management Ahmedabad need not consider itself as the sole custodian of management education. D.R. Gadgil's arguments carried the day. The project remained with the cooperative department.

What should be the name of the new institute? Gadgil was keen that the institute should be named after the late Vaikunth Mehta who had dedicated his entire life to the furtherance of the cooperative movement. It was also under his chairmanship that a committee first mooted the idea of such an Institute. So I put up the proposal that the Institute be named "Vaikunth Institute of Cooperative Management". Annasaheb Shinde who was Minister of state in the Ministry suggested that it was essential to call it "National Institute." So ultimately it was decided to name the Institute as "Vaikunth Mehta National Institute of Cooperative Management". Its shortform "VAMNICOM" agreeably suggested "why many come?" to a good cooperative institute.

Appointment as Director VMNICOM

Now the time had come to set the project on the ground. The first step was to select a person to be the founder Director of the Institute. D.R. Gadgil suggested that since I had been the one who had prepared the project report and had seen it through, I would be the best person to take up the responsibility. Gadgil had been my teacher when I studied for my M.A. in Economics in Pune University, I could hardly say "No". Moreover after joining the Mysore cadre of IAS I was totally out of Pune where I had studied and the Marathi culture and atmosphere in which I had grown. Personally I thought I would like to have the opportunity of spending sometime of my working life in Pune, where I would normally never have been posted and which opportunity Gadgil's offer gave me. So I accepted the offer. Gadgil wrote a formal letter to the Ministry.

But people in the Ministry were hardly interested in the project. Cooperation had become a part of the Ministry of Agriculture and Secretary B. Shivraman apparently did not care much for the project. On the other hand, since I had already completed my five year tenure in the Ministry including my one year at LSE he was thinking of repatriating my services to the state. My earlier experience with eosonophilia in Bangalore was not happy and I would go to Pune rather than Bangalore. I took an appointment with Shivaraman and indicated my preference. Shivaraman showed indifference as if it mattered nothing for him and told me if that were to be my preference he would not come in the way. But I had an uneasy feeling that he did not appreciate my choice.

Any way, ultimately the clearance came. Obviously, the Union Government succeeded in getting the clearance of the State Government which was necessary. I would get the same selection grade of Director which I drew in the Ministry.

In mid May 1967 I left Delhi for Pune after spending four years in the Central Government.

My stay in Delhi had one memorable event in my personal life—The birth of my son on 25/07/1965 at the Lohia (then Willingdon) Hospital in the afternoon hours. Delhi came to have further association with him in his later life. During my second spell in Delhi, after standing third in India in the entrance examination my son completed his degree course in computer science at IIT, Delhi.

CHAPTER 12

Founding Director, Vaikunth Mehta National Institute of Cooperative Management (1967-71)

Building up a New Institution

Shift from New Delhi to Pune was a sea change. By mid May Delhi had become extremely hot. For four years we had lived with Delhi's long hot summer and extremely cold winter. But when we reached Pune we were greeted with pleasant pre-monsoon climate. Pune's short summer had already ended and cool breeze heralded the arrival of monsoon at the end of the first week of June. Mornings and evenings were particularly pleasant. Returning to Pune, where I had my education and had spent childhood and adolescence, after 14 years away from Pune and Maharashtra appeared like home-coming after '*Vanavas*'. Immersed as I was in my official work all the time and dealing with the problems of family life in an unfamiliar environment with which I had to cope after every transfer, I had forgotten the homely Marathi atmosphere. Return to Pune made me realize how much I had missed. When we arrived at Pune station, we were welcomed with fragrant mogra flowers by V.S. Patwardhan, Dy. Director Research, at the National Cooperative College which was to be the nucleus component of the new institute which I had to build. Next day morning I went from the suite in the Treveller's Bungalow to 5, B.J. Road to take over charge. I could see a completely changed atmosphere in which I had to work. From the huge, formalised bureaucratized administrative structure I had come to a small homely training institution of which I was the head. There was no stifling bureaucratic atmosphere, no layered hierarchical framework, in which supervisors and their supervisors were breathing down the neck all the time, where one could not decide for oneself but had all the time to work for others according to their priorities, where there were no clearly defined goals for which one worked. Here I knew what I had to do, *viz.*, build up a new business management institute for the cooperative sector whose blueprint I had prepared.

The Tasks

The tasks I had set to do from day one were: 1) start the 9 month diploma course in cooperative business management, 2) Shift the CIMCOB from Bandra, Bombay to Pune, 3) Integrate it with NCC and 4) reinforce the existing faculty by recruiting new faculty in various aspects of management like organizational behaviour, personnel, finance, systems etc and subjects like agricultural economics. For accomplishing task 1, I had to complete tasks 2, 3 and 4.

I went to Bandra and visited the CIMCOB. It was located in flats at various floors in a multistory building It was conducting courses in various subjects and techniques relating to modern management of consumer business through cooperative stores. viz procurement of supplies, their display, inventory building, bulk breaking, pricing, pre-packing etc. It had a small faculty headed by Prof. S.B. Rao. I had to explain to them the new shape of things and the need for shift. There was some reluctance.

But for shifting the Institute from the multistory structure at Bandra to Pune I had to locate for it a suitable accommodation in Pune. I went round and ultimately fixed on the bungalows of Sangli State in the aristocratic Koregaon park locality. The latter had a unique prestige of its own. All plots were large—an acre or more on which spacious bungalows with beautiful gardens in front were built by big and small Maharajas and leading industrial families, many of them Paresees. We were lucky in getting the two-story spacious bungalow of ex-Sangli Maharaja. It had enough space for classrooms, office and hostel. The rent was fixed. The only condition that Sangli family insisted upon was that their bungalow staff, *viz.*, a gardener and a boy servant should be employed by the new occupants of the bungalow, to which we readly agreed. The boy servant, Shanker was suitable to work on the personal establishment of the Director and soon became a welcome aide useful in many ways. He learned driving on my car and was later absorbed, after I left, as a driver in the Institute

The CIMCOB had an Ambassador car which as an asset of the institution ought to have been automatically passed on to us. But while Shri S.S. Puri, the Managing Director NCDC was happy to be relieved of bearing the financial burden of running the Institution, he was reluctant to pass on the car to us. It required application of a great deal of pressure and persuasion before the car came in our custody. The National Cooperative College had only a jeep and the possession of a black Ambassador car was very welcome.

We needed another building for running the newly designed one-year course on cooperative business management which was going to be the flagship of the Institute. So I was on the hunt for another suitable building which I soon located. The old building of Napier Hotel which was no longer run by its owner Mazada was available. It had a large hall, several rooms and another attached building with a series of rooms which could serve as a hostel. The building located at the entry of East Street like the Sangli bungalow at Koregaon Park, was not far away from 5, B.J. Road. So it was hired. I had to work simultaneously from three places *viz.* 5, B.J. Road, Koregaon Park and Napier Building.

While buildings provided the infrastructure, the more important thing needed was the academic faculty. I issued advertisements and interviews were held at Mumbai by the Selection Committee chaired by D.R. Gadgil. D. Zha was selected as Professor agricultural economics while M.N. Rudrabasaraj from Coimbtore and Metha from Bombay were selected for Management posts. K.K. Taimni and A.S. Desai were selected for the posts of readers. For the post of Registrar Wing-Commander Joshi was recruited. I had thought that a retired army officer could bring better administration in the Institute. That was also apparently a generally accepted idea. The army officers retired at an early age and had years of active service ahead of them. Their rich experience in the army, one would have thought, could bring better discipline and system in the civilian administration but I was in for a disappointment. Joshi had no feel for civilian administration. He was not good in handling files nor in grasping procedures. Nor could he bring in the so called army management techniques for quick decision making. I reluctantly came to the conclusion that the pre-conceived notion that retired army offices would automatically prove to be competent civil administrators was hardly valid. Not all the army officers can adjust to the administrative responsibility in civilian set up. A proper scrutiny has to be made as in the case of general candidates. Our choice may not prove right. Selection of a good human being is a difficult task. But without a team of good competent people, an institute could not be built.

Of all the faculty member newly added M.N. Rudrabeserraj was the most enthusiastic and was active in making preparation for the course on cooperative business management. Amongst the old faculty of NCC, R.V. Nadkarni was a veteran with sound knowledge of cooperation. Dr. G.S. Kamat returned after one year at the Cooperative College, Loughborough, England. Both of them were full members of the team of faculty, which I readied for handling the new course on cooperative business management. I held a series of faculty meetings and allocated subjects.

Above all I prepared myself academically. I did not believe that as Director my job was purely administrative—dealing with files, acquiring accommodation and recruiting faculty. Nor was it only of directing others. In my view Director had to be not only an academic leader but also an active faculty member. I therefore started making an intensive study of literature on cooperatives, particularly cooperative principles and management principles. As a result of the study, I developed deeper understanding. My understanding of cooperation was not like that of Registrar of Cooperative Societies, purely administrative in terms of government department of cooperation and government scheme of promoting cooperative activity. I looked upon cooperation as an economic system historically evolved as an alternative to capitalism and socialism. I also asked for myself the question is " Cooperative Management" a contradiction in terms? Are cooperative principles compatible with the principles of management? Or, is there an inherent contradiction because cooperation is an ideology with social content? As a result of my study and reflection, I formulated a paper under the caption "Cooperative and Management Principles" which was published in the *Indian Journal of Public Administration* and the *Journal of Cooperative Review*. Shri R.G. Sarriah, the veteran co-operator read the article and when he met me he specially expressed his appreciation.

My Book on Principles and Philosophy of Cooperation

Even in advance of the introduction of one-year course on cooperative business management, I started lecturing on cooperative principles to the on going regular course on cooperation for senior personnel. I also took up the subject for my own lecture to be delivered to the course on cooperative business management. Once Dr. M.N. Namjoshi, my friend from student days, who was working in the Gokhle Institute of Politics and Economics heard one of my lectures and suggested that my treatment of the subject was distinctive and I should bring out my lectures in the form of a book. I took his suggestion seriously and prepared my book under the caption "Cooperative Principles and Philosophy". D.R. Gadgil who, by the time of publication of the book, had shifted from Pune where he was Vice-Chancellor, Pune University, to Delhi on his appointment as Deputy Chairman of the Planning Commission, found time to write a two and half page foreword which he concluded by saying that "Dubhashi had rendered a real service to the cooperative movement by writing this book". In my introduction I pointed out that the distinctness of my treatment of cooperative principles lay in taking the principles back to basic philosophical ideas and forward to their application specially in Indian conditions. Instead of entrusting the publication of the book to a private publishing agency I brought it out as the Institute's publication. I claimed no royalty. The book had a good get up. Young Surjit Patwardhan spared no efforts in providing a good layout. Every chapter had at the beginning, a short summary as in the American textbooks. The book was used for teaching not only in the training institutes but also in universities where cooperation was taught as an academic subject. Years after I left the Institute I got a letter from a reader in AP, that the book was "Gita, Bible and Quran" of cooperation. Some visitors in Indonesia told me that the book was in use there. Once a trainee in VMNICOM working in Assam sent the book for getting my autograph. These appreciations of my book brought me great happiness. I had dedicated the book to Prof. D.R. Gadgil at whose feet I had learnt the art of analytical thinking and logical presentation of ideas.

Inauguration of Business Management Course

But I have gone ahead of the event of the inauguration of the first course of cooperative business management which effectively marked the inauguration of the V.M. Institute of Cooperative Business Management. The course though of long duration had a good response from the cooperative departments and institutions all over the country. Some outstanding cooperative officers came – amongst them P.G. Koranne who was Deputy Registrar in Govt. of Maharashtra and was later inducted in the IAS and S.T. Bhide, who continued to work actively in the cooperative field after his retirement in the area of cooperation and was Secretary of the Committee on Cooperative Law and Administration appointed by Govt. of Maharashtra under my Chairmanship.

For the inauguration of the course I invited Prof. D.R. Gadgil, and for presiding over the occasion Prof. D.G. Karve. The latter had been the Principal of the Brihan Maharashtra College of Commerce, Vice-Chancellor of Poona University and Chairman of the Commission on Reformulation of Cooperative Principles appointed by the International Cooperative Alliance who gave its report in 1966 which provided input to my book. He was also the Founder Director of the Indian Institute of Public Administration.

Even as I was looking forward to the inauguration day, a sad thing happened. Prof. Karve suddenly passed away. I invited Vice-Chancellor of Poona University Dadasaheb Pataskar at short notice. He readily agreed as also on subsequent occasions whenever I invited him to the programmes of the Institute.

I had fixed the programme sometime by September end. I was happy I had completed the job of making a start with the course in cooperative business management within a few months of my taking over as the Director. The National Cooperative Union had recommended my name for participation in an international seminar in Berlin. I denied myself the opportunity because I did not deem it fit to postpone the inauguration of the course. My sense of duty and commitment did not permit me to do so. The inaugural address of Prof. D.R. Gadgil gave the course a good start. The course was my *Guru Dakshina* to him.

A Variety of New Programmes

I wanted to diversify the courses, organize a series of seminars and reinforce training with research and publication programme. I started a journal of the Institute called *Cooperative Information Bulletin*. I desired that instead of publishing articles of transitory nature which often appear in magazines of this sort, solid information should be provided. I had specially recruited Shri Datar with M.A. (Statistic) who was teaching at Shivaji University so that there would be continuous statistical support to teaching and research work of the Institute. I wanted him to publish statistical information about cooperative development systematically covering all sectors. But Datar could not sustain it nor even keep his commitment to his subject. After I left, the journal was named *Cooperative Perspective* publishing sundry articles on cooperation.

Amongst the new programme I started was SPUITC Special Programme for University Teachers in cooperation. It brought together University teachers teaching cooperation from all over the country. The programme not only helped in linking the Institute to

University Departments in cooperation thus opening the possibility of joint programmes but also served to make university teaching closer to the ground realities. Another fruitful seminar was COMET—Cooperative Management, Education and Training. This was organized by Shri Rudrabesraj who invited a number of experts in management in private business sector whose inputs provided valuable material for management training programme of the Institute. A book containing papers and proceedings of the seminar was published. Another publication was on *'Leadership in Cooperation'* based on research by Shri Dinesh, a Research Officer.

I gave a great deal of attention to strengthening the library of the Institute. A substantial budget was allocated for the Library and its management was strengthened by appointing an Assistant Librarian to help the Chief Librarian.

I invited a number of distinguished persons to the Institute like Prof. V.K.R.V. Rao who was then Union Minister for Education, Shri V. Kurian, Managing Director AMUL, who had ushered in milk revolution in the country, and Shri P.N. Damry, Deputy Governor of the Reserve Bank of India. Their visits were a source of enlightenment and inspiration. Prof. Marshall, Principal Loughborough College England, visited the Institute, spent some time, met the faculty and gave lectures.

With cooperative business management course at Napier Hotel premises, consumer management course at Koregaon park, and old higher diploma course at 5, B.J. Road, and seminars, research and publication, the institute started implementing a diversified programme in an integrated and purposeful manner. In course of a single day, I would move to all the three places, participating in the three streams with full zest and making my presence felt.

Reserve Bank Initiative

But more opportunities were round the corner. The Reserve Bank of India had completed a magnificent set up of self-contained buildings for a large training institute on its large plot prominently situated along the University road but did not know how to use it! The RBI offered the premises to the newly established National Institute of Bank Management which was working in hired premises in Mumbai but the latter was not interested in shifting at that time from Bombay to Pune and so new premises appeared to be without a user. For the inauguration of this new building Shri L.K. Jha the Governor of the Reserve Bank had arranged a get-together of a few persons amongst whom I was one. The get-together was at the "guest house" on the first floor of a building, the ground floor of which was meant to be the residential quarter of the Principal of a training institute intended to be set up in the new building. The guest-house was tastefully furnished with curtains and furniture by Smt. Jha who was associated with the promotion of cottage industry products. It was at this get-together that having failed to induce the NIBM to shift to Pune and use the new building that the Dy. Governor P.N. Damry broached the idea that I should shift the VMNICOM to the new premises; further more, I should also assume the responsibility as the Principal of the newly set up College of Agricultural Banking functioning in a tentative manner at Bombay. I liked the idea and accepted the additional responsibility. The RBI would pay me a token monthly allowance of Rs. 500/-. This was a tremendous confidence reposed in me by the RBI, specially its Dy. Governor, Shri P.N. Damry who later became Secretary of the World Bank. Once the idea got the clearance of the Committee of Cooperative Training and the Government of India I vacated all the three premises and shifted the three components of the VMNICOM to the brand new buildings of the RBI, which was a most convenient arrangement in every way.

For my residential purpose, I had, after coming to Pune, started residing at the Ghaswala Building near Mhasoba Gate not far away from the RBI premises. But now I too had to shift to the Principal's quarter of RBI building. That too was an excellent place to stay with three bed rooms, a dinning room and a living room of modest propositions but very compact and convenient. There was an attached garage. My father came from Bombay to stay with me for a while.

The RBI had started the new College of Agricultural Booking following the decision of the Government of India that the commercial banks should not confine their activities to city centres and trade and industry but also extend to rural areas and to agriculture. The new policy went by the name "social control over banking".

The commercial bankers were new to the area of financing agriculture and rural development. They were used only to financing industry and trade. It was therefore necessary to provide them a new orientation – not only familiarity with the requirement of agriculture and the rural economy but also the new techniques of lending to and recovery from farmers and operating and nurturing small accounts. This was an extremely important pre-condition for the success of the new policy.

I took up this additional new responsibility with my usual enthusiasm and great gusto. I had as my colleagues, six officers of the RBI who were given residential accommodation in the flats of a multistory building on the campus itself. One of them Shri Bhuvanchandran was designated as the Vice-Principal. I had to play the role of the leader of the RBI task force of six. I prepared the syllabus and training material for the one month. course for reorientation of the commercial bankers for agricultural banking. But I found the approach of the RBI personal rigid and unimaginative. They felt that training meant explaining the circulars of the RBI. My approach was entirely different. I wanted the orientation related to the fundamentals of the rural economy and sociology to which the rural finances had to be related. Before reorienting the trainees I had to reorient the training faculty of the RBI itself and I found that not very easy. The RBI staff was steeped in orthodoxy and did not have the flexible mindset of a trainer. Training has less to do with the contents of circulars of instructions and more with the basic concepts and ideas that lie behind them.

Though the RBI training staff was, as it were, working under compulsion under an outsider like me, I found the trainees, the officers from various commercial banks, quite enthusiastic. They were quite excited about this new venture of commercial banking. They came in large numbers and were quite open to new ideas. So one more dimension was added to the combined set of training programmes I was directing—four streams at a time.

It was quite extraordinary that I was simultaneously accountable to three institutions at the same time—the Government of India, the National Cooperative Union of India and its Committee of Cooperative Training and the Reserve Bank of India. All the three authorities had reposed their trust in me and I had no difficulty in reconciling my accountability to three sets of authorities. While keeping them informed of my activities, I retained full institutional autonomy.

Autonomy of VMNICOM

I got constituted a special committee of VMNICM headed by the Chairman CCT, of which President of NCUI was the chairman and Director VMNICOM the member secretary. In running VMNICOM, the Director would have the full delegation of powers as that of Member Secretary of the CCT. That meant there would be no interference whatsoever of the Member Secretary of the CCT sitting in Delhi. But that was exactly what happened, after I left as Director, the Member Secretary started interfering in activities of the Institute.

For the College of Agricultural Banking there was a separate committee headed by the Deputy Governor of RBI. Here too there was clear unhappiness at lower levels in RBI that "their" institution was headed by an "outsider".

A Combined Institutional Set-Up

Despite the possibility of conflicting forces creating disharmony, I maintained completely harmonious functioning at the institutional level. There were four separate class rooms assigned to the four streams and two separate messes – one for the RBI and the other for the VMNICOM since the mess charges and standards were different. For running of the RBI's College of Agriculture I hired additional clerical staff. My attempt was to make the faculty work as a combined team but in that I could not succeed completely though I did try to use VMNICOM faculty in Economics, Cooperation and Management for the courses of the College of Agriculture Banking.

My objective was to turn these entirely fortuitous arrangements of the two institutions working together on the same campus under one Director into a permanent institutional system. I had a grand vision of all the training programmes pertaining to the cooperative and rural economy as a whole, coming together in one system supported by the combined resources of the Government. of India, RBI and the NCUI – all reinforcing each other. I even prepared a paper proposing to set the ad hoc arrangements under which the two institutions could work together on a permanent footing. Eventually they could grow into a Cooperative University. But that was not to be. Soon after I left the fissiparous tendencies gathered strength and under Dr. A.U. Shaikh the management fell apart. But one cannot be responsible for what happens after one leaves. One cannot shape the future which is inevitably determined by those who follow. Great dreams, visions or deigns can only be sustained if they are upheld by the successors.

While VMNICOM was comfortably housed on the premises of RBI, I wanted VMNICOM to eventually to have its own independent premises if the combined functioning could not be put on a permanent basis. I thought of VMNICOM linking up with Poona University in an organic manner. Physical propinquity could help in this development. How nice it would be if the VMNICOM could be given a plot on the periphery of the University land – I wondered. I had a fortunate circumstance. Prof. D.R. Gadgil had become V.C. of the University. I mooted the proposal to him. He was of course favourably inclined. When I made the proposal formally, he placed it before the Syndicate of the University and got it approved I then got in touch with university's estate officer and on either side of the hillock got demarcated two portions – one for the administrative offices and classes for the training courses etc and the other for residential purposes. The plot was demarcated and handed over to the Institute. It is on this plot of land that the VMNICOM is now having its complex of buildings.

The Intellectual Nerve-Centre of the Cooperative Movement

I visualized the VMNICOM as the intellectual nerve centre of the cooperative movement. But the visions had to be shared by the leaders of the cooperative movement. Most of them were chairing the apex cooperative banks in various states. I brought them together at a seminar. The redoubtable Vasantrao Dada Patil who later became the Chief Minister, Maharashtra, was the host Chairman. All these Chairmen expressed their interest in the development of VMNICOM. I told them that after I leave, the VMNICOM could fullfill its promise only if it had the enlightened support of the cooperative leaders. They promised such a support at the seminar but it only remained a promise. There was hardly any permanent commitment of cooperative leaders to VMNICOM. They left it to NCCT of the NCUI which was steeped in cooperative politics.

Seminar in Sweden

After I had setup VMNICOM at the RBI premises, I got an opportunity to participate in a one month training seminar in Sweden. It was an excellent opportunity for me. Sweden was considered to be at the forefront of consumer cooperative movement. It had its own federation known as K.F. It was a rich organisation and had supported the regional office of the ICA at New Delhi. The seminar was held at a resort in Sudatellye a few miles from Stockholm, the capital of Sweden. The arrangements were excellent. Residential as well seminar facilities were available at the same premises. There were lectures, discussions and visits. It was September and quite cold but rooms and even buses were centrally heated and one was quite comfortable. After supper and huge quantities of coffee we often went down town to have enjoyable walks. Food was served on a huge table which is a

Swedish institution known as "smorgasbord". One thing which one liked most was a huge jug full of milk and very mild wine-like drink available in limitless quantities.

The idea of the seminar was to make the participants familiar with the organisation and techniques of the consumer cooperative movement in Sweden. The federal body of the Swedish movement was K.F. It was a very strong organisation. Its motto was "∞" which stood for infinite protection to the consumers from the exploitative practices of the private trade and act as price leader in the market. The department stores with "∞" sign could be seen every where in Sweden. They provided full consumer protection. An article purchased by a consumer could be returned later and the amount paid refunded. An article bought at one place could be returned to another store in another city if the consumer was dissatisfied. This was what one of the participants actually did. This experience was in strong contrast to what we experience in India where the stores followed the principle of "caveat enptor" – "beware, the consumer buys at his own risk".

Sweden was well known as a welfare state as well as a developed economy with a high standard of living for its population of some eighty lakhs. As a result, it had also become an egalitarian society.

The consumer cooperative movement was closely connected with the movement of adult education. Great deal of attention was paid to continuous consumer education. The approach to education or training was not through long courses but brief courses year after year focussing on precise information and knowledge related to specific roles and functions. While K.F. was the leading institution in the field of consumer cooperation, the leading institution in the field of adult education was *Braves Sceholan*. Its correspondence courses covered virtually the entire adult population of Sweden. The idea was that in a dynamically changing environment the working population should be continuously equipped to acquire new knowledge, techniques and information.

Following the month long seminar at Sudatllye, visits were arranged to Stockholm and Malmö in southern Sweden from where we made a visit to Copenhagen, the capital of Denmark. It is a most impressive city with many ancient buildings and canal system but what I liked most was the walking-street where pedestrians can do shopping and have coffee and eatables at restaurants without bothered by transport vehicles.

What was even more memorable was the visit to Finland. Sweden, Norway, Denmark and Finland are known together as Scandinavian countries. While Sweden, Norway and Denmark are close to each other, Finland abuts Russia and separated by the Baltic Sea. In an overnight journey in a well appointed ship we crossed the Baltic sea to be greeted in the morning by the "White City" – that is what Helsinki is known as – which was in sight across the horizon. I had known the Finish as a brave people who during World War II had taken on the might of the Russian Red Army and defended its freedom. We visited the impressive memorial to the brave soldiers of World War II.

Finland was impressive in many ways. There was artistry in making of furniture and apparel. We toured through many small towns and were impressed by the progress of cooperative tourism, restaurants and insurance which were for me new fields of cooperative development with which we were not familiar in India.

Finland and sauna go together, I had read that even Cabinet meetings in Finland were held in sauna bath chambers. I had my first experience of sauna bath in Finland. One sat in a steaming hot chamber absorbing heat in the body and jumped thereafter into a pool of cold water. The effect was extremely exhilarating on body and mind.

Karnataka Calls Me Back

After a very enjoyable and rewarding stay of five weeks in Scandinavian countries, I returned to Pune after a brief visit to Loughborough and Hamburg. My return was just on the eve of Diwali. The day following my return, early morning P.N. Damry, Deputy Governor of RBI, dropped in, unannounced. I was quite surprised. But that was typical of him. He told me that my term of three years was coming to a close but he would like me to stay on. He wanted to know whether I was agreeable. It was a pleasant surprise for me. If somebody wanted me to stay on, why not agree? Specially when the institutions which I had established were coming up well? And a place where it was a pleasure to stay? Damry took up the proposal with the Government of India and the state Government. I was told that Shri L.P. Singh, Union Home Secretary, felt that it was high time that I returned to the "mainstream". It would not be in the interest of my career development to stay on the side-line. But he reluctantly agreed. But it was the state Government which started being adamant. They said that they wanted "their" officer back who had stayed away well beyond the normal period of deputation to the Centre. They further said that they wanted my services urgently. They had already appointed me as Secretary to Government. in the department of Development, Housing, Panchayati Raj and Cooperation. The Secretary to Chief Minister, Shri Christopher Lynn, went on phoning to Damry and pressuring him. Damry a seasoned officer as he was, was a gentlemen as well. He found it difficult to resist.

But he came with another offer. He could work out a proposal for my permanent absorption in the services of the Reserve Bank of India if I could leave the IAS. My absorption would be at the level of Joint Chief. This proposal was hardly acceptable to me. I could hardly leave a secure position in the IAS almost at the middle of my career with possible promises in the future for a position in the Reserve Bank of India at not too high a level and then get stagnated. I told Damry that though it was nice of him to have thought of the proposal I could not accept it. So it was only a matter of time for me to lay down my office as Founder Director of VMNICOM and the first Principal of College of Agricultural Banking after it was set up in Pune and bid goodbye to Pune where normally I could not have had an assignment as an IAS officer on Karnataka Cadre.

CHAPTER 13

Secretary to Government of Karnataka: Dealing with Mountain of Files and Many Ministers

Secretary to Goverment is an important position in the administrative set up—infact it is the highest level in the administrative ladder. It is at the policy making level. The Secretary is the principal advisor to the Minister who as a member of the Cabinet decides the policy, obtaining whenever necessary, the approval of the Chief Minister and the Cabinet. Every IAS officer covets the position of Secretary whether at the State or the Centre. There is of course no parity between the Secretary at the State level and the Secretary at Union level. The Secretary at the State level was then considered to be equivalent to Joint Secretary at the Central level.

An Omnibus Department

The department assigned to me was an omnibus department—DHPC—development, housing, panchayati raj and cooperation. This was considered to be a department appropriate to my background. Development meant rural development and I had already been Deputy Development Commissioner in the state Government and had dealt with community development and Panchayati Raj programme in the state. As for cooperation, I had worked as Director in charge of cooperative training in the Union Ministry and later became the founder Director of the Apex Institute of Cooperative Management though I had not worked as Registrar of Cooperative Societies. Housing was a new subject for me and certainly too important a subject to be tagged on to community development and cooperation. But that is how it was. Besides there were other departments not explicitly referred to in DHPC—*viz.*, department of Weight & Measurement and Department of Marketing. The combination of all these departments was indeed a formidable assignment and required a lot of attention. No single individual could take these matters at one go. At present each of the subjects would have an independent Secretary.

While all these departments were concentrated in a single secretary, they were looked after by three different Ministers—C D and P R were with one minister, Cooperation another & Housing third—each in charge of a separate Minister and I had to report to them. Every Minister expected the secretary to fully attend to him. The secretary was like Draupad of Mahabharat—he had to live with administrative polyandry. The Minister for Housing Basavalingappa, belonged to schduled caste and was particularly a strong personality. Fortunaitly I had good relationship with him. Alva the Co-operative Minister was in contrast pleasant courtous and mild though not effective. Taking care of three Ministers and attending to them simultaneously was no mean task!

On the other hand I found that as Secretary I had not the feeling of independence which a Secretary must have. I was accountable to the Development Commissioner who was like a Super-Secretary overseeing Secretary DHPC and Secretary—Agriculture. The post. was next only to that of the Chief Secretary, perhaps bracketed with Revenue Secretary G.V.K. Rao, my old superior when I was Deputy Development Commissioner, held the position of Development Commissioner. He had developed greater maturity and self confidence. Though he was the most agreeable person one could have as a superior, my spirit of independence would not relish working under a superior even after occupying the position of a Secretary. Were the concepts of consolidation at the administrator level and dispersal at the ministerial level and that of a Super-Secretary administratively sound?

A Mountain of Files

Any way in administration one has to come to terms with a given situation and work within it if one cannot change it and that is what I set about doing. As I started settling down to work I discovered that a mountain of files would start appearing on my table and daily disposal of files itself became a burden—let alone finding time to give a new direction to the departments under me. I was new to the subject of housing. There was public sector housing for low and middle income groups taken up by the Housing Board whose Secretary was a Superintending Engineer, who reported to me. The Department of Cooperation was headed by the Register, a post held by Maharudrayyah who had succeeded me as Deputy Development Commissioner when I was shifted to Delhi. While I was trying to get a grip of the situation, my first worry was how to get the better of the flood of files. They would come in a haphazard manner in a relentless flow leaving little time for thinking. I had to get over the file work. Files are the embodiment of red-tape which is the hall-mark of government administration. I was determined to get over the red-tape. I realized I could not do it in normal working hours where time would be taken up by meetings with Development Commissioner and calls of Ministers.

This burden of files worried me even while I was settling down as a family hunting for a house and admitting children to schools. I put my daughter in Sophia Convent and son in the Central School. I had to take the daughter to school at early morning hour. I decided to come to the office straight from the school and find additional undisturbed time to dispose of the files.

The files were all mixed up and the PA did not take care even to separate them department wise. As I started handling the files I realized that it was all a case of velocity in the movement of files without any body attending to dispose them off finally. Secretariat departments acted as post masters in this merry go round of the files. If a proposal came from the head of the Department—a field position—it would be promptly passed on to the Finance Department or Law Department for their "views" and when after a few days they returned with some queries, they would be passed on to the departmental head for their clarifications And when the files came back again after clarifications on queries raised, the process would be repeated with new queries raised! The secretariat department had become a post office between the field agency and the Law Department and Finance Department. The latter department could take only a technical view without touching the substantive matters involved. The only way to stop this unending merry go round was to go through files carefully, examine issues in depth and give them a decisive shape. This is what I set about doing. My new approach soon yielded dividends. The to and fro movement of files was replaced by decisive disposal. The meaningless movement of files without final disposal came to an end and the load of files on my groaning table miraculously went down to my great relief. I could find time for reading literature relating to my several departments to enable me to give higher level guidance and direction as also to look into field problems and seek solutions, as all my departments were field oriented. Secretarial work had no meaning except in terms of improvement in the quality of work at the field level. The intensive inter-connection between secretariat and fieldwork is often overlooked. That is the main shortcoming of our secretariat level administrative system.

Field Orientation

Cooperation is entirely a subject of field administration. Cooperative institutions in various sectors like rural credit, supply of agricultural inputs and marketing of agricultural output, agro-processing, consumer distribution, housing etc. were setup in post independence era with massive state support but were often lacking in performance because of poor management. Since public funds were involved, it was the duty of public administration to see that the cooperative institutions worked properly. As Secretary (cooperation). I was an ex-officio member of the Board of Management of State Cooperative Bank and State Land Development Bank. Often because of other preoccupations government officers do not attend the meetings of the Board. But I made it a point to attend to them and take active part in discussions on various items on the agenda. The Managing Director of the state Land Development Bank was Shri Angol, an IAS officer who took interest in his work and did not take his work as a deputation to a cooperative institution with a sense of reluctance if not resentment. It is often stated that the system of deputation of government officers to cooperative institutions should cease as a rule. But if the officers during their tenure of deputation of 3 to 5 years work with zeal and dedication, the system could work to the advantage of cooperative institutions which can get the highly qualified services of an experienced officer of the IAS.

I took interest in other cooperative institutions as well. In particular I remember my initiative in the recovery of a cooperative oil-pressing unit in Gadag, which was not functioning. The plant was lying idle. I visited the plant and found that the main reason was that the plant had been managed with indifference and no attempt was made to collect groundnut produced by member farmers which provided raw material for the factory. There was no officer working as the manager. The post was lying vacant. I persuaded a state civil service officer to accept the post and guided him in a detailed manner. Initially he lacked confidence but soon he geared up his work and succeeded in effecting a turn around.

The raw material was collected and the plant started processing to its capacity. There was no particular problem in selling the final product.

Political Turmoil in the State and Imposition of President's Rule

Even while I was setting down in Bangalore to which I had returned after nine years (I left it in 1962 and returned to it in 1971) at the insistence of the Chief Minister Virendra Patil, who was apparently very keen to have my services returned by the Central Government to State Government, I felt rumblings of strange political happenings. Despite the majority of the Congress party in the state legislature, Virendra Patil's government was finding the stability of his government threatened by internal dissidence. Devraj Urs had raised the banner of revolt. In this political horse-trading, the Chief Minister was hardly in a mood to give appointment for a courtesy call by the officer who had newly joined as Secretary. Unable to hold on to majority despite effort, he resigned leaving the state in turmoil. Suddenly the Governor, a retired civil servant, Dharma Veer, who was spending time playing golf, became the focal point of the political scene. He had earlier been Governor of West Bengal. There too after the fall of Ajay Mukharji government, he had to handle the situation. He recommended President's rule and when it was imposed he administered the state. Now in Karnataka he was placed in a similar situation. Here too he recommended President's rule which was soon imposed. Governor's administration started. He replaced the council of ministers as the final decision maker. All files were to be submitted to him for final decision-making.

I had a slight but pleasant experience of meeting him. when he was working as the Cabinet Secretary and I was Deputy Secretary in the Ministry of Community Development. He had convened a meeting in his office at the Rashtrapati Bhavan and I was asked to attend it on behalf of the Ministry. When I went to attend it, I found that the meeting, for some reason, stood cancelled. But instead of asking his PA to convey the message as was the wont, he himself received me and told me about it and to compensate for the trouble I had undergone to go to his office, he graciously offered me a cup of cold coffee which in the summer of Delhi I relished. I remembered the event with pleasure because it was such a rare experience. Normally in the hierarchical atmosphere of bureaucracy an officer as senior as Cabinet Secretary could hardly offer such courtesy to an officer as junior as Deputy Secretary who had come to attend a scheduled meeting.

Governor – Shri Dharma Veer

Dharma Veer was a person of very short stature but had risen high in the administrative echelon. He had come close to Jawaharlal Nehru as his Personal Secretary and got one assignment after another, higher and higher in the administrative echelon and now for a second time he was heading a large state as Governor at the helm of administration in President's room. Soon I came into personal contact with him and came to know his qualities of head and heart as an administrator. I had already experienced his graciousness in Delhi and that I received throughout the six months period of President's rule. He was not intellectually brilliant but he had sound commonsense. He could grasp a problem, listen to the advice tendered and arrive at a balanced conclusion. Commonsense and robust balanced outlook, good interpersonal relationships are qualities perhaps more important in an administrator then mere intellectual brilliance.

I found working under the President's rule an agreeable experience. The work was going on in a smooth way. Files would come back from the Governor without delay. There were no abrupt calls from the Ministers breaking into work time – nor undue pressures. Decisions could be taken in an objective manner on merits of each case. Elections to cooperative institutions which were held up because of political interference could take place. Visitors with political clout who would normally go to Minister now came to the Secretary. I remember Shri R Gaudurao who later became the Chief Minister once came to see me for a personal case of his, perhaps related to a cooperative institutions in which he was an officer bearer.

While I was satisfied about the short break in democratic Government, my friend Shri Mani Narayanswami who was Finance Secretary felt otherwise. He thought that it was only in the regime of democratic Government that real interaction of administration with the common people takes place and he found it missing under the President's rule. He was perhaps fundamentally right. But I was in charge of a people oriented department and did not feel the absence of public contact. I rather welcomed absence of 'undue interference'.

World Bank Project

The period of President's rule became memorable for one reason – the clearance of a World Bank project for a loan of $ 40 million to the state for construction of irrigation wells all over the state. The loans were to be given to farmers though the State Cooperative Land Development Bank for the purpose. Shri Vishwanathan was the President of the Cooperative Land Development Bank while Shri Anaglo, was the M.D. The latter had to provide field information and information regarding institutional functioning needed for the formulation and implementation of the project. Shri G.V.K. Rao, the Development Commissioner was the over all coordinator. I was a member of the team as Secretary in charge of cooperation. The World Bank team visited the state to assess the project. The team consisted of some five experts including an irrigation engineer and financial analyst etc. They visited several parts of the state and held continuous discussions ending in a meeting with the Governor who gave them a grand dinner. In due time the project matured for a final pilgramage of the state team to the World Bank. The team led by G.V.K. Rao included me, Shri Vishwanathan and Shri Anagol. This was my first opportunity to visit USA and participate in negotiations with World Bank. American capital, Washington with its broad roads was quite impressive but I was quite surprised to find the element of crime floating in the air. Once while walking back together in a group from the World Bank after day's discussion we were accosted by a gang of black hoodlums whom we just ignored and moved on.

The negotiations were of routine character where members of World Bank team sought clarification and assurances which were duly given. The leader of the team which had visited the state was the real active member of the World Bank team.

The Bank was then headed by the redoubtable Robert McNamara who provided vigorous leadership for reorientation of the Bank in the direction of 'direct assault' on poverty. He brought considerable augmentation of the resources and loaning programmes for 'soft loans for poverty allleivation' which earlier were mostly available for 'hard projects' like infrastructural constructions of roads and bridges. During the visit I tried to call on McNamara but he could hardly give a appointment to a member of a negotiating team from the state for a small project and all I could do was to leave my visiting card with a copy of my book "Principles and Philosophy of Cooperation" which he did not even acknowledge! Perhaps it was a futile expectation.

On return from successful negotiations regarding the World Bank project I immediately set down to lay the foundation for yet another World Bank project on agricultural marketing. I had a feeling that with the success of the green revolution, the problem of agricultural marketing would grow in importance. I had written and published an article "*Marketing the Theme of the Seventies*" in which I had set out my ideas. I wrote down a note that Karnataka should work out a comprehensive plan to strengthen the system of agricultural marketing both by way of the infrastructure of regulated markets and for stregnthenic the presence of cooperative marketing societies in these markets so as to ensure better return to the farmers for their agricultural crops. As Secretary in change of marketing and cooperation, I was the one who had to take the initiative which I did. Eventually, the project was submitted to the World Bank and the state was successful in getting the financial support from the World Bank. But by that time, I had moved to another department.

I made some contributions to the smaller departments of Marketing and Weight and Measures as well. They were neglected. There were not even basic cadre and recruitment rules which I got prepared and approved.

Housing

The housing programme was limited to low and middle class housing by the Housing Board. They built some houses which were then sold to persons of that category. What was needed was a massive housing project both in rural and urban areas where housing shortage was severe. Once Shri K.P. Singh, a bright young IAS officer working as SDO Chitradurg came with bubling enthusiasm to tell me how he helped poor villages to build their own houses with local material and limited financial help from some local development fund at his disposal. I immediately felt that was the right approach to mass housing in rural area I prepared a scheme on that line to be introduced all over the state. The housing Minister Shri Basavlinppa welcomed the scheme. That was perhaps the precursor of nation wide scheme known as Indira Awas Yojana.

Shift to Public Works and Electricity

I had worked for just a little more than a year when I moved to another Department on promotion. While I was working as Secretary DHPC and was still on the senior scale of IAS. I had completed 18 years in IAS and was due to be on the super-time scale which was already delayed I was promoted to it 1972 in my nineteenth year of service. But for that to happen I had to change my assignment to take up a post, which was earmarked as a super-time scale post. Not all posts of secretaries were on super-time scale. The super-time scale post to which I was promoted was Secretary, Commissioner, Public works and Electricity. That was indeed a huge portfolio compressing various building activities, *viz.*, roads, bridges irrigation works etc., which at present are treated as independent departments with separate secretaries in charge. In addition to the works programme mentioned above I had the charge of electricity for which the agency incharge was the State Electricity Board. This is now known as 'Power Portfolio'. This was yet another huge area of work. As though this was not enough, I was also in charge of ports. Since I belonged to Karwar, I was particularly interested in this activity. I thought that Karnataka's coastline could be dotted with a series of good ports—major and minor which could handle substantial cargo and passenger traffic.

A Conflict Between Senior and Junior Ministers

The Minister in charge of the department was Shri H.M. Channabasappa the same Minister who had phoned to me from Bangalore late at nights when I was Deputy Commissioner, Raichur, accusing me of playing politics. But now he appeared to have cleared himself of all prejudices against me. He cordially welcomed me as his new Secretary. Obviously he thought I was an honest and impartial officer needed for his department. Well might he have needed such an officer, because soon I realized that while Channabasappa appeared to be a powerful Minister incharge of a department with vast empire and capacity to do a lot of visible work all over the state, he had his own political handicaps. The Chief Minister Devraj Urs considered him as political rival and wished to checkmate him in his exercise of unfettered power in the department. And as a Machivellian wily politician, Devraj Urs had appointed a Minister of State to snipe at his senior Minister all the time. Shri H.N. Nanje Gowda was given the irrigation portfolio. Channabasappa was a Lingayat and Nanje Gowda, a Vokkaliga—two rival castes of Karnataka. There was no love lost between the senior minister and the junior minister. Not only that Nanje Gowda did not seem to care a damn for his senior and never attended a meeting called by him in his room. They did not seem to be even on talking terms. For the matters in his portfolio of irrigation he would report to the Chief Minister rather than the Minister of the Department. Channabasappa should not have accepted such a situation—a junior minister not only disagreeable to him but also not answerable to him. But such are the compulsions of politics that he accepted the arrangement The rivalry between the two ministers should not have mattered per se to the Secretary and to other civil servants but for the fact that, as I soon realized, it spilt into day to day work. Once after several sittings Channabasappa approved of a long list of transfers of PWD engineers. The orders of transfers were issued. As soon as a copy of orders reached Nanje Gowda he kicked up a big row. His argument was that some of the engineers who were transfered were working in "his" department of irrigation and could not have been transferred without his approval. The orders had to be withdrawn and reissued after the changes suggested by him. The "strong" Channabasappa had to put up with this humiliation. For me too it was an unpleasent experience.

The baleful Nanje Gowda did not stop at this. He started taking serious exception to the behaviour of the Deputy Secretary, Shri Purshottam in charge of administration. He sent for me and expressed his displeasure with him. Shri Purshottam was a Secretariat service officer. A mild-mannered officer he typically worked like a secretariat service official acting according to rules. He had done nothing wrong and Nanje Gowda had no business to find fault with him. But he was a man of strong likes and dislikes and pressurized me to take action against Purushottam. But I could not oblige him for no fault of the officer. He sent for Purshottam and reprimanded him. He came crying to me. I tried to console him. The incident left a bad taste.

Getting a Grip Over Work

I tried to ignore this tension between the two ministers and decided to work as a professional civil servant. I had a huge portfolio and had to get thoroughly acquainted with various subjects of which I was in charge. In my usual way I started reading literature on the subject to give depth to my knowledge which in my way of working was essential for getting a grip over the work. I first took up irrigation which most interested me. Huge irrigation projects were taken up on the rivers in Karnataka, *viz.*, Kaveri and its tributary, Hemavati, and Ghataprabha and Malaprabha, tributaries of Tungbhadra. The project had to completed on time and their irrigation potential fully developed. As Deputy Commissioner Raichur I had already had some acquaintance with the Tungabhadra project and now I had to deal with several other irrigation projects. An exclusive Chief Engineer Shri B.C. Angdi was in charge of the irrigation projects. As part of reading I came across a wonderful book by Henny Hart called "Rivers of India." It gave an account of all the first generation irrigation projects taken up by free India. I found the book not only interesting and informative but also inspiring. Here was a living account of what Nehru called "temples of Modern India" The book was written as a Ph.D. theses but unlike the ordinary work of a Ph.D. student in India it was of high order, almost a classic, and I thought it should have been compulsory reading for every official who had anything to do with the irrigation projects. But none of our officers, engineers included, were even aware of the existence of the book much less reading it. I also read the report of the Irrigation Commission. This reading enabled me to have a wider perspective and indepth understanding of the irrigation projects. For more specific information I tried to get hold of the project reports and read them. Apart from the irrigation dams, another big dam was on Kali *nadi* in North Canara (Uttar Kannnda) district to produce power. A separate power corporation was established to be in charge of the project. I decided to personally visit the irrigation projects in North Karnataka, the Hidkal dam on Ghateprabha and Soundatti dam on Malaprabha and its cannel system I found these visits a thrilling experience.

Corruption

But there is always an unsavory aspect of the big construction projects costing crores of rupees, i.e., corruption that goes with it. PWD is notorious for corruption and I was the Secretary in change of the department. But surprisingly enough the contractors never came to me to offer any bribe in return for a favour. Did that mean that there was no corruption? Obviously it had bypassed me. Shri I.G. Makdum was Engineer in Chief and Additional Secretary and was reportedly in direct touch with the Chief Minister Devraj Urs who was in charge of irrigation. Devraj Urs was said to have institutionalised corruption and Makdum was said to be his associate. After I took charge, Makdum once called on me but later never kept in touch with me. He had his own office as Engineer-in-Chief. The subterranean passage of corruption remained unknown to me.

But an incident happened which was directly to affect me. Complaints came that hand pumps being installed all over the state under the scheme for rural water supply were defective and did not function. The huge amount of funds spent on installation of pumps was simply wasted. I tried to get information to face responsibility. I came to know that a firm called Nirmala

Engineering Works was responsible for installing these faulty pumps which not only led to waste of public funds but also deprived the poor villagers of the most essential need of human beings, *viz.*, drinking water. I put up a note informing the Minister of the scandal and proposed that the firm be blacklisted immediately so that no further orders would be placed with it and no work given to it. The Minister without any hesitation approved the proposal and orders were issued accordingly. No one approached me or spoke to me to take back the orders or modify them. But I seldom realized the corrsequences that would follow and I would have to pay the price.

A Bolt From the Blue

I had hardily spent six months in the challenging job of Secretary-cum-Commissioner PWE, still trying to get a grip over the huge department in all its aspects when like a "bolt from the blue" orders came shifting me from that post and appointing me to the new post of Administrator, Malaprabha and Ghataprabha Projects with HQ at Dharwad. Even the minister was taken by surprise as he had no inkling of it. He very much wanted me to continue and told me in so many words but was apparently utterly helpless. He was said to be No. 2 in the Cabinet but could not even register his protest. Such is the compulsion of politics; such is the bizarre working of administration and its effect on the fortunes of civil servants who are up right but have no God-fathers and who work strictly within the rules of administrative and code of civil servants.

The order posting me as Administrator in a mofussil town was clearly seen as demotion. The post was outside the main-stream and had no "power" or privilege associated with it. Moreover it had come at a very odd time at the end of the academic year when children ware preparing for examination. My daughter was to appear for the final year school leaving examination. Here was an officer who only a year and half ago was specially needed to work as Secretary and was brought back by the State Government from a post in which RBI was keen to see him continued and here was the same state government shifting him to a field post without any compunction. The Government had changed and was in no way bound by the act of the previous government. Moreover a civil servant has no right to hold any particular post and is required to go to any post to which he is posted. It is the privilege of government to transfer a civil servant any time. But this theory, as I maintained in my writing, was not correct. The transfers have to be in public interest and not accordingly to the will of the politicians with brief authority. Unfortunately the trend of arbitrary transfers of civil servants at the will of the politicians has only increased to the detriment of administration and demoralistion of civil servants.

I found myself sadly helpless in this situation. I approached K.H. Patil another important Minister whom I knew well to intervene but he was as helpless as my own Minister since he too belonged to the camp opposed to the Chief Minister and could hardly protect an officer from utterly arbitrary orders.

So I decided to meet the Chief Minister himself. I got an appointment to meet him at his house. He came after making me wait for a while with a beaming smile on his face. I asked him bluntly why I was suddenly transferred. He benevolently told me that he was sending me to a very important assignment. Only a few days earlier, Shri D.P. Dhar, the Deputy Chairman of the Planning Commission had visited the state and wanted the state government to take up a plan for Command Area Development under Malapraha and Ghateprabha projects and the Chief Minister felt that I was best person to undertake the responsibility. I could see the wily Chief Minister talking with tongue in the check but by giving a sound reason for my transfer, he made it difficult for me to put my case except for personal reasons, which I was unwilling to do.

Why Dharam Vira was Eased Out

The one person who could have possibly helped was Governor Dharm Vira. It was on his time that I got promotion in normal course. He had already left the state in unsavory circumstances. While still running the state under the President's rule, he made some statement to which strong objection was taken by congress politicians who had brought about the fall of Virendra Patil government. It was not an ordinary rift. Virrendra Patil and Ramakrishna Hegde, the two politicians who in tandem ruled the state were followers of Nijalingappa, the Congress President and father figure of Karnataka. He was the one who had dared to oppose Indira Gandhi. The latter took up cudgels on the "Syndicate" leaders and threw them out. The fall of Virrendra Patil was one of the outcomes of this political war between "Syndicate" and "Indicate". Dharma Vira had good relations with Virendra Patil and especially Ramakrishna Hedge with whom he played golf. So Devraj Urs and his supported had suspected all along that the Governor was on the opposite side. They carried tales to Indira

Gandhi who became suspicions of Dharam Vira and probably had decided to remove him. One remark reported to have been made by him appeared to have angered her. It was in the context of Central grants to be made available to the state. He publicly announced that he would not allow the Centre to overlook the legitimate requirements of the State and would fight for the interest of the State. It was hardly an objectionable remark. A Governor in charge of the State under the President's rule cannot be faulted for talking on behalf the State, albeit perhaps in a somewhat combative manner. But that was the pretext for the all-powerful Prime Minister to show her displeasure. Dharam Vira went to Delhi to meet the Prime Minister and remove the misunderstanding. He waited for three days but got no appointment with the Prime Minister. He returned to the state defeated and dejected and soon resigned. This was indeed an unceremonious ouster of a respected civil servant from the post of Governor. He returned to Delhi and settled down in Greater Kailash as advisor to the House of Lala Shriram. At his house he arranged dinner parties to which I was invited when I came to have my posting in Delhi later. Sometimes people in position of influence like the redoubtable Pupul Jaykar, the cultural czar of Indira Gandhi, came. But I was unable to think of using those occasions for establishing useful "connections". I just could not think that way. Dharma Vira was kind and gracious. He matured in old age in a graceful manner and his New Year greeting card was always a reminder of his graciousness. I myself never sent greeting cards but always acknowledged his. Once I sent a copy of my published paper on the reconstruction of India's political, economic and social system after 50 years of independence and he not only acknowledged it but also sent a thoughtful reply. Just a few years before he expired at the ripe old age of ninety, the Government conferred on him Padma Vibhushen. I sent a letter of congratulation. As it is bound to happen when such honours are conferred late in life, he was hardly excited and said so in his reply.

The connection between my backlisting the Nirmala Engineering Works and my removal from the post of Secretary Public Works and Electricity became quite clear when I read in the press sometimes later a report of the Public Accounts Committee which noticed that the government had restored Nirmala Engineering Works despite the fraud it had committed on the rural people in Karnataka. Despite this indictment, the politicians responsible for the misdeeds went scot-free as it often happens in the Indian politics.

After my meeting with Devraj Urs, I reconciled to shifting from Bangalore to mofussil Dharwad. For any other senior officer this would have appeared as a personal calamity. But not for me. I had no attachment to Bangalore. I had no house. I had never taken to Bangalore. The weather though pleasant did not suit me. For a second time, eosinophilia had returned requiring resumption of medical treatment. The work environment was also not very pleasant. Working with people like H.N. Nanje Gowda could be quite an unpleasant experience. So on receiving orders I left in the car for Dharwad with my wife and two children to start a new life.

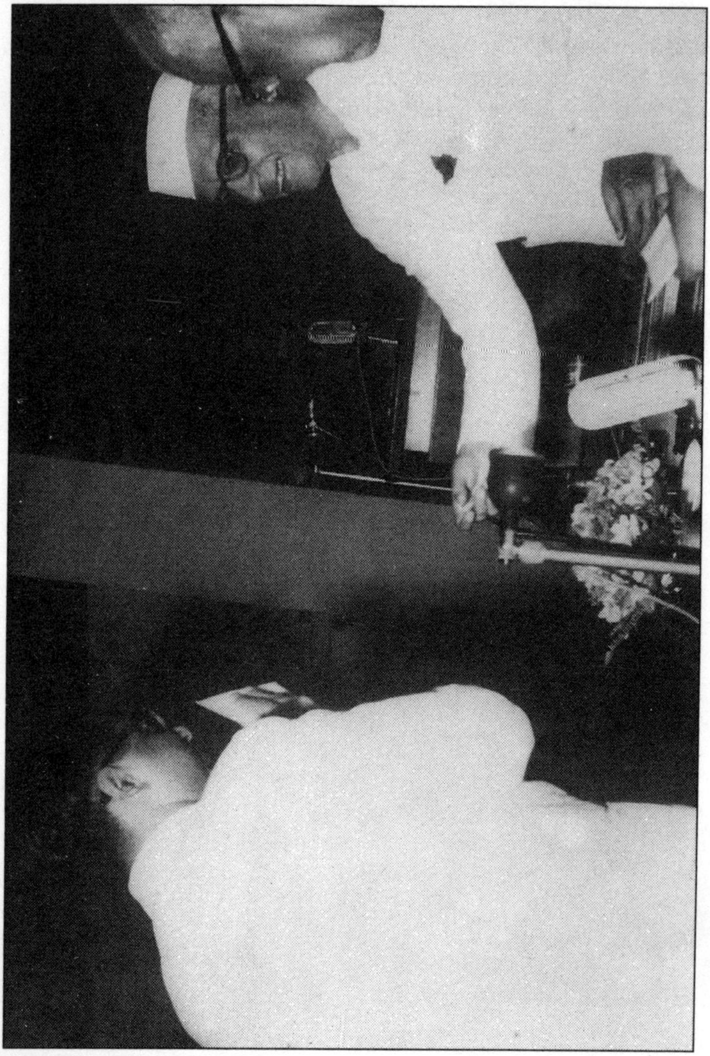

With Pandit Jawaharlal Nehru -- receiving prize at his hand awarded for the essay on "Teaching of Public Servants in a Developing Economy" which was selected in IIPA's Annual Essay Competition

With Smt. Indira Gandhi who is glancing at the author's books which he presented to her on the occasion of the visit of officers of all India and Central Services participating in the Advanced Professional Programme of Public Administration (APPPA)

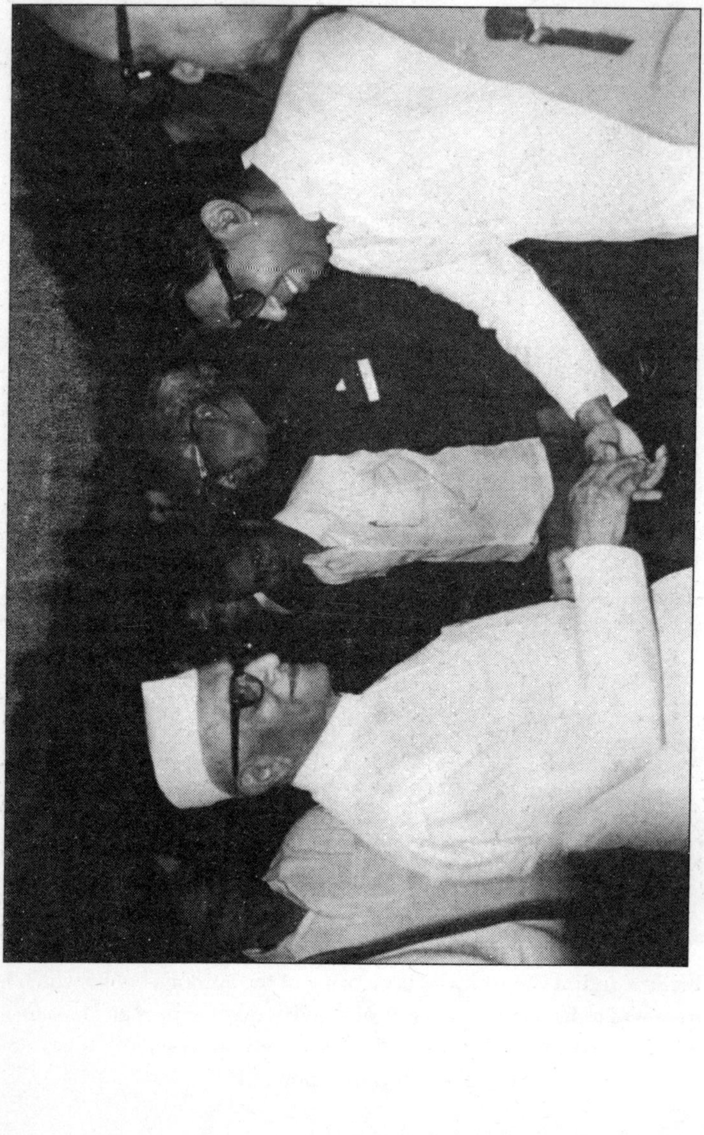

Receiving Morarji Desai as he arrives at the Asian Conference on Agricultural Credit

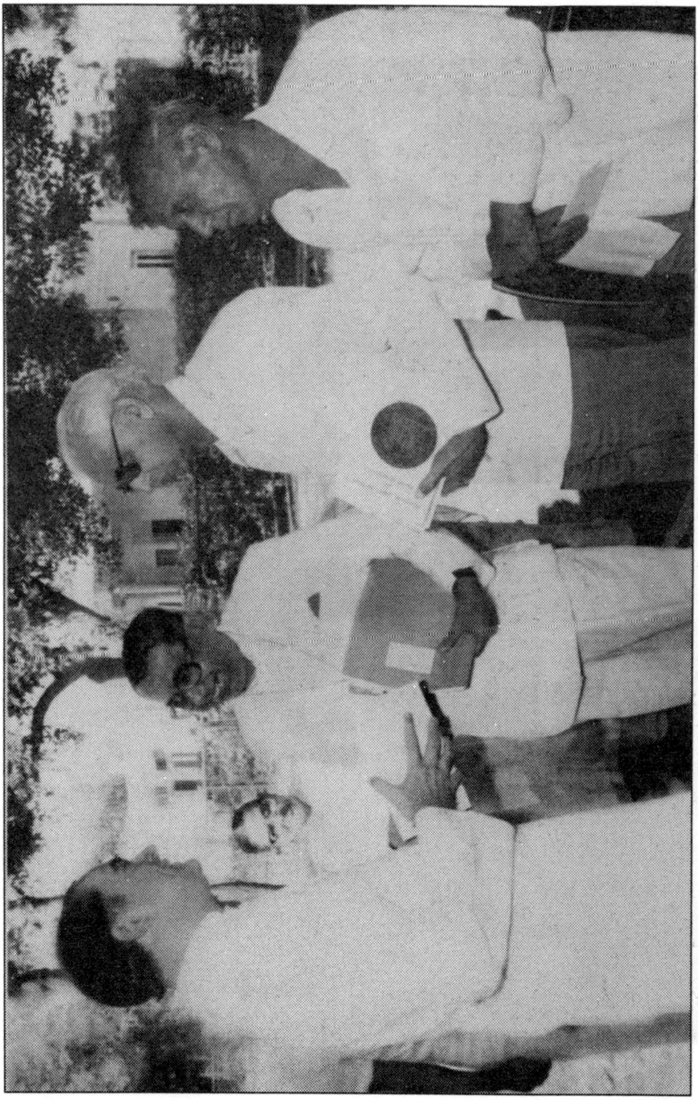

With Shri Rajiv Gandhi presenting him with a copy of author's book on Administrative Reforms

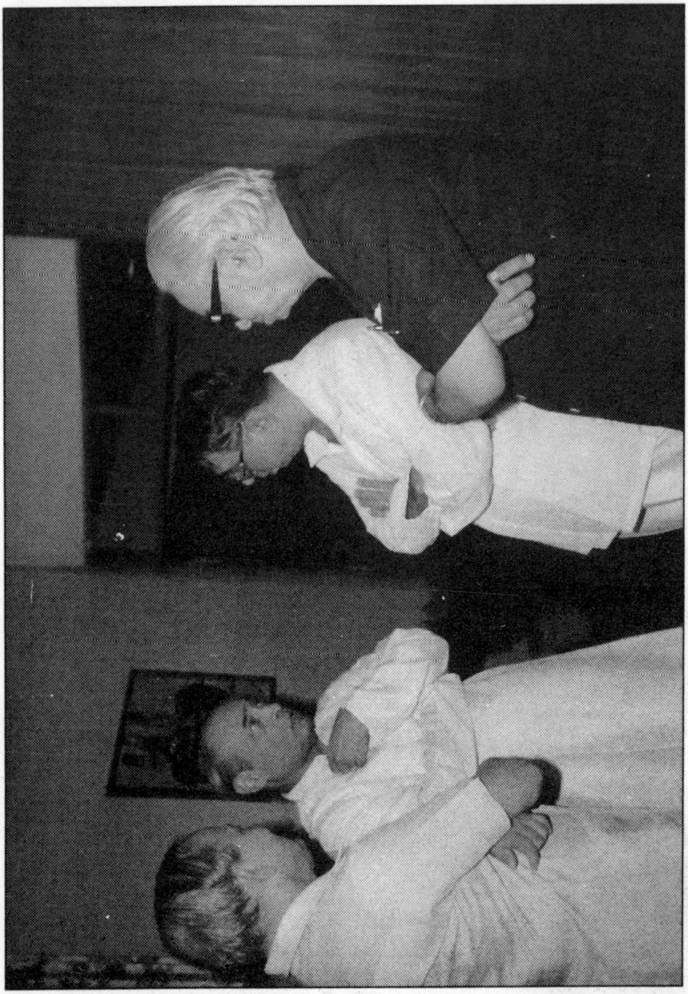

With Shri Narsimha Rao at a Get-together

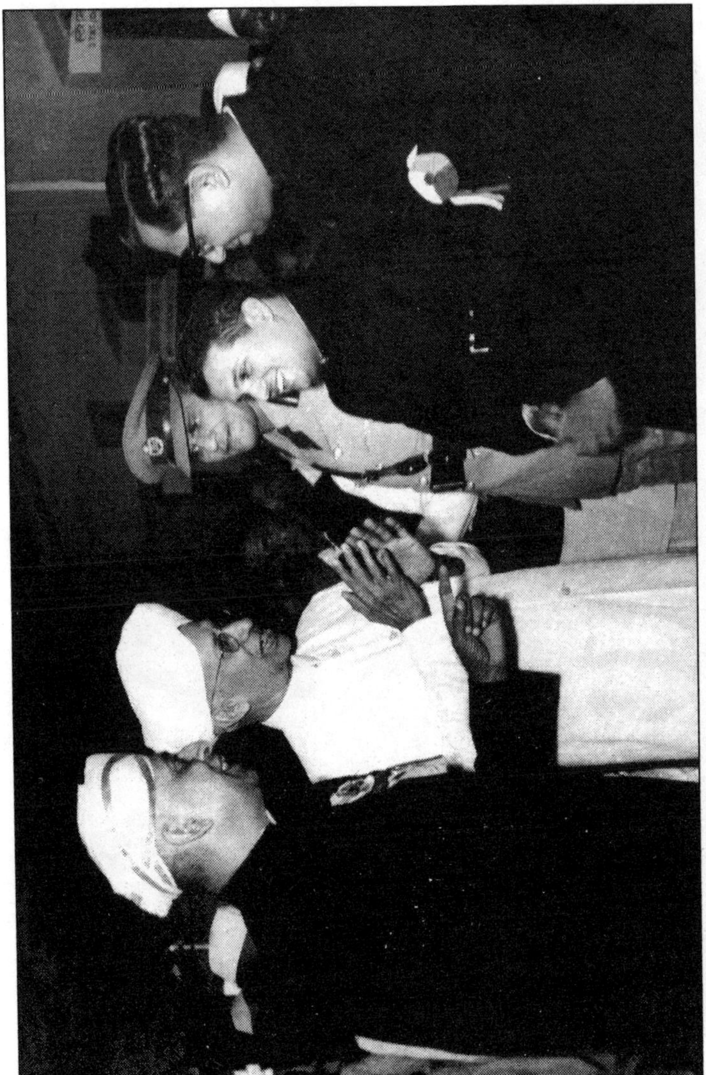

With Dr. Radhakrishnan at the time of visit to Gulbarga, Karnataka

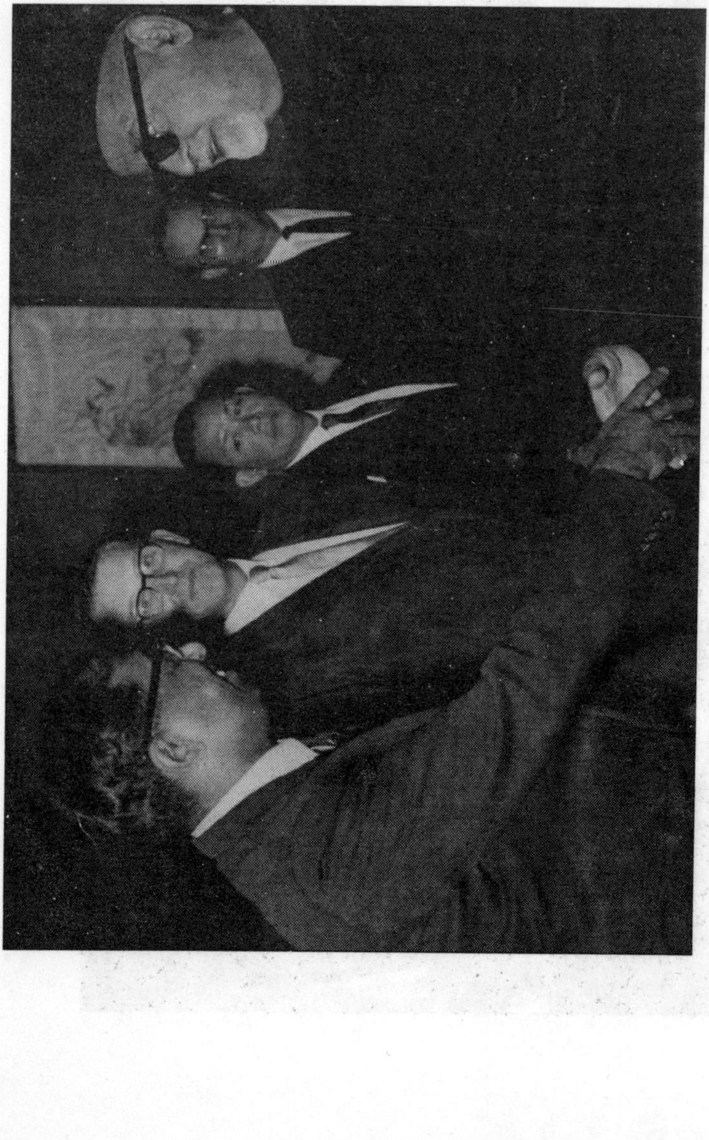

With Dr. Zakir Hussain -- Receiving him at the Asian Conference on Economic Co-operation

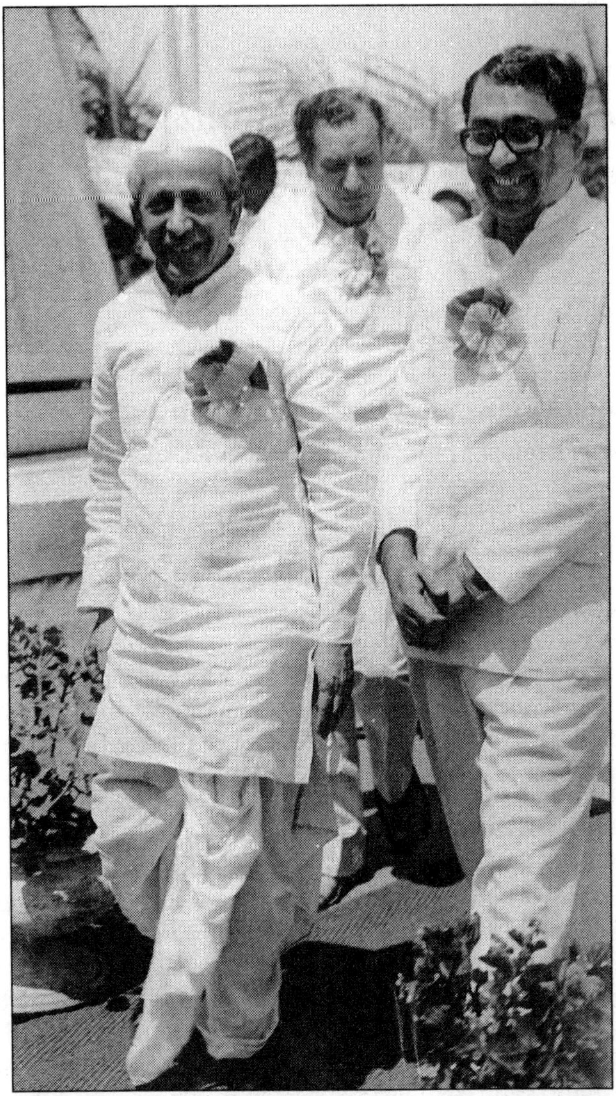

With Shri B.D. Jatti, Vice President (who later officiated as President) during his visit when the author was Divisional Commissioner, Belgaum (Shri M.Y. Ghorpade, Finance Minister is seen in the background

CHAPTER 14

Administrator, Malaprabha and Ghataprabha Project (1971-72)

Pioneering Command Area Development

I was a victim of a premature transfer. The Karnataka Government had specially asked for my services and got me back even though RBI Dy Governor was keen the I should continue. They posted me as Secretary Development, Housing, Panchayati Raj and Cooperation where I had just completed a year when I was shifted on promotion as Commissioner Secretary, Public Works Dept. and Electricity. I had hardly completed six months when I was shifted to a new post for which Chief Minister Devraj Urs could not find any other officer. So I had to pack up and go at an odd time in the academic year of children. Transfer, I realized, was indeed a punishment—a punishment for honesty and uprightness.

Importance of Dharwad

Dharwad was a small district town known for its salubrious climate. It was located, like many other good cities like Belgaon and Hubli on Bangalore-Pune highway. Its importance as District Head Quarters was increased when the Karnataka University as well as Agricultural University were set up at Dharwad. This gave Dharwad the status of the educational centre of North Karnataka. Mallikarjun Mansoor the great musician and D.R. Bendre the great Kannada poet of Marathi origin were also living there as well as many other cultural and intellectual luminaries. One of them was the well known Marathi story writer G.A. Kulkarni who became a legend. Once, very causally, Joshi, a local well known resident, introduced me to him at the Dharwad club where he used play cards regularly while I played badminton. Dharwad's old Karnataka College had an excellent reputation. It was a coveted district even during the British days, hence the sprawling bungalow of the Deputy Commissioner.

No Office and No Establishment

One morning we left Bangalore in my car and reached Dharwad in the evening. For the first time I had to go to a post which existed only on paper. There was no office and no "establishment". Only one post was created in advance of my joining—*viz.*, that of Deputy Administrator to which Shri Dattatrey Rao, a BDO promoted to a higher post in the development cadre was posted. He was a local person and had his own house at Dharwad. He had arranged for our temporary accommodation in a wing of the sprawling bungalow of the Deputy Commissioner. Shri P.D. Shenoy was the Deputy Commissioner whom I had known.

Irrigation Development After Independence

I had to begin from the beginning, start from a scratch. My job was command area development under Malaprabha and Ghataprabha projects. I had started studying the subject before leaving Bangalore. It was a new subject which I found fascinating as well as very important. After independence, India had from 1951 onwards embarked upon a planned process of economic development. The successive five-year plans provided for investment in development projects of which irrigation projects were the most important. India is a land of rivers. But the copious waters of these rivers were not harnessed and went down to the seas while the land remained parched in summer specially in periodic droughts leading to famine when mansoon rains failed.

Dependable agriculture required irrigation. Only 6 per cent of rain water was stored and used. The rest was not available in the absence of storage. Out of 340 million hectors (m.h.) of land only 22 m.h. were irrigated. It was estimated that 122 m.h. could be brought under irrigation through major, medium and minor irrigation projects. Amongst minor irrigation projects were wells and lift irrigation projects and small tanks. Old Mysore was dotted with more than 33000 tanks created by small bunds erected by village communities along descending points in the vallies. It was traditional customary obligation of the village community to maintain these tanks. Unfortunately with modernisation, the traditional obligation was slowly going into disuse. But the emphasis in our plans was on errecting new gigantic irrigation projects with vast potential. This gave scope to engineers and contractors to design and erect huge irrigation projects of which Bhakra Nangal, the tallest dam was the pioneer. These dams with vast reservoirs looked very impressive but often were not productive since the irrigation potential was not put to use.

In the purely engineering approach to irrigation, the task of utilizing irrigation potential was overlooked or neglected. There was a large time gap between creation of irrigation potential and its utilization in the absence of the distribution and conveyance system and agricultural extension work needed to prepare the farmers for irrigated agriculture. Both the tasks were not easy. The farmer required construction of distributaries and channels reaching right down to his own plot. This irrigation development involved a transformation of rain fed agriculture into intensive agriculture involving not only agricultural change but even a cultural change, a change in the farmers, way of life. It implied technological change as well as organizational change needed for enhanced application of inputs like improved seeds, fertilizer and pesticides. The concept of command area development meant conscious attention to all those aspects. It was a new concept in Indian administration.

Personal Problems

As always I was taken up by the new idea and as soon as I took over the new assignment I started working on it. But first I had to settle down and set up my new office. I had difficult problems regarding my children's education. My daughter had all along been in the stream of Indian School Certificate, earlier known as the Cambridge Certificate examination. In Dharwad there was no school preparing for that examination. So I had to change her over to the State Board School Certificate Examination. That required her to take Sanskrit as a new subject. All this abrupt change disturbed her educational arrangements and caused a great deal of anxiety. As regards my son, he was in the Central School, none of which existed in Dharwad. One Central School existed in the twin city of Hubli—some 9 k.m. away and for a small child to commute every day was not easy. We had to wait anxiously every day for his safe return.

Locating Premises for The Office of Administrator

Then there was the problem of finding a place for the new office. I started scouting for premises but in a small town like Dharwad none was readily available. The office of Administrator was a new one with neither any field agency nor any power of patronage. My only help was Deputy Administrator—Shri Dattatrayrao. After some searching we came across a new building coming up at the corner of the ridge on which the Bungalow and office of the Deputy Commissioner were located. The new building was meant for a new circuit house at Dharwad. It was a two story building and I immediately surmised that it would suit my purpose – the ground floor as office and the first floor as my residence.

I immediately sent a proposal to Government for allotment of the new building to the administrator for office and residential purpose. The department of public works of which I had till recently been a secretary had to agree to the proposal, albeit as a temporary arrangement – some mercy for an officer who had been suddenly uprooted to set up a new office all by himself.

Functional Set-up

I had then to work out arrangement for a new office. I decided to have a functional set up for the office of Administrator – not the routine set up of a district office. The functional division would be:

1. Development of water conveyance systems and distribution of water to individual farmers
2. Land Development
3. Agricultural extension
4. Supply of inputs – seeds, fertilizers etc.
5. Marketing of produce and
6. Auxiliary enterprises like dairy development, forestry and fishery

I decided to have a planning officer to help me in the task of planning the development of the area under irrigation. The work of Administrator was essentially one of contact with farmers, coordination of activities of various departments and providing a sense of direction to the efforts of different departments concerned. That the goal of constructing huge reservoirs was to transform the rural economy and lives of the farmers was itself not well recognized. The job belonged to none – no administrative department was concerned with it. There was a Superintending Engineer, with huge staff like Executive Engineers, Assistant Engineers and administrative accounting and clerical staff working under the chief engineer of irrigation project based in Belgaum. The engineers were concerned with construction and contractors not with farmers and supply of water to their fields. The department of agriculture was concerned with extension but of the traditional sort. It was not geared to the undertaking of huge extension effort involved in preparing the farmers who for centuries were engaged in growing rain fed crops like jawar for growing irrigated crops requiring high yielding seeds like paddy, sugar cane, hybrid cotton (Varlaxmi) and new varieties of groundnuts and sunflower. These irrigated new crops required arrangements for supply of new seeds and fertilizers and much additional finance for leveling of land and procurement of inputs. This was a job for which the cooperative credit and marketing institutions as well as commercial banks had to be galvanised. The new high yielding seeds would generate additional yield which had to be marketed at a satisfactory price. The agricultural produce marketing committees had to provide physical arrangement to handle the produce while the cooperative marketing societies had to ensure that the farmers get a good price for their produce and not exploited by the *adatias* – the middlemen. All these new and important tasks required thinking and planning and above all concern for farmers and their problems.

I set up working groups on each subject or aspect under my chairmanship consisting of officers of department and agencies concerned. I convened meetings of these groups in which I tried to develop approaches and plans concerned with each of these aspects or subjects. The whole set up of field agencies of a variety of departments was being mobilized to get results from the huge investment made in the irrigation projects and indeed to change the face of the rural economy. What bigger challenge can be to an Administrator than this? I had to put life and energy in somnolent departments to undertake a difficult but an exciting task. The departments that used to follow their lonely track on routine lines had to undertake energetic team work of planning and execution.

Field Tours

As soon as I got a staff car for my office I undertook field tours in Ghataprabha and Maleprabha project area to get in direct touch with the farmers and understand their problems. The irrigated area under the Ghataprabha project (prior to construction of Hidkel dam, based on diversion of waters) was developed seventeen years ago in 1956 and I wanted to know whether it was fully and properly developed. I was amazed to find that farmers had innumerable complaints regarding water conveyance. Water was simply not flowing to lower reaches which were officially said to be irrigated. During all the seventeen years no body had taken note of these problems. This was either due to absence of field channels or excessive drawal of water in the upper reaches. The engineers had "completed" the project and "brought" the area under irrigation and had no longer anything to do with it. This was not the problem of the agricultural department either since it fell in the jurisdiction of the engineering department. The revenue department with its existence throughout the rural area was concerned with the collection of land revenue and enhanced water rates-whether water actually reached the farms or not was not their concern. In one word a legitimate problem remained unattended for 17 years and no department addressed itself to it. My visit to the area opened the lid. Farmers found that somebody was visiting the area precisely to look into their problem of lack of or inadequate supply of irrigation water because of deficiencies of water conveyance. They waited for me in large numbers as I travelled along the irrigated area. I stopped at every spot, went to the fields and noted the reasons and defects with precise survey numbers etc. At the end of the tour, I issued tour notes in which I indicated in details the shortcomings of the irrigation system. I sent one copy of the tour notes to the Superintending Engineer with a covering letter asking him to set right the defects. I sent a copy to Shri G.V.K. Rao, the Development Commissioner. He received several such tour notes, went through them and felt that this was precisely the kind of work that needed be done but was not done. Once he told me that I had stirred up the entire area. I did not stop at issuing tour notes. I took up all the points in the meetings of the working group on water conveyance and pursued these points with Superintending Engineer and his subordinates till the short comings were set right.

In the Malaprabha area the water conveyance system was still being built. The engineering staff typically attended to the construction of major distributaries but ignored the construction of small water courses and field channels. That was the problem under the Tungbhadra project also which I had noticed fourteen years earlier when I served as Collector/Director in Raichur District and the same was the problem under Ghataprabha/Malaprabha projects as well. The problem was particularly acute under the Malaprabha project. It was a black cotton soil area where the water courses and field channels would simply not stabilize. The soil would expand as soon as water would start flowing and obstruct its smooth flow. It would break the sides of channel and would flow in a wayward fashion and accumulate leading to salt formation, spoiling the soil. Irrigation instead of being a boon would become a bane. The obstruction to the smooth flow would be particularly acute where level of land changed. In such cases cement concrete drops had to be provided. All this small detailed work proved irksome to engineers but unless this was patiently and systematically attended to, the benefits from the irrigation project would simply not accrue.

For even spread, of water the land had to be level or else water would accumulate at lower levels while it would not reach higher levels. Land levelling had therefore to be undertaken. This would require use of tractors which were not evailable with the farmers in the area. I thought of land levelling on a cooperative basis. I mooted the idea but farmers would not readily take it.

Motivating Farmers for Irrigation Development

Farmers were generally apathetic and would take time to do what needed to be done to develop irrigated agriculture. My job was to hasten the process I had seen the problem in Tungabhadra. The department of agriculture had to arrange exhibitions and field demonstrations to disseminate information regarding irrigated crops. Above all farmers had to be motivated. I myself visited several villages and held meetings with farmers whose land would come under irrigation and told them to avail of irrigation facilities as early as possible by changing their cropping pattern and cultivation practices. I remember one particular village Alagwadi where 10000 acres were to come under irrigation. I visited the village several times and it had the desired effect. In two-three years time the entire command area was irrigated. In another village I set up a village planning commission to bring about all sided development which should follow irrigation and consequently generate enhanced income.

I wrote an article on administration of command area development which was published in the *Indian Journal of Public Administration*. My work of systematic command area development was indeed of a pioneering nature though, in the absence of publicity, I did not get due credit for it. A UNDP official who visited me appreciated my work and the pattern of integrated command area development that I had evolved. Later on the same approach was institutionalised by the Union government and the State government in the form of establishment of command area development authorities, i.e., CADA all over the country under 55 major irrigation projects. I had already done so in the form of my working groups and coordination committees related to various facets of command area development.

Meeting with Prime Minister Indira Gandhi

As Administrator, Malaprabha and Ghataprabha project I got an opportunity to participate in a meeting in the Conference Hall of Vidhan Soudha addressed by the Prime minister Smt. Indira Gandhi. She was very much concerned about the need for raising agricultural production and it was at her initiative that the State government had convened the meeting. The meeting began by an address by the Prime Minister. She spoke extempore and I was surprised by the grip she had over the subject and her awareness of its various facets. I had also an opportunity to speak and presented at some length the efforts made to develop the irrigation potential under the two projects I was in charge. She as well as others appeared to have appreciated my presentation.

Linguistic Trouble

While I was immersed in my work of command area development, disturbing events were taking place around the area in the form of Kannada, Marathi conflict. It was simmering over years in the border area between Maharashtra and Karnataka and suddenly flared up. Several areas near the borders of the two states are of bilingual nature and in the reorganization of states on linguistic basis, language groups found themselves left out and placed in the state of another language. Nippani, Belgaum, Khanapur and Karwar area were included in Karnataka State though they had substantial Marathi population. Both the states agreed to refer the dispute to the Mahajan Commission which, while appreciating that there were Marathi pockets in these areas, had placed them in Karnataka state taking into account the predominant language of the District. The Marathi people felt aggrieved and started agitating against the award of the Mahajan Commission. The Chief Minister of Maharashtra Shri Vasantrao Naik, who had earlier agreed to abide by the finding of Mahajan Commission, reneged when the recommendations went against Maharashtra. But Karnataka was firm on Mahajan Commission's recommendations and would not budge. That was the genesis of the dispute which took the form of agitation by Marathi speaking people whose centre was Belgaum where they set up Maharashtra Ekikaran Samiti which set up candidates for the Assembly who got elected. The agitation often created law and order problems. The Karnataka police were often harsh on Marathi agitators and beat them up with lathi charge. The immediate spark for flaring up of the agitation was provided by rumours reaching Karnataka area that some Kannada women prostitutes were de-robed and raped in Kolhapur. Houses in Marathi areas were set on fire in which a prominent Marathi businessman lost his life. The Pune—Bangalore high way was blocked at various places and buses and other traffic could not ply.

In my position as Administrator Malaprabha, Ghataprabha projects, I was hardly concerned with these untoward events. It was for the Divisional Commissioner Shri K.R. Ramchandran, the Deputy Commissioner and the police officers to handle the situation. But it was as a citizen that I experienced the fury of the language agitation which had suddenly flared up.

One afternoon my little son who was to return from Hubli after attending his central school did not return at 2.30 P.M as expected. We anxiously waited and when he did not turn up we sent a driver with a car to fetch him. The driver returned saying he could not proceed to the school because the highway was blocked on the outskirts of Hubli. We became desperate. What do we do? The little boy was held up without lunch and we could not reach him. Where would he be? What might happen to him in the midst of this violent agitation? I decided to go myself. All during the half-hour journey my mind was full of anxiety. When I reached the outskirts of Hubli. I saw huge boulders across the highway blocking the movement of vehicles. Neither the police nor any body else could dare remove the boulders and restore the traffic on the highway. I took the instant decision to stop the car at that point and walk the distance to the school. I walked fast and what a relief it was that my little eight year old son was waiting in the class room unharmed. None was with him to take care of him. I took him out and started walking back. I asked him not to talk and converse in Marathi because this could infuriate some Kannada language fanatics. It was a relief to reach the car and getting into it felt like getting into sanctuary! In a few minutes we were back home safely. Security in times of turbulence is so precarious.

We had another experience of this in a few days. At mid night while we were sleeping a sound of heavy footed movement came from the ground floor where the office was located. We stayed upstairs. The office of the Administrator had no particular status and was entirely unprotected. There were no guards.! As I woke up in the bed I could not figure out who could be there at that unearthly hour in the thick of night. Could they be some miscreants coming to attack and do harm? I was entirely unprotected and had no weapon—never thought of having one. I waited anxiously in the bed for quite some time till I heard the sound of people walking away and was greatly relieved. Perhaps they were the police on the night beat.

For quite a few days there was tension in the atmosphere. I strictly enjoined my two children not to speak a word in Marathi outside lest it should enrage some language fanatic. That in a gentle town like Dharwad fear should grip us only shows the terror that fanaticism born out of chauvenism, linguistic or otherwise, can generate. Slowly the frenzy subsided.

Tragedy of Life

But I was to undergo a double tragedy in life. One day a phone call came from Karwar that my wife's mother had died while asleep. We went to Karwar for the last rites; and soon after her brother and my father passed away. Father was staying at Bombay and suffered from blood pressure and had even a mild heart attack though he had kept away from me that information. My brother, a doctor was keeping a strict watch on his health. His movement was also restricted. He was not travelling. Once, Prof. Kogekar, my teacher met him and told him how nice his son was! Prof. Kogekar had come to Dharwad as a member of the Forward Market Commission along with the Chairman Shri Vaghaiwala ICS to visit the agricultural market committee. When he came to know that I was posted at Dharwad, he and Vaghiwala visited me and had a lunch. He went back and told my father of his visit and my hospitality. He spoke extremely well of me and my work. My father felt that if others could visit his son why not he? So he simply made up his mind and on the eve of Makarsankrant in 1974 he along with my mother flew to Goa-Dabolim airport and went by bus to Mangeshi, the seat of our family deity. He wrote a letter to me from there saying that he had peace of mind there and found happiness in the presence of Lord Mangesh. That was to be his last letter to me. From Mangeshi he went to Karwar our native place which he loved so much. He had a hearty fish curry lunch which he relished, but that was to be his last meal. Even while he was chatting after lunch he had a heart attack. My uncle Dr. Shripad Pikle attended to him but the equipment was limited and the treatment could not have been adequate. He tried to hold the oxygen mask to his nose but he could not inhale or breathe and he passed away.

When the news reached me on phone at Dharwad after I had just returned from tour I was devastated. Here I was looking forward to his visit to me at Dharwad and what I had to hear was the news of his death. I was shocked and was sad beyond measure. This was the first tragedy of my life. I immediately left for Karwar. The few hours of journey found me crying within myself. And when I reached Karwar and saw his dead body draped in white cloth I could not contain myself. My mother was inconsolable. She looked so vulnerable without my father. We waited for my brothers who were to come from Bombay and as soon as they arrived, we took the father's dead body on our shoulders and cremated it on the sea shore. My greatest mental support had gone. He always had high expectations of me and the desire to fulfill them was the main motivation of my effort. The inspiration had gone and a chapter had ended.

But life waits for no body's tragedy. I went back to Dharwad only to see a letter from PWD asking us to vacate the premises as they wanted them back for the circuit house. I told the Minister that I had just undergone a personnel tragedy and was in no positron to make alternative arrangement.

But the problem soon solved itself. I was posted to Belgaum as Divisional Commissioner and the office of the Administrator was also shifted to Belgaum. I held both the positions. I was happy about the change since the post of Divisional Commissioner was of importance in the administrative hierarchy as compared to the post of Administrator I had held.

CHAPTER 15

Divisional Commissioner Belgaum (1974-77)

Creating People Oriented Administration

As soon as I got the orders, I left for Belgaum and took charge of the post of the Divisional Commissioner. Shri K.R. Ramachandren my predecessor had vacated the bungalow since he was posted to Bangalore and so left at the earliest. I had all the time for myself to arrange according to my convenience. The old colonial type sprawling bungalow of the Divisional Commissioner was located at the magnificent Hulme Park full of mango and jamun trees. One went deep inside from the road to reach the bungalow. The house was furnished. So I could stay in the bungalow without any inconvenience. I stayed for a few days all by myself before returning to Dharwad to pack up and shift to Belgaum with family.

The Hulme Park Bangalow and the Vintage Office

After one year's stay at Dharwad I had again to settle down in a new place. But this time I did not have to start from a scratch. A well-furnished bungalow was here for residence and an old well established office with a large staff and three personal assistants to help in work, and a chauffeur driven car. That gave a sense of security and comfort. The office of the Divisional Commissioner was located in a magnificent nineteenth century stone building and my own office was on the first floor. It was a large deep hall and served as the court-room of the Divisional Commissioner as well. A number of appeals against the orders of the Deputy Commissioner as well as appeals in Municipal cases came to the Divisional Commissioner. Just behind the seat of the Divisional Commissioner was the room for my P.A.s—Sharhatti and Jakati. Shirhatti was quite an efficient and experienced personal assistant and could be relied upon in working out schedule of work and appointments.

The shift from Bangalore to Dharwad had created severe problems for the education of my children – Medha and Devdatta. Medha, despite change of the stream creditably passed the school leaving examination of the Karnataka Board. It was decided that she should join the commerce course and was admitted to Gogte College of Commerce. As for Devdatta, there was no Central School in Belgaum but there was an equivalent Military School which he joined. The latter was well established and had good reputation and standing and had also good discipline and campus.

I had joined soon after a severe linguistic agitation of which Belgaum was the centre. I had to feel my way carefully. I was a Marathi speaking person and was of course well conversant with the state language Kannada. My name "two language speaking person was" well justified. But was this an asset or a liability? I was soon to learn from experience.

Exposed to the Charge of Favouring Marathi

On the very first day after assuming office, Shri Rambhau Potdar, Chairman of the Regulated Agricultural Marketing Committee invited me to an official function. I readily accepted his invitation. He welcomed me in Marathi and I responded in the same language. Ever since Belgaum became a part of Karnataka, this was the first time that an incumbent of the post of Divisional Commissioner spoke in Marathi at a public function. When I was welcomed in Marathi, I saw no objection in responding to it in Marathi. But Kannada protagonists were wide awake and noticed this "lapse". Next day at my bungalow I got a copy of *Nadoz,* a local Kannada newspaper of small four pages with little circulation which carried the news of my public speech in Marathi and characterised me for that reason as a Marathi *pakshpati* – a Marathi protagonist. Though the newspaper had a small circulation, I could see that it was a warning to me. The newspaper was edited by Shri Arvind Joshi (a Marathi sounding name) and his son Raghavendra Joshi. I later came to know that Arvind's another son Vasu was active in Marathi literary activities. But that is how things were in Belgaum – bilingual families with one foot in Kannada and another in Marathi.

Actually bilinguism or even multilinguism is an asset rather than a liability in India. But once xenophobia overtakes a people an asset becomes a liability whether in the case of linguistic diversity or religious diversity. I myself always held that an educated Indian should be multilingual. Belgaum itself has been traditionally a bilingual city. It was considered to be a mini Pune and was a centre of Marathi culture. Marathi dramas would be enacted very often and Kannada people would be in the audience because they appreciated them. The Kannada people would be able to converse in Marathi but the converse was less true Nevertheless there was hardly any linguistic chauvenism or antagonism.

However all this changed after this formation of Karnataka which involved merging Kannada districts of Belgaon, Dharwad, Bijapur and Karwar which were, during the British rule, a part of Bombay province in the newly formed Karnataka. This was not to the liking of the Marathi people who felt stifled. Instead of assaugaging their feelings with a liberal policy of allowing them to use their language, a bilingual approach in the conduct of administration, e.g., Application forms in both the languages, allowing Marathi medium schools and giving due scope of the continuation of cultural activities, some misguided administrators started a drive of Kanndification. The Marathi people interpreted it as a hostile attitude of Karnataka Government to them. They established an organization called *Marathi Ekikaran Samiti* whose express goal was to join the Marathi speaking area of Nippani, Belgoan, Supa and Karwar to Maharashtra. It became a fighting organization with the veteran Baburao Thakur at the helm. His small local newspaper *Tarun Bharat* read widely in Belgaum became the mouthpiece of the Marathi movement. The *Ekikaran Samiti* put up candidates for the Legislative Assembly who were elected, election after election. This was taken as a true indication of the support to merger with Maharashtra. The representatives of *Marathi Ekikaran Samiti* would wear saffron turbans and shout slogans in Marathi in the Karnataka Legislature Assembly to advocate their cause.

Shri Sainak was the legislator from Belgaum. As soon as I took over, Baburao Thakur accompanied by Sainak and other local Marathi leaders called on me. I talked in Marathi amicably with them. This was a new experience for them. Ever since 1960 when Belgaum became a part of Karnataka, they had for the first time a sympathetic hearing in administration. All these years they had faced much hostility especially from the police. The DIG Shri Lewis had become the symbol of such hostility. He would order merciless lathi charge on Marathi slogan shouting processions. This was not conducive to developing any affinity between the Marathi speaking people and Karnataka administration. My attitude appeared to make a difference.

But at the same time I realized that I had to watch my steps because I was under the watch of the Kannada *chaluvaligars* (agitators). I had of course no difficulty with Kannada Language or Kannada people. As an IAS officer of Karnataka cadre I felt privileged to serve the Kannada people in whatever capacity I was called upon to serve. I had become well versed in speaking in Kannada with the common people. Indeed, I spoke much better Kannada then the Kannadigas of Belgaum whose diction was mixed up with Marathi vocabulary especially the numbers which they mentioned in Marathi style. I had therefore little to learn from the Kannadigas of Belgaum.

But chauvanists are never reasonable and are always on the look out to cause trouble. Soon after I took over, Shri Phadnis, Principal of the Rani Parvaibai College, came to invite me to unveil the oil painting of Shivaji Maharaj. I readily accepted the invitation since it gave me the opportunity to visit a leading educational institution of Belgaum. But I had not reckoned with the reaction of the Kannada chauvinists. The very next day *Nadoz* carried the news and warned me against accepting the invitation. What was the objection? First, Shivaji was the Marathi Chieften and second, Rani Parvatibai College was run by Marathi people. I found this attitude utterly despicable. But I had to understand the reality. The area had just emerged out of a major linguistic trouble and as the Divisional Commissioner, it was my responsibility that I did nothing to inflame the situation or provide the spark for a fresh disturbance. I decided to consult with DIG Shri Garudachar, a Kannada officer who had been in the area for some time (his jurisdiction was also the range covering Belgaum Division.) I met him at the club and told him about the invitation. He took an alarmist view and asked me not to accept any invitation from Rani Parvatibai Devi College which was a den of anti-Karnataka Government Marathi agitationists. I was surprised at this assessment but I had been just for a week in Belgaum which had only recently experienced bad disturbances caused by conflicts between the two linguistic protagonists and I did not want to queer the pitch. So I phoned up Principal Phadnis and told him that because of the opposition of some Kannada chavernists it would not be proper on my part to keep up the appointment lest it should add fuel to the fire. He appreciated my difficulty.

But I felt bad about the whole incident and decided to make my own assessment in future and not go by the advice of the police officers which was nothing but preconceived prejudice and only led to disaffection amongst the Marathi speaking people whom I continued to treat in the same cordial manner as I treated Kannada speaking people. This had a desirable effect. The Marathi people of Belgaum people started feeling that they were not given step-motherly treatment. There was a request of people from Khanapur taluka, a Marathi speaking area for Marathi medium schools in the countryside which was needlessly opposed as it was felt by Kannada agitationists that it would provide encouragement to Marathi. This was quite an absurdity, I supported the request and the schools were sanctioned to the happiness of Khanapur people.

I had seen during my visit to Helsinki, the capital of Finland, that even 7 per cent Swedish minority was cared for by giving street names both in Finnish and in Swedish. Here in Belgaum, the Marathi speaking population was much larger in percentage, were citizens of the some country and state and yet same people felt quite wrongly that they should be discriminated till they agreed to be Kannadigas.

After the Rani Parvati Devi incident, about which I felt bad, I decided to throw away the advice of police officers and started accepting every single invitation of Marathi speaking people and spoke freely in Marathi at all those public functions. At the same time those who approached me in Kannada, I would deal with them in that language without once using a Marathi word. The Belgaum Knnadigas started appreciating this and held no grudge against me for speaking in Marathi while dealing with Marathi speaking people. The majority of the Indian people, I thought, were quite liberal, only busybodies and politicians mislead them. There was a prominent lady with Marathi type name, Smt. Asha Potdar, who always sat by the side of Smt. Usha Gogte, the wife of a prominent local businessman Raosaheb Gogte, a Marathi supporter, whenever a Marathi drama was enacted. She would invariably speak with me in Kannada and I invariably replied in the same language without a word of Marathi and obviously she could have no grudge against me! It was my good fortune that not once did the Karnataka Government reprimand me or even took objection to my speaking in Marathi. On the other hand, they must have been happy that with my coming the Marathi agitation had in fact subsided. For example there were no inevitable clashes on the *Rajyotsava day*, the day the Karnataka State came into existence. This had always been the day of clashes between the Kannada processionists observing it as a celebration day and the Marathi people taking out a protest procession observing it as a black day.

I told Baburao Thakur and MLA Sainak that they could have their procession before the official *Rajyotsava* procession which I would have to join in my official capacity. They accepted my advice and conflict was avoided.

The Kannada protagonists tried to test me and put me in the wrong. Once as I was hearing cases, I heard some slogan – shouting outside. On enquiry I was told that the Kannada leader Siddan Gowda Patil had come leading a protest of Kannada students against the neglect in the maintenance of Kannada schools in Belgaum city. Without hesitation I came out and assured the students that I would personally look into their grievance and do the needful. They went away peacefully and never again did the matter come up. I had asked the local Municipality to provide the needed funds. Genuine grievance no matter by whom expressed should be immediately attended to – that is the first principle of good administration which is often forgotten leading to trouble.

Two occasions came when the linguistic antagonism could flare up. One was unveiling the statue of Shivaji Maharaj and the other of Jagatjyoti Basaveshwar, the founder of Lingayat sect. The statue of Shivaji was made by the famous sculptor Ravindra Mistri with the encouragement of Ranajit Desai, the famous Marathi auther of historical novels. The statue was to be inaugurated at the hands of Shri Devraj Urs, the Chief Minister. Shri Shivajirao Kakatkar, the Marathi speaking mayor belonging to the ruling Congress party and not *Marathi Ekikaran Samiti* was to preside over the function. I was asked to welcome. The police were quite nervous. They feared some kind of trouble and wanted to keep the people behind the barricade as far away from the dais as possible. I had not quite appreciated their point of view but the police had their way on ground of law and order. The programme of the function included welcome by me, speech by Ranajit Desai, unveiling of the statue and the speech by the Chief Minister and Presidential speech by the Mayor. In what language should the entire programme be conducted? To insist that the whole programme should be entirely in Kannada would not be to the liking of the predominantly Marathi audience emotionally attached to the memory of Shivaji Maharaj. Eventually I spoke in English (avoiding both Kannada and Marathi which could have been controversial), Ranajit Desai spoke in Marathi, Devraj Urs in Kannada and Kakatkar in Hindi – raising no objection from anybody. The function passed off peacefully to every body's great relief. That this was quite an achievement I came to realize later when Shahaji Raje of Kolhapur came to Belgaum to attend an Air-Force function. He told me that in Kolhapur it was widely feared that there would be trouble in Belgaum on the occasion since Kannada protagonists would violently protest and would not allow the function to pass off peacefully. Nothing of the kind happened. Fears are often misplaced and themselves become a source of trouble.

A few months later came the function of unveiling of the statue of Basaveshwar at the hands of Shri B.D. Jatti then Vice-President of India. I had known him earlier as CM of Karnataka. He was a very devout Lingayat invariably flouting Vibhuti on his forehead and a proper dignitary to unveil the statue of the founder of his sect. Basvanna's sayings like *Nudidante Nadeyavanu* (similar to Tukaram's *Bole Taisa Chale*) or in Sanskrit "*Mansayekam Vachsyeskm Karyamekam*" words and actions of good people match or *Kayakwe Kailasa* (physical labour iself is the hevanly bliss) show how the same thoughts have been expressed in all languages over centuries and have provided the ethical code for not only the Lingayats but all people in country. In speeches his sayings were often quoted (even by me!). The Municipal Commissioner Shri Patil, himself a Kanadga and Lingayat, was very enthustic about the occasion and had arranged to erect the statue on the spacious ground near the Municipal swimming pool on the border of the city and the cantonment. No trouble was expected, as Marathi people could not have any objection. I had to perform the function of welcoming the Chief Guest. The entire function had to be conducted in Kannada and I too gave my welcome speech in Kannada, which went off very well. Later, I was told that some people in the audience were heard commenting "He speaks in Kannada" and then later "oh! He speaks very well." So this established my credentials amongst the Kannada people.

Once I was asked to inaugurate a seminar on Kannada's folklore. For this occasion too, I got myself acquainted with Kannada folklore tradition to deliver an appropriate speech. As a result of occasions like this and my fluency in Kannada not only in daily conversation with people who came to see me for official work but also on occasions like the functions mentioned above, I became quite acceptable to the Kannada people. My speaking in Marathi on numerous public functions made no difference. Throughout my 3½ years stay I attended innumerable public functions in Belgaum conducted by Marathi People. After all Belgaum was an important centre of Marathi culture. This had one good effect – Marathi people felt nearer to administration. It is with some pride that I can say that throughout my stay in Belgaum not a single skirmish took place between Kannada and Marathi people nor any lathi charge which had become a regular feature. I thought the linguistic bitterness had ended, but not quite so. Xenophobia and prejudice were deeply rooted and could emerge any time. This is what I realized almost at the end of my stay. I had attended the 75 years celebration – Platinum Jubilee *Amrut Mahotsav* of *Vangmay Charchya Mandal* to which I was invited as the Chief Guest I went without hesitation and enthusiastically participated in their literary programme. But this was not to the liking of Shri Patil Puttappa the editor of *Vishal Karnataka, Hubli* who was later appointed as the official watchdog of Kannada's language and in that capacity carried on a relentless campaign for exclusive exhibition of Kannada name boards on all establishments in Belgaum and elsewhere and exclusive use of that language in all official administrative transactions no matter what inconvenience it could cause to non-Kannda people. In his newspaper he poured venom on me for participating in the celebrations of *Vangmay Charcha Mandal* asking how could an official of Karnataka Government participate in a Marathi function and an official who dared do so should be transferred forthwith. I was taken aback by this vituperative reaction. Patil Puttappe had known me well. In an earlier function at Hubli for the inaguaration of a theatre to which both of us were invited, he publicly praised me for speaking so well in Kannada though I belonged to Pune. I had to remained him that I hailed from Karwar which after state reorganisation came from Bombay province to Karnataka. Not much notice was taken of Patil Puttappa's vituperations. Karnataka government did not call for my explanation.

But this did not mean that Karnataka government was entirely free from bias. I wrote to the Chief Secretary Shri G.V.K. Rao that on the occasion of the Platinum Jubilee, this organisation which was carrying on good literary and cultural activities should be given a handsome donation by government of Karnataka. I was surprised that the proposal was turned down on the ground that the organisation was promoting Marathi language and culture! G.V.K. Rao had served earlier as Divisional Commissioner, Belgaum, and could have shown better consideration.

On another occasion too I was at the receiving end of anti-Marathi bias. The big Kalinadi Power Project which was to produce large quantity of electricity for the state was to submerge the Taluka Town of Supa and 36 neighbouring villages. For the state of

Karnataka, the people had to lose every thing—their lands, ancestral houses, properties and settled way of life. For their sacrifice, I thought the uprooted people of this area should be treated generously. I planned a new Ramnagar village for the affected people. Some of them requested for building sites in Belgaum city. I thought that the request was reasonable and got the Rehabitation Committee under my Chairmanship to approve allotment of some 40 sites to them. I was shocked to get a letter some time later from the Chief Secretary turning down the proposal on the ground that it would upset the linguistic balance in Belgaum! Such was the paranoia of Karnataka Government regarding Belgaum that the need for being generous to the people who had to sacrifice their ancestral lands and houses to provide electricity to the state was entirely overlooked. I was pained but did not fight lest it should provide official stamp on my being branded as a pro-Marathi Officer. Once I was shocked to see the extent to which police officers could go in their anti-Marathi activities. Some papers came to my notice in which the DIG had proposed rebordering of the electoral wards in Belgaum for Municipal elections so that Marathi candidates could be defeated and Kannada candidates elected. Clearly ward demarcation was none of the jobs of the police officers and they had no business of indulging in gerrymandering. And this was done at the back of the Divisional Commissioner keeping him in the dark though he was the supervising officer of Municipal administration.

On the representation of the Belgaum people the Commissioner for Linguistic minorities appointed a language official in Belgaum to report on the grievances of Marathi linguistic minority. He met me on arrival. I helped him to set up an office in the fort area of Belgaum. I do not know to what extent he could help the Marathi people in border areas in removing their grievances on getting their due.

At Peace in Belgaum

Because of the absence of skirmishes on the ground of linguistic antagonism, complete peace prevailed throughout my 3½ years stay in Belgaum and I could concentrate on my administrative and developmental work to my heart's content. For many reasons I could feel totally at home in the Belgaum division. First, my own native district Karwar or North Canara renamed, as Uttar Kannada, was a part of the division. *Konkani* my mother tongue was spoken in the district and I very much liked speaking in that language whenever that was appropriate in public functions and of course in course of contact with the people. Though I was attached to Karwar emotionally, I had no links or vested interest which could create problems in my administrative work. I had never lived in Karwar except during summer holidays in my childhood.

Belgaum was indeed a wonderful division. Two districts Belgaum and Dharwad were on the borderland between *"Maidan"* (flat plateau) and *"Malnad"* forest area. The Pune-Bangalore highway dividing *Malnad* and *Maidan* ran through Belgaum and Dharwad. The eastern part of Dharwad district as well as Bijapur district were in the rain shadow area and hence drought-prone. Bijapur city was of historic importance and was the capital of Adilshah dynasty. It had historical buildings like the Gol Gumbad and the tomb of Ibrahim Shah. Thus, the division had coast, forest and platau was and full of diversity. Hubli, Bijapur and Jamkhandi (from which Jatti came) had some sprinkling of the Marathi people while Karwar district had some Kokani speaking people.

Belgaum was a charming little city with a wonderful exclusive club established during the British days. I played tennis regularly in the bracing morning weather in Belgaum. It had a golf course as well, though to my regret I did not play the game feeling that it could take too much of my time. There was the big aluminum factory INDAL on the outskirts of the city and its General Manager Raj Bhargav became a close friend. He arranged badminton tournaments which I attended and had the privilege of meeting top class players like Prakash Padukone and others, Belgaum division was also the home of top class musicians—Gangubai Hangal who lived in Hubli, Mallikarjun Mansoor who lived in Dharwar as also Basavraj Rajguru and Kumar Gandharv or Komkali. Kumar Gandharv hailed from Belgaum though he lived in Dewas, M.P. Once, for some work, Gangubai visited me at my house and so did Marathi author Ranjit Desai and Girish Karnad the celebrated author of drama, who hailed from Sirsi in N.K. district. Once Basavraj Rajguru was honoured with a shawl at a music festival at Kundgol from which Savai Gandharva, the guru of Bhimsen Joshi hailed. My speeches at public functions were widely reported especially in *Tarun Bharat* and made me very popular and quite well known locally.

One of the institutions to which I felt attached was the Institute of Comparative Philosophy and Religion established by no less a person than the great philosopher saint Rambhau Ranade. He was a Professor of Philosophy with many books on philosophy to his creditand and was also the Vice-Chancellor of Alahabad University. But what was more important was that he had the grace of god and a touch of divinity. That is why Prof. Radhakrishnan said of him "while we taught philosophy, he lived it" The Institute in Belgaum in Hindwadi area was run by a kindly retired revenue officer, Shri Parulekar who often invited me to the spiritual programmes. I came to read Ranade's life and was greatly impressed. It left a permanent stamp on my mind. I also read his philosophical works and also visited the ashram he had put up in Nimbal in Bijapur district.

The division of Belgaum which was my jurisdiction was inhabited by almost one crore people. To visit the districts like Bijapur and N.K. (Uttar Kannada) or Karwar I had to cover large distances of over 100 miles. But I had planned to systematically cover every part of the division. Every month I would visit the talukas in two districts. The administrative rules stipulated inspections of all the district officers and a portion of taluka offices by the Divisional Commissioner I took these instructions seriously. The inspections gave me the opportunity of reviewing the entire administrative work of the district covering revenue and non-revenue aspects.

The New Approach to Rural Development

The position of Divisional Commissioner gave me the unique opportunity of personal involvement in every single scheme of development introduced in the seventies. The approach to rural development had undergone a total transformation since the days I worked as S.D.O. and Deputy Commissioner in the fifties. Then the approach was of a general nature, multipurpose in character, as embodied in the community development programme. Then came in 1959 the Ford Foundation repart on food emergency and how to meet it. The rural development programme came to be focussed on agricultural development programme as embodied in the Intensive Agricultural Development Programme (IADP). Under that programme all the village level workers were transferred to the agriculture department which became responsible for immediate and drastic increase in food production. In 1967 was started the new agriculture policy with the introduction of high yielding hybrid seeds, intensive dosage of fertilizers and application of water made available not only through distribution under major irrigation projects but also under minor irrigation projects like wells, lift irrigation projects and tanks.

A major change in approach to rural development took place in the seventies following Indira Gandhi's slogan of *garibi hatao* That itself was in response to a situation in which it was realized that bulk of the benefit of rural development had accrued to the larger farmers and small and marginal farmers and agricultural labourers had been left out. This was established with facts and figures by the Rural Credit Review Committee report (1960-69) produced by Shri B. Venkatappayya who in 1951 was also a member of the Rural Credit Survey Committee on whose recommendation was established throughout the country the three-tier system of cooperative credit institutions. To take the credit programme to the left out sections of the farming community, the committee recommended the establishment of SFDA (Small Farmer Development Agencies) and MFAL (Marginal Farmer and Agricultural Labour Agencies). Under the auspices of these agencies subsidised credit was to be provided by the cooperative credit institutions to small farmers (owning less than two hectares) marginal farmers (owning less than one hectar) and landless agricultural labourers – the last category benefiting by acquisition of assets like milch animals and poultry as supplementary ways of earning a livelihood.

Another approach suggested was the establishment of special programmes for drought prone and desert areas which were in rain shadow and also for dry farming in unirrigated areas. They were special programmes for conservation of water and soil.

In the wake of the new agricultural policy of 1967, a multi agency approach to rural credit was adopted. The cooperative credit institutions were considered to be inadequate and could not be solely entrusted with the responsibility to provide rural credit. The commercial banks were called upon to provide rural and agricultural credit as well. A National Credit Council was established to exercise social control over the commercial banks. But this did not satisfy Prime Minister Indira Gandhi. She wanted to do something dramatic so that she could be looked upon as the messiah of the poor. This she did on 19th July 1969 when against the advice of the Governor, Reserve Bank she nationalised at one stroke 14 large commercial banks. Moraji Desai who did not agree with the step was summarily stripped of the Finance portfolio. Consequently, he resigned. The nationalized banks were instructed to earmark a certain portion of their lending (40%) to "priority sectors", *viz.* agriculture, small industry and export and also open branches in rural areas to finance agriculture. At the same time on the recommendation of the Narasinhan Committee report a new type of banks called "Regional Rural Banks" combining the best features of cooperative banks, *viz.*, accessibility and the best feature of commercial banks, *viz.*, professionalism were also established under the latter's auspices. Banks started becoming active partners in rural development. They added a new dimension to the work of the rural administration.

Galvanising Development Programmes

I with my enthusiasm for rural development plunged headlong in these new programme as I had done in community development almost two decades earlier as a young IAS officer. I was now holding senior most position in field administration and was in charge of a much larger area. I had leadership role to play as Chairman of committees in-charge of these programmes, *viz.*, Committee of SFDA in Karwar and MFAL and DPAP (Drought Prone Area Programme) in Bijapur district. I was disappointed to find that the dynamism needed in implementing these innovative rural development programmes was missing. The enthusiasm for development of the fifties during the early years after independence in the Nehru era was missing. The development administration had fallen into a rut despite the existence of Panchayati Raj Institutions. I decided to galvanize the machinery for implementation of programmes. The first step regarding SFDA and MFAL was to identify the small and marginal farmers as had to be done later on in the wake of anti-poverty employment programme of those below the poverty line. Having identified the families, they had to be given loan and subsidy for acquiring assets to improve their earrings. I found that in Karwar 36,000 families were identified as "small farmers" but only few of them had benefited. They had to be individually approached and helped, which the field workers were not doing. SFDA and MFAL had project officers but no field staff of their own. They had to use the same VLWs and extension officers who had been appointed under the CD programme. They did not consider themselves accountable to the project officers.

The administrative principle of single line of command and obedience was missing. I decided to introduce dynamism and accountability by asking the sub-division officer in whose jurisdiction were three or four blocks to take responsibility for these new development programmes. To my surprise they were not associated with these programme at all. While twenty years ago as a young SDO I considered "development" as the main content of my work, now twenty years after independence, it had seized to be the focus of work of young IAS officers taking their first jobs as SDOs. They were doing routine work as revenue officers. My decision to associate SDOs with the new development projects like SFDA had a dramatic effect. The coverage of small farmers under the programme rapidly improved. I set up sub-division level committee of the SFDA under the Chairmanship of the SDO. The district was too large a unit and small unit – like subdivision meant more intensive application. I also found that small and marginal farmers were sometimes by themselves unable to acquire and optimally use an asset like irrigation well. I introduced the idea of "group landing". A number of small or marginal farmers could join together to get a loan to dig a well. This approach also was successful. Some of these of innovative ideas gave a push to the programme which in the absence of necessary interest had become moribund.

DPAP was even more difficult. The water-shed area approach was the right approach to conserve water in rain-shadow areas. But it had yet to be established. Bijapur district was notorious as drought prone. It was therefore a good laboratory for DPAP. A young IAS officer Shri S.K. Hazra was deputy commissioner of the district. I encouraged him to identify such water sheds and take up projects like farm ponds for harvesting and conserving water and tree belts to check wind erosion. A programme like this can bear fruit over a long period. So while a beginning was made, immediate re-usable results could not be expected. I discovered that in the rain-shadow areas, horticulture crops could be an alternative to normal agricultural crops. Indi Taluka in Bijapur district was well known for producing lemons. The area under lemons could be increased and could provide a productive alternative. The success of this approach was demonstrated in later years by the growth of area under *Ber* in dry area of Solapur district in Maharashtra.

I enthusiashcally participated in the work of setting up the Malaprabha Regional Rural Bank as the representative of the State Government on the Bank's board of management. I emphasized close association of the Bank with the development agencies of governmental administration for the formulation of bankable projects.

Coordination

The divisional commissioner has to coordinate the activities of various departments at the divisional level. Most of the departments had independent officers at the divisional level with whom I came into contact in course of official work. The Coronation Committee at the divisional level was intended to solve interdepartmental problems if any and promote cooperation between them for the attainment of common goals. In addition to the departmental officers at the divisional level, the Deputy Commissioners of four districts were also invited to participate in the meetings of coordination committee

I felt that holding one coordination meeting of all the departmental officers did not serve the purpose since the number of participants tended to be too large and the agenda too long and hence the whole exercise too unwieldy. Not all officers were concerned with all the items and I felt that their presence, when those items were discussed, served no purpose. I therefore decided to break the coordination committee into subject matter groups such as: (i) Revenue, (ii) Development, (iii) Social Welfare, (iv) Urban Administration, (v) Civil supplies, and (vi) Law and Order. This proved to be an effective mechanism and saved the time of officers and at the same time led to more intensive consideration of issues. I however found that two-departmental officers Police and Forest, both belonging to All India Services started resenting the ascendancy and the coordinative role of the Divisional Commissioner developing ideas that they do not have to suffer the hegemony of the Divisional Commissioner. Such attitude were hardly conducive to coordinated administration.

When Shri P.G. Halarnkar succeeded Shri Garudahchar as DIG, I invited him and his wife for dinner at my house. The bungalow of the divisional commissioner in Hulme Park had been bifurcated into two and one portion was earmarked for the residence of the DIG. This might have contributed to a sense of equality between the Divisional Commissioner and the DIG, which Halarnkar from the very beginning was keen to show in whichever way he could. He would not attend the meeting of the coordination committee and apparently persuaded the Divisional Conservator Forest also not to do so. The latter whose attitude to the Divisional Commissioner in the beginning was quite cordial suddenly became quite assertive. Both of them insisted that their CRs should not be commented upon by the Divisional Commissioner. When I brought this to the notice of the Chief Secretary he preferred to do nothing about it and I concluded that it was not worth while pursuing the matter and one had only to put up with limitations to coordination. Things were slowly falling apart and the traditions of colonial administration according to which the police was certainly required to recognize the senior role of the Deputy Commissioner/Collector at the district level and Divisional Commissioner at the divisional level were getting eroded. The Deputy Commissioner could no longer "inspect". the police stations which were strictly out of bound for him. Shri Halarnkar as DIG would not appear in uniform before the Divisional Commissioner as a mark of his "independence". Once when I was appointed by government to inquire into capsizing of a boat in Krishna river near Bagalkot, I summoned Halarnkar to appear before me. He chose to come in *Mufti*. As another token of his assertion I suddenly found one day that the policeman who had been traditionally guarding the bungalow of the Divisional Commissioner at the entrance was removed. I noticed the occurrence but chose to ignore it because I thought it demeaning to take up such a trivial issue with the DIG or the SP. But attitude such as this eroded the integrity of law and order administration whose standards have progressively fallen. If the IPS officers wanted to be independent of IAS officers, their subordinates, *viz.*, the inspectors and sub-inspectors wanted to be "independent" of their superiors and sought patronage of the politicians. The rot that had set in only worsened in later years.

Weird Experience

Looking to the attitude of the DIG I decided that I would not look to police for any "protection." Soon I had a weird experience of this lack of "police protection". The Revenue Minister Shri Huchmasti Gowda on a petition to him regarding some alleged construction at an *Idga* in Gadag, a sub-divisional HQ in Dharwad district, observed that the Divisional Commissioner should personally visit and enquire into the allegation and report. I considered that the matter was hardly of any importance to warrant a personal visit of the Divisional Commissioner. The local tahsildar's visit and report would have been quite adequate. However since the Revenue Minister's noting on the petition was quite categorical I fixed a visit to the spot. The President of Gadag Municipality and the local SDO accompanied me when I visited the *Idga*. Apart from the *Mutavalli* in charge of the *Idga* some local Jan Sangh workers were also present. Apparently, they were the ones who were at the back of complaint to the Minister regarding "illegal" construction within the *Idga* compound and had made their appearance at my spot inspection though not invited by me. After visiting the *Idga* site and noticing the construction, I started walking out of the compound of the *Idga* towards my waiting car when I suddenly felt some disturbance at the back. Turning around I saw that the *Mutavali* had given a blow to the Jan Sangh leader whose spectacle had flown away. The Jan Sangh workers, who had accompanied the leader, were quite excited. I calmed them down and admonished the *Mutavalli* for his behaviour. As I sat in the car, the Municipal President by my side and the SDO by the side of the driver, and the car started moving, I suddenly found that a crowd had gathered from nowhere and had encircled the car which could not move. I asked the Jan Sangh leader to see that the crowd made way for the car but the crowd would not listen to him. The Municipal President also made an appeal but without any effect. In the meanwhile the crowd had swollen every minute and became menacing. Some of them started banging on the bonnet of the car. Many in the crowd were workers who at the end of a long day were fully drunk and had a ready situation for rowdy behaviour. They could have set the car on fire. I came out of the car and saw a single policeman at a distance helplessly watching the crowd which could have even lynched me! I asked the policeman to get the crowd dispersed to enable the car to move but a single policeman could not cope with a crowd and went away to get some re-enforcement. Fifteen minutes passed but he did not turn up. The sunset and darkness descended. Here was the head of administration of the division on his official duty who was left entirely unprotected at the mercy of a hostile crowd though the programme of my visit was issued well in advance of which a copy as usual was marked to the police authorities. The situation was hopeless. The only saving grace was that somehow I had not lost my composure and had not turned panicky. In a flash I realized that the only way out of the situation was to get out of the car and simply walk away. This is what I set out to do. I walked away and the SDO and the Municipal President followed. We first reached the office of the SDO where I got into a jeep and kept my next appointment before returning to the Circuit House. Soon the driver came with the car. He was unharmed and the car had only a small dent.

When I tried to find out why there was no police *bandobast* at the time of the spot inspection, I was told that the entire police force had gone to HQ at Dharwar to participate in some sports event. Later Shri Raghuraman, SP Dharwar, called on me and explained the absence of the police. I sent a report to the Secretary, Home, but I was not informed about action taken if any I convinced myself that absence of the police was a blessing in disguise because they would have lathi charged and the crowd could have run berserk worsoning the situation giving rise to unsavory publicity in the press.

Dubious Value of Police Reports

As Divisional Commissioner I was a regular recipient of confidential weekly police reports. They contained no information that I did not already have and in a more accurate manner. I realized that an administrative officer in close contact with common people and whose doors are always open to all is much better informed and does not have to depend on police reports. The latter could even be biased as I realized once at my own cost. On a Republic Day I took salute at an NCC parade which was a grand show. The driver Laxman had put the national-flag on the bonnet of the official car without my asking him to do so. Perhaps he did so as a normal practice on the Republic day. I noticed the flag fluttering as the car left the porch taking me to the function which went off very well. There was quite a good attendance. In the police report following the function, I was alarmed to find a comment that there was public resentment at the fluttering of the flag on the car of the Divisional Commissioner. That was the privilege the police thought probably of only the Ministers. There was no public reaction which I had noticed nor was there any mention of such reaction in any of the local press. Then where did the police notice the reaction? Obviously it was a jealous reaction of some senior police officers who wanted to embarrass the Divisional Commissioner or even put him in serious trouble. The police report goes right to the Home Secretary and the Chief Secretary and they could have picked it up and started an unending unsavory correspondence and inquiry. Fortunately that did not happen and my decision not to take up the matter myself turned out to be the right one. I am glad that under the orders of the Supreme Court, on a public interest application, the unreasonable order regarding the restrictive use of the national flag which gave opportunities to the police to show their clout has been done away with and the citizen of the free country has been given his right to use the national flag.

The advice of the DIG, when I had newly come, not to accept the invitation of the Rani Parvatibai College to unveil Shivaji's portrait, his sending proposal for gerry-mandering the constituencies for the municipal elections so as to ensure that the *Maharashtra Ekikaran* candidates do not get elected, the fuss made by the police to keep away the public at a function of installation of the portrait of Shivaji, their utter neglect of the security of the Divisional Commissioner at the time of spot inspection at Gadag, the sudden removal of the police from the gate of the Divisional Commissioner and the adverse report against the Divisional Commissioner himself in the secret police report—all convinced me that a civil administrator should never rely on the police for the assessment of a situation. He must make it himself which he can do if he keeps in touch with the people and always keeps his doors open. The members of the public themselves provide true and correct information—more reliable than the police reports. Often police themselves are a part of the problem rather than solution. Their merciless lathi charging over the years on the processions of *Maharashtra Ekikaran Samiti*, in my judgement, had needlessly antagonised the Marathi people against the government. The police have neither a correct understanding of the situation nor do they act with necessary restraint. This has happened on many occasions. If instead of understanding the causes of social unrest and removing them, the administrators start relying on police reports and advice, the "law and order" situation gets "created" and goes out of hand.

This has happened often in recent years as administration has gone more and more away from the people and has started resorting to coercive practice. The attempt of the police to be independent of the civil administrator has made them more dependent on local politicians who have misused the police machinery for partisan purposes. The Home Ministry at Delhi had also contributed to the weakening of law and order administration by adopting the single track approach of sending more and more police forces and greater and greater resorting to coercive processes as the essence of tackling the law and order situation. This approach is totally flawed. Soon after independence, we talked of turning a "Police State" of the colonial days into a "Welfare State" Fifty years after independence all that we notice is the pervasive presence of the police state guarding the rulers of dubious standing and alienating the common people.

People-oriented Administration

I was always keen that decisions as far as possible should be taken after consulting with all concerned, and administrators should show patience and understanding and should not be trigger-happy and impose their decisions on unwilling people. Once a case arose of the location of a cooperative sugar factory at Gokak. There were two parties each having its own location in mind and opposing the choice of another. What was involved was the loss of agricultural land, which affected the interest of the two parties. I visited both the sites but succeeded in locating a third site, which was a non-agricultural land and hence did not adversely affect any body's personal interest. The decision was welcomed by both parties and the factory came up rapidly. An attempt to support either of the two parties could have created a "law and order" problem.

It is important that the administrators keep their doors open at all time for the people to present their grievances and solve them as far as possible. If for some reason a decision could not be taken in their favour, the reasons should be explained. This applies to even influential people like MLAs. Once I effected transfer of some BDOs and an MLA came with a request to stay the transfer of some individual officer The officer had completed his tenure and was due for transfer. I explained this to the MLA and even told him that under the rules the officer in whose favour he has tried to interfere is liable to be proceeded against for bringing to bear outside influence on official transfer. All this I explained in a friendly manner and the MLA understood. He did not hold it against me.

Systematic Disposal of Routine Work

I was also very keen on systematic disposal of routine work. Often officers neglect the routine in trying to do something spectacular but in my view, prompt disposal of files was greatly conducive to solving the problems of the people. Files should never pile up and decisions should be taken quickly and matters not allowed to hang on. This applies to court cases as well. As Divisional Commissioner, I was the appellate authority under a variety of laws including revenue, municipal, cinematography etc. I had fixed timings for court hearings on three days in a weak at 2.30. p.m. and never changed the schedule. After reading Justice M.C. Chagla's autobiography "Roses in December" I decided to deliver judgements in open court at the end of hearing and did not reserve the cases for delivery of judgement at a later date. Nor did I allow mere than one adjournment in a case at the lawyer's request. This brought a great deal of discipline and promptness in court work.

Court Hearings

Once the Chief Minister Shri Devraj Urs was to visit Belgaum. I was to receive him at the Circuit House at 10 a.m. Actually, as is often the case, his arrival was delayed by several hours. He made his appearance at nearly 1 p.m. I was already upset that my precious time was lost. I received him on his arrival and after some preliminary conversation I requested him to allow me to excuse myself from accompanying him during his afternoon engagements since I had to hear cases in the court which were already fixed. I was relieved that he promptly agreed since his afternoon engagements were of a populist nature. I had hurried lunch at my house and punctually appeared in court and announced cases to be taken up. No lawyers were present But I started dictating judgement in the first case to be taken up on the basis of papers available in the file including the appeal petition setting out arguments. Soon the lawyers came rushing in and expressed their surprise that the court hearing had started as usual though they had felt that in view of CM's visit I would be with him and not in the court. I stopped my dictation and allowed the lawyers to set out their arguments. This was how public business was not interrupted just because CM had come on a visit. But this was an exception rather then the rule since no government officer could dare tell the Chief Minister about the priority of official work.

Corruption

I was keen that administration should be totally corruption-free and all offices including my own and those of Deputy Commissioners (Collector) should be clean. I used to get general complaints that Deputy Commissioner of NK district, a promotee from the state civil service nearing retirement habitually took bribes but there was no specific allegation. One could not go by general complaints. I was looking for an opportunity to book him. It came with a signed petition alleging corruption in the allocation of supplies to flour mills. I promptly fixed a date for hearing complaints. All the complainants were asked to appear before me individually. I was amazed to find that in spite of the chance of individual and confidential hearing that I had given to each petitioner, none of them came forward with any evidence. Most denied that they had even signed the complaint petition. I was shocked but lost the opportunity to book an allegedly corrupt district head. It had rightly been said that people get the government and administration which they deserve.

On the other hand I myself got caught in the net of allegation of corruption. I had taken leave travel concession and the family decided to visit Kerala. An itinerary was worked out and was casually mentioned in the club to some friends of whom Mahaveeranna Patil, a well-established businessman was one. Over a long period; we had come to know him as a decent person who never approached for any official favours. When he learnt that we will be undertaking the journey in our personal fiat car, he said that long journey in a small car won't be comfortable and offered his own big car for travel. With some hesitation I accepted the offer. I soon realized how wrong it was on my part to have accepted the offer. Ten miles out of Belgaum, the car developed trouble and we had to make a hasty return. As an alternative arrangement I phoned Shri V.S. Shirgaontor, owner of a private sugar factory at Ugarkhurd on the border of Karnataka and Maharashtra. He was a decent person and readily agreed to spare a car, which came in no time. But I had not reckoned that a trouble was in store for me. In our first stop at Mysore we had a halt at the guest-house of the Administrative Training Centre where K.P. Singh, a young IAS officer had come to participate in a course. While I was talking with him a person apparently drunk came in inquiring whether a car of the Ugarkhurd Sugar Factory had come. K.P. Singh hastily told the stranger that it was that of Divisional Commissioner Belgaum. He took the stranger out of the room and came back a while afterwards. We resumed the journey the next day. But on return from our tour I was shocked to find a copy of the CBI letter to the Chief Secretary that Shri P.R. Dubhashi as Divisional Commissioner had misused his official position to use the car of a sugar factory for personal use. The Chief Secretary had asked for my comments. I felt shaken by such a letter which I considered a blot on my spotless career and self-image. I had put in petrol in the car myself and paid the hire charges for the car to Shri Shirgaokar who was reluctant to accept and got a receipt, so I felt in no way obliged. I wrote accordingly to the Chief Secretary and heard no more in the matter. Later I learnt that Chief Secretary Rao had written to the CBI that there was no truth in the allegation and the integrity of the officer could not be doubted. But who could have given the information? The drunken person who had barged into my room at Mysore or K.P. Singh who had taken him out? The latter I considered as my protégé, a young officer who had worked in my division as SDO before being transferred to Bangalore. I had occasion to enquire into an anonymous petition alleging that he had with the collusion of a forest officer cut forest tree and taken wood for the bungalow he was constructing at Bangalore. Since the petition was anonymous no action could be taken nor could the allegation be established. But I leant that (i) one should not be misled by unsolicited advice of an outsider in a personal matter, (ii) there could be a hidden enemy around (iii) no body should be trusted and no help should be taken even though offered without strings; one had to be extra careful. This is for the scrupulous. For others there are no limits to corruption indulged in with impunity.

Emergency

My tenure as Divisional Commissioner Belgaum from 1973-74 overlapped a most traumatic period in national life – the imposition of emergency on the nation on June 25,1975. I had just completed a year as Divisional Commissioner and things were quite even and peaceful without the kind of tension that had gripped North India as a consequence of *navanirman* movement in Gujarat and JP's movement in Bihar against Indira Gandhi's "dictatorial" rule. There were signs of trouble in the shape of nation-wide railway strike, which was put down by government with an iron hand. As Divisional Commissioner I was asked by government to keep in touch with the railway authorities particularly to ensure safety of railway property against any kind of sabotage. I visited Hubli, the centre of railways in the division and met with railway officers. No untoward incident took place before the strike was ruthlessly put down.

But then came the bolt from the blue on June 25, 1975, when Jayprakash Narayan, Moraji Desai and many other opposition leaders were arrested and whisked off to various jails. The action was triggered off by the decision of Justice Sinha declaring Indira Gandhi's election invalid because of corrupt practice (mostly of technical nature because her private secretary Yashpal Kapoor, a government servant, had put up an election platform for her election rally) and his opponent Raj Narayan was declared elected. On an appeal to the Supreme Court Justice Krishna Iyer ruled that though Indira Gandhi could continue as PM she could not vote in Parliament. This completely eroded her prestige and authority and Indira Gandhi could not bear it. She was in a mood to lay down her office but her belligerent son Sanjay Gandhi who had already emerged as a political force would not hear of it. After consulting with her constitutional expert Law Minster, Siddharth Shankar Ray, she decided to clamp down Emergency and got President

Fakhruddin Ali Ahmed to sign the declaration without even consulting her Cabinet which had become a rubber stamp.

I came to know of these nocturnal events only next morning from *Tarun Bharat*, the local daily, which carried the news. The radio confirmed it. We hardly knew the implications at the field level of this unprecedented development in the constitutional, governmental and administrative system of the country. There were no communications to the Divisional Commissioner either from the Central government or the State government about the changes in administration which Emergency required. It was said in the press and elsewhere that thanks to Emergency, government employees started coming to offices on time and doing their work regularly without wasting time in chit-chat. This might have been true in Delhi offices but so far as distant Belgaum was concerned, we were already working on time. I, as Divisional Commissioner would come on time regularly to my office and so would the rest of the staff and did not need an Emergency regime to make us do our duties. Rigours of Sanjay Gandhi rule were felt in Delhi and around in the northern belt but in the revenue division of North Karnataka the tremors were hardly felt and it was business as usual. As Divisional Commissioner, I was determined not to create "Emergency Atmosphere" in my division—no oppressive climate. I believed in "people friendly" administration and wanted to continue it and succeeded in doing so. As Divisional Commissioner I wanted to play no role in the "Emergency". I did not want to be its active agent. On 15th August, the first independence day after the declaration of Emergency, I had to unfurl the national flag in front of the office of Divisional Commissioner and say a few words to the gathering of civil servants. I recalled the famous words of Rabindranath Tagore from *Gitanjali*—"Where the mind is without fear and the head is held high, into that heaven of freedom my father let my country awake". I deliberately chose these lines as a protest against the suppression of liberty during emergency. That was as far as I could go. There was a fear that these words could appear in the police report, but they did not.

But in spite of me, the suppression of liberty was taking place. I learnt that a number of people from Belgaum were rounded up and locked in Hindalga Jail. Who were these people—either on the left or the right who were political "threats" to Emergency. Actually there was no provocation given no anti-Emergency rallies takenout. Under whose orders were they rounded up?

I got to know of the procedure of detainment only when I, in course of routine work, inspected the office of the Deputy Commissioner, Belgaum. While inspecting the judicial branch, I came to see a number of cyclostyled orders of detention singed by the District Magistrate. I asked the latter whether he had collected or seen any evidence before signing the detention orders. He had none, he had signed them at the instance of District Superintend of Police who in turn got a list from the State government who in turn must have prepared the list on the basis of police intelligence reports. Later on, once, while talking to G.V.K. Rao who was Chief Secretary I learnt that he tried to tone down as far as possible the harsh emergency measures being suggested from Delhi for suppression of freedom of expression and protest movements. Many opposition leaders like Advani and Vajpayee were detained in Bangalore jail while the main opposition leader in Karnataka Shri Ramkrishna Hegde, I learnt, was lodged in Hindalga Jail in Belgaum.

I wanted it to meet him and other detainees in Hindalga Jail and asked the jail officer to arrange my visit and meeting with the detainees. By the time, the visit was scheduled Hegde was removed from Hindalga to Bangalore and I could not meet him. But I met quite a few people from Belgaum including one Shri Kulkarni who ran a small industry. He was active in public life who often met me. I also met one young girl named Marathe who was a lonely figure in the female ward and also her old father who hardly looked like a threat to Emergency. First I thought that I would spend only half an hour in jail but as it happened my visit extended from 10.30 a.m. to 2.30 p.m. during which I had friendly chat with detainees regarding the inconvenience they had to undergo in the jail. They wanted small conveniences like books to read and films and documentaries to be shown and home food provided. These were small requests and I assured them that I would try to see that they were provided. At the end of my visit I prepared a short note of these requests and wrote to jail officer to see that they were provided. I followed up the letter by personal inquiring to see that the needful was done. I felt somewhat relieved that I could do such small things to mitigate the hardships of Emergency imposed on people without reason.

It was during Emergency that Indira Gandhi introduced her famous "20 point programme" to give people the sweet fruits of Emergency. Many welcomed this as Indira Gandhi's bold new initiative for the welfare of the people though she herself had described it as a product of "few stray thoughts" that she had placed before the Congress Working Committee meeting. But her Congress followers excelled each other in singing the paeans of praise of the 20 point programme. One Chief Minister Shri S.B. Chavan went to the extent of saying that it was Geeta of the twentieth century. On going through the programme I found that it was a hotchpotch of a variety of programmes most of which were already in existence. The field publicity officer arranged a big seminar at the city auditorium on the twenty-point programme to which officers of all departments and many others were invited I was the chief guest. I had no hesitation in saying that the twenty point programme was the collection of several programmes most of which extant. They had to be implemented with efficiency.

One of the programmes was related to family planning. It had caused havoc in North India because of much coercion used in its implementation. In Belgaum division too family planning camps were organized. In some villages there was cent percent coverage, i.e., all eligible persons mostly women had undergone the operation. I visited camps and appreciated that the programme was implemented without compulsion but with voluntary compliance.

It was during the height of emergency that Indira Gandhi's law Minister Shri H.R. Gokhale came on an official visit. I accompanied him on his tour. He did not utter one word about the Emergency or how effectively it was enforced. It was business as usual.

Throughout the Emergency, there was not one occasion for me to change my people-friendly style of administration or show the coercive face of administration. Belgaum was far away from Delhi and Sanjay Gandhi's remote control was not felt. There was no Jagmohan-type Turkman Gate operation.

Rehabilitation Work

I was keen all the time that administration should be carried on without the use of coercion and by willing cooperation of the people even when some unpleasant work had to be undertaken. One such was the trans-shipment of people coming under the spread of water of the huge reservoir created by the Hidkal Dam on Ghataprabha. I heard stories of villagers herded in trucks and removed like chattel just when, with the onset of the mansoon season, waters threatened to flood the villages. I did not approve of this method of "rehabilitation". Some more villages were threatened with inundation as the addition to the height of the dam stored greater quantities of water. I decided to take action well before the onset of the mansoon. I visited the villages, met with the villagers and discussed with them the need for orderly evacuation well on time. I told them of the new location where they would be shifted and the assistance and compensation to which they would be entitled. In one village, an ancient temple was coming under inundation. The villagers were attached to it by long tradition. I told them that the temple would be transplanted brick by brick to the new location. I told them the plan for evacuation and its time-table. After considerable discussion the villagers agreed to the plan which was carried on time without last minute shift with the use of the police. I firmly believed that as far as possible police and their coercion should be kept away from the normal administrative operations.

My three and half years as Divisional Commissioner Belgaum, was a happy and worth while experience. I came into close touch with people and gave a people oriented administration. Despite the glitches caused by the initial hostility of extreme Kannada elements, I became a "popular" Divisional Commissioner. I gave a smooth and fast moving administration. By normal standards of tenure in a government office, it was a long stay except that it was interrupted for a day by the appointment of Shri P.R. Nayak as Divisional Commissioner relieving me of additional charge (I continued to be Administrator, Maleprabha and Ghatprabha projects). I was taken aback by the government order. Nayak, a junior to me in IAS by a year, came post haste and took charge. He had come on promotion. As soon as he arrived junior officers like Municipal Commissioner abandoned me and received him. It turned out to be only a drama. Nayak returned to Bangalore as quickly as he came. His posting was only to give him promotion in a "substantive" post, before he was deputed at that level to Power Corporation as its Managing Director. One never knows how a government moves in posting of civil servants. I wished government had kept me informed of its intention so that I could have been saved from an embarrassment by an order summarily removing me from an additional charge of Divisional Commissioner.

The Role of Divisional Commissioner

Often the post of Divisional Commissioner in the field-administration is described as a redundant one. The State government could run the administration by being in direct communication with the Deputy Commissioners (Collector) of districts. But how could there be 'Deputy Commissioners' without 'Commissioners' in position? That apart, my experience showed to me that Divisional Commissioner does play a useful role of coordination and over all guidance to Deputy Commissioners who are often young and inexperienced. I collected some additional information regarding the situation existing in neighbouring states like Maharashtra and their orders regarding delegation of powers and functions of Divisional Commissioner. On the basis of that information and my own experience, I wrote an article (in my usual way of administrative writing based on experience) on the "Role of Divisional Commissioner in Indian Administration" which was published in the *Indian Journal of Public Administration*. It is perhaps a rare piece of writing on subject.

Deputation to Centre

The government in the usual routine way had asked me whether I would be prepared to go on deputation to the Centre. I had already done my central deputation for nine years and had returned to the state because the latter badly needed my services and now the same State Government considered me for yet another deputation when several IAS officers, specially the "Sons of the soil," the officers of Mysore State Civil Service inducted into IAS had refused to leave the comfortable postings in Bangalore. They wanted to be in IAS and yet wanted to avoid central deputation. That is how the functioning of IAS was distorted by the "Local Officers" and their god-fathers in local politics.

Despite this inequitable position, I had agreed to yet another central deputation. And the consequence was an intimation from the state government about my appointment as Joint Director of the Lal Bahadur Shastri Academy of Administration at Mussorie. This is the apex institute for training of recruits to IAS and other all India and Central services. The appointment was at the level of Joint Secretary to the Government of India. My daughter was college going and there was no college at Mussorie. I would have to put her in a hostel, say at Delhi. I was reluctant to do so. The other alternative would have been to be alone at Mussorie and leave the family at Delhi or any other place. These alternatives, I was reluctant to explore. To overcome my reluctance it was indicated to me that I could be elevated in the near future as Director with the rank of Additional Secretary. Along with the incentive, there was disincentive too. If I failed to accept the offer, I would not be considered again for deputation to Centre.

I was put in a quandary. I asked for a posting at Delhi but the Establishment Office was apparently bent on forcing on me the Mussorie posting. I decided to try the informal channel. I spoke on phone to Shri Mohan Dharia who was then Minister of Commence in Moraji Desai's Janata government. I thought I had known him well when I was posted at Pune as Director, Vaikunth Mehta National Institute of Cooperative Management. I was attending the discussion group of Shri Prabhakar Padhye where Dharia too came and had appreciated my review of Galbraith's "The Affluent State" which had just appeared. But power changes a man. When overcoming the queries of his P.A. I got to talk to him, he assumed high and mighty officious position and ticked me off that it was irregular on my part to have approached him in that manner. I was taken aback. I knew which the formal channel was. But also knew that informal channels did exist. But Dharia wanted me to believe that it was gross impropriety on my part to have explored it.

In the meanwhile people of Belgaum come to know that I had personal difficulties in going to Mussorie and wanted to help me. Shri Madhu Dandavate who was Railway Minster in Morarji's government had come to visit Belgaum. He had many personal friends in Belgaum—the socialist minded Marathi leaders who suggested that I meet him at the private house of his host, a decent prominent Marathi person. I did so. Dandvate's attitude was also similar to that of Dharia. I made no request to him or made no mention of my personal difficulties regarding the central posting offered to me. Despite this he started lecturing that in Morarji government there was no scope for interference in personnel matters. It appeared to me that both Dharia and Dandavate were either hypocritical or scared of Morarji who was supposed to be a stickler for rules and unbending in his attitude.

In any case, my personal request was eventually considered and my posting at Mussorie was cancelled and instead I was posted to Delhi as Joint Secretary in the Ministry of Commerce and Cooperation headed by the same Mohan Dharia!

Farewell Functions

Many small functions arranged to bid me good-bye. At one of the functions, Shri Siddan Gouda Patil, the local Kannada *chaluwaligar* leader was present. In the course of his speech, he, who had as Kannada protagonist often questioned my "friendly attitude" to Marathi people, generously expressed his appreciation of my administration as Divisional Commissioner Belgaum. He said he learnt two things from my administration. First, it was not necessary to go to Bangalore to solve local problems. They can be solved at the level of the Divisional Commissioner. Second no matter to what department a case pertains, one can always go to the Divisional Commissioner who can take it up with the department concerned and provide a solution. He further said that when I came to Belgaum it was a volcano; when I was leaving, it had become an iceberg. I thought he correctly summed up my 3½ year achievement as Divisional Commissioner, Belgaum.

My Acquaintance with *Jnyaneshwari*

Soon after my arrival in Belgaum, as reports of my speeches started appearing in *Tarun Bharat,* the local Marathi daily, on old person made his appearance at my bungalow one fine morning and introduced himself as one Shri Yardi. He gratuitously asked me to take bath that very evening and start reading Jnyaneshwari, the great commentary of Saint Jnyaneshwar on the Gita in Marathi. I thought it was a good suggestion and complied with it. I acquired a copy and during my stay in Belgaum, I went through the work twice over. Undoubtedly in terms of philosophy and literary merit, the long commentary running into some 1800 verses is the first and the loftiest work in Marathi language. The work greatly lifted me mentally and morally.

Somehow my interest in *Jnyaneshwari* became known and one day I was surprised to get an invitation to talk in Kannada on *Jnyaneshwari* to a gathering of *warkaries* taking place at Saundatti. The invitation was at the instance of Shri Venka Reddi Huli, known as Ajja, the grand father, an ex-MLA of 85 years and a person of great influence and himself of *warkari sampraday* whose members went on foot to Pandharpur on *Ashadhi Ekadashi.* I picked up some selected verses from different chapters in *Jnyaneshwari* and wrote down their original Sanskrit *shlokas* and their Kannada translation in order to convey the main idea and message of Gita. When I arrived, I was wonderstruck to find a magnificent pendal accommodating some ten thousand *warkaries.* Before this visit I never realized that the Varkari sampradaya existed in such large numbers in the Kannada territory. But I soon remembered *Jnyaneshwar's* own description of *Vitthal* of Pamdharpur as a Kannada deity in the famous verse sung by Asha Bhosale – *Kannada Vitthalu Karnataku* This only shows how close are the people of Maharashtra and Karnataka and the thread of unity that runs in our common people throughout the length and breadth of our country. The talk itself was for me an exhilarating experience and I felt one with that vast Kannada congregation. The Lingayat *swami* who presided greatly appreciated my discourse and said that the *Pasaydan* in which Jnyaneshwar expresses his good wishes not only for all human beings but for the entire animate and inanimate world, should be displayed in United Nations for pursuing peace in the world. At the end of my stay, I delivered another *pravachan* in the town at the invitation of Shri Digamber Parulekar.

Astrological Pronouncements

When the news of my transfer to Delhi became known, Shri Yardi came and took away my horoscope. He soon predicted that in the near future I had *Gaj Kesari Yoga* in my fortune which meant that my stars were very bright. I had till that time never shown my horoscope to anybody nor tried to ascertain my future. But Yardi's prediction undoubtedly made me somewhat happy. At the same time Yardi warned me that the good turn of fortune in the immediate future is bound to create enemies for me. While his warning was clear, I did not try to find out from Yardi what I should do to defeat the evil designs of my enemies. Obviously I did not take his warnings seriously. I did not bother about my future and always dealt with the present. Also I had a naïve outlook of optimism in my mental make up. Perhaps future events were to show that I should have taken Yardi's warning more seriously!

CHAPTER 16

Joint Secretary in the Department of Cooperation (1977-78)

Formulating Cooperative Policies

A transfer is a dreadful experience in the life of a civil servant especially when it is one such as from Belgaum with its security and comfort to the impersonal anonymity of Delhi. At Belgaum I held the highest position in the administrative system. Because of my participation in innumerable social and cultural functions, some 500 in 3½ years, I had become a familiar and even a popular figure. There was an atmosphere of friendliness and even appreciation and acclaim. In addition, there was of course the support system available to the privileged position of the Divisional Commissioner—a vast bungalow in a park, servants at home, a chauffeur-driven car, all eager to serve. In Delhi, I had to be on my own. I had to start from a scratch—find a place to stay, admit children to school and college, personal effects to be packed, transported, unpacked and rearranged on securing a residence. I left Belgaum full of anxiety and unease. No body counts this kind of price which a civil servant has to pay as a professional hazard!

As an IAS officer I could find temporary accommodation in the Guest-House of the state government Karnataka Bhavan in Chanakyapuri, where a number of state governments had their guest houses on the outskirts of the palatial buildings of the embassies and High Commissions of foreign countries. A fairly comfortable room was allotted to me where I stayed with wife and two children. Catering was available and we could have, meals, tea and snacks in the dinning hall of the guesthouse.

Though I was a Joint Secretary in the Ministry of Commerce and Civil Supplies and Cooperation, I was allotted to the latter department which was considered to be a poor relative of the prestigious department of commerce. The latter was concerned with foreign trade and apparently agents of trading houses made a beeline to officers for favours to be granted by bureaucracy in the era of license permit raj then prevailing with full force.

Joining Department of Cooperation

I reported for duty in the Department of Cooperation located in Krishi Bhavan. Shri Thapar, a senior IAS officer of Rajasthan cadre, was the Secretary. The Department of Commerce was headed by Dr. P.C. Alexander who later rose to higher positions. Krishi Bhavan was a familiar place because it was here that I had worked in my earlier central deputation to the department of Community Development.

A Gory Incident

I had first to secure admission to children in the educational institutions. The new academic year was to start soon and I had to take quick action. My son was in the Central School stream and I tried first in the Central School at Gole Market. At the time of my visit, the Principal was, for some reason not available and I could not arrange the admission of my son. Shri Chakku who was still there in the Cooperative Department suggested that I try the reputed, Delhi Public School on Mathura Road, which was well established. I went to the school and met its tall Principal Shri Deendayal who appeared to be quite friendly. When I showed him Devdatta's card of his performance at Belgaum school, he was quite impressed with his marks and said that there should be no difficulty in admitting him but formalities required that he gave an entrance examination. For that he directed me to the Vice-Principal, an ex-army officer. The day for the examination was fixed. It was to last from 8 am to 11 a.m.—quite a long stretch of time. I brought my son Devdatta to the school right on the dot and left him to be examined. The Vice-Principal told me to come at 10.30 a.m. to pick up the boy. When after spending some time in the office, I reached the school not far away from Krishi Bhavan right on time, I met the Vice-Principal in his office. He said that the examination was still going on and in the meanwhile offered me a cup of tea which I readily accepted. While taking the cup of tea, I was looking anxiously at my watch and it was 10.45 a.m. I again enquired whether the exam was over. The Vice-Principal enquired and told me that the exam was getting concluded soon. When after a few minutes, I again asked rather impatiently, the Vice-Principal checked up and told me that the examination was over and the boy had left. But when the boy did not come back to Vice-Principal's room, enquiry started why he had not turned up. Perhaps he had gone down. I rushed to the ground floor and made enquiries with the Receptionist, a talkative but a presumptuous lady. She coolly told me that the boy had gone out! The boy was to be brought to the VP's office on the first floor just across the corridor, from the hall where the examination was conducted and now the lady said the boy had gone out. Where? I searched in the compound till the gate but he was nowhere to be found. Where had he disappeared? Lady said that the boy might have gone with a friend. What friend? We had landed in Delhi only a few days back and there were no friends. With whom could he go? The boy was only twelve years old and he was now allowed to be lost in an unfamiliar city when the VP of the school had promised him to be delivered at the end of the examination and the father was waiting with the VP himself to take delivery of the boy. Suddenly I felt panic as never before in my life. I rushed to the Principal Deendayal who suddenly lost his friendly attitude and coolly told me that the school took no responsibility for the wards and I could complain to the police! I became desperate. I rushed to my office perhaps he had gone there. He knew the office but he was not there. Covered with cold sweat, I rushed to the Karnataka Bhavan where we were still staying. What a great relief it was when I saw Devdatta. He had just returned I asked him why he did not come to the room after the examination. as I had asked him to do. He told me that after the examination, he was escorted out and asked to leave the school forthwith out of the gate! What a height of irresponsibility! Out of the school compound, he started walking towards the India Gate and asked a pedestrian the way to Karnataka Bhavan. The person who happened to be a decent citizen and not a crook told him *"Bacha, wo to kafi door hai, rickshaw karo"* Devdatta had no money with him. But he hired the vehicle which dropped him at the Karnataka Bhavan. The rickshaw driver also happened to be a normal law-abiding person. If any of the two were to be a crook, anything might have happened. A boy of twelve, a total stranger to the city, could easily have been abducted for a demanding ransom. At about the same time, a gory incident had taken place. Chopra children (Chopra—an Air Force Officer), a brother and a sister were abducted and later on killed in Buddha Jayanti Park by criminal Billa. The motivation—just some amount as ransom.

I got so appalled by the incident that I suggested Devdatta to reject the admission to Delhi Public School and join some other school. But he would have none of it. He insisted on continuing in Delhi Public School, Mathura Road. In the meanwhile, I secured accommodation after about a month's stay in the Guest-House, in Motibagh. It was an excellent ground floor flat, with a lawn in front, a garage and servants-quarters. Not far away was the Delhi Public School branch of Ramakrishnapuram. But Devdatta did not change the school. He continued to go to D.P.S. on Mathura Road and eventually passed his School Leaving Examination from the school before joining the IIT.

An Educational Problem

Daughter Medha's admission to the Commerce College proved more problematic. She had completed at Belgaum her first year of the B.Com. course. At Delhi University, they insisted that she join the first year again, since Delhi University had an integrated course of three years. This meant she had to lose one year for no fault of hers. I could see how the lack of uniformity in the educational system on an all India basis could render havoc with the education of children of the transferable government servants. We were not prepared to give up so easily. We decided to take up the matter with the University authorities. Shri Chakku's brother-in-law Shri Wanchu was the Registrar of Delhi University. We addressed a letter to him explaining Medha's case and asking for her admission to the second year as she had passed the first year examination and she should not be made to suffer for no fault of hers. After much effort, the Delhi University conceded to the argument and agreed to admit her to the second year of the B. Com. course as an exceptional case. This was a great relief. Medha joined the Vankateshwar College of the southern campus of Delhi University.

My Charge

Meanwhile I was settling down in Krishi Bhavan. I got a good room for my office. There were two Joint Secretaries in the department. Apart from me there was the other Joint Secretary Shri Balkrishnan (who was Registrar of NICD Mussorie) was in charge of the Department of Civil Supplies which at that time was engaged in building up a network of public distribution system. Though I was in charge of Cooperation, NCDC (National Cooperative Development Corporation) was not in my jurisdiction. Shri V.B.L. Mathur was its Managing Director and dealt directly with Secretary Thapar, both belonging to Rajasthan cadre. I had a competent Director as my deputy Shri Krishnamuthi—who later became Chief

Secretary West Bengal under the Marxist Government. As J.S., I was Government's representative on the Board of Directors of IFFCO. The competent and experienced Paul Pothan was its Managing Director. It had fertilizer factories in Kalol, Kandla, Kutch in Gujarat, which were run with professional competence and did better than public and private sector fertilizer factories. It produced urea and other chemical fertilizers. As a Director, I always supported Paul Pothan in managing the enterprise in a professional manner.

Soon after I took over I called on Shri Nirmal Mukarji ICS, who was the Cabinet Secretary. It was only a formal call. During Indira Gandhi's days he was the Home Secretary. When the Judge, Sinha declared her election as invalid, Mukarji convened a meeting of officers to consider how the post-judgement situation should be handled. This did not endear him to the Prime Minister who summarily removed him from the powerful post of Home Secretary and appointed him as Secretary Civil Aviation. Now when Indira was out of power and her opponent Morarji became Prime Minister, Mukarji was selected as Cabinet Secretary. Morarji earlier had known him when he was Chairman Administrative Reforms Commission and N.K. Mukarji the Secretary. Thus personal connections have much to do with the appointments of civil servants!

Soon on my joining, a meeting of all officers in the Ministry – some sort of get together – was arranged. I was one amongst many. It was summer and I was wearing a long sleeve Khadi bushshirt. At the get together, Dr. P.C. Alexander, Secretary, Department of Commerce, addressed deferentially to me as "Sir". I was surprised. He had mistaken me as the Deputy Minister (or Minister of State) in the Ministry. Later on he realized his mistake. But it betrayed his attitude to politicians in power. It was this attitude that took him far in later life. But for the time being he was in trouble. He was an Emergency recruit to IAS. He belonged to Kerala cadre but had managed to stay at the centre without once serving in the cadre state. This was a clear violation of the IAS stipulation of rotating the postings of civil servants – serving partly in the state and partly at the centre. So as soon as the non-Congress government came, his was one of the names included in the list of officers to be repatriated to the states. This was not obviously to his liking. He managed to get selected for a UN job in the Trade Centre of Geneva under GATT. At a farewell function he boasted that he would return to a higher position in government. It was not an empty boast. He returned as Principal Secretary to Prime Minister Indira Gandhi when she returned to power. It was not an appointment that took place in the normal course. Alexander had cleverly worked for it. In his book "My days with Indira Gandhi" Alexander recalls how he sought on opportunity to meet her during her visit to Geneva when she was out of power and narrated her the tale of his "victimization" by the Janata Government. This is how clever civil servants play on the sensitivities of the politicians – the "victimised" politician was sensitive to the plight of a "victimised" civil servant.

On Alexander leaving the post of Secretary Commerce, Thapar, who was Secretary Cooperation and Civil Supplies, quickly jumped to occupy the "Coveted" post and Shri Anil Muzumdar of 1949 batch of Maharashtra cadre who was holding the post of Additional Secretary, moved up in the post vacated by Thapar. In the function felicitating both the officers, I, speaking on behalf of the Dept. of Cooperation (Pratap Kaul who was Additional Secretary in the Dept. of Commerce spoke on behalf of that department) asserted that it was a pity that the post of Secretary Department of Commerce which dealt with the exporters who were interested in profit is considered to be "coveted" while the of Department of Cooperation and Civil Supplies which dealt with the fortunes of the common people – farmers and ordinary consumer – was considered to be a poor relative. It was my usual frankness of expression but it may not have endeared me to the powerful civil servants in the Dept. of Commerce and I should have realized it.

As Joint Secretary I missed very much the touch with the people that I had as Divisional Commissioner. I felt it as a climb down from the lofty position of the Divisional Commissioner in the local administrative set up to the position of one among many Joint Secretaries in the vast empire of Government of India. But now I had the opportunity to contribute to the policy formulation at the level of the Central government.

Cooperative Policy Resolution

The opportunity came when it was mooted to convene the annual conference of the Ministers of Cooperation preceded by that of the Registrars of cooperative societies of all the states. I always liked working on All India canvas. I decided to set up a path breaking agenda rather than routine items before these conferences – in the shape of a comprehensive national policy on cooperation. Last time this was attempted was way back in the year 1958 when the National Development Council approved a resolution on the subject but it was confined to the setting up of Reiffeisen type of small primary credit cooperatives in the villages as against large size viable primary cooperatives recommended by the Rural Credit Survey Committee report. The ambit of that resolution was limited. What was required was a comprehensive guideline-type statement regarding cooperative development in all sectors of the economy. Two decades had elapsed since 1958 resolution. During that period notable cooperative development and diversification had taken place as a part of planned process of development in different sectors of the economy. Sectoral developments and inter-sectoral links had to find a place in the first comprehensive resolution on cooperation after independence. I attempted such a formulation. A diversified and developed cooperative movement needed managerial upgradation and human resource development. A resolution should not just chalk out goals. It should also deal with implementation. A policy should be translated into action. I therefore, prepared a 42-point action programme as a follow up of the policy resolution. I prepared the two papers single handedly without any support from the office.

When Thapar, the Secretary, got my papers he approved of the idea of a comprehensive cooperative policy resolution being placed on the agenda of the forthcoming conference. He made verbal changes in the formulation but retained its essential structure. Minister Dharia also approved. The resolution was duly discussed at the two conferences and passed. Dharia as Minister, took credit for this achievement and gave a prominent place to the policy resolution and 42 point action programme in his budget speech in Parliament. Thus the policy resolution got the stamp of approval of the Parliament itself. But Dharia never felt like giving credit that was due to the author of the resolution. This is often the fate of civil servants who do not tomtom their achievements.

Another initiative I took was a proposal to set up a cooperative commission. The cooperative movement was completing seventy-five years of existence. It was time to critically and comprehensively review its performance, identify its shortcomings as well as achievements and opportunities for future development and chalk out future course of development. Secretary Muzumdar supported the proposal and Dharia as usual enthusiastically took it up with the Cabinet. But there it remained pending and no decision was available. I felt disappointed.

Many years after he was no more a Minister, Dhania in his retirement years in Pune took credit for both the cooperative policy resolution and proposal for Cooperative Commission as highlights of his achievement as Minister for Cooperation at the Centre. He explained that when the proposal for the Commission was about to be taken by the Cabinet, Morarji Government collapsed.

Promotion

While I was just a year old in my job as Joint Secretary in the department of Cooperation, I had a pleasant surprise. I got a phone message that I should see Maheshwar Prasad, Secretary (Personnel). When I went to see him, he told me that I was being appointed as Establishment Officer in the Department. This was a post at the higher level of Additional Secretary. I was the first in my batch of 1953 to be appointed to the post after 25 years in the IAS. A sense of exhilaration ran in my being at getting this promotion without any effort. How would I account for this stroke of good luck when a crucial promotion came so unexpected? Moreover E.O's was considered to be a coveted and powerful post. Obviously Yardi's *Gaj Kesari Yoga,* which he predicted for me while leaving Belgaum was making itself felt! But Yardi had also predicted that the stroke of good luck would also create enemies. In the euphoria of unexpected promotion. I had forgotten that.

CHAPTER 17

Establishment Officer (1978-80)

Working for the Appointments Committee of the Cabinet

The job of the EO has been to deal with appointments under the Central Government. The appointments of all officers at the level of Deputy Secretary and above are made by the Appointments Committee of the Cabinet. The funny thing about this committee is that it never meets though few people outside the system know this! The EO is the Secretary of this important committee which never meets. But as Secretary, it is he who submits proposals regarding appointments for the approval of the Appointments Committee which normally consists of the Prime Minister, the Home Minister and the Minister concerned.

Independent Department of Personnel

The office of the EO is in the North Block next to the room of the Home Secretary. For the first time I had my office in the North Block. The very location of the office was a matter of prestige! The two massive buildings of red stones in front of the Rashtrapati Bhavan facing each other are known as the South Block and the North Block. They house the most powerful ministries of the Central government, the South Block houses Ministries of External Affairs, the office of the Prime Minister and the Defence Ministry while the North Block houses the influential Finance Ministry and the powerful Home Ministry.

For a long time the portmanteau Home Ministry was also in charge of establishment matters. It was the Administrative Reforms Commission (1967-70) which recommended the creation of a separate Department of Personnel working directly under the Prime Minister. But the PM, the Chief Executive of the Government of India, has so many important responsibilities of overwhelming nature that he could hardly have any time to attend to a department like that of Personnel. A separate Minister for the department was inevitable. A Minister of State—a minister of the second rank was entrusted with the day to day work of the Department When I joined, the post was held by Shri Sonu Singh Patil of Chalisgaon. He was known to Morarji Desai since his earlier days as the Chief Minister of Bombay Province. Since those days he was in oblivion. Morarji obviously never forgot his old associates and remembered them when he came to the helm of office. Sonu Singh was one of his old associates and so was Tapase, the Harijan Minister in his Bombay government who was almost forgotten till Morarji made him Governor of Haryana. Sonu Singh was old type Congressman wearing a Khadi cap and a dhoti. Soon I called on him. I found him a pleasant agreeable type of a person. I learnt that it was to Sonu Singh that I owed my appointment and through whom the *Gajkesari* yoga fulfilled itself! When I called on him and Cabinet Secretary Nirmal Mukarji, I realized what had happened. Mukarji put up a list of first ten officers of 1953 batch who were due for appointment as Additional Secretary and it was Sonu Singh who picked up my name from the list. Sonu Singh after going through the list might have chosen a Marathi speaking officer—a fact which he might have gathered from the personal files put up to him. Sonu Singh had not sent for me before selecting me and so for as I was concerned, I felt free to work as I liked without any sense of personal obligation to Sonu Singh Patil. Nor did I feel it necessary to reflect his wishes in my proposals or recommendations nor see him oftener then necessary. Sonu Singh obviously was not fond of the Personnel Secretary, Maheshwar Prasad, and would have liked me to be his counterweight and help the Minister to checkmate him. But I was too straight forward a person either to understand the situation or to be of help in this unstated desire of the Minister.

Appointments are a matter of vested interests. So every body wants to take interest in it and bring to bear influence on appointments. Mukarji knew this and had told the Prime Minister that his personal staff should not interfere in matters of appointments. Mukarji's finger was obviously towards PM's powerful Secretary Shri V. Shanker. He was a retired officer of the ICS of Bombay cadre and had served Morarji when he was Chief Minister, Bombay. He was known as close to Sardar Patil and a powerful civil servant. But by getting Morarji's assurance of non-interference in personnel matters, Mukharji had effectively neutralized him. Morarji's Personal Secretary was his loyal old servant Shri Y.V. Tonpe. He was a Marathi person from Solapur. He was a pleasant low lying person doing his job unlike Dhavan,

Indira Gandhi's personal secretary who had become so powerful during Emergency days that it was widely talked that even senior civil servants of the IAS aspiring to be Secretaries had to first call on him before being considered!

So being free from the baleful influence of interference, I could do my job without being required to succumb to influence. Some months later Mukarji told me that he was snooping on me and found that I was a straightforward officer who did not come under the influence of power or money in appointment matters. I was somewhat amused that he should think it necessary to snoop on me and himself tell me about it. But it indicated how it is believed that people in position to make appointments could misuse the authority. Obviously I was innocent of all such possibilities.

Importance of EO

But for civil servants, approach to the EO was of importance. My own predecessor Shri U.C. Agarwal of Orissa cadre 1952 held that position for quite some time and had become an indispensable EO. He was one of those officers who was removed under the Janata rule and had reverted to the state Government. He was the one who had desired to penalize me for refusing to go to Mussorie by removing my name from the list of officers acceptable to the Central government. He called on me soon after I took charge. Obviously he had been surprised by my selection for the post and had never expected it. He told me that EO's was a thankless task. Another unexpected visitor was Shri Romesh Bhandari of the Indian Foreign Service. He was then Additional Secretary in the Ministry of External affairs. When he entered in my room the fragrance of the rich perfume wafted. He was obviously given to rich style of living and atter and perfumes were a conspicuous part of it. He had no particular work but wanted to be acquainted with a civil servant holding the august position of EO. Another officer who came for no reason was Shri S.V.S. Juneja, Joint Secretary in the Ministry of Economic Affairs. He just wanted to know the officer who was holding the position of EO.

My own batch mates were obviously jealous about my being the first to be appointed as Additional Secretary and remained to be the only one to hold the position for five months. The first in my batch was Shri S. Venkitramanan then Managing Director SPIC. He came all the way from Madras to see me. Another to come was Smt. Pratibha Trivedi of Assam cadre. She tried to probe as to how I was selected – whether I had brought to bear any special influence.

I told her that first ten names were considered and I was selected. I realized later that my candidness in telling her so proved to be my undoing. Yardi's forecast of machinations of colleagues jealous at my *gaj kasari yog* was to come true.

My smooth and timely elevation to the post of Additional Secretary made me complacent. I started feeling that my road to the eventual elevation to the post of Secretary was open. I had only to work with my usual zest, commitment and honesty and God will take care of me. But I had not reckoned for the jealousy and manipulation of my own batch mates. With change in political government, I was to realize this

Central Staffing Scheme

But I am anticipating. Let me go back to my job as EO. On my appointment as EO I immersed with full zest in my work. I had never previously worked in the field of personnel administration though in all my previous positions I, as head of variety of offices was concerned with it in one way or another. But now I was holding the position concerned with higher appointments in the whole range of offices and organizations coming under the preview of Central Government. The appointments were under what was known as the "central staffing scheme". The scheme envisaged that the Central Government would draw on the cadres of All India and Central Services to fill up the positions. The prominent All India Service is of course the IAS whose officers though distributed amongst various state cadres are deputed to central government in course of their careers. But there were two other All India Services, *viz.* Indian Police Service and the Indian Forest Service which being functional services (as compared with the IAS which has been a "general service") had a delimited scope in holding positions. The same was the position regarding the central services like the Audit and Accounts services, Income Tax and Revenue Services and the Postal Service. The position of Central Secretariat Service was somewhat different. It was specifically meant to provide officers to hold junior positions in the Central Secretariat but they did aspire to rise higher and hold senior positions in the Central govt. One exception was that of Shri Prem Kirpal who rose to become Education Secretary. Another example was that of Shri V.P. Menon who rose from position of a stenographer to become the most powerful Secretary in charge of reorganization of states under Sardar Patel. But his was an exceptional case. Generally all the All Indian Services and Central Services resented the dominant position of the IAS in the Central Government. They got the opportunity when they succeeded in getting one of the working groups of the Administrative Reforms Commission recommend that for IAS also a functional role should be defined so that officers of the service do not have a free run. It was N.K. Mukarji then Cabinet Secretary who was the Secretary of the Commission. He belonged to the last batch of the ICS and had enjoyed all the privileges of the dominant position of the ICS and particularly the sudden opportunities available to them after the vacuum created by departure of British officers of the ICS but for strange reason appeared to be reluctant to provide the same opportunities to IAS, the successor to ICS. As Cabinet Secretary, he wanted to appear to be fair and sensitive to the aspirations of the non-IAS services—so that in every case of promotion to the position of J S and above there would be some non-IAS officers. When I was promoted to the position of Additional Secretary there were two other non-IAS officers simultaneously promoted. I did not particularly appreciate this bending backward position of N.K. Mukarji but I did not want to be unfair either. I rather thought that the basic point was not to pay attention to inter-service rivalries but match the requirement of positions with the qualifications and experience of an officer. In the inter-service rivalries and the manipulations of ambitious officers with the help of supporting politicians, basic considerations were overlooked and the country did not get the best out of their services. I considered appointments not as isolated episodes but part of career development of an officer from recruitment to retirement so that his or her talent flowers with experience, and the nation gets the best benefit of its human resources available in civil services.

There was a system of selecting officers from various services and including them in the panels of officers suitable for the positions of Deputy Secretary and Joint Secretary. For the higher positions the panels would be prepared on the basis of scrutiny by committees of officers. Mukarji did not feel it necessary to have such panels for the post of Additional Secretaries and Secretaries.

There was the Establishment Board under the Chairmanship of EO and Senior Establishment Board under the Chairmanship of the Cabinet secretary of which Personnel Secretary was a member and the EO, the Secretary. These Boards dealt with issues relating to the appointments at respective levels.

EO's Independent Position

Though EO was in the Personnel Department, he worked in an independent fashion and did not send his papers to the Cabinet

Secretary through the Personnel Secretary. This distinguished him from other officers in the department. There was an Additional Secretary in charge of Administrative Reforms and Training and a Joint Secretary in charge of personnel matters. Under the EO there was a separate foreign assignments section which maintained a bank of information relating to officers suitable for and interested in foreign assignments. A senior Deputy Secretary was in charge of this section.

The daily stock in trade of the EO consisted of files relating to appointments. First in consultation with departments concerned, proposals for appointments were worked out. The department notified to EO the posts falling vacant and asked for suitable names. The EO's office would look into the list of officers cleared for appointments and suggest a few names. The department could go through the suggested names and make their choice. Sometimes they could ask for more names. The Department would finally make the choice in which Minister had the ultimate say.

On receipt of the final recommendation of the Ministry, the proposal would be put up on file to the Appointments Committee of the Cabinet. It would consist of the Minister of the Department concerned, the Home Minister (Shri Charan Singh at that time) and the Prime Minister. For sometimes after the appointment of H.M. Patel, Home Minister was not a member and I would put up the proposal directly to the Prime Minister. The files would generally come back promptly with the signature of the Prime Minister Morarji Desai. There was a time when the number of posts at the level of Deputy Secretary and Joint Secretary was very small. But over years the number had grown and there were some 500 posts of Deputy Secretary and more than 200 posts of Joint Secretary. PM needed hardly to be bothered regarding appointment to the post of Deputy Secretary.

After some experience I realized that a number of files regarding appointment at the level of Deputy Secretary need not really go to the Prime Minister. But this needed an amendment to the rules regarding the jurisdiction of ACC which everybody was reluctant to make and I did not initiate the proposal.

Sonu Singh Patil once described the procedure of appointment as similar to matrimonial matchmaking. That appeared to be an apt comparison. The work of the EO appeared to be of routine character. Shri U.C. Agarwal called it a "useless job".

Human Resource Development

Nevertheless selecting a right person for a job was an important task which could not be considered as an ordinary routine. The whole performance of a department and ultimately of the government. as a whole depended on the right choice of a person. A square peg in a round hole would not do. He could bring down the level of performance. But the importance of a right choice was often ignored in the routine working of government. Indeed a single appointment is a stage in the "career development" of an individual officer. But the concept of career development and its relation to administrative performance and standard was overlooked in government. Job performance, job rotation, on the job and in service training are all elements of a dynamic process of human recourse development in government. But what existed in government was careerism rather than career development. Sustained programme of human resource development for raising administrative performance had no conscious place in governmental administration.

Apart from the posts in the government proper, there were also posts in the Public Sector Enterprises. For selecting persons for these posts, a Public Sector Enterprise Selection Board (PESB) was constituted. When I was EO, Shri Rajadhyaksha formerly Chairman Hindustan Lever and later member, Planning Commission was the Chairman PSEB. The PSEB would send the proposals based on the selections to EO to getting clearance of the ACC. Normally there was not much to do except to submit the proposal to the ACC. In rare cases where presumably some influential persons approached the PMO, the proposal would come back unapproved asking the PESB to reconsider.

Meeting with H.M. Patel

Sometime after I became EO, Shri Yashwant Rajawade, Private Secretary to the Finance Minister Shri H.M. Patel met me and suggested that I pay a courtesy call on him. I did so. H.M. Patel had a huge reputation as a competent and effective ICS officer who worked indefatigably to deal with post-partition problems of administration. But when he was Finance Secretary, he got involved in Mundhra Scandal and had to retire from ICS in disgrace. But he made a comeback in politics first as an active person in Swatantra Party led by Rajaji and later joined the first non-congress government at centre of Janata party headed by fellow Gujarati Morarji Desai. When I called on H.M. Patel and told him that I was holding a position once held by him, he pompously told me that the post was then very important (implying that it was no longer important now). I felt touched to the quick and told him that the EO has now to deal with many more posts and services besides the newly created Foreign Assignment section. Patel was not the one to brook any resistance much less from a junior like me. A few months later on the departure of Charan Singh from Government he became the Home Minister but for some strange reason was not appointed as a member of ACC and I had to send the proposals directly to PM. He resented this and held it against me. Later he took it on me in some meeting he had called for discussing some case of deputation to a foreign assignment. When I cited a circular in relation to a point he was making, he suddenly flared up and before everybody including the Personnel Secretary shouted at me "Don't talk nonsense." H.M. Patel was known as an aggressive type and I got the heat. I did not walk out of the meeting in protest nor did I argue further with him. But calmly carried on. In retrospect I wonder whether I should have meekly borne the insult. Lokmanya Tilak had once said that half the salary of a civil servant is for bearing the insult. Patel did not think it necessary to apologise at least later for his incivility to a younger officer who was only doing his duty. He behaved like a high handed village headman which name he bore!

Establishment Manual

The work of EO, I found, was governed by a large number of orders and circulars and felt that they should all be brought together in the form of an Establishment Manual. I did so and sent a copy to Cabinet Secretary Shri N.K. Makarji. I thought I was the first EO to produce such a manual systematising the instructions regarding various aspects of establishment matters. A few days later he sent it back appreciating the effort but cautioning that codification might cause rigidities. I felt disappointed at his reaction. In administration initiatives and innovations are rare and when made are not always appreciated.

Cases of Some Individual Officers

Officers, senior and junior, belonging to all services often met me with their requests for placements or foreign assignment. They belonged to all services. My door, as always, was open to all and I was courteous and considerate to all – with none of the high headed posture of EO in a position to bestow favours. Once Smt. Kiran Bedi came with a request for deputation under some foreign assignment opportunity. I was impressed by her personality and recommended her name but Sonu Singh for his own reason turned it down. I did not go and tell Sonu Singh to change his orders. Somehow I did not relish doing that when I had made my recommendations on an objective basis why should it be necessary to do a personal pleading?

Once Shri M. Varadurajan a senior officer of the IAS phoned me requesting for an appointment at home. I gave it to him. He came shedding tears on his personal predicament due to family trouble. His wife had been difficult – a harassment and he sought escape by getting a posting in Indian High Commission in London. I helped him and he got the posting. But when as Director Indian Institute of Public Administration, I had to on a occasion to briefly visit London he hardly remembered the favour done to him and did not feel it necessary to show any courtesy such as inviting me for lunch. I learnt later that he abandoned his Tamil wife, married a Kashmeri Muslim woman and became a member of the Minority Commission. His son Siddharth Varadrajan became an assistant editor in *Times of India* always writing vigorously for the rights of minority and in favour of secularism and taking every opportunity to attack BJP government. at Delhi.

Another senior officer whom I helped was Shri A.F. Couto, my batch mate in getting a job in the Commonwealth Secretariat. He went on phoning me, addressing me as "boss" to flatter me. He got the job but after he got it, he hardly ever remembered me. Such are the ways of the world.

Did Not Help Myself

While I was keen to help others, I was unconcerned about helping myself – leaving it to God. Many people felt that now that I had got into a crucial position I should be able to get a UN job with a fat salary. Once UNDP asked for a panel. Sonu Singh picked up several names putting me at the top. We forwarded the panel. I thought automatically, in the fullness of time I would be picked up and did nothing more. I found my confidence and optimism misplaced. I waited but nothing happened. Later on, when I spoke to Secretary External Affairs Shri S.K. Singh, he said that a word should have gone from PM's office to Bradford Morse, Administrator UNDP for the proposal to fructify. Later on I felt that if only I had asked

Sonu Singh he would have definitely put in a word for me. But my reluctance to use political influence came in my way. Meanwhile Shri R.K. Dar whose name figured down in the panel suggested, was picked up. The realization of what I should have done dawned on me far too late. By that time Sonu Singh had gone out of office after the collapse of the Morarji government.

Fall of Morarji Government

The fall of Morarji Government was a shocking development of the sordid political drama at the Center. Internal bickerings became the undoing of Morarji government. Ambitious Charan Singh walked out of Morarji government with his supporters. Sanjay Gandhi engineered the breach with a promise of Congress support to a government headed by Charan Singh. The latter was lured and fell into the trap. Morarji not given to underhand dealings and political manoeuvring lost the vote of confidence. At the last moment even George Fernandes who gave a thundering speech in Morarji's favour deserted him. Charan Singh with Congress support became the PM fulfilling his life-long ambition. Congress (O) joined his government. Their parliamentary leader Shri Yashwantrao Chavan became the Deputy Prime Minister. Morarji government, the first non-congress government at the Center lasted for just a couple of years.

But Sanjay made a fool of Charan Singh. As soon as he was sworn in as PM, Congress withdrew the support and his government came into a minority. Shri Sanjeev Reddy, the President should have dismissed him and given a chance for an alternative government to be formed under the leadership of the Harijan leader Shri Jagjeevan Ram waiting in the wings who had every chance of forming an alternative government. But President Reddy gave him no such chance. Charan Singh knowing that he would not be able to get the vote of confidence in Parliament did not face Parliament even for a day. Instead he asked the President to order fresh elections. He lingered on for five months as Prime Minister till fresh elections were held. Such was the mockery of Indian democracy!

Charan Singh was himself responsible for his unenviable position as PM. He could not have expected Indira Gandhi to support his government. It was he who had treated her in a ham handed fashion and ordered her arrest. To be sure, Shah enquiry had brought out the misdeals of the Emergency rule. But apparently there was no legal evidence available enough to warrant her arrest. Indira took full advantage of Charan Singh's revengeful but foolish act and from the day of her arrest she was on the comeback trail. With Sanjay's advice, she designed her crafty plan of bringing down Morarji's government, thanks to the ambition of Charan Singh to be PM which made him blind to Indira's real intention. In retrospect it appeared that Charan Singh had no regret or remorse and was happy that he could be even a lame duck PM. Equally thoughtless was the otherwise balanced Yashwantrao Chavan who agreed to join Charan Singh and got the consolation prize of being Deputy Prime Minister. There was hardly any love lost between Chavan and Charan Singh and no meeting of minds and it was only a marriage of convenience. But hunger for power made Chavan agree to an untenable arrangement.

Charan Singh Government – A Travesty

Charan Singh government had no political legitimacy. It was reflected in governance which became a travesty. The government. lacked leadership and direction and could not take any initiative. It was living from day to day carrying on administrative chores without any sense of purpose. For full five months this pretence of governance under discredited leadership went on. There was a distinct anomie in administration. I carried on submitting papers to the ACC, i.e., Deputy Prime Minister and Prime Minister. It often happened that proposals approved by Dy PM were not agreed to by PM and some other name was approved. As was the practice in the past, PM was the final authority and his orders were acted upon. We did not stop to resolve the contradictions between the Dy PM and the PM, One day Shri Sharad Kale, Private Secretary to Shri Chavan, the Dy PM, sharply reminded me that it was a coalition govt. and PM's orders which went against the approval given by Dy PM could not be treated as final. I pointed out my predicament and suggested that in such cases it was for the Dy PM to take up such matters with PM. But he never did, because Dy PM himself knew of the nature of his government and lacked the will to take up such cases with Charan Singh with whom he did not seem to have any relationship – cordial or otherwise. Chavan was sitting only a few rooms away in the chamber of the Home Minister and never held officers' meeting. He never sent for me nor did I seek an appointment to meet him which in retrospect I feel was a great pity. As a Marathi speaking person, I could have established immediate rapport. But somehow the underlying feeling in my mind of revulsion against him for joining the illegitimate government of Charan Singh in number two position, made me feel that I should not go near him.

Change of Appointment

It was during this listless period that the Cabinet Secretary, Shri Mukarji once sent for me and suddenly broached the proposal of my appointment to position of Additional Secretary in the Department of Culture which was falling vacant. I had completed only about a year as EO and Mukarji's proposal was unexpected. He made it clear that I should not take it as a proposal to remove me from the post of EO – that I was unwanted. It was only an offer for a change for me to consider. I met Shri A.C. Gill holding the position of Additional Secretary (Culture) – he was being appointed as Secretary of the Minorities Commission – and asked him about the advisability of my joining as AS (Culture). He was distinctly unenthusiastic and discouraged me form taking the post. All that he had to do is AS (Culture) was to face the fiercely contending claims of ambitious artists and "culture vultures". He did not tell me that it was an independent charge in the Ministry of Education and there were opportunities for travel abroad for signing cultural agreements. I perhaps wanted to stick on to what was considered to be an influential position. I did not ask Mukarji to consider me for an alternative position as say AS in Economic Affairs which would have suited my economic background. I simply told him that I was not interested in his offer. He did not try to dissuade me from my position nor did he try to point out the opportunities available to AS culture. But in retrospect I feel he had reasons to offer me the post. He had sensed the end of the lame duck government and return of Indira Gandhi to power and wanted me to go to a less visible position. But he did not share with me his reasons for making the offer I might as well have taken his offer. Opportunities once lost never return. But my mood then was that opportunities were always there waiting for me!

It was soon after the fall of Morarji that Shri Kailash Prakash of the Indian Postal Service, who soon after my appointment as EO started seeing me, frequently suggested that I meet Morarji whom I had not met when he was PM. As Secretary of ACC of which he was the Chairman in his capacity as PM, I should have sought an appointment and met him. But I never went to PMO and met neither V. Shankar his secretary or Shri Tonape his Private Secretary, nor of course the PM. I did not feel it necessary. But this again was a mistake. It was my failure to deliberately cultivate relationship with influential politicians that cost me dearly. Now Shri Kailash Prakash told me that politicians out of power were easy to meet. I was tempted and went to meet Morarji. As soon as I arrived in his presence, he with his shining head without the Gandhi cap brusquely asked me whether I had kept away from my office work to meet him. I told him that I had come to give a lecture in a nearby building in the Army Officers Staff College and thought of paying him a courtesy call. He said nothing further and after some uneasy time with him, I took my leave. Even out of power, Morarji was his usual self.

Indira Gandhi's Comeback

The inevitable happened. General elections took place and Indira Gandhi returned in triumph. The impossible happened. No one had imagined that Indira Gandhi so thoroughly discredited during Emergency could make a comeback so soon. But the squabbling politicians of Janata Dal made that possible. They brought down their own government and made way for Indira Gandhi.

From the day, she assumed office, Secretary (Personnel) Shri Maheshwar Prasad became shaky. He started saying that his was the first head which would be on the chopping block. Obviously being of UP cadre he had previous connections with Indira Gandhi and was probably not her favourite. It was only after she lost power in Delhi that he could come to Delhi as Secretary with the blessings of Charan Singh. I felt no such fears because though I had been elevated to the post of Additional Secretary during Janata Dal regime, I had approached no politician for such favour. But perhaps perceptions of others were different and I was to prove wrong.

Maheshwar Prasad always appeared to me of a secretive nature. Sonu Singh did not trust him and in his confidential report described him as "not clubbable "! I wondered where Sonu Singh had picked up this phrase. I had not much occasion to interact with him as my work as EO was of an independent nature. But occasionally according to his convenience he held internal staff meetings to which two Additional Secretaries and the Joint Secretary Mattoo were invited. These meetings had no subjects on the agenda. He had some files to decide upon and sounded the officers on the decisions relating to the files. He kept the files to himself and without going through them it was not correct to express any opinion but this was exactly what he solicited. Once he raised the question regarding the rule which laid down that an IAS officer who sought to change his cadre should be put below all other officers of the same year of recruitment to IAS. Smt. Pratibha Handa – had joined Assam Cadre of her husband P.H. Trivedi and was ranked accordingly – below her husband who had been much lower in the IAS list of successful candidates of 1953. But when Pratibha learnt that my appointment to EO was on the basis of consideration of candidates from the first ten of 1953, she got the hint. She went and argued with Personnel Secretary Maheshwar Prasad that though she was lower in rank in the Assam state cadre, she should be restored to her original position in the All India list. Shri Maheshwar Prasad was trying to push the idea of separating state level decisions relating to IAS officers from the center level decisions. Thus though an IAS officer was not approved for inclusion in the panel of Joint Secretary, at the Centre, he could be promoted to the same super-time scale level in the state. One rule for State and another for the Center for the officers of an All India cadre was perhaps not a sound approach. But he stead fastly followed the approach. When he raised the point at the meeting, it did not immediately strike me that the point was raised at the instance of Shri Pratibha Trivedi. It could go against me by placing her above me in the All India list. I came to know it when in the revised list of All India seniority she was shown above me I did not immediately protest feeling that the change would not make much of a difference. But I was wrong. It did affect my future adversely. Too late did I realise that one could not afford to be complacent or less than vigilant and fail to take counter action on time. If I had protested with cogent arguments I could have got the decision reversed and my seniority restored. That was not without consequences. It had a bearing on my promotion to the position of Secretary.

In the meanwhile 1980 elections saw Indira Gandhi returning in triumph. People disgusted with the internal squabbling of Janata politicians brought her back with a thumping majority. With her assumption of the office of PM, bureaucratic changes were bound to follow. The first to go, it was expected, would be the Cabinet Secretary, Mukarji. But Indira Gandhi kept him though with diminished power, influence and stature. On the other hand, Maheshwar Prasad's fears came true. He was unceremoniously repatriated to UP to hold the position of Chairman, Revenue Tribunal. But in my self complacency I thought I would not be touched. I kept on doing my work as usual. One of the first appointments I had to handle in the new dispensation was that of Shri R.K. Dhavan as Joint Secretary in PMO. When the proposal came I asked the Under Secretary to collect and provide information regarding his qualifications and experience to see whether they met with the stipulations laid down for the position of Joint Secretary in Government of India. But even before the information was made available to me pressure started building up. Personnel Secretary Shri Maheshwar Prasad who had not yet been repatriated phoned me asking me to expedite the case. I could see the importance of a normal scrutiny of the case. But at the same time I could also see that the posts in PMO were not treated as normal cases and were given a special treatment. Even in Morarji Government. that was the case. His Secretary Shri V. Shankar had long superannuated and therefore was not in the eligible group as also his Private Secretary, Shri Y.V. Tonpe who had retired long back but was brought back to hold a position in government. I therefore thought the better of it and issued orders regarding Dhavan's appointment.

Giani Zail Singh Gets his EO

There was excitement in the South Block as to who would be the Home Minister, Indira Gandhi appointed Shri Giani Zail Singh, previously the Chief Minister of Punjab. A thoroughly provincial politician, he had never worked before at the Center. He was a reputed speaker in Punjabi but was not supposed to be very familiar with English. After taking over as Home Minister, his very first act was to rush to Anandpur Saheb for thanks giving and seeking blessings of the Guru. He was expected, as Ministers do on assuming office, to hold a meeting of all officers in the Ministry but he did not feel it necessary to do so.

Instead, it was I who had a surprise in store. Zail Singh brought his own officer form Punjab Shri I.S. Bindra as his private secretary. He was known to me as Registrar of Cooperative of the State when I was Joint Secretary (Cooperation). After I issued orders of his appointment he called on me. I was glad that I had a known officer to go through to reach Minister when necessary. But the first thing he did was to convey to me his Minister's wish that he would like to have his own EO. I was shocked. A minister chooses his own private secretary. But he does not choose his senior officers according to his liking. This was a new theory being introduced in Indian Administrative system. The prevailing theory had always been that a Secretary is Secretary to Government and not to a Minister. But Gianji had little to do with it. His choice was a Punjab civilian Shri S.P. Bagla who was not even an officer of the level of Additional Secretary. His appointment had to be at the level of Joint Secretary. Bindra graciously added for my consolatory satisfaction that Minister had spoken to Agricultural Minister Rao Birender Singh, previously Chief Minister Haryana for my appointment as Additional Secretary in his Ministry. Zail Singh did not think it necessary even to meet me before making up his mind. I thought it an utterly discourteous treatment of a Senior Officer. Since he had already made up his mind, I did not think it necessary to meet him. Soon the file came of my transfer from the post of EO to that of AS in the Ministry of Agriculture. At the end of the proposal made on the file were letters in red ink "Indira Gandhi"—signature of the Prime Minister giving the stamp of approval to the transfer.

The journey back to Krishi Bhavan was not particularly unwelcome. I was familiar with the subject instead of going to "Culture" as proposed by Shri Nirmal Mukarji only a few months ago—a subject which I had not handled earlier, I was going to "Agriculture." What galled was the uncalled for transfer just because the minister wanted his own officer. This personalized approach to administrative transfer was the dangerous precedent of the ways to management of personnel administration which was likely to destroy the objectivity of Indian administration. The trend only increased in the years that followed.

As was my wont, I wrote an article on EO which was published in *IJPA*. It was an authentic article on that position not available till then in literature on Public Administration in India.

CHAPTER 18

Additional Secretary, Ministry of Agriculture (1980-81)

When I joined the Ministry of Agriculture as Additional Secretary, all my colleagues considered it as a demotion, a punishment and a loss of favour of the new government. I was blissfully unaware of all these implications. I took the transfer in stride. To be sure, I was in the job of EO for less than a couple of years. But perhaps that was enough. I was always interested in programmes of real development. But I was disappointed by the subjects allotted to me. There was the same old subject of cooperation with which I was concerned as Joint Secretary and Director of Cooperative Training and as Director VMNICM and would have liked something different. Besides, the Secretary of the Department was the Vice-Chairman of the National Cooperative Development Corporation of which the Additional Secretary was not even a member. That kept the real meat of cooperation out of the scope of work of Additional Secretary. It galled me but it was not my nature to ask for things to work for and manipulate to get them. I was content to do well what I had. In addition to cooperation there were smaller things like Agricultural Census and export of agricultural commodities. The latter was an important subject and was substantively handled in the Ministry of Commerce. The subject came to Agriculture Ministry only peripherally specially where cooperatives were to be involved in export business. Rarely did files on the subject came to me. Smt. Satyabhama of Tamil Nadu cadre was my Joint Secretary. She was also in that capacity, the Central Registrar of the cooperative societies. She was quite a competent and well informed officer but somewhat rigid in attitude. The Joint Secretary Smt. Snehlata Puri looked after the subject of agricultural exports. She appeared to be a law into herself and worked in her own way. The officers at lower levels in the

Department of Cooperation were the old ones whom I had known for years.

Dealing with a Scientist Secretary

The Secretary of the Department. was the well known agricultural scientist, Dr. M.S. Swaminathan. Working under the non-IAS secretary was a different experience. He was an extremely pleasant and courteous person and had excellent abilities to communicate. He had a PhD from Cambridge University and was an expert in genetics. With the association of the famous scientist Dr. Norman Borlough he helped in ushering the green revolution with Mexican varieties of hybrid wheat and Taiching and Tainan varieties of rice developed by the International Rice Research Institute. The revolution was brought about under the political leadership of Shri C. Subramaniam, an energetic Minster placed by Indira Gandhi in charge of agriculture. Swaminathan's entire career was in the Indian Agricultural Research Institute (IAPI) of which he became the Director after the retirement of Dr. B.P. Pal. I wondered why Swaminathan chose to move to the administrative job of Agricultural Secretary rather than the other job available in Ministry, *viz.* Secretary in charge of Agricultural Research. One reason could be that the former was considered to be the Senior Secretary. But the other reason was that he apparently desired to gain administrative experience which he thought would be useful in climbing to higher position. Though outwardly very mild in personality, obviously fierce ambition lurked behind as his future career was to show. Whatever that be, it was a pleasant experience to work with him.

As soon as I joined, after calling on Swaminathan I sought an appointment with the Minister Rao Birender Singh. I was surprised that I could not get it for quite a few days—hardly a proper way of treating a senior officer joining his Ministry. The meeting was only for a short time when some others were also present. Obviously, he had an air of authority of a political boss traditionally developed by Ministers in Haryana and Punjab. I later learnt that even to a distinguished scientist like Swaminathan he displayed the same kind of attitude. However I must say that neither at this first meeting nor later throughout my stay in the Ministry, was he particularly unpleasant to me. However he did give me a hint that I was eased out by Zail Singh and he had "accommodated" me.

Leading Central Task Force in Assam

Though holding a position of Additional Secretary, I did not find that I had responsibilities commensurate with my position. My job did not appear to be sufficiently challenging. However an opportunity came to undertake a challenging task. Prime Minister Indira Gandhi was for sometime concerned with growing unrest in the border state of Assam. Her conclusion regarding the cause of unrest was the lack of adequate employment opportunities for the youth. That led to the rise of the organization of Assam Student Union which got growing support amongst the people and threatened the traditionally unchallenged domination of the Congress party. As a political leader Indira Gandhi had to counter the trend. She thought—perhaps she was so advised—that the best way of creating employment opportunities was to boost the agricultural economy of Assam which was stagnating.

She decided, perhaps on Swaminathan's advice, to appoint a Central Task Force to visit Assam and produce a comprehensive report recommending measures for boosting the agricultural economy of Assam. Soon after the decision was taken, Swaminathan sent for me and asked me to suggest a name of an officer to lead the Task Force. I suggested several names. Swaminathan listened and turned towards me and suggested that I lead the Task Force. He had already made up his mind and taken his decision. His consulting me was only his way of broaching the proposal. As Additional Secretary in the Ministry I had of course to accept the proposal; which I did without hesitation. It was in my nature to accept responsibility in matters of national importance with enthusiasm. Swaminathan set up a truly multi disciplinary task force with representation of the various disciplines in the Indian Council of Agricultural Research—Dairy, Fishery, Horticulture, besides various inputs of agriculture like seeds, fertilizers etc. There were officers of Planning Commission as well who included Economist Smt. Barthakur, a Punjabi lady married to an Assammese who advocated Assamese cause with vigour. Apart from technical aspects, the task force had to attend to organizational aspects as well—administrative machinery, Co-operatives, Panchayats etc.

I had to complete the work of the Task force at the earliest. I, therefore, lost no time in convening the first meeting of the Task force at my office in the Ministry. Some 22 members of the Task Force—all professionals and experts in their own subjects attended. I told them of the task assigned and asked each member to produce tentative outlines of papers on the aspect with which they were concerned in the reorganization of the agricultural economy of Assam. Most of the members were able to prepare these outlines with the data available. At the second meeting which I convened after going through the papers, I worked out a plan of the visit to Assam. The team was divided into two groups—one concerned with Districts in the Brahmaputra valley and another with the hill districts. The itinerary covered every district in Assam.

On the appointed day, we landed at Guwahati. We camped in the circuit house on the bank of the mighty river Brahmaputra whose vast stretch from one bank to another with several islands made an impressive appearance. Our task force was reinforced by the officers of Assam Government in each of the areas of work. Cars were placed by the State Government at the disposal of our Task force.

We had planed for a punishing schedule of visiting all the districts. We would get up early morning, visit rural areas and hold detailed discussions with the district officers of all departments. The work would go on till late in the evening. We travelled by road from Guwahati to Nowgaon, to Shivsagar on to Dibrugarh and to North Lakhimpur to the north of Brahmaputra. I remembered a huge gathering in a village few miles from Dibrugarh where I addressed a meeting of villagers on various aspects of work of the Task Force. The sharp turn which Brahmaputra takes at Dibrugarh was a sight to see. The local newspaper *Assam Tribune* extensively reported on our work. We had of course a little diversion from rigorous work by way of visit to the famous Kaziranga Sanctuary where we moved on elephant's back to see the rhinos and tea factory at North Lakhimpur. The small packet of Assam tea that was offered to us was of high quality which produced tea which we greatly relished. We saw various stages of processing tea and tea tasting.

We concluded our itinerary with a meeting with Governor Shri L.P. Singh at Shillong in which officer of North East Council participated. Through all the visits and discussions at District and state levels, we collected a lot of information and ideas which provided valuable inputs to our report.

At the conclusion of our work we returned to Guwahati for taking a flight back to Delhi. But because of a strike called by the Assam Students Union, the flight was cancelled and we had to stay put at the circuit house—extending our stay. Instead of getting annoyed at this forced stay, I asked members of the Task Force to use the compulsory leisure to produce draft chapters of the Report. It was an excellent use of our spare time where members could do solid work at the quiet Circuit-House undisturbed by normal office work.

After return to Delhi, I met members of Task Force individually and in group and got individual chapters finalized. I myself wrote a chapter on cooperatives, panchayati raj institutions and administrative toning up as well as an introductory and a concluding chapter. Since I had held a number of meetings from the time the Task Force was constituted there was a great deal of meeting of minds among members. This enabled a certain consistency of approach among all the writers of separate chapters – so that the report became one consistent whole. We all realized that Assam had imminence potential – what was needed was streamlined and determined approach. The main idea was conveyed by the following words – "Assam is green but green revolution has not touched Assam." The consumption of chemical fertilizers and use of credit was lowest in the country. The cooperatives in rural areas were concerned more with the public distribution of consumer goods rather that supply of inputs. Agricultural investment was woefully inadequate and subsoil water potential was hardly tapped. Assam had one crop agricultural economy though two or even three crops could be easily grown. Horticulture in Assam had immense possibilities – a variety of fruits – pineapple, oranges, bananas could be grown in large quantities and processed but there were no fruit processing units. I prepared a twenty-five point action programme – points arising out of conclusions of individual chapters. This came handy for newspapers to publicize the findings and recommendations of the report of the Task Force.

Secretary of the Department, Dr. M.S. Swaminathan was happy with the report. We had done justice to the task entrusted to us. The report was comprehensive and yet pointed in its conclusions. It had chalked out a definite plan of action. What was remarkable was the fact that the report was presented in a fortnight of the return of the Task Force from Assam. Because the Task Force was appointed at the instance of PM herself, there was a top-level interest in government and administration. Minister Rao Birender Singh called a press conference at which all the members of the Task Force were present. I was asked to present the main finding of the report – which I did. Dr. Manmohan Singh, Deputy Chairman Planning Commission asked for two copies of Report. Overnight I came to be recognized as expert on Assam. Shri H.C. Sarin, who succeeded Shri L.P. Singh as Governor Assam, told me that he went through every chapter of the report and gave directions for follow up of various recommendations. I had every reason to feel satisfied with my mission as the leader of the Task Force, which I completed with a high degree of professionalism. Very few task forces or committees had such an achievement to its credit. I thought that the way in which the task was accomplished should be placed on record and widely shared. So I wrote a paper—*"Leading Task Force in Assam"* which was published in the *Indian Journal of Public Administration*.

But there was one aspect which was not covered in the report, *viz.* the political aspect. The atmosphere in Assam was greatly disturbed by the apprehension created in the public mind by continuous infiltrations from Bangladeshi Muslims from across the border. They had occupied villages after villages and taken control of land. Bangladesh was overpopulated and such infiltration could only be expected. Indeed immigration was not new to Assam. Because of the easy-going nature of the Assamese, hard working labour had immigrated from neighbouring states. The tea planters had employed Bihari labour force. And now Bangladeshis had taken to rice cultivation in several villages. The Assamese politicians like Sadulla and Fakhruddin Ali Ahmed had systematically encouraged the infiltration of Muslims which proved to be a solid vote bank Since Assamese were not alert, they had to blame themselves. Now that infiltration had assumed big proportion, they had woken up. During our visit to Assam a big literary gathering of *Assam Sahitya Parishad* was taking place at Nowgong where a resolution was passed for the repatriation of the infiltrators who were disturbing the demographic balance in Assam.

While presenting my report to Dr. Swaminathan, I brought this aspect to his notice. Since the appointment of the Task Force itself had a political background it was proper on my part to do so. I told him that the people of Assam had faith in Indira Gandhi. But they wanted her to change the Congress policy of ignoring the infiltration and take strict action to throw out the infiltrators.

Swaminathan was close to the Prime Minister and promptly conveyed this to her while giving her a copy of the report. PM took notice of this. While I was in Bombay to attend a regional conference on agriculture, I got a message from the PM's secretariat to immediately return to Delhi to meet the PM. So I took the first flight back to Delhi—only to be disappointed as it often happens in government. Krishna Swami Rao Saheb, secretary to PM said that the meeting had already taken place, Shri Vaishnav who was adviser in the Planning Commission and deputy leader of the Task Force had attended it and I did not have to meet PM. I felt disappointed and cheated!

My political advice, however, had its own impact. Indira Gandhi had almost decided on a crackdown on the student movement in Assam. But she postponed it at least for the time being.

After all the initial euphoria on my report, and Governor Sareen's interest, like all government. reports it also gathered dust on shelves and disappeared in the limbo of the oblivion. The elected government, which followed President's rule took no interest in the follow up action. I left the Ministry and was not in position to take follow up action.

Ten years later I had occasion to visit Assam as a member of NABARD's Expert Committee on rural credit. I tried to trace my report from government "archives". It was traced. I tried to get it circulated at the seminar on rural credit, which we had arranged. The local Development Commissioner was aware of the report. That was some satisfaction.

The Agricultural Census

Another notable event during my tenure as Additional Secretary, Agriculture was the conduct of the third census of agricultural holdings. From the point of understanding of the agricultural economy, this census was of great significance. It was carried out by local administration in the states and I had no direct role in actual conduct of the census. But I got an opportunity to go through the previous census reports. There were clear trends—the number of agricultural holdings was rapidly increasing, the average size was getting smaller, the number of large holdings was diminishing while that of marginal and small-holdings was increasing. I wrote a paper on the census which was published in the *Financial Express* and included in my book—"Essays on Development Administration."

KRIBHCO

A third important development was the establishment of KRIBHCO—Krushak Bharti Cooperatives to set up a giant fertilizer plant at Hajira in Gujarat. The entry of cooperatives in fertilizer business started with IFFCO—Indian Farmers Fertilizer Cooperative with its plants at Kalol-Kandla in Gujarat and Phulpur in UP. I was a government director on this cooperative both earlier as Joint Secretary and later as Additional Secretary. It was a success story. The fertilizer factory in the cooperative sector compared favourably with those in the public and private sectors. The credit went to its Managing Director, Shri Paul Pothen and several of his associates. KRIBHCO spawned out of IFFCO since it was felt that IFCO was already large enough and a separate cooperative for another large plant would be in order. It was to be a large fertilizer plant with 4 units each producing every day 1100 tons of urea with an investment of about Rs. 1,000/- crore. Government. had to nominate the first Board of Directors. The Minister Rao Birendar Singh could have nominated a non-official to be the first Chairman of the board. Posts of this type are often treated as a political patronage at the disposal of the Minister to favour their own people. But Rao Birendar Singh decided to appoint an official and the honour fell on me. I became the first Chairman of KRIBHCO. Paul Pothen the veteran fertilizer executive with long experience first in FACT in Kerala and then as first MD of successful IFFCO became the first MD of KRIBHCO. With him as the executive, the project was destined to succeed. All I had to do as Chairman was to give him full support. We could draw on the experienced personnel of IFFCO. From the beginning we laid down high standards of management with complete objectivity and professionalism. I must say to the credit of the Minister that he allowed us to do so and never once interfered in our work or asked us to hire *his* people. But that was during my tenure which proved to be short. About that later.

Though the Minister never interfered, there was interference at a higher level. Along with KRIBHCO another big plant at Thal Vaishet in Konkan in the public sector was to be set up. The two plants among themselves were a big opportunity for foreign fertilizer consultation companies to have their slice of cake. I was surprised to know that India had no technology of fertilizer production and had to acquire it from foreign firms. This was a case of technological dependence. India had to make a choice between firms which could offer such technological consultancy. The committee of experts which went into the matter recommended Pullmen Kellog and C.J. Brown. The recommendation was accepted by the Fertilizer Ministry. But things were being manipulated at a higher level. The figure of Ottavio Quattrochi, the Italian representative of the firm Snam Projeti, had started making his baleful presence on the Indian business scene. Through the PM's family's Italian connection, he was reported to have come close to

PM and started using that influence to make business deals in favour of his firm. The business climate became thick with rumour—which came true and became a scandal and it got reported even in the American press. In the face of unanimous technical opinion, the cabinet committee headed by ever helpful Vasant Sathe decided to supersede the technical opinion and rejected C.J. Brown and replaced it with Snam Projeti and Halder Topso, a Dutch firm. The Secretary of the Department, Shri K.V. Ramanathen was helpless and had to defend the superior political decision before a Parliamentary committee which went into the deal. When a reference came from the Parliamentary Secretariat, Secretary S.S. Puri avoided dealing with it (such was the fear of going against Quattrochi) and it fell to me to draft a reply, which I made purely factual. This was but one example of Quattrochi's interference. He was also involved in the Bofors case and when things became hot and Rajiv Gandhi and Sonia Gandhi were out of power, he simply vanished from Delhi where he had enjoyed living for many years and migrated to Kuala Lampur. India started a long and up to now unsuccessful process of extraditing him.

In the meanwhile World Bank loan had to be negotiated for KRIBHCO. The proposal for a loan to Thal Vaisheth Project was postponed because of the scandal but the case of KRIBHCO was allowed to go through. A delegation headed by me and consisting of Shri Sharad Kelkar Joint Secretary in the department of Fertilizer, Shri Jain, Director in the department. of Economic Affairs in the Ministry of Finance and Paul Pothen, MD went to Washington to negotiate the loan. I found I had little role to play and the matter was taken over by Kelkar and Jain who had negotiated such loans in the past. All that I had to do, was to feel happy that the delegation headed by me could obtain a loan of $ 400 million—till that day the biggest loan ever sanctioned to a single project. I was the first to return to Delhi and sent a note informing the Secretary and Minister of the happy outcome of our negotiations.

Review of Co-operative Development

As Additional Secretary, I had the opportunity to comprehensively review the state of cooperative development in the country. I held a series of zonal meetings to which I invited the Registrars of Cooperative societies in the states. The series of meetings was extremely useful in pinpointing the strengths and weaknesses of cooperatives societies in different parts of India and suggest remedial measures.

Agricultural exports was one of the items in my jurisdiction. The work was looked after by one Joint Secretary—Smt. Snehlata Puri. She did not sit in Krishi Bhavan but in Udyog Bhavan. She rarely met me and hardly sent me any files. I was therefore kept ill informed of the subject. There was a Joint Secretary in the Commerce Ministry—Shri Vinod Pande in charge of the subject. Since he was substantively dealing with the subject, Agricultural Ministry was only on the sidelines. I found my pathetic ignorance of the subject, when a matter regarding export of viscose fiber and its effect on the export of cotton fiber came up for discussion at the Parliamentary committee of the Ministry. I found Smt. Puri advising the Minister on the query raised. A lack of clear-cut allocation of responsibility can be a source of administrative weakness.

Minister Rao Birender's Approach

My Joint Secretary in charge of Cooperation was another lady—Smt. Satyabhama of Tamil Nadu cadre. She was an intelligent and competent lady and had worked as Registrar in the state and had field experience in the subject. Yet she was somewhat of an obstinate nature. She was a member of a high power committee on rural credit under the Chairmanship of B. Sivaraman. She as Joint Secretary was also the Central Registrar of Co-operatives. Because of her straight forwardness and may be her obstinacy, she came into conflict with the high handed Minister who started alleging that she was showing favouritism in appointing auditors for multi-state cooperatives and was even taking money! He wanted me to look into the matter. On some preliminary discussion with her, I felt that there was no basis for such an allegation. There was a standing list of approved auditors from which the appointments were made. I cautioned her to be careful. But she was not the one to take such advice in proper spirit. Her combativeness would not permit any compromise and I could see an inventible clash to her disadvantage.

Rao Birander Singh was feudalistic in attitude with Haryana background of politics. Not for him any cooperative idealism of equality and economic democracy. Even to a cooperative stalwart like Shri Verghese Kurien he gave a rough treatment. Once Kurien met me and gave ideas to make Multi State Cooperative Bill then on anvil more liberal. I believed that the law should be consistent with cooperative principles and a repressive law which allowed undue government control and interference in cooperatives would be to the detriment of cooperative development. I had, therefore, no difficulty in agreeing with most of Kurian's points. But when I sat with the Minister and made these points in relation to several clauses in the Bill, Rao Birender Singh would have none of it. He wanted full government control over the cooperative movement and there was nothing I could do about it.

Rao Birrender Singh was quite an intelligent person. He could remember and assimilate facts. His performance on the floor of Parliament, (unlike that of Shri S.K. Dey, elsewhere eloquent, but floundering on the floor of Parliament), was very effective. But he gave short shrift to his Scientist Secretary Dr. M.S. Swaminathan who shifted to Planning Commission as member. A senior bureaucrat like Shri S.S. Puri successed Swaminathan. He was also reluctantly shifted to the post of ambassador at European Economic Community Brussels after he was overlooked for the post of Cabinet Secretary. Shri Krishnaswamy Rao Saheb was appointed to the post instead. Shri S.P. Mukarji serving as Additional Secretary in the Ministry succeeded Shri Puri. He was 1952 batch officer senior to me by only a year. There was no occasion for Rao Birender Singh to ill treat me even once but I felt that the atmosphere in the Ministry was generally suffocating. Rao Birender Singh's feudal attitude could not allow any atmosphere of freedom. In fact I generally felt unhappy with government and felt I could move out for a while till I got an appointment as Secretary to Government which I thought would come to me automatically. Events were to show how unrealistic I was in my expectations and how much I was out of touch with the machinations of my own colleagues many of whom had become my enemies as predicted by the old man Yardi of Belgaum! Anyway I was carried away at that time by my revulsion of atmosphere in government and was looking for placement outside government.

Moving Outside Government

The opportunity came when Shri T.N. Chaturvedi, who was holding the post of Director Indian Institute of Public Administration (IIPA) moved as Secretary (Education). I had known him well and congratulated him and expressed my interest in the post. It did not occur to me that Chaturvedi had treated the post as an entry point to get the job of Secretary whereas I was moving out of government instead of using my position in government to get the post of Secretary. I had twice been an elected member of the Executive Council of IIPA, and had contributed articles over years for the *Indian Journal of Public Administration* ever since 1956 when I first contributed an article on coordination in rural development In 1959 and 1960 I had received from the hands of Jawaharlal Nehru prizes for essays in the annual essay competition held by IIPA. I phoned Shri Venkatappaiha a retired officer of ICS who was Chairman of the Standing Committee of IIPA and had the main role to play in choosing the new incumbent to the post of Director. He was also the Chairman of the Social Development Council whose office was located in a building adjoining India International Centre. He invited me for lunch of IIC dinning hall and welcomed me to the post of Director IIPA .He indicated to me that he would soon speak to Cabinet Secretary Shri Krishnaswami Rao Saheb. He did that but there was no initiative from Rao Saheb. I learnt that government. was not ready to release my services. What came in the way was that Chaturvedi was holding the position at the level of Secretary and the batch of 1953 was not yet taken up for elevation. I called on Rao Saheb He told me that government. was not interested in releasing me. But if I was keen to move, I could do so only at the level of Additional Secretary. I could be elevated to Secretary level only after 1953 batch was cleared.

At that time I was so much taken up by the desire to move out that I did not mind moving out even at the level of Additional Secretary. I was certain that as soon as 1953 batch was cleared, I would have no difficulty in getting the elevation in the post itself, as there would be no difficulty from the IIPA side, which was ready to take me at Secretary level at the time of joining itself. I therefore, called on Cabinet Secretary and conveyed my consent to accept the post of Director of IIPA at Additional Secretary level.

I had not spoken to my Minister, Rao Birender Singh, about all these developments. When he came to know that, at some occasion of a meeting he looked at me in a meaningful manner, but did not open the matter at all. But he was unlikely to take kindly to me. He set about installing a substitute for me at the earliest. There was no problem in getting a substitute. I realized that officers are ever ready to pounce upon a suitable vacancy in the Ministry. Even before I replied to a letter from the Joint Secretary in the Ministry asking me whether I would like to accept the post of Director IIPA on a deputation basis, the officer who had an eye on my post Shri P.S. Kohli then working in the Food Corporation asked me when I would like to hand over, since the orders of his appointment have already been issued. Obviously he was practically working for it all the time. If there was any case of unseemly haste, it was this. I suddenly realized how dispensable I was made to look. When I called on the Minister, he said I should go because I would get lots of "allowances" – when all the extra I was really getting was free residential accommodation on the campus of IIPA.

When I went to see the accommodation I was sorely disappointed. It was a non-descript flat in a run down building in which other flats were occupied by faculty members. Nearby was a thermal plant spewing out huge quantities of smoke. One look at it and I decided that I would not shift from my existing accommodation in the sylvan surrounding of Pandara Park. I immediately told Shri Venkatappaiah – that I would join on one condition, *viz.* I would be allowed to continue to stay in my present accommodation and IIPA would bear the cost. Since IIPA was keen to get me, my condition was agreed to. Some non-descript furniture of IIPA was shifted to my Pandara Park flat because I was entitled to free furnished accommodation.

I suddenly realized that on being relieved I had lost all leverage in the government. But I wanted to go to a place where I could breathe freely – which was hardly possible under a Minister like Birender Singh. But I must say that even at my parting meeting with Minister he was reasonably courteous. But he was too proud to ask me why I was leaving the Ministry. Perhaps he was convinced that I was attracted by "allowances" which hardly existed.

I sought the appointment as Director IIPA because at that time I had an overwhelming desire to leave the bondage of government and seek freedom. But I had not decided to leave the government. On the other hand, even before completing my deputation period of three years, I was looking forward to return to government in the position of Secretary. But I got the impression that most officers – my batchmets as well as others – were certain that an incument of the post of Additional Secretary was not wise in voluntarily leaving powerful position in the government, if he had the ambition to be a Secretary to the government. They tooked it that I went out only because I got an appointment at secretary level and were relieved that I, who was the first in the batch to be Additional Secretary, had not again got the better of his colleagues by being the first to be elevated to the post of Secretary. Actually Shri S.S. Gill of 1952 batch who had never been in touch with me phoned me to confirm that I was going as the Additional Secretary and when I confirmed he said – "it is only a lateral move" I should have realized that "bondage" is a condition which government servants should not only accept willingly but should show that they do so, if they wish to thrive in he government.

CHAPTER 19

Director, IIPA

IIPA—The Vision of Prime Minister Jawaharlal Nehru

The Indian Institute of Public Administration was established in 1952. On the recommendation of the report of Paul Appleby report, an American expert on Public Administration. He was invited by Jawaharlal Nehru to examine India's system of Public Administration and make recommendations. Jawaharlal Nehru, the first Prime Minister of free India was keen that India's administration system, a legacy of the British Colonial Rule, should be reformed to meet the needs of free India as a democratic polity and a welfare state. The administration of the colonial government, it was generally felt, was confined to law and order functions of a "police state". The attitude had generated amongst civil servants was that of *mabap sarkar*. It had to be transformed to undertake the functions of a welfare state in a democratic polity. Appleby came to the conclusion that Indian administration was one of the twelve best in the world. But it had to undertake new tasks and for that it had to learn new skills and develop new capacities. He made many broad recommendation but the two specific recommendations of his were (i) establishment of an Indian Institute of Public Administration and (ii) O&M Organization in Government. Both the recommendations were accepted. Shri S.B. Bapat, an ICS officer from West Bengal cadre, who was Joint Secretary in the Ministry of Home Affairs and also the Establishment Officer as well as Principal of the IAS school running at Metcalfe House, Delhi, acted as Appleby's counter part in the Central Government and took keen interest in the establishment of IIPA. It was conceived as an apex body devoted to the promotion of a scientific discipline of Public Administration and its application to actual conduct of public administration. To that end it should undertake research and training in Public Administration. It was expected to enlist membership from the practitioners and teachers of Public

Administration, indeed from all those citizens who were interested in the promotion of sound Public Administration. In the early years practising administrators including many ICS officers like D.L. Muzumdar, H.M. Patil, P.R. Nayak, L.P. Singh took keen interest in the working of IIPA.

Jawaharlal Nehru made a conscious effort to set up national level institutions in various fields as a part of nation building. He not only took initiative in setting up such institutions but gave his great support to develop those institutions buy personally associating himself with them. IIPA was one such institution. He was its founding President and made it a point to preside over its Annual General Body meetings and delivering his thought provoking addresses. These have been brought together by the IIPA in a separate publication. In these addresses he dealt with various facets of administration but the one point to which he gave greatest importance was peoples' participation in public administration. That is why he gave greatest importance to fostering Panchayati Raj Institutions. Said he – "Let the Panchayats make mistakes but give them responsibility. It is by making mistakes that they would learn". This indicated his faith in the common people of India as the foundation of Indian Public Administration. It was at such general body meetings that I got prizes at his hands at two successive general body meetings for my two essays – one on "*Scope and Implications of Democratic Decentralization*" and another on "*Training of Public servants in a developing economy*". Not understanding that PM's time is precious and should not be wasted, a member would get up and go on wrangling with some out of place remarks against the IIPA. Nehru would look at him with indulgence till his patience would not take it and the speaker would be asked to end his speech.

Nehru's daughter Indira Gandhi was not the one to put up with such nonsense. It was after such experience of IIPA, AGM, that she probably decided to withdrew her association with the IIPA. The PM ceased to be the President of IIPA. That position was taken by the Vice-President and the tradition continues till this day. The PM's withdrawal of this association with IIPA could not but affect the clout of IIPA in Indian administrative system.

Directors of Institute

Prof. D.G. Karve, an academic economist from Pune, formerly founder Principal of the newly established Brihan Maharashtra College of Commerce in Pune was the first Director IIPA. He stayed there for a short time before moving on to be the first Director of the Programme Evaluation Organization in the Planning Commission. When I joined the IAS training school in 1953, I got the opportunity to meet him. He was staying alone at the guesthouse in Dholpur House. He had a suite of rooms with an attached Kitchen. As I was a student at Pune, he took kindly interest in me. He invited me for dinner at his room and personally served a delicious meal of Dahikadhi and rice. I was touched by the kindness shown by a senior academician to a youngster joining the civil service. It was he who personally gave me the IIPA membership application form, got it filled and made me one of the earliest life members of the Institute. From that early time I took continuous interest in the working of the Institute. I contributed several papers to the *Indian Journal of Public Administration* starting with one on coordination in development administration based on my direct experience of working as project executive officer in charge of community development blocks. I made it a point to attend the general body meetings of the Institute whenever I was in Delhi I had the privilege to listen to Nehru's extempore addresses on that occasion.

Prof. D.G. Karve was succeeded by Prof. V.K.N. Menon, an academician, who was Director of Public Administration Institute in Patna. Smt. Laxmi Menon, Minister of State in the Ministry of External Affairs was his wife. He was there for about six years and is often remembered as the founding Director of the Institute. He was followed by Dr. J.N. Khosala who was in Indian Foreign Service and had served as Indian Ambassador in Romania. He was said to be close to V.K. Krishna Menon who was close to Jawaharlal Nehru and owed his appointment to that relationship. He stayed there for many years and was participated in the work of the Administrative Reforms Commission with which IIPA was associated. It was in 1967 when I was Director Cooperative Training that he invited me to join the IIPA project for the commission. The offer did not materialize because of the attitude of K. Hanumanthaih who succeeded Morarji Desai as Chairman of the Commission. Prof. Ishwar Dayal who was professor at IIM, Ahmedabad, succeeded Khosla. He tried to bring "management culture" in the IIPA but did not succeed and left the Institute in disgust because of the manner in which he was treated during the meetings of its Executive Council. He was succeeded by T.N. Chaturvedi who used the post of Director as a stepping stone to become secretary to the Government. I followed him with an appointment for three years.

The Role of Director

Because of my association with IIPA over several years, I was quite enthusiastic about the job of Director, though few of my colleagues in government thought that it was comparable in terms of prestige to the job of secretary to the government. A letter of congratulation from the well known economist Prof. V.K.R.V. Rao gave me some encouragement. He expected me to make some worthwhile contribution in the job. The task of the Director was two fold – first as the professional head of a training and research institution and second as the member secretary of a society with nationwide body of membership of people interested in public administration. In the former capacity, the Director had to organize, guide and support a variety of training programmes and research and consultancy projects. The faculty consisted of more than twenty persons at various levels – Professors, Readers and Lecturers. They belonged to various disciplines – Economics, Political Science, Public Administration, Management, Computer Application etc. From time to time for one reason or for another, a vacancy would occur and the Director had to recruit new faculty members through a Recruitment Committee. So the Director was also acting like Public Service Commission.

In discharge of his associational responsibilities the Director has to act as member secretary of the Executive Council, arrange its meetings every quarter, prepare agenda for such meetings, issue proceedings and take action on its resolutions. There are also a number of subcommittees including standing committee and academic committee. The executive council consists of elected and nominated members. The members are elected every two years for which the Director has to arrange elections through postal ballot. So the Director is also one-man Election Commission of IIPA.

There was quite some competition for getting elected to the Executive Council. This led to enlistment of new members with an eye on building up a vote bank. Slowly this led to malpractices which assumed an acute from years after I left and a committee had to be constituted to look in into the malpractices in election and take remedial measures.

The General Body Meeting of members had to be held every year in October. Surprisingly quite a large number of members from all over the country attended especially from Bihar. The meetings of AGB are held in Institutions auditorium Railway concession are made available to the members to attend the General

Body Meeting. Coinciding with the General Body meeting is held the Annual Conference on some important subjects relating to Public Administration. The lead paper is prepared by a faculty member. Also a meeting of the office bearers of regional and local branches is convened. So the two to three days with a series of events keep the Director very busy.

The agenda for the General Body meeting is set by the Director and is more or less of a standard nature – discussion on the Annual Report submitted by the Director, approval of the audit report and proposal, if any, for the amendment of the constitution. The latter if urgent would require convening of the special general body meeting. During the election years, the newly elected and continuing members of Executive Council meet soon after the General Body and elect the co-opted members. Thus, General Body meeting starting at 6 p.m. in the evening would go on till 8 pm on beyond.

The General Body meeting is presided over by the President. In my days the President was Mr. Justice Hidaytulla, the retired Chief Judge of the Supreme Court who was holding position of Vice President of India. He was a learned, gracious person and I felt happy to be associated with him. He was followed by Shri R. Venkatraman, veteran politician who was earlier Minister in Madras (Tamil Nadu later) and then held important positions in union cabinet. He was also a genial personality with vast experience in administration and keen on administrative reforms. The Presidential address is an important feature of the Annual General Body meeting. I have referred to Jawaharlal Nehru's extempore addresses. Hidazatullah and Venkatraman delivered written addresses. A convention was establishment that after the Presidential address formally inaugurating the AGB, he would leave and the chairman of the Executive Council would be in chair and carry out the proceedings.

In my time at the time of my appointment Babu Jagjiven Ram was the Chairman. I remember my courtesy call at his residence. He received me with courtesy but in course of the conversation he did not fail to mention that the Institute had let me continue to stay at the Govt. accommodation. There was a hint that this was a special concession shown to me – in return for which I should feel grateful. This was the politician in him manipulating a civil servant. I resented this but could hardly express my resentment. That his patronizing attitude was not without practical implication became clear to me when on his behalf some request was made to me about some administrative matter. This was an interference in administration which I did not like. Of course I did not oblige.

Soon I had a new Chairman in Shanker Rao Chavan who was the Minister for Education. He was Chairman throughout my tenure. I had excellent relationship with him—he later rose to be Deputy Chairman Planning Commission and Home Minister. He treated me with respect. Whenever I sought an appointment on official business, he would give it immediately and would deal with my subjects in a business like manner. We would speak in Marathi and that increased rapport between us. He was known as "Head Master" in Maharashtra and brought to bear the same attitude when he chaired Executive Council meeting. He would not allow the discussion at the meeting to wander away from the agenda. This business like approach resulted in the meeting not lingering for hours on.

I was keen that AGB was held with dignity. During AGB, the Director would sit by the side of the chairman listening to the comments and observation of the members on the Annual Report and other items on the agenda. Often these comments would be critical. The members wanted to exercise their democratic right of free expression—no matter on basis of half-baked information. Sometimes the critical comments would be engineered by a disgruntled faculty or staff member. I never resented any such comments nor did I intervene when the comments went on. I would diligently record all points, classify them under several headings such as training, research, consultancy, administration, constitution etc and then reply to them point by point, when my turn to reply came at the end of the discussion. The audience would listen to me in pin drop silence and the report would be approved unanimously. It is with some satisfaction that I recall that as a result of my approach all the AGBs during my period of five years were conducted in an orderly and dignified manner—with never a discordant note which would rankle in heart. I was told that ABGs after I left often turned out to be disorderly and disgraceful affairs.

I also gave considerable encouragement to development of regional and local branches. The J&K branch had become dormant. I revived it. It became quite active. I have vivid memory of my visit to Shrinagar where a largely attended meeting of the regional branch was held. Another branch that became active was the one at Ranchi. The Maharashtra Regional branch at Mumbai continued to be the leading one claiming larger portion of grant meant for the regional branches.

For the conduct of the Annual Conference, I successfully introduced the innovation suggested by Prof. M.V. Mathur of holding regional and local conference as a prelude to the Annual Conference and placing the ideas generated at these conference for the national annual conference.

Research and Training Programme

This associational work was only peripheral to the main work of the Director, *viz.* running the Institute in a professional manner. Over the years the training, research and consultancy programmes of the Institute had evolved. The Director had to direct the work in a sustained manner and if possible add to it. Training course on performance budgeting for example had been carried on year after years. In the beginning it was an innovation. Later on it became a routine and it was churning out trainees without making a qualitative difference to administration. The goal of performance budgeting was to relate expenditure to achievement or outlay to outcome. The budget itself was to indicate the physical performance expected to result from financial expenditure. But once it became a routine while the budget provided the information, the qualitative change was not visible. Administrative innovations and reforms are lost in the desert sand of routine and dead habits. However once such courses are established it is not possible to give them up. It was Prof. M.J.K. Thavraj who had initiated the course which was carried year after year. Another such course on Project Management, Proper formulation and management leaves much to be desired in India. There are, time and cost overruns which a poor country can hardly afford. This is because of bad project formulation and implementation. Projects must be scientifically formulated, rigorously followed up and supervised and competently implemented. The course is therefore of great importance for upgrading knowledge and skills of administrators interested with such projects. If the personnel interested with the task of project formulation and implementation are given training, there could be some improvement. The course invariably had good response, Shri Thyagarajan, ex-engineer was in charge of this course. A third course which evoked good response was on Management Information System (MIS), important for all programmes and projects. This course was conducted by Shri Jagdish Kapoor and was always well attended. Shri Sachdev conducted courses on the use of computer in administration. Apart from such courses related to functions and techniques, there were courses in subject matter areas like law and order and criminal justice administration, rural development and urban administration. I remember a largely attended seminar on collective violence. It was held against the background of anti-Sikh riots in Delhi after Indira Gandhi's assassination by her Sikh guards. Julio Reibero who was then special secretary in the Home Ministry participated in the seminar. Minister in charge of internal security Shri Arun Nehru gave the valedictory address. In a variety of courses on Rural Development different aspects of integrated rural development and poverty alleviation programmes were dealt with, with an emphasis on the effective delivery system and it was intended that the benefits reached the people for whom they were meant. This was an area in which I had long personal experience both at the field level and policy making level. These courses were handled by Prof. Kamta Prasad, Shri R.K. Tiwari and Shri S.N. Mishra. The courses relating to Municipal Administration and urban development were handled by the Centre of Municipal Administration. It was established as a separate centre and had been functioning for years. It brought out a separate journal called *Nagarlok*, apart from the IIPA's Indian *Journal of Public Administration*. In this course, we dealt with general municipal administration as well as specific functions like solid waste disposal.

I initiated courses in two new areas, *viz*. Administrative Ethics and Environment—both at the instance of Shri Shekhar Singh who later become an activist and well known thinker in the latter field. Both these areas had become extremely important and our courses were of a pioneering nature.

Apart from a variety of short term courses some of which are mentioned above, whose number in the annual calendar of programme exceeded to sixty, we had a long term course known as Advance Professional Programmes in Public Administration (APPPA) for a whole year in which officers of IAS and Central Services took part. I soon realized that most of the participants joined this course to extend their stay in Delhi for a year at the end of their tenure with central government. Whatever that be, some officers who later held high positions had participated in these courses. The course had a broad focus and after dealing with political, social and economic environment of administration, it went on to analyse, the essentials of administration. The course included an overseas visit and that was a special attraction of the course. The course director went with the participants on this tour. I myself went with one of the courses to Indonesia which was then about to have a general election. Our ambassador there met the participants and explained how the Golkar Party of the President "managed" the outcome of elections and made a mockery of democracy in Indonesia. We visited rural development programmes. They used Sanskrit nomenclatures to describe their development programme. A visit I could never forget was to the Museum and Jakarta. It contained a rich treasure of statues of Hindu deities and *Rishis* such as Ganesh Yama, and Agasthi the like of which may not be available even in India.

Having regard to the standard of the course, I was able get help of the Vice-Chancellor of Punjab University, Shri Ramchandra Paul to get the course recognized as equivalent to M.Phil. These gave an additional incentive to officers joining the APPPA, which could be a stepping stone to Ph.D. as well.

Association with Prime Minister Indira Gandhi

The IIPA had lost the association with the PM when she refused to be its President for her own reason. Someway, I wished to restore the Association. I thought of requesting the PM to address the officers participating in the APPPA course. I established contact with Shri Sharda Prasad, the press secretary to PM, whom I knew. I was glad when the PM complied with our request. The PM would not come to IIPA but the participating officers would go to 10 Safderjang Road. The PM's official residence. We were quite excited. I led the team of officers to visit the PM's residence. The meeting was arranged at a pandal erected on the lawns. We went exactly on time. The PM was punctual to the minute. She was in a pleasant mood. It was October 1982. The weather was pleasant. Before PM's address, I spoke a few introductory words recollecting that the IIPA owed its origin to the vision and initiative of her father – Jawaharlal Nehru. I also told her about the unique nature of the APPPA course. I presented her a bouquet on behalf of the participants and also a set of books published by the IIPA including the book containing the addresses delivered by Jawaharlal Nehru every year at IIPA's AGB meeting and also my own book "Grammar of Planning". The PM had suggested that rather than giving a monologue, she would rather respond to questions. She responded to all questions in a candid manner. I had asked all the participant to raise questions about the salient aspects of Public Administration arising out of their own experience and reflection. One of the questions related to Emergency. PM was not upset and responded in an imperturbable manner. The meeting lasted for over seventy minutes. We felt absolutely elated. After the meeting PM went to meet people waiting for her. In our mood of elation we forgot to ask her to pose for a group photograph. So we waited till she returned after meeting the people. When she saw me, she asked good naturally. "are you still here?" I told her that we were waiting to have a photograph with her. She graciously agreed. We returned with a great sense of satisfaction. It was clear how important it was for the IIPA to have a link with the head of Indian Administration – the Prime Minister. I had kept notes of questions and answers as a historical record of our meeting. The event was repeated next year as well. This time the meeting was fixed a little later in the month of November. It was cold. The situation created by Khalistanis under Bhidranwale had taken serious turn. The PM had reason to be worried. Still she gave us time. She came in a black heavy overcoat followed by her faithful secretary Shri R.K. Dhawan. This time too she gave 70 minutes and responded to all question with the same imperturbability as during our previous meeting. But the pall of gloom was there, she was not as cheerful as at the last years; meeting. But even then, the PM was not oblivious to the convenience of the visiting officers. She asked for heaters to reduce the cold in the pandal. This time too I took notes. Later on, on the basis of my notes I prepared an article – "Indira Gandhi and Public Administration". It was first published in "*Management in Government*" a journal of the Government of India Department of Personnel and later on included in my book "Recent Trends in Public Administration" along with another article under the caption "Jawaharlal Nehru on public administration". The article brought out Smt. Indira Gandhi's burning desire to make India a strong country in the comity of nations of the world which would not go down before a super power like the USA.

That was to be our last engagement with PM Indira Gandhi. Next year she was tragically assassinated by her own Sikh guards whom she kept despite warnings of the intelligence agency. Her son Rajeev Gandhi became the Prime Minister. He was a pilot in Air India and was inducted as Indira Gandhi's political assistant after the death of his younger brother Sanjay Gandhi in an air accident. At that time, a faculty member Shri Sadashiven through his acquaintance a fellow malyali, Shri V. George, who was Rajeev Gandhi's PA, tried to get him invited to IIPA on the occasion of Jawaharlal Nehru's birth anniversary, *viz.* Nov 14. He had agreed.

When that became known, another faculty member, Prof. S.R. Maheshwari, met me and registered his protest". Who was Rajeev Gandhi to be invited to IIPA? We protest," I was taken a back at his ill will and negative attitude but chose to ignore it. Ultimately, however, Shri Rajeev Gandhi did not keep the engagement. If he had visited, a contact would have been established which would have been helpful when he became PM.

Prime Minister Rajiv Gandhi's New Initiative

As PM Rajeev Gandhi took great interest in training. His professional background accounted for this. He started joint programme for ministers and civil servants at top levels in institutions like Tata Management Centre, Pune and Administrative Staff College, Hyderabad. I remember participating in a programme at the latter centre which was also attended by Shri K.C. Pant and Shri Sukhram who later became notorious for piles of a currency notes in his bed room. Obviously training is no antidote to corruption! I also participated in course at the Tata Management Centre, Pune. Rajeev Gandhi envisaged a series of courses for IAS and central service officers at various levels, courses for Joint Secretary level officers on policy making and courses on programme and project management for middle management level officers. These courses were allotted to various training institutions which by that time had sprung up in large numbers all over the country. The IIPA and Lal Bahadur Shastri Academy of Public Administration, Mussorie were called upon to conduct courses on policy making. I greatly welcomed the opportunity. I had great interest in the subject of policy making which I considered as the most important function of public administration which at the same time was most neglected. I prepared an outline syllabus for one month programme of training and held a meeting with Director, Lal Bahadur Shastri Academy, at the institute and finalized the syllabus. At the end of lectures and seminars, the participants were expected to prepare policy document regarding various sectors of public administration such as law and order, agricultural and rural development, water conservation and management, urban administration, infrastructure development etc. In subsequent months several programmes on policy making were arranged. A large number of joint secretaries in the Union Government. and secretaries in the state governments (they were equivalent to Joint Secretaries at the Centre) participated in the programme.

It is out of his interest in training that Rajeev Gandhi arranged a conference of Directors of training institutions. It was well attended. P. Chidambram, Minister, Department of Personnel, was sitting by the side of Rajeev Gandhi. Amongst the participants were Director, Academic Staff College, Hyderabad and Tata Institute of Management, Pune (the preferred institutions of Rajeev Gandhi?) I spoke in my usual candid and forceful manner. I said that public administration is often ineffective because it deals with symptoms and deeper issues, social, economic and Political are overlooked. Unless they are tackled, programmes, policies and approaches would not be effective. The civil servants are often not properly acquainted with these issues. The training course ought to be focused on the basic issues behind the administrative problems. As I held forth, I saw Chidambram visibly squirming in his seat. He appeared to feel uncomfortable that a mere Director of a training institution should be addressing the PM himself on the basic issues of public administration and how training should deal with them. Later on I felt that frank talk was not expected from a Director. On the other hand, I should have eulogised the PM on his initiative in introducing the three level design of the training courses.

Research Projects

Apart from the training programmes, the institute undertook a number of research and consultancy projects in various fields. Prof. S.K. Goyal had a large project to collect and store in computer information regarding business companies. When Shri B. Venkatappiah raised objections to the project being taken up in IIPA since it could not be considered as relating to public administration. I thought it was too late for him to raise such an objection since it was taken much before I had joined. Prof. Goyal used the information to raise the question "How private is private enterprise?" The project related to the functioning of our mixed economy and the place of private sector in the mixed economy and the extent to which they should be supported by public funds from financial institutions. A project I very much remember was the one related to the motivation of the civil servants especially the police. Their remuneration is low, their working environment poor, there working hours long. All this led to their alienation from their families and from themselves. It would be difficult to expect commitment from police working in such an environment. Working environment should be improved if we are to expect better performance. Another project I remember related to the working of District Rural Development Agency (DRDA). Did this organizational innovation serve any purpose? Another huge project related to the public distribution system taken up by the Prof. K.N. Kabra with a view to find out whether this should be target oriented.

Faculty

The quality of training and research and indeed the overall performance of the Institution depended on quality and commitment of the faculty. IIPA had large faculty of professors, readers, lecturers and research officers but I could not help feeling that its collective performance left much to be desired. Indeed. IIPA did not give the impression of a high quality institution contributing significantly to public administration. The faculty consisted almost entirely of those belonging to the academic world. There were no practicing administrators on sabbatical leave taking upon themselves the task, out of their own choice, of training and research in public administration. The rat race amongst the civil servants to move forward in influential positions in government, did not motivate them to take sabbatical leave to work in IIPA. IIPA had an excellent library and gave unrivalled opportunities to civil servants to come on sabbatical to do in-depth study of various aspects and problems of public administration. But Indian administration has been mostly superficial doing fire-fighting work all the time without tackling the basic problems. IIPA was expected to provide depth to the approaches of the administrators but this never happened. IIPA was not expected to be a mere "ivory tower" institution to provide positions to academicians who could not find a place in the academic institutions. IIPA was to combine the best of academic approaches and practical insights of administrators. But in fact it managed to get done the worst-low quality academic work and isolation from actual experience of administration.

There was absence of stimulating atmosphere in IIPA. Training courses were continuously churned out as a routine. Research and consultancy projects were handed down by agencies of government. I took interest in all these programmes and gave not only inaugural addresses to the courses and distributed certificates at the end of the courses but also whenever possible took lectures. I also went diligently through all the drafts of research projects and gave suggestions. I was totally immersed in these activities but never felt satisfied.

In the lax atmosphere of the institute both administrator and academic standards left much to be desired. All that could be done was to see that things would not further slip, I did my best to create a new stir, a new commitment in the faculty. I started holding full faculty meetings to discuss freely and frankly all aspects of work training, research, consultancy, publication and administration. The faculty did attend the meetings. The attendance was good. But I found that I had to raise subjects and points and did all the talking. There was hardly any feed back from the faculty. The basic reasons for this strange attitude was that the institute had fallen in a rut and nobody wanted to raise it to a higher level.

Over the years, a thick crust of insensitivity and cynicism had settled over the faculty mind. There was no stimulating and creative interaction though the faculty was diverse and belonged to various disciplines, economics, political science, sociology, management etc. There was little institutional commitment. Each for himself was the motto. Each pursued the motto in his own way. There was neither the pressure of fear nor the stimulus of creative work. All that Prof. S.K. Goyal did was to hold on to his computerized company information bank. Prof. S.R. Maheshwari considered himself bigger than the institute. He had no qualms of conscience in using Institute time and facilities to write text books on public administration, sell them through contacts developed through years and make a hefty sum through royalties. Shri Thyagarajan sold his book on project management to course participants through the course budget. When I objected to this practice as unethical and stopped it, he felt bad and went on pestering me and ultimately I relented. Many of the faculty members were more interested in getting invitations as guest lecturers in other institutions and making money from lecture fee rather than giving all their time and energy to the institute's work. Normally they should have taken permission to accept invitations but they seldom did so. It would have been possible to go after the faculty members indulging in such lapses but that would not have yielded much result. A Director would have to waste all his time and energy and face only a hostile faculty. The change has to come from within and that is what I set out to do by encouraging every one to take up more work. Ultimately even diehards like Maheshwari and Goel took up responsibility to conduct courses on policy making.

When commitment to the institution itself, from which the faculty members drew their bread and butter was lacking, there could be no question of loyalty to the Director. If there were to be any problems it was for the Director to solve. He alone should face the Executive Council and the Annual General Meetings and take all the initiatives needed. It was for him to get grants from the reluctant Ministry. In the past some faculty members had gone to courts and the institute had to face litigation. The faculty disloyalty was compounded by a wholly unsound provision in the constitution of the institute according to which the faculty members could stand for elections to the Executive Council of the institute. As faculty members they were answerable to the Director but as elected members of the Executive Council they would hold the Director answerable to them. The dual position was indeed quite untenable and unhealthy. They would often join hands with the scheming members of the EC in making unjustified comments and creating a hostile adversarial climate. They did not contribute anything at all to take the Institute forward. Instead of strengthening the hands of the Director they tried to weaken him and make his position uncomfortable in the Executive Council. They felt that it was only by weakening the Director that they could increase their importance. Their meaningless charade of comments could only drag on the meeting of the EC. Starting at an inconvenient time of 6 p.m. (perhaps it was so fixed to enable practicing civil servants to attend the meetings) they could drag on till 9 pm or even beyond. Fortunately Shri Shankar Rao Chavan who was known as " Head Master" when he was the Chief Minister of Maharashtra was a no-nonsense man and the EC could work in a business like manner and conclude early.

My appointment was in the first instance for a period of three years. I had hoped to return to Government as Secretary at the end of the period. My three years tenure passed quickly. Infact Shri Venkatappiah expressed surprised that the period was already over when I told him about it.

Extension of Term

While the initial three years period in IIPA was quite smooth sailing, in my personal career it proved painful. In 1983, our batch of 1953 was taken up for consideration for secretary level postings. We in the batch had completed 30 years of service and had five years of service left. When I was appointed in 1981 as Director IIPA, Cabinet Secretary, Shri Krishnaswamy Rao Saheb, told me that while I could not straightway take up the post at secretary level and when 1953 batch would be cleared for secretary level posting, I could be elevated automatically and he expected no hitch. But unknown to me dark clouds of hostility had gathered to create difficulties for me.

First I found that Shri Ganapati of IIAS 1951 batch and Shri P.K. Basu of management pool were appointed as Secretaries. Obviously they had done a lot of manoeuvring and brought to bear influence. They were appointed as Additional Secretaries along with me but though I was of the IAS, I was left behind. I saw Rao Saheb. He said that 1953 batch of IAS was taken up and I would get my chance. I soon realized that it was a mistake that I took his assurance at face value.

My batch mates had started their manoeuvring. Smt. P.P. Trivedi phoned me saying that we should see the Secretary to PM for pressing our claims. I did not respond as I had an assurance from the Cabinet Secretary. I did not know that in the new dispensation, Cabinet Secretary had no decisive voice though he was supposed to be the head of the civil service and so far as civil service postings were concerned his word should be considered decisive. At a dinner gathering of 1953 batch mates, they started talking of secretary level postings for them but there was no mention about my elevation. I and my wife felt uncomfortable. A few days later, while on a visit to Lal Bahadur Shastri Academy of Public Administration, Mussorie, I came across Shri R.K. Shastri, my batchment. Looking in my eyes he menacingly asked me "*Dilli me kya ho raha hai*?" he did not explain his intriguing question nor did I pursue it, carrying with me an uncomfortable feeling.

That uncomfortable feeling turned into gloom when I saw orders elevating three of my batch mates but no elevation for me even in my present job. I phoned Krishnaswamy Rao Saheb but he started giving evasive replies forgetting all his previous assurances. I felt badly let down. I came to know that "screening" for elevating 1953 batch for secretary level postings was made by a committee of three. i.e., Dr. P.C. Alexander, Principal Secretary to PM, Krishnaswamy, the Cabinet Secretary and T.N. Chaturvedi, the home sanitary. Since I had known the last well, I enquired with him but he too was evasive and seemed rather to relish my discomfiture. Shri G.V. Ramakrishna, Secretary Petroleum, (who later become chairman of the disinvestment Commission) who had never visited me, came to my house to meet me and find out what had happened. I found that believing always in my good luck and never given to maneuvering, I was totally unprepared to face the set back at the last stage of my career. I just did not know what had struck me.

Shri P. Chidambaramm, Dy. Minister in charge of Personnel had visited IIPA. He was quite impressed by our performance. I had given him a written statement about my career and claim for the post of Secretary. But he too was not candid when the crunch came.

I asked for on appointment with the secretary to PM, Dr. Alexander. When I did not get it I went early morning to his house. He was quite unprepared and said we could meet in the office. I later got a phone call from his office giving me an appointment. When I met him, he greeted me saying: "I know why you have come?" in a hostile manner which quite unnerved me. A rightful claimant, I felt, was being reduced to an abject supplicant. I could hardly reconcile to my position in which, at the fag end of my unblemished career and indeed dedicated work of over thirty years, I had to explain my work and press my claim! I could quite see that a coterie of officers had reduced me to a miserable position.

In such a predicament my own only solace was Shri Shankarrao Chavan. He was Chairman of the Executive Council and held the position of Dy. Chairman Planning Commission. He had appreciated my work as Director IIPA. He had written a laudatory forward to my book "Grammar of Planning". When I explained the injustice dome to me, he agreed to see the Prime Minister. He kept his word and after the meeting told me that he had a feeling that the PM was convinced and would do the needful. His assessment was correct and a few days later I received orders regarding my promotion. The announcement was also made on Doordarshan.

Though with effort, I got my last elevation in civil service it became a harrowing experience. I felt slighted. I was ill treated despite my outstanding performance. My own colleagues, I suspected, had turned enemies (as predicted by old man Yardi) and had given the impression to the powers that be that I got undue advantage during the Janata regime and had to be punished. I would not be surprised if they had dug up my published articles like "Commitment in civil service" in which I had, though in a dispassionate manner, criticised India Gandhi's concept of political "Commitment of the Civil Servants". Krishnaswami Rao Saheb went on raising red herrings. That created doubt and fear in my mind. "Was our (second) visit to Indira Gandhi a disaster? Did I do any thing to lose her favour?" Actually nothing had happened and the visit had gone very well. I had lost three months of elevation and should have asked for retrospective promotion. But I had lost not only my complacency and optimism but also self-respect and self-confidence. But in the huge juggernaut of Government,. feelings of honest, straightforward, devoted civil servants do not matter. What matters are maneuvering, currying favour, lobbying and all the baser operations which should not have any place in a healthy civil service tradition. Since these traditions have not been maintained in post-independence India, the standards have steeply fallen. The civil service had been politicised and has become non-professional. The politicians in power consequently do not get free and frank views and objective impartial advice because they encourage pliant civil servants. Every thing gets biased and wrong decisions taken. No wonder the nation is ill served. Mistakes are made and problems created and not solved. They linger and turn into disasters.

At the end of my three years, Dr. Venkatappaih felt that I should continue for a further period of two years. The Institute had no substitute in mind. Nor did they think of any. I had provided good leadership and the Institute was running smoothly. It had not only gained stability but was on the ascent. In order to pressurize me to agree to continue, Venkatappaih told me that the Cabinet Secretary had told him that they had no position for me under the centre and I would have to go back to the state. Instead of keeping my feelings or difficulties to myself, I told him that my children are studying in Delhi and at the critical stage of their education, I would not like to leave Delhi I would therefore agree to a two year extension of my tenure as Director, IIPA. The Government agreed to the proposal. The IIPA's Executive Council had to pass a formal resolution to that effect.

They insisted that I must shift my residence to the campus which I was unwilling to do. The extension was on existing terms and conditions and the Institute was not justified in changing them. Realizing that some of the members were bent upon imposing the condition, I talked to Shri Shankar Rao Chavan, the Chairman. He was sympathetic and agreed to my continuing with the existing residential arrangement. When the matter came up in the meeting of the Executive Council I left the meeting because my own "case" was to be discussed. I was not sure about the outcome. I feared that the meeting may prolong. But Chavan came out shortly thereafter and proceeded to the lift to leave. But his face and the down cost face of Venkatappaih and others told me that he had done what he had promised. Later on I learnt from him that when Venkatappaih raised the point and persisted with his arguing (quite falsely) that my staying on the campus was essential for proper running of the Institute, Chavan gave him a dressing down saying that he had no business of changing the existing terms and conditions.

I was relieved but I realized that hereafter I should expect hostile postures. I indeed had enough of IIPA and would have liked a change but it was not available. I felt trapped. I even expressed my feelings to Chavan. But for the time being I continued.

But more trouble was in store for me. Once at a wedding reception on the lawns of India International Centre, Cabinet Secretary, Rao Saheb accosted me and airily told me that he was giving me "marching orders" I was aghast. Why should he say so? What was the point of sending me back to the state after agreeing to my continuation? I told him that I was on deputation to IIPA for two years more with the consent of Central Govt. and my return to the state would not arise. I was hurt that he should raise the matter so casually at a wedding reception. A person who could deal with a senior officer in such a cavalier manner was hardly fit to hold the position of the Cabinet Secretary. I also realized that it was because my position in the Government. had become weak, that I had no political support that some bureaucrats could feel that they could take liberties with my posting.

While I was ready to leave the Institute what I desired was a posting as Secretary to Government. to which I was entitled. But several vacancies occurred like Secretary, Department of Agriculture or Rural Development for which I had a proper background but I was overlooked. Obviously some bureaucrats with their proximity to ruling politicians were determined to keep me out. I realized this when suddenly one day Shri P.K. Kaul who had succeeded Rao Saheb as Cabinet Secretary sent for me. I thought he would be offering me the post of Secretary. Instead, what he offered was the post of Director General of the National Institute of Rural Development, Hyderabad I promptly told him that I was not interested in shifting from one Institute to another and in all fairness he should "accommodate" me in a post of Secretary to government of India.

In my extended two year term, I continued my good work in IIPA though I could sense the hostile attitude in the Executive Council which could not stomach the slight given to Shri Vankatappaya and those who instigated him in forcing me to move to the campus. But I had to bear it.

International Conferences

The IIPA was member of two international association, *viz.* Association of Schools and Institutes of Public Administration and EROPA – Eastern Regional Organisation of Public Administration. The Director IIPA got invitations to attend the annual meetings convened by these bodies. I attended these meetings and took active part in their deliberations. The meetings were held, I remember, in Bangkok, Seoul (South Korea) and Indiana (USA). I was even elected as one of the Vice-Presidents of the Institutional Association. My active participation in all these meetings helped me to be in touch with recent trends in public administration one of which was globalisation. I also remember a discussion held in Nagoya, Japan on development administration convened by Shri Shabir Cheema and attended by Prof. Milton Esman, the well known academician from Cornell University, USA. I also attended an expert consultation on Development Administration at the Asia Pacific Centre, Kuala Lumpur. In connection with all these conference, I produced a number of papers.

As on three previous years, I ran the administration of the Institute in a smooth, manner. There were no mishaps and contretemps though because of developments over the years the atmosphere was by no means healthy. The Institutions tend to develop a cramped atmosphere with internal mutual jealousies. Each member of the academic community had his or her own idiosyncrasy and they were often not on talking terms with each other. Once, in the residential flats two members and their families came to blows. My general approach was never to get involved in any these petty jealousies and encourage each to make his or her maximum contribution. For example a faculty member Dr. Jaideep Singh (son of Shri Tarlok Singh of the ICS, who was well known for his contribution to Planning Commission) had found himself out of work – whether training or research. I interested to him the work of preparing case studies. He took interest and brought out under my guidance the volume of case studies on the delivery system.

The Administration of IIPA

The administration of Institute was quite pedestrian. The chief administrative officer was the Registrar. The post was held by Shri Brijbhushan Khare. He was from Madhya Pradesh. He was fairly efficient but one could not help feeling that he was clever and could not give unstinted loyalty to the Director. Perhaps he had to be like that because he had also to deal with members of the Executive Council and had to survive in the internal politics of the Institute.

The members of the Institute's Executive Council were also not beyond using their clout for taking undue advantage. For example Prof. Shanti Kothari who was also a member of the Rajya Sabha started asking for the staff car. The Institute had only one staff car and he had to be told that he could not have its services. The stay in the hostel was supposed to be limited to seven days at a time but Shri M.K. Chaturvedi an IAS officer of MP Cadre stayed for more than a month on the pretext of some work of the Institute and insisted on daily allowance for all those days. He had a prolonged stay actually for attending to the work of his house. Shri T.N. Chaturvedi phoned me to put word in his favour. I placed the case before the Executive Council drawing attention to the rules. The EC which otherwise would be very critical in granting even a petty concession, generously approved of Shri M.K. Chaturvedi's demands. Obviously he had done the necessary lobbying.

One unhealthy feature of the Institute's governance was that a faculty member could stand for election to the EC. A faculty member, once elected to the Council would think that he instead of being answerable to the Director would instead hold him accountable. He would provide "inside knowledge" to the other members and even gang up with them to create difficulties for the Director in EC. The experience of seeing IAS officers ganging up with academic members over petty matters was not very edifying. But what could not be cured had to be endured. Banning faculty members from standing for elections would have been the right course of action but concession once given could not be withdrawn and would have been easily dubbed as undemocratic. After I had left; over the years, this conflict assumed serious proportions.

The faculty behaviour could sometimes assume a strange character. Once, Raj Nandi, a junior faculty member though not junior in age, was suddenly found squatting outside the chamber of the Director with some demands. I told him that he could meet me if he had any problems but should not squat which was unbecoming but he was adamant and persisted. There was nothing particularly significant in what he asked for. He considered it a waste of Institute's resources that fruit juice was served when a parting dinner was arranged at the end of the courses. I had not initiated the practice and a glass of juice in the menu could not be considered extravagant. Obviously, Nandi was set up by somebody else who tried to put in a word on his behalf. When I remained firm in my stand that I could discuss any matter with Nandi but could not be bullied by squinting, he climbed down and ended his strike.

The administrative staff, as in all institutions had their association and like every association, they had their small demands and like all heads of institutions I had to face them. Through all my five years, I managed to have good relations with them and there was no unpleasant event of any sort. One of the demands of the association was that the lower level staff had no opportunities for promotion through long career stretching over 30 years I considered their demand sympathetically. It was certainly degrading that they had nothing to look forward to throughout their career. I formulated a proposal that every 10 years every staff member, in normal circumstances will have a promotion to a higher scale in their existing place even though no vacancy were to be available in the higher scale. The proposal was accepted by the EC. This was greatly conducive to staff satisfaction. Years after I left the institute, on a rare chance visit, an attendant in the hostel remembered the kindness shown in introducing the scheme and said that I was the only one Director who cared for the staff.

An important part of the Institute was the guest house and catering facilities there. Both were available at very reasonable rates. In the nation's capital such facilities were difficult to come by and could be availed of only at great expense. They were highly prized and indeed a major attraction to membership; in spite of the standard of the hostel rooms and their maintenance Rs. 25/- per room per day was a pittance. The IIPA could do with more funds. I raised the tariff to Rs. 50/- per day and despite murmurings, was accepted and contributed to the permanent addition to the flow of internal resources of the Institute. The caterer Shri Katiyar provided sumptuous breakfast and two meals at a very reasonable rate of Rs. 50/- per day. He also provided special meals on special occasions. Despite this some members of the faculty found fault with his services and wanted to end his "monopoly" over many years. I gave careful consideration to this complaint. I realized that it was not easy to get a replacement. None could have come forward to provide the catering at that rate. He stuck to the Institute because the Institute stuck to him and gave him steady business. He had employed *pahedi* staff who worked for him with loyalty and at low compensation. People have a tendency to run down what is available. I constituted a committee of faculty members to monitor catering and if possible find a better substitute. The committee could suggest some improvements in catering from time to time but, as I expected, it singularly failed to arrange an alternative caterer.

Whether in the faculty and staff management or in the conduct of courses or development of research work or in the associational activities like conduct of meetings of EC and other committees or the Annual General Body Meeting or the Annual Conference, there was smooth sailing without a hitch through all my 5 years. There was no untoward happening; there was stability and steady improvement though not a spectacular transformation, which I realized was impossible in an old institute settled in grooves and working in constraints imposed both by the organizational set up and financial resources. Once several years after I left the institute and the civil service career, Prof. Ramesh Arora of Rajasthan University met me at a conference and told me that my administration of the IIPA was remembered as the best—fair and efficient.

Review Committee

The IIPA had completed more than three decades of working but its work had never been comprehensively reviewed. A committee was therefore constituted to take up such a review. I, as Director, was the convenor of the committee and wrote the report single-handedly. And yet Prof. M.V. Mathur started mentioning it as "Juneja" Committee. I once corrected him telling that Juneja was only a member. In the report, Institute's training, research and consultancy programmes as will as its organisation and administration were all reviewed. Mathur and some others had sometime suggested the constitution of various centres within the Institute like the Urban Administration Centre, which already existed, and others such as rural development centre, criminal justice administration centre etc, I did not see any merit in such an organisation. The various subjects already existed and the faculty for those subjects was already in position. Nothing could be gained by calling them centres except to create some rivalries and bickerings on issues such as who would be the head of these centres. On the other hand I was more keen on giving faculty some experience of actual administration by short period placements and the induction of practicing administration for tenure in the institute. Such a cross fertilization was absolutely essential for a realistic development of the subject of public administration. Unfortunately, in India this has not happened and consequently teaching of the subject is purely academic in character while the practice of public administration is not strengthened by theoretical insights.

Eminent Visitors

Many important persons visited IIPA during my tenure apart from Minister in Government. Amongst them were Nobel Prize winner British Economist of Oxford Prof. John Hicks and his wife Ursula Hicks. Their books "Value and Capital" and "Public Finance" respectively I had read during my student days. I wanted John Hicks to speak but he insisted on his wife giving the lecture. Both were mature, highly respected personalities in tune with each other in the evening of the their lives. They did us the honour of staying in our hostel. Another distinguish visitor was Harvard economist John Kenneth Galbraith who as usual gave a scintillating talk. The 6½" tall Galbraith was an imposing personality. He advised me to visit John Kennedy Institute of Public Administration at Harvard, which I could never make. Dr. V.K. Rao. also gave a well organized lecture on India's Economic problems. Prof. Amartya Sen (who was then a candidate for the Nobel Prize) visited Prof. Kanta Prasad, his former student for a meal at his flat. Sen was simply dressed and was courteous in his manners.

Carpentier, the head of French Ecole Nationale public administration also visited. He wanted some relationship to be established between the two institutions, which however could not be done during my tenure. Riaz Khokar from the Pakistani High Commission also visited. He was suave in his behaviour but later on found to be a committed anti-Indian in his outlook. He became foreign secretary of Pakistan in the Musharraf regime. Perhaps against his own inclition, he had to play an active role in the peace process between India and Pakistan.

A notable American academic thinker on Public Administration F.W. Riggs spent a few days at the Institute. He stayed at the hostel as the guest of the Institute and delivered a series of lectures on recent thinking in public administration. He had earlier visited IIPA when Prof. V.K.N. Memon was the Director. He then introduced the concept of ecology of administration. His lectures were brought out as a publication of the Institute.

Consultancy Projects

Over and above the work of Institute, I also completed a number of small consultancy projects. They started with a project of IFAD (International Fund for Agriculture Development) based in Rome. A team of 5 members headed by a British was given the responsibility to prepare a development project for Badulla District.

I found that Sri Lanka had every district covered by foreign aid for rural development either by multilateral aid or individual donor countries. I was one of the members of a five men team set up by IFAD. I was concerned with institutional development which included financial institutions, cooperatives and local govt. institutions. We stayed in Colomto's Inter-Continental Hotel and also visited some places like Talemanner, a small port town in the north, and Anuradhapur, Kandy and Nuaraelia (mentioned by Pandit Nehru in his autobiography) This was my first visit to the peaceful island of Sri Lanka before the peace was brutally shattered by the rise of the ferocious LTTE in defence of the Tamil interests which were cynically and callously overlooked by the successive Singhalese rulers.

In course of our field work in Sri Lanka, we interacted with a number of Sri Lanka officials in banks and government departments. I found that they had little incentive to work as the administration was thoroughly politicized. Every district had a minister in charge and the "agent" and equivalent to a collector or Deputy Commissioner in India had to work under the orders of the District Minister.

The cooperative had acquired a bad name and were looked upon as institutions to be shunned. All this was hardly an encouraging scene.

At the end of the field work we went to Rome for writing and submitting the report to IFAD authorities. I stayed at a nearby hotel with my wife and went to IFAD office for work. While in IFAD office I met Sartaj Aziz, a Pakistani who was Vice-Chairman, IFAD. He was all praise for China. Aziz later became Finance Minister in Nawaz Sharif government and was briefly under arrest in General Musharraf regime.

I took up three other expert consultancies, *viz.* a development project in Tonga, small irrigation project in Burma (Later known as Myanmar) and a third for development work of voluntary organisations in Philippines and Nepal all of the Asian Development Bank, Tonga is a small island right on 0' longitude in the Pacific Ocean. The sun rises first on the island. The island is inhabited by Tongans, a Polynesian race with average height above 6´´. When the Tongan king nearly 7´´ tall visited India, a special bed had to be fitted for him! The Tonga team was headed by an American, an employee of ADB who was not particularly highly qualified but quite genial offering lemonade all the time to quench the tropical thirst. We all stayed in a single hotel that was available. I greatly liked Tonga because it had the same atmosphere as my native place Karwar or Goa. Tonga had to be reached via Auckland, the largest city in New Zealand. En route Tonga I spent a day on that spread out city. I saw a number of *Maoris,* the natives of New Zealand. They appeared to be moving freely without any particular restrictions. Tonga had little institutional infrastructure. I recommended in my part of the report that this may be set up.

The Burma experience was particularly trying. It was ruled ruthlessly by a military dictatorship which had snuffed out all semblance of freedom. Students who had demonstrated against the military rulers were mowed down by the army. During my stay, I managed to visit the place of carnage in the University campus. No political activity was allowed in Burma. There was no free press either. Only a single sheet was brought out by the military administration which contained only the account of local visits and speeches by the members of the military government. I lived in the Soviet built Inya lake Hotel. In sharp contrast to the bright hotels of Bangkok, it had all the darkness of a socialist country. Indeed Burma's combination of militarism, socialism and Buddhism was lethal to any economic development, social freedom or political development. The tell tale signs of stagnation were writ large every where. The buses of pre-world-war II vintage were invariably over crowded with passengers hanging from the bars. The airport was run down and there were no distinctly coloured taxis. On arrival I managed to get one run down vehicle carrying passengers to the city. As the taxi drove to the city, the driver suddenly stopped in a shady area and offered to convert my dollars into *quats* the local currency at double the official rate. I was alarmed but was tempted not so much by any monetary gain but to get an experience of black market prevailing in strict socialist military economy. I exchanged a small amount but brought a lot of needless worry. I had while entering filled up a currency form giving every detail of currency brought in and I was afraid that while leaving. I might have to account for the currency spent. I even shared my small worry with the Indian Ambassador Shri I.P. Singh. I had not reckoned for the Socialist inefficiency of which I had an experience on arrival itself. My luggage was missing and came later. But when I went later to the airport to claim it, I had to fill up a number of forms to salvage it. My luggage was before me but I could not take it till the procedures were completed!

For collecting information regarding small irrigation project in Burma I visited the public works department in the secretariat. I soon realized that for attaining senior position the civil servants had to join the political outfit of the army. There was no such thing as administrative neutrality. The Burmese government had appointed an Assistant Engineer as my Liaison officer. Through him appointments were fixed which was not always easy. The Liaison officer soon became friendly and once requested me to buy for him some cheese from the *Foreign exchange store* from which such delicacies could be brought which were not accessible to the local people! Their plight was indeed pathetic. I was asked to do my purchases for jades for which Burma is famous from the Scots Market where black marketing, I was told, flourished. I decided not to buy these precious stones lest the functionaries of military government check up my luggage while leaving and detain me for smuggling out precious stones! In spite of the miserable plight of the common people, there was a creamy layer of the select few who were near the people in authority as was seen at "receptions" (marriage or otherwise) which were regularly held at the Inya Lake Hotel. The food at the hotel was extremely drab—the same standard insipid menu for lunch and dinner. As a part of my work, I visited Mandalay. There I requested for a visit to the jail where Lokmanya Tilak and Netaji Subhash Bose were detained. The visit on some excuse, was denied to me. At one time, the Indians were a flourishing community in Burma. Cities like Rangoon and Mandelay were dominated by them. But now most of them had fled and those who remained were in a miserable state without any economic or political clout. I was glad to finish my work and leave Burma, starved as I was of both food and freedom!

On Tonga, Philippines and Burma I wrote general articles which were published in the magazine *Caravan*.

My fourth expert consultancy mission was in relation to the NGOs engaged in development work on Nepal and Philippines. It gave an opportunity to visit a number of NGOS in both the countries. As compared to India in those days, NGOs development activity was prominent in both theses countries. I was surprised to find this but it was to be expected. It was the consequence of the fact that in India. Government had undertaken a number of development programmes while in these countries the field was wide open to NGOs who received funds from donor agencies in the developed countries. Nepal at that time had a Panchayat Raj system under the tutelage of monarchy. It was therefore the queen who was the patron of many of theses voluntary agencies. On paper at least their activities were notable and diversified. During my stay at Kathmandu I took the opportunity to visit the Tribhuvan University I also called on Shri Arvind Dev who was our Ambassador in that country. He had quite an impressive residence. But what I was more impressed with was the US Embassy that I visited. It was like a fortress and the Ambassador was like an emperor. I did not seem to relish this area. Though the proliferation of NGOs both in Nepal and Philippines initially impressed me a great deal, but later on I got a suspicion that the NGOs might well be a conduit for foreign funds reaching the hands of influential people and people in power. Bangladesh has also an impressive array of voluntary organisations whose representatives I met later at a World Bank seminar at Delhi. India in more recent years disenchanted with the performance of government agencies has taken to canalising development funds through voluntary agencies. This is a definite break from the mould of the welfare state with which we started after independence. While voluntary agencies with genuine spirit of service could do better than government agencies, those set up purely for obtaining funds from government, could be a happy hunting ground for self-serving people using public money for their own advancement.

My fifth consultancy project related to Rural Sanitation Project in Malaysia. Here I dealt with severe problem of sanitation in coastal habitations in Malaysia and came out with some innovative proposals.

My five consultancy projects gave me an understanding of development process in Asian Countries—two of them concerned with integrated development as in Sri Lanka and Tonga and with specialised areas as small irrigation projects in Burma and rural sanitation in Malaysia.

My Ph.D. Project

During my five year tenure as Director, IIPA I also did work for my Ph.D. and obtained a doctoral degree from Pune University a year before I laid down my office. It was 1962 when I went for higher studies to LSE as a British Council Scholar that my teacher Prof. S.V. Kogekar had suggested that I work for my Ph.D. But I had only a year's scholarship for completing the postgraduate diploma in a course in Economic and Social Administration and Public Administration. Ph.D. would have meant extending my stay by another two years, which was difficult for a serving civil servant. Moreover a Ph.D. at that time did not appear to be particularly relevant for a civil service career. But the seed of the idea remained in my mind and sprouted when I became Director, IIPA. I explored the procedure and found that I had first to register for Ph.D. with a University and an authorised Ph.D. guide. I thought of Pune University whose M.A. degree I had and asked my contemporary Prof. Nilkanth Rath, an agricultural economist whom I knew well in my student days. For my Ph.D. I did not find it possible to do field work. I wanted my Ph.D. to be based on Library work and had thought of the subject of evolution of agriculture and rural development policies and programmes in post-independence India. To my disappointment Rath declined to be my guide and so I approached Dr. N.R. Inamdar, head of the Dept of Public Administration of Pune University. He agreed and I duly registered. I worked out an outline of my research work. The approach was to do reading on public policy making, identify the ingredients of sound policy making and see to what extent they could be found in evolution of policy in India in regard to agriculture and rural development. I had not only worked in this field and had personal acquaintance with policies and programmes in this sector of administration but had also contributed papers. But Ph.D. work had to be rigorous and there had to be some theoretical framework. After reading a large numbers of books on policy making I realized that policy making related to the conscious formation of measures for the transformation of a given environment into a preferred environment for realization of predetermined goals. The policy making field in agriculture and rural development related to: (a) building basic institutional infrastructure, (b) supplying technical knowledge and inputs, (c) promoting investment, and (d) providing market and structural incentives.

The first included development related extension, community development cooperation and Panchayat Raj, the second related to rural financial institution including cooperatives, rural branches of commercial banks and regional rural banks and the third related to Land Reforms, sound marketing and price incentives. With this basic framework, I did extensive reading and slowly worked out chapters for the thesis.

For my Ph.D. I did not take leave. Reading and writing was part of my work as Director IIPA. The work I did myself, without seeking guidance from the Ph.D. guide who was for away in Pune. However Inamdar did insist on a lengthy introductory writing on the basis of theoretical literature on policy making. This helped me a great deal in designing and conducting courses on policy making assigned to the IIPA under Rajeev Gandhi design of training. Thus my Ph.D. work coalesced with my work as Director IIPA.

After effort of over four years my thesis was finished and bound as required and sent to Pune University for acceptance as Ph.D. dissertation. The material ran over 400 pages. I was asked to appear for a public interview (a system newly introduced by Pune University). After the successful interview, I heard from the University that I was duly awarded the Ph.D. On receipt of the degree, when I changed my name board, academics like S.R. Maheshwari questioned it only to be told that the degree had been duly acquired. None of the academic colleagues or members of the Executive Council thought it necessary to congratulate me.

As a second string to my bow, I had sent my book "Grammar of Planning" and other published books to Bombay University for the award of Doctor of Letters. But there was no response from them for a long time. Shri V. Subramaniam had been awarded the degree for the book "Parched Earth" though as Prof. S.V. Kogekar once told me, the book was based on official work and material available to him in his official capacity and could not have been considered for the award of degree of Doctor of Letters.

Once I enquired with the Vice-Chancellor Smt. Bangalee who told me that the matter was being processed. I was irked by the delay but I could do nothing about it. But in the meanwhile I got a Ph.D. on the basis of my written thesis from Pune University and forgot all about D.Lett. Till one day a pleasant surprise came to me after my retirement when I had settled down at Pune. Shri S.R. Rairikar conveyed a message to me from his brother Prof. B.R. Rairikar, member of Bombay University's academic council that the degree of D.Leitt has been award to me. A few days later a letter duly came to me from the office of the Register that the degree has been awarded to me and that I should collect it from the office on payment of a small sum of Rs. 135/-. I asked my brother staying in Bombay to collect it on my behalf.

My double doctorate got some significance when on retirement; I became Vice-Chancellor Goa University. On my official visiting card, I could proudly mention my two doctoral degrees!

My Ph.D. thesis, I thought deserved publication. I approached Shri Tejeashwar Singh of SAGE publication whether they would like to publish the book. They readily agreed and the book came out in both hardbound and paperback editions. The book got excellent reviews in the *Indian Economic Journal, Indian Journal of Agriculture Economic* and the "*Hindu*".

Memorial Lectures

I was invited to deliver lectures on various aspects of administration. At the invitation of Prof. M.A. Muttalib I delivered a lecture on "Centre State Local Government relationship" at Osmania University, on "Administration Reforms as John Mathai memorial lecture at Kerala University, Janmbhoomi Endowment lecture at Bangalore University" on "responsive administration and on administrative ethics" at Administrative Training Centre of Kerala government. at the invitation of Smt. Padma Ramchandran, its Director. All these lecture were published.

Though I worked with full vigour and enthusiasm for all the five years as Director IIPA, I was not happy with the atmosphere at the IIPA which for reasons mentioned above was the effect of deep rooted tendencies in the Institute developed over the years, *viz.* the tendency of EC members to indulge in petty minded discussion of nuisance value without making any positive contribution and the faculty of the Institute to be concerned only about themselves rather than the Institute. My friend and batch mate Shri Somiah who went from strength to strength in the Central Government. occasionally phoned to remind me that I had to "run a Department". I was by no means averse to it – in fact hoped for it but there was some "block" which came in the way. What exactly was the block and who was responsible for it, I could never discover! Apparently, that I was first from my batch to get promoted to the A.S. level by Janata govt. was held against me. All that I knew was that it had blighted my career in the last and the crucial phase despite a dedicated and meritorious performance of duties. And this was done by a coterie of civil servants who for their own reasons were inimical to me. I frequently wrote articles on public administration which were published in IJPA but also in newspapers like *Statesmen* in which I frankly analysed the administrative situation and expressed my views. I was never officially questioned but that might have been held against me. Once I held in the IIPA a seminar on administrator – politician relationship. That was highlighted in the *Statesman* and I was mentioned as one of the independent minded civil servant who stood for independence of administration untrammelled by political interference. Whatever it be, I felt frustrated. When one suffers but cannot identify the cause of suffering this happens.

Work of Expert Committee

One of my notable assignments during this period was membership of the Committee on District Planning under the chairmanship of Prof. Hanumantha Rao, the economist from Delhi University. The Committee was appointed by the Planning Commission. The subject of District Planning was one in which I was interested for years. Way back in 1959 as Deputy Commissioner, I had done the exercise of preparing the District Plan when "planning from below" was first attempted. I had read Prof. D.R. Gadgil's, R.R. Kale memorial lecture on District Planning based on his Wardha District plan. I had myself delivered a lecture on the subject of local planning. As a member of the committee on District Planning, I contributed the chapter on the methodology of District Planning.

I also contributed to the G.V.K. Rao Committee on district administration in the context of Panchayati Raj set up.

Going Back to Government

While I was expecting the offer for post of Secretary to Government, Shri P.K. Kaul the Cabinet Secretary sent for me and he offered me the job of Director General of NIRD, Hyderabad. I told him that I was not interested in it but in the job of Secretary to Govt. but he did nothing. He left the job of Cabinet Secretary on his appointment as Ambassador to USA and Shri B.G. Deshmukh, who was then serving as Chief Secretary Maharashtra was appointed in his place. I had known him as Additional Secretary in the Home Ministry when I was Establishment Officer and Additional Secretary in the Department of Personnel. We worked in the same building *viz.* the North Block. He would often drop in connection with some appointment in the Home Ministry. When his appointment to succeed Kaul was announced and he was to visit Delhi, I decided to lose no time to call on him. My wife said that though I might have known him, he would ride a high horse— which he did! On his taking over I wrote a letter to him drawing attention to the circular issued at Rajeev Gandhi's instance that those who served as trainers would be given an assignment of their choice at the end of their assignment. My letter had some effect.

When I was at Asian Development Bank (ADB) office at Manila in connection with my consultancy assignment, I got a wire from my private secretary, Shri Malhotra informing me of my appointment as Secretary (Coordination) in the Cabinet Secretariat. I felt happy. Here was an opportunity to get out of IIPA where I had worked long enough and which no longer attracted me.

On my return I sent a note to Shri Vankatappaiah informing him of my appointment and telling him that I would be laying down my office of Director, IIPA and the EC should appoint a successor. An IAS officer who was also a member of EC—Shri M. Subramaniam of Maharashtra Cadre was available. He was Secretary (agriculture). For some reason the Minister Shri Buta Singh had fallen foul of him. He felt that as Secretary, Subramaniam was not loyal to him, had kept him in the dark about some development and had in fact worked contrary to his wishes. He was unceremoniously relieved of his post and was without a job. The job of Director IIPA came handy to him. The EC passed a resolution approving his appointment. But it was now the Govt. of India which started dragging its feet. They would not approve of his appointment as Director, IIPA and without Govt's approval. The IIPA could not act on their resolution to appoint M. Subramaniam as Director. It was the Minister again displeased with Subramaniam who had put his foot down and insisted that he should not be allowed to hold any post under the Central Govt. This was a striking example of how a civil servant cannot afford to clash with politicians in power. This was not only a blow to Subramaniam but also a great discomfiture for IIPA, particularly to Venkatappiah, who as Chairman of the Standing Committee had handled the appointment.

Seeing that Subramaniam's appointment was getting into difficulty, Venkatappaiah suggested that I stay on for some more time till a successor could join. But I had enough of IIPA. I told him that I had already accepted the offer of the Union Govt. and had to join the Union. Govt. by the end of the month and I could not accept his suggestion. I was glad to leave the IIPA.

Was it Worthwhile?

I always wonder whether it was worth my while spending five valuable years at a crucial stage in my administrative career. I wanted to leave for a job of Secretary to Govt. which was my due and of which I was cheated by persistent opposition of my enemies whom I was unable to pinpoint and whose motivations I could not fathom. Once Prof Ramesh Arora of Jaipur University said—"You are a threat to Cabinet Secretary", you are "threat to Home Secretary!" I wondered what made him say so. But that perhaps indicated the type of undercurrent of hostility against me. I had never aspired for these "august" posts of doubtful value. It would be difficult to recollect what concrete contribution was made by the civil servants occupying these posts except to preside over a continuous deterioration in the standard of governance and administration and deterioration in law and order after independence.

However not everything was lost for me. Years after I left IIPA, I would meet officers who had served different organizations and belonged to different services fondly remembering the time they spent attending some course and listening to my address. Only recently as I had gone to attend a music recital, I met a person who accosted me and said—"you remember me—I had attended the APPAA course! There had never been another dynamic Director like you after you left." Perhaps that was my award.

Later I wrote an article. "Why Institutions fail?" Which was published in the *Indian Express*. In that I argued that institutes succeed when they work in a healthy atmosphere and fail when the atmosphere turns sick. I mentioned some factors which lead to organizational sickness. Amongst them was self-serving people on the governing board, who do not allow the Institution to function to fulfill its avowed goals.

CHAPTER 20

Secretary (Coordination) Cabinet Secretariat (1986-88)

A Ring-side View of Cabinet Government

I was happy to be back in government—back from the Institute where I had to bear all responsibility with no support, in an atmosphere which sometimes gave me the feeling of claustrophobia.

Office in the Rastrapati Bhavan Campus

The office of the Cabinet Secretariat is located in one wing of the Rashtrapati Bhavan. It is uniquely different from any of the huge departments of Union Government, located in the sprawling spread of various Bhavans in New Delhi. It is small, compact, almost homely and in the isolated splendour of the Rashtrapati Bhavan. The main office room on the first floor is that of the Cabinet Secretary right in front of which is the Committee room. Just nearby by is the room of Secretary (Coordination). The physical environment in which one works has a bearing on one's official personality. I certainly had a sense of elevation working in that office. From the window of my room I had a view of the tall guards of the Rashtrapati Bhavan in their coloured uniforms parading on the ochre soil and the flowered garden neatly laid round the lawns. Every time I entered through the iron gate of the Rashtrapati Bhavan to my office, I had a sense of thrill and that happened over less than two years from July 1986 to March 1988.

A Missed Opportunity

The day I took charge I had a phone from PM Rajeev Gandhi's office that I had sought an appointment (as Director IIPA) and would I like to meet him. That appointment I had sought for a posting in Government. That reason no longer existed. I had taken my assignment in Government. I thought I would settle in my new job and I could call on him sometime later. My direct and simple way of thinking has been my undoing. The appointment never came and I missed an opportunity. My belief that opportunity would always be available, if one is missed another would come, was optimism often misplaced. The lesson is that if an opportunity does come it should be grabbed with both hands.

I did seek opportunity to meet the PM when my book on "Administrative Reforms" was published. I wanted to present him a copy. I was given an appointment but that was during his "morning Darshan". He had hardly any time as he moved from person to person. All that I got was a photo with the Prime Minister which was published by the publisher on the front page of his publication brochure. So I had in my possession photos with three Prime Ministers of the same lineage—with Pandit Jawaharlal Nehru when he presented me the prize for my essay in the annual essay competition of the IIPA, with Indira Gandhi when I presented her a set of books at the time of my leading the APPPA participants to her residence and now when I presented a copy of my book on "Administration Reforms" to Rajeev Gandhi. I expected him to go through the book but probably he never found time to do so.

The Role of Cabinet Secretariat

The Cabinet Secretary holds the highest position in the civil service hierarchy. The Cabinet Secretariat itself was comparatively of the recent origin—during World War II. Shri H.M. Patel was then the Secretary to the Cabinet though holding the rank of the Joint Secretary in Government of India. Later the position was elevated to that of Secretary and came to be looked upon as the senior most position in the civil service.

When I joined the Cabinet Secretariat as Secretary (coordination) the position was held by Shri B.G. Deshmukh of Maharashtra cadre. He once asked me to write a paper on the role of the Cabinet Secretariat which I did. It was published in *Management in Government* which was probably the first published paper on the subject. As I pointed out in the paper, the role of the Cabinet Secretariat was to serve the Cabinet—to fix meetings of the Cabinet, to prepare agenda, to circulate it, to record the outcome of the Cabinet meetings, to circulate proceedings to those concerned and to take follow up action. The proposals for discussion at the Cabinet came from all the Ministries. According to government's rules of business, certain items like policy issues or external relations or investments in large projects had to get the approval of the Cabinet. The Ministries have to send policy papers to the Cabinet Secretariat to get the Cabinet approval. Before sending the paper, the Ministry was supposed to incorporate the views of the other departments.

Often before the issues were placed before the Cabinet, they were discussed at meetings of Committees of secretaries. These were attended by the secretaries of the departments concerned and chaired by the Cabinet Secretary.

The position of the Chief Secretary in the state is considered analogous to that of Cabinet Secretary. But there is a difference. The size and sweep of the State Government. is much smaller than that of the Central Government. The various departments of the State Government. are located in the same building (now that is also changing as the size of state administration is expanding with the proliferation of departments) while the various Ministries of Union Government. sprawl over a large number of Bhavans apart from the original South Block and North Block where "crucial" Ministers of External Affairs, Defence, Finance and Home are located. The Chief Secretary can therefore exercise a much tighter control over Secretaries of various departments than the Cabinet Secretary. Indeed there is no such tradition of control over departments by the Cabinet Secretary at the Centre. However the Cabinet Secretary does have a voice in the appointment of Secretary in a department. The secretary in trouble with his Minister can seek the help of the Cabinet Secretary.

The Ascending Role of PMO

But in recent years the position of the Cabinet Secretary has been affected by the rise of the PMO headed by Principal Secretary to the Prime Minister. The institution of PMO did not exist in the days of Jawaharlal Nehru. Shri M.O. Mathai was only the Private Secretary to the PM though even he occasionally wielded influence. But it was when Lal Bahadur Shastri succeeded Jawaharlal Nehru that he needed the support of a high level administrator and appointed Shri L.K. Jha a renowned ICS officer to the post of Secretary to Prime Minister. Slowly the post became influential. The aura and the over riding position of the Prime Minister gradually passed on to the Secretary to the PM as well. As more and more specialist officers – such as those in charge of law and order, science and technology, and above all of economic affairs and external affairs etc came to be appointed either as Joint Secretaries or Advisors, the PMO proliferated and soon became a parallel government. The influence of the Principal Secretary to PM reached its peak when Indira Gandhi appointed Shri P.N. Haksar, a Kashmiri pandit and previously an officer of the Indian Foreign Service as her Principal Secretary. The latter is by the side of the PM all the time. He is with the PM when the day breaks out and also when it ends whereas the Cabinet Secretary could meet PM only on appointment. It was said that even when a competent, ICS officer like Shri B. Sivaraman was appointed as Cabinet Secretary, he could see PM rarely and it was the Principal Secretary, Shri Haksar who carried the day. The civil servants who are more interested in watching the balance of power in government rather than their own work, soon sensed the difference and adjusted themselves, whereas a civil servant like me who is always immersed in his own work and goes by the formal institutional position had to pay the price at the time of elevation to Secretary. I found that the Cabinet Secretary, Shri Rao Saheb could be neither effective nor dependable. The overwhelming position of the P.M. and the PMO soon transformed the Cabinet form of government into Prime Ministerial Government. The transformation was not unique to India. It look place in the country known as the origin of Parliamentary Democracy, *viz*. UK where the transformation became pronounced under the powerful personality of Margaret Thacher. P.N. Hakser's position waned when he clashed with Sanjay Gandhi but the institutional change became permanent and survived even the end of dynastic rule and one party dominance at the centre.

Compared with PMO, the Cabinet secretariat remained small. Besides me as secretary (co-ordination), there was an additional secretary's post (filled by Shri Rajamani of AP cadre who was earlier Joint Secretary in PMO) and a Deputy Secretary below him. The whole paraphernalia of the intelligence agencies, *viz*. RAW, joint intelligence wing etc., supposed to be part of cabinet secretariat worked from elsewhere and their presence was not felt in the small building of the cabinet secretariat.

The Role of Secretary (Co-ordination)

The post of secretary (coordination) was created to assist Shri T.T. Krishnamachari when he was appointed as Minister in charge of economic coordination. That ministerial position ceased to exists after TTK's exit but the post of secretary (coordination) survived and continued. I did not come across any precise definition of the post (such formal delineation of duties does not always exist in government) nor did I try to define "coordination" of which I was supposed to be in charge. I realized that in the system of parliamentary democracy, the PM himself or herself is the converging point of administration and of coordination which position became more pronounced after the cabinet government became the Prime Ministerial government. While the cabinet secretariat to continued play the modest role of serving the cabinet meetings, the PMO proliferated and became more influential with finger in every pie. The ministries started looking to it to know which way the PM was inclined. So as secretary (coordination) I had to do what I was allowed to do. Any stronger desire and attempt towards coordination was not practical. Coordination could be done only through the cabinet mechanism.

Cabinet secretary Shri B.G. Deshmukh found out a neat way of sharing work with me. As cabinet secretary he had to attend meetings of the cabinet and its two principal subcommittees, *viz.* Cabinet Committee on Political Affairs (CCPA) and The Cabinet Committee on Economic affairs (CCEA). But the cabinet often appointed Groups of Ministers (GOM) to examine in depth issues or proposals coming before it as part of cabinet agenda wherever doubts were raised or where issues were complex or ambiguous and decision could not be taken by the cabinet on the basis of material placed before it. In Rajeev Gandhi's days the number of GOMs proliferated and reached nearly fifty. Obviously the Cabinet Secretary could not personally attend to the meetings of all the GOMs and assigned the work to me. So far as the GOMs were concerned, I had to service them. When I started the work, I could realize that the conduct of meetings of so many GOMs could be a daunting task. The number of GOMs started only growing! The convenience of Ministers who were appointed as chairmen had to be ascertained, meetings fixed, proceeding recorded and the decisions remitted back to the cabinet, which in the first instance had appointed them. The simultaneous existence of a large number of GOMs could become unmanageable. But by systematically organizing the work of GOMs I was able to get the work of GOMs completed and their number eventually came down considerably.

The Working of GOMs

GOMs brought me in close touch with many ministers who had acted as chairmen of these groups Shri P.V. Narasimha Rao, HRD Minister who later became PM, Shri Buta Singh holding the important portfolio of the Home Ministry, Shri P. Shivshankar, the Law Minister, Shri Narayan Dutt Tiwari, the Industry Minister, Shri Vasant Sathe, Minister information and Shri Madhavrao Scindia, then young and upcoming minister close to Shri Rajiv Gandhi etc. They all seemed to be quite cautious lest they should take a wrong step and do something which the PM may not approve of. I remember one example. The case of the factories of The National Textile Corporation. They ware running into losses and the experience had clearly shown that no amount of additional investment would make them viable. The only alternative was to denationalise them. They were wrongly nationalized in the first instance by Smt. Indira Gandhi in the name of protecting employment and became a bottomless pit for the public exchequer and yet Tiwari would not recommend denationalisation. Since no less then Smt. Indira Gandhi had nationalized them! I gave him the example of Mrs. Margaret Thatcher who had shown the boldness to go headlong on the road to privatisation. But her example was not sufficient for him to muster courage. Ultimately the GOM came up with some wishy washy recommendation. Another GOM I remember was on the formulation of Policy on youth. I myself prepared a draft based on the draft sent by Department of youth, drawing on my past thinking while serving as Director, youth. Shri Sathe who was chairman of the group appreciated the draft but when it came up for discussion members like Shri Madhavrao Scindia and Smt. Sheela Dixit started raising objection. In my draft I had recalled the statement of Pandit Jawaharlal Nehru that the "present generation is sentenced to do hard work " and had exhorted the youth in the manner of John Kennady that they should ask "not what their country would give them but what they would give to their country". But they were not prepared to go with this. They wanted to go soft on the youth and give them sops only! Scindia wanted English of the draft to be improved (!) I did not tell him that I was a winner of the Hughlings prize of Bombay University for proficiency in English. The youth policy languished in the face of such objections!

CCPA and CCEA

On occasions I attended meetings of CCPA and CCEA as well as the full Cabinet, sitting by the side of Rajeev Gandhi. I found that he would come armed with little notes from the officers of the PMO and was inclined to go by the advice of the officers of the PMO rather than go by the recommendation of the cabinet note prepared by the Ministry concerned. The Cabinet would generally go by PM's inclinations and the contribution of the Ministers would generally be muted. This was bound to happen. Ministers owed their position to PM rather than to their own political strength.

CCPA was a very small group. It was an inner circle of Government consisting of Defence Minister and Home Minister in addition to PM. I remember a meeting when it was decided to give

Goa the statehood. Rajeev Gandhi remarked that since the language controversy is now finally settled (with Konkani recognized as the state language), the state could be brought into existence.

I remember another meeting when the question of sending peace keeping force to Sri Lanka was discussed. Rajeev Gandhi was in two minds but Shri P. Chidambaram who was called in egged him on saying that India as the regional super-power should be equal to its responsibility. It was a bad advice which not only led to the eventual return of the IPKF in ignominy but also ultimately culminated in his tragic assassination when he was no longer the PM but was actively campaigning in Tamil Nadu for return to power.

In yet another meeting to which I was suddenly summoned Shri Rajeev Gandhi was battling with a grave situation when reports came that corpses of Muslims brutally killed flowed in the Hindon canal on the outskirts of Delhi. Shri Rajeev Gandhi was not sure as to what to do; should this episode be allowed be publicized and government's reaction clearly stated or should be suppressed as far as possible. Tragic killings of Muslims had taken place during communal riots at Meerut and their dead bodies thrown in Hindon canal. The tragic event was serious and government should have taken a categorical stand without fearing the back lash which the publicity of the event might have produce. His grandfather Pandit Jawaharlal Nehru had advised his daughter never to fear the light and never do anything in darkness. But after consulting Shri Veer Bahadur Singh, CM of UP, on phone, Shri Rajeev Gandhi decided to suppress the event rather than to publicize it and boldly state the government's stand. It was only slowly that the newspapers brought out various facts regarding the tragic events. This was not so much a systematic meeting of CCPA as a PM trying to tackle a delicate situation.

The Shadow of Bofors

In his early days as PM, Shri Rajeev Gandhi had the image of "pleasant Mr. Clean" – but certain events happened and he lost the image. The shadow of Bofors fell on him like that of a dark cloud. The newspapers broadcast the report from the Swedish radio that government was involved in a big scam in the purchase of guns for the army. The response of Shri Rajeev Gandhi did not inspire confidence. He first tried to suppress the scam and then denied his personal involvement. When the pressure grew, he appointed a Parliamentary Committee under Shri Shankaranand of dubious reputation whose method of investigation did not inspire confidence. To add to Rajeev's woes his relationship with the once loyal Shri Zail Singh installed in the position of President became visibly strained. Shri Zail Singh was upset that Rajeev did not see him at all in order to slight him and did not perform the constitutional duty of the Prime Minister to "inform" the President. Shri Zail Singh expressed his displeasure in various ways including withholding Presidential approval to a Post Bill to amend the postal law which was referred to him by government. conferring on government. officers powers of surveillance over postal correspondence. This was rightly looked upon by people as emergency type regulation depriving them of the fundamental right of liberty given by the constitutions. The action of the hostile President received popular approval to the discomfiture of the Prime Minister. Soon rumours started floating that this step was but the beginning of the extreme step which President intended to take to dismiss a "corrupt" Prime Minister. This would have created a constitutional crisis of the first order in the history of independent India. Fortunately the President was persuaded not to take the extreme step. But the popularity, authority and credibility of the Prime Minister and his government were thoroughly compromised despite the unprecedented majority that Shri Rajeev Gandhi enjoyed in Parliament. That asset was eroded and the government lost confidence of the people if not Parliament. The tremors were clearly felt not only in our office situated in the Rashtrapati Bhavan itself but in the entire swathe of sprawling Bhavans of central government administration. It appeared that the whole administrative process came to a grinding halt by the single issue of Bofors. The opposition took full advantage of Bofors incident to malign the Prime Minister. Shri V.P. Singh who as finance minister was numbers two in the Cabinet himself raised the banner of revolved against the Prime Minister. He was shifted to Defence but there too he intensified his attack and added purchase of submarines from Germany as yet another example of scam. He was forced to resign but became popular and led the attack on Rajeev Gandhi.

The Humiliation of Secretaries

No wonder in this kind of atmosphere, the hopes and euphoria of the early years of Rajeev Gandhi evaporated. The PM's mood changed. He became irascible and often vented his ire on the civil servants. Two secretaries Shri C.S. Shastri of the Department of Agriculture and Shri D. Bandyopadhya of the Dept. of Rural Development became victims of his ire. They were asked to give presentation of the work of their departmental activities. The PM was thoroughly disappointed with their performance and gave them a public dressing down. The discomfiture of the secretaries was complete when the whole event was splashed in the press next day. The hapless secretaries ran to Shri Sam Pitroda advisor to the PM whose presentation the PM had been thoroughly appreciated when he first appeared like a comet on the horizon of Indian Administration, to get lessons in the art of presentation. The Pitroda's help proved useful and the second presentation by the two secretaries passed muster.

Another secretary was in for even a greater shock. That was Foreign Secretary Shri A.P. Venkateshwaran. He was certainly a very intelligent and outspoken officer of the IFS but Rajeev Gandhi apparently was not keen (perhaps for those reasons) to appoint him as Foreign Secretary. But after appointment him he did not find him on his own wave length. Once in a press conference on PM making a statement in relationship to Pakistan, the press correspondents drew attention to a contrary statement made earlier by the Foreign Secretary. The PM not only disowned it but declared in the full glare of the press conference that they would get a new Foreign Secretary. Audience in the country watching the press conference on the TV, particularly in the nation's capital were shell shocked! Shri Venkateshwaran had no alternative but to resign the very next day.

The two events involving top bureaucrats were not conducive to norms of proper relationship between the ruling politicians and the civil servants. Those relationship have to be confidential in nature and are not meant to be publicised. Such publicity can destroy the very basis of confidence. Civil servants must have the confidence to express their views and give their advice without fear. After these two incidents which secretary would have the requisite confidence?

These incidents apart, the fact that the civil servants had no self-confidence to express their views frankly became obvious to me at a private meeting with secretaries over dinner at Hyderabad House, arranged by the PM. This was during the days before PM became irascible, a few days before Bofors issue burst on the scene. Perhaps PM was aware of the shape of things to come. Because as the secretaries gathered round him at a meeting, The PM out of the blue, as it were raised the issue of corruption. "Why do people believe so easily in the allegation of corruption against government" asked the PM. There was silence as no secretary was prepared to stick his neck out. I was not in charge of any department and hence had no connection with any possible event of corruption and perhaps not qualified to talk about corruption. Nor did I stop to contemplate the reason behind the stunning silence of the secretaries. In my usual style of rushing where the angels feared to tread, I said "Believing in rumours is in our blood from Ramayan days. Even Sita was not spared by rumours spread about her chastity when she was held captive by Ravan. To ward off allegations, we must establish traditions of incorruptibility. In recent years we have hardly established such traditions. How can then we expect that the people would not believe in the allegations of corruption in government." I don't think my frank talk was well taken though the PM did not give any reaction nor did any other IAS secretary who wanted to play safe. They did not express any views on the sensitive subject. Only the scientist Dr. Arunachalam, Chief Scientific Advisor to the Defence Ministry, spoke making some general observations. Surely the conclave of over 40 secretaries to government of India did not make PM any wiser regarding the issue raised by him. Did the PM have any premonition of Bofors? Confining the question to me only "did I speak out of turn? Were the other secretaries wiser in their silence?"

In course of my work, I could not have any day to day interaction with the Prime Minister. The PM mostly had it probably with his own staff in PMO and perhaps the Cabinet Secretary. For the post of Cabinet Secretary he had picked up mild mannered Shri B.G. Deshmukh, obviously he would not have an assertive officer in this place. Intellectually strong civil servants are rarely relished or tolerated by the politicians in power unless they are more sure of themselves. As his principal secretary, Rajeev Gandhi picked up Smt. Sarla Grewal of the Punjab cadre who was then holding a comparatively less influential position of secretary, Health and Family Planning. I had met her and her husband who rose to the position of Cabinet Secretary when I was studying at LSE – She was also doing some course in social welfare. I had also some contact with her when I was Establishment Officer. She was not known for her intellectual prowess but had some reputation for being a "no nonsense" civil servant who would wield a hunter when needed. Perhaps Rajeev Gandhi needed such a civil servant. It was said that Rajeev Gandhi did not relish long notes to be submitted to him. He was not like his grandfather who was an intellectual with a flare for analysing national issues. I had read all the volumes of his letters to the Chief Ministers which showed how meticulously and objectively he would analyse national issues, bringing out and balancing both the limitations and possibilities and alternatives. I had in course of my work as secretary (coordination) came across a long note which he himself recorded on the subject of administrative reforms. No such note could be expected from Rajeev Gandhi. Perhaps an ex-pilot, he relished technological precision rather than any elaborate analysis. But national issues hardly lend to such technological yes or no precision.

However Rajeev Gandhi liked that line and therefore preferred a rank outsider like Sam Pitroda – a technologist who had immigrated from his native Gujrat to USA and had many patents to his credit in the field of telecommunication. He had demonstrated successfully the strategy of the spread of telephone facilities all over India even in rural areas through franchised booth system, which provided thousands self-help employment opportunities as well. The same "technology mission" mode was extended to other areas like oil seed production which too became successful. Once after listening to me on TV participating in a conversation with Lt. General Chibber, then Director, Management Development Institute, Gurgaon on the importance of training administrators, he felt impressed and phoned to me in office conveying his appreciation. But I failed to capitalise on his appreciation by developing relationship with him, though it was in line with my general approach of keeping to myself, doing my job well and leaving everything to fate though I started realizing that that was not always the best approach.

The Officers of the PMO

The PMO contained several officers in charge of specialised areas of administration. They were large enough in number and of such influence that PMO came to be known as the real government. One of them was Shri Gopi Arora a UP civilian in charge of perhaps law and order and confidential matters, another was Shri M.S. Ahluwalia (who had served in World Bank) in charge of economic matters; a third was Smt. Otima Bordia of Rajasthan cadre who looked after the social sector, Shri H.Y. Sharda Prasad was the information advisor to the PM. They were all on positions of Additional Secretary. They were aware of their influence and were not readily accessible but generally did not throw about their weight or stick their neck out. But not always when it came to their own interest. I had a strange experience of this when one day quite sometime after I joined, when I was at my residence, I got a call – quite unexpected from Shri Gopi Arora. He peremptorily told me that the PM had approved of his posting as secretary in the Department Information and the orders should be issued. This was a strange way of communicating PM's decision to appoint a secretary. This was a matter about which the PM or Principal Secretary to PM should have spoken to the Cabinet Secretary and not the officer concerned to Secretary (coordination) in the cabinet secretariat. It is a well known convention that the handling of an appointment of an officer is made by another officer of the relevant department or organisation and not by the Officer himself. Shri Arora should have known of this wholesome practice but did not care to follow it when his own case was involved. I did not feel it necessary to tell him about this because it would have served no purpose. I simply heard and did not respond. I had, of course, no doubt that he would not have spoken to me without PM's clearance. It was a holiday and I spoke to Shri Rajamani at his residence and told him that the information given by Shri Gopi Arora may be processed.

The same Gopi Arora was involved in Bofors scandal case. I had no personal knowledge about this involvement. But I saw how he was handling the Bhopal Tragedy. This is one of the worst scandals in post-independence India when the main culprit Mr. Anderson, Chairman of MNC Union Carbide was allowed to go scot-free and the unfortunate victims were given a short shrift by even the Supreme Court by withdrawing all criminal cases against Union Carbide in subordinate course for reasons, which could not be appreciated. A scientific committee was appointed to find out facts. The committee had given its reports but was simply allowed to continue its existence. The case came to me. I met Shri K.R. Narayan, Minister of State for Science and Technology (who later became president of India) and told him that the committee having given its report had no reason raison detre. He agreed with me with some hesitation which could only be attributed to his lack of confidence. He would not speak out categorically. Perhaps the committee was being used as a fig leaf to avoid a categorical decision being taken. That was why when after meeting Narayanan, I gave an unambiguous recommendation to wind up the committee, it was continued, perhaps at the instance of Gopi Arora. To my simple minded logical thinking the decision was un-understandable except for some ulterior reasons. So much for transparency in government!

In the days when Rajeev Gandhi, "the pleasant" was not eclipsed by the Bofors shadow, I once sat by his side in a meeting of CCEA and whispered in his ears "many happy returns of the day" as that was his birthday. He glowed with happiness and Ministers wondered what magic I had exercised to make PM so happy.

But when his mood turned irascible due to Bofors and when secretaries became the targets of his dark mood, I too had an unpleasant experience. I was sitting by his side in a meeting to consider the drought situation. I was quietly sitting by his side taking notes. As mentioned earlier Rajeev Gandhi appeared allergic to notes, while they were the stock in trade of civil servants; looking at me menacingly he suddenly asked "what is it that you have taken down?" For a moment I felt unnerved that he should ask such a question in such a manner. But I gathered wits and glancing over my notes not always legible of discussion not always coherent, I started blurting out the main points. Rajeev Gandhi had no patience to listen and continued the meeting without any further flare up.

Nocturnal Exercise of Cabinet Expansion

But I had an experience of Rajeev Gandhi' strange method of working when suddenly at about 9 p.m. I had a phone from Smt. Sarla Grewal, his principal secretary that I should immediately arrive at PM's residence to help in a rather large exercise of Cabinet expansion. A car from PMO was to pick me up. I got ready. I was picked up and reached the PM's residence in tight security. The Cabinet Secretary Shri B.G. Deshmukh was away at Hydrabad and hence I had to take the responsibility in his place.

I sat in a small room in the PM's house where Smt. Sarla Grewal was present and so were two other Ministers *viz.* Shri Buta Singh and Shri M.L. Fotedar who were perhaps summoned by Rajeev Gandhi to help him in the exercise. Suddenly Rajeev Gandhi arrived and some names were mentioned with their possible portfolios. He again went back to his chamber to dart in a little later to add some more names. Again he went back. This back and forth movement went on for quite some to time. And I was hard put to it in keeping track. Being engaged in this work, I could not always get up when he would briskly make an entry, as Smt. Sarla and Buta did! Suddenly Rajeev Gandhi turned to me and asked—"What is it you are taking down?" I told him that I was noting the names which he was mentioning. The strange nocturnal exercise went on till 2 a.m. when it was completed at long last. I read out the outcome of the exercise to Smt. Sarla and Buta Singh. The exercise of expansion of ministry was finalized. The new ministers were to be sworn in at the Rashtrapati Bhavan next day morning at 9.30 a.m. When I returned home from the PM's house, my wife wondered what I was doing all these hours at night! It was said of Morarji Desai that he would go to bed sharply at 9 pm and would not like to be disturbed by state affairs. Rajeev Gandhi much younger and with an entirely different background had a different mode of working.

Next day early morning I phoned Deshmukh and told him about the swearing in ceremony. He was surprised but said he would try to be at the swearing in ceremony. When I arrived at the swearing in hall at Rashtrapati Bhavan, I was surprised that Rajeev Gandhi appeared very fresh with not a trace of fatigue left by the nocturnal exercise! The newly to be sworn in ministers obviously felt very happy one of whom from Karnataka called on me at my residence as a token of his gratefulness! Surprisingly Deshmukh could also managed to arrive at the swering in function!

Whirl of Meetings but Little Sence of Direction

All the less than two years that I worked in the cabinet secretariat were spent in attending meetings every day – meetings of secretaries of GOM and occasionally of the cabinet and its sub committees. As my friend Dr. V.A. Paipanaudikar observed, in the last phase of my administrative carrier. I got a ring-side view of administration and government at the apex. This was indeed true. How did it look? As far as I could see, there was hardly any sense of direction in the whirl of activities – any sense of priorities. All was grist to the mill. Even bizarre items would certainly turn up – such as starting casinos on off shore ships to attract tourism or produce arms in defense factories for export in order to earn foreign exchange. Were they only kite flying exercises or serious proposals? In Jawaharlal Nehru's days there was clearly a sense of distinct and definite sets of polities – planned economic development, self-reliance and nation building promotion of science and technology as the foundation of development, decentralization through panchayati raj and cooperation, non-alignment, and secularism. Nehru himself was the policy maker and would himself draft policy documents. As the Israel public administrative expert observed, there has to be a "mind of government" which should be reflected in policy making. In Nehru's days the "mind of Government" could be clearly seen. Since his days things had changed. An overseeing mind giving a sense of direction was missing and hence casinos could find a place along with the proposal to set up a council for forecasting and assessment of scientific development. Professionalism in policy making also appeared lacking. Policy papers emanating from Ministries often were loosely drafted. Policymaking should be treated as a science. Policy is an instrument for the transformation of a given environment into a preferred environment for achieving definite objectives. Policy makers in government, i.e., those at the helm of Ministries seemed to be lacking this awareness. Hence the inclusion of contradictory objectives, failure to link policy instruments with policy objectives and confusion of policies with programmes. The Textile Policy or the Drugs Policy that came up before the Cabinet were of this sort. They appeared to be a bundle of contradictions and one would not know what they were aiming at.

Policy Making—The Achiles Heel of Government

The job of policy making is the most important responsibility of government at the highest level. Without clear policies there is drift. Policies must have clear objectives. They are not a pious set of desires. They have to be translated into action. Policy must clearly delineate the means and instruments of reaching objectives. Policies should be regularly evaluated. Without such evaluation policies get outdated in a changing environment. Socio-economic realities, constantly change and thereby bring about changes in environment. In the day to day disposal of files and decision making, Ministries and even government as a whole lose the larger sense of perception. Who should do the job of policy making and evaluation in every Ministry—the Minister or the secretary? Both should do this but both are too busy to find time to focus on this primary responsibility of policy making. They have no "mind" of their own.

It is the PM and the Cabinet Secretary who should do the meta-policy making. They should have a clear sense of direction and of priorities in government. Nehru had it but his successors—Indira and Rajeev perhaps did not have his comprehensive perspective though they did try to carry out his legacy. But times were changing and needed a proper response though some of the old problems left by Nehru himself persisted like relationship with USA, China and neighbouring Pakistan as well as the domestic challenge of improving the rate of economic growth. Both Indira and Rajeev had sensed that Nehruvian socialism had led to economic stagnation and took faltering steps towards liberalization. But in the absence of a comprehensive policy making perspective those were inadequate compared with liberalization in China initiated since 1979 by Deng Xiao Ping, the supreme leader and his policy of four modernizations. Consequently China's economic reforms and resultant rate of economic growth turned out to be faster.

The Cabinet Secretary himself hardly appeared to play a positive role in policy making. Servicing the Cabinet and responding to the directions of the Prime Minister perhaps took all the time. Perhaps the initiative in policy making had shifted to the PMO from the Cabinet secretariat. I could not help feeling that the Cabinet secretariat should play a major role in policy making. Rather than merely holding meetings of secretaries and servicing the Cabinet, it should do its own thinking on policy making and take initiatives. But this hardly happened. The Administrative Reforms Commission had recognized the importance of policy making and had recommended a cell in every Ministry on policy making. Such cells were established in some Ministries under a Joint Secretary. But in the absence of Minister having suitable perspective, he hardly gave any importance to this cell and could not creatively use it for policy making. The Joint Secretary became yet another aide to the Minister. This drift in policy making is a major deficiency in government. This needs to be corrected and suitable mechanism should be created. The Cabinet secretariat must emerge as a powerful instrument of proactive policy making all the time responding to the changing environment with an alert and agile mind. But if the "mind" is lacking mere mechanism would not serve the purpose. In the absence of both the mind and the mechanism the work of coordinated policy making suffered. There was piecemeal policy making in Ministries—often at cross purposes with each other. This was the supreme task of "coordination" which I as Secretary (coordination) was hardly in any position to undertake.

Intelligence Reports

The same lack of mind was seen in the use of the reports of intelligence agencies. Prolix reports would emerge from time to time from intelligence agencies like IB and RAW. I got copies of these reports and read them avidly. In addition to the special reports, there would also be regular reports. They often contained insights but to take action on them they needed to be more precise. That precision was lacking. Some threat to security would be indicated but where exactly it would occur or what exactly would be its nature would not be indicated. Also the high-up had to have the time to go through the reports, interpret them and take some positive measures. This did not appear to be happening. One simply did not see any action following the reams and reams of reports of intelligence agencies. Sometimes I would send brief notes based on my reading to the Cabinet Secretary who pressed them on to the Home Ministry. What the Home Ministry did was not known. Perhaps they did not appreciate the "interference" in their work. Over the years the Home Ministry was given to creating new types of police forces, increasing their number and deploying them to the spots where the trouble occurred, rather than preventing their occurrence by taking timely preemptive steps.

Like security intelligence reports there had to be "economic intelligence" reports but they were not received. There was a "committee on prices" headed by Minister for Civil supplies which took note of rise in prices of commodities as they occurred but the committee's work was not related to macro-economic policies which were the province of the Finance Ministry.

A Missed Opportunity of Foregoing Assignment

While I was busy working as secretary (coordination) I had an opportunity to take a foreign assignment which I had missed despite my being in charge of the foreign assignment section as EO. A vacancy had occurred in the post of Director, Asia Pacific Centre at Kuala Lumpur, Malaysia. The incumbent, a Malaysian, was retiring. I had known him well. I had spent some time at the centre for an expert consultation meeting and he had visited me when I was Director, IIPA. He had good relations with me and I thought he would be helpful in supporting my candidature. The Cabinet secretary, Shri B.G. Deshmukh was able to get the candidature approved by PM and it was duly sponsored. But for it to be finalised, it required to be supported by the Asia countries represented on its Board of Management. The support had to be mobilized by active canvassing. I spoke to Shri A.N. Verma who was then secretary in the Commerce, which was the nodal functionary in government who had to lead mobilization on behalf of government. Shri Varma appeared to be lukewarm (later Verma became Principal secretary to Prime Minister Narasimha Rao and came to be known as A(bhi) N(ahi) Verma!). Deshmukh felt I should go to Kuala Lumpur to myself whip up support. Accordingly, I went and immediately contacted Indian High Commissioner who had to contact the representatives of other governments. I asked him whether he could arrange my meetings with them but he asked me to hold on. But next day he told me that the Board meeting had been held and the nominee of South Korea has been selected. South Korea had a more dominating influence. I felt disappointed. I wondered whether the Commerce Ministry and the External Affairs Ministry had done enough. Earlier when Institute of Race Relationship in Sri Lanka had invited me to attend a seminar Secretary of the Department of External Affairs Shri Venkateshwaran had come in the way saying that time was not opportune for a senior officer of government. to visit Sri Lanka. Strange indeed, I thought, are the ways of the Ministry of External Affairs which can hold up but not support when needed. I returned to Delhi, crest fallen. My being in Kuala Lampur served no purpose!

Post Retirement Job of Vice-Chancellor

My date of retirement came. I was given a send-off by the little group of officers of the Cabinet Secretariat. Deshmukh who was older had stayed on because he was given extension but I had to retire. I had completed 35 years of service and had no reason to feel disappointed.

However at 58, I still felt completely fit and at the top of my faculties. I therefore asked both Shri Deshmukh and Smt. Sarla Grewal for a possible post-retirement assignment. But while they said they would try, they were not particularly serious about it.

My son was doing his Ph.D. at Cornell University, USA and we had to visit him. I was in touch with Prof. Upoff of Cornell University who was the Head, Rural Development Division. He invited me as Senior Fellow (though without monetary benefit—only facilities) I had decided to work on Drought (India was said to have had in 1987 the worst drought of the 20th century) My stay was to be for a short period of 4 months. I did extensive reading and prepared a long paper which was presented and commented upon. On my return, I sent the paper to "*Economic and Political Weekly*" which duly published it. In a later issue, the renowned economist Dr. S.R. Sen published an article in which he greatly appreciated my contribution.

Though government did not give me any post-retirement assignment, an excellent assignment came my way. Dr. V.A. Pai Panandikar, Director, Centre for policy Research in New Delhi persuaded me to send my bio-data to the Chief Secretary, Goa for a possible of the post of Vice-Chancellor of the newly established Goa University. Several months later as I was just settling down in Pune, I got a phone call from Governor of Goa making the offer. I accepted it. The five year assignment was to my liking. I have given an account of my five years as Vice-Chancellor, Goa University in my book—"Building up a new University" brought out by Allied Publishers, Bombay.

CHAPTER 21

Epilogue

Finished Innings of Thirty-five Years

I spent full thirty-five years as an officer of the Indian Administrative Service. I retired on superannuation on 31st March 1988 on completion of 58 years. (The retirement age for IAS officers has since been raised to 60 years) It was not a case of "unfinished innings" as in the case of Shri Madhav Godbole!

Each of the chapters of my account deals with a specific post that I held and the specific assignment that I had completed in that post. Each chapter therefore is like a case study in Public Administration. Each chapter of my account relating to each post I had held, focused on a particular theme of administration with which I was concerned in my posting. I have given sub-titles to the chapters which define the main theme. These themes would show how administration after independence assumed very different character. The new concerns of administration gave a new meaning to the work of civil servants

Changing Profile of Administration

My account of 35 years in the Indian Administrative Service may be taken as a case study of the changing profile of administration in the years following independence when political power was transferred from British Colonial Administration to the elected representatives of the people. My 35 years saw five Prime Ministers at the helm of Indian Administration—three from the Nehru dynasty which assumed a unique place in Indian political firmament which it has not yet lost. Jawaharlal Nehru was Prime Minister for seventeen years. His daughter Indira Gandhi had also a long period of fourteen years broken into two spells because of the consequence of imposition of emergency which led to her loss of power. After her tragic assassination, her son Rajiv Gandhi became Prime Minister. He could not return to power after his first term of five years because of the Bofors issue. Jawaharlal Nehru was succeeded by Lal Bahadur Shastri. His integrity, simplicity and grit in times of war with Pakistan made great impression on the people. Unfortunately he met pre-mature end in Tashkent. Morarji Desai became the first non-congress Prime Minister at the Centre. He could not complete his term because he was ditched by the number two Minister in his cabinet, Shri Charan Singh, who was consumed by the ambition to become Prime Minister. He had to pay the price for his treachery. Congress withdrew support and he could not face Parliament even once. These momentous changes left their mark on administrative environment in which the civil servants had to function. In days of Nehru there was air of self-confidence and atmosphere of stability and the civil servants knew where they stood. The relationship between the minister and civil servants was that of mutual trust. After Nehru's death, politics became turbulent and times became uncertain. The civil servants had to watch their steps. The change in politics at the centre had it effects on state politics as well. Both at the Centre and in the States there was growing politicisation of the civil service.

Postings at all Levels of Administration

The career of a civil servant consists of a series of postings. During my 35 years of service I had some sixteen postings. I must consider myself fortunate that I did not have a larger number of postings. Some civil servants had 30 postings with an average of one year per posting. Short durations make it impossible for an officer to make any contribution or to do justice to any assignment much less to leave a footprint. My average was more than two years. In two postings namely Director IIPA and Director VAMNICOM, I spent five years and as Divisional Commissioner Belgaum I spent more than three years. My postings with tenure of less than one year were as Director, Studies, at National Institute of Community Development at Mussorie and Secretary PWE in the government of Karnataka. My other postings had tenure of one to two years.

Of the thirty-five years of service, I spent more than half the career with the Centre (probation 1953-54 one year; 1962 to 1971 nine years and 1977-88 eleven years, total 21 years), nine years at earlier and eleven years at a later stage of my career. Of the fourteen years in the State, eight and a half years were in field assignments (1955 to 1959, 1973 to 1977), four years at junior level and four and half years at senior level. At the junior level I worked in two subdivisions in two different parts of the old Mysore state and four and half in two assignments in North (Bombay) Karnataka. In my administrative career I thus worked at all the echelons in higher administration in India without missing any level .I was Assistant Commissioner (Assistant Collector), Deputy Commissioner (Collector) and Divisional Commissioner at the graded levels in field administration, head of several heads of field departments (as Administrator, Maleprabha and Ghataprabha project) and Deputy Secretary and Secretary in the State Secretariat and Deputy Secretary, Director, Joint Secretary, Additional Secretary and Secretary in the Central government. Most officers of the IAS miss one stage or another, I did not miss any. I may therefore claim to have had a "Complete" administrative career."

A Trainer as Well

But I had something more than that. I was also a trainer and headed four national training institutions, *viz.* National Institute of Community Development (Mussorie) which later become National Institute of Rural Development, Hyderabad Vaikunth Mehta National Institute of Cooperative Management (of which I was the Founder Director) and College of Agriculture Banking of the RBI (of which I became the first Principal after it was shifted from Bombay to Pune in its new premises in Pune) and Indian Institute of Public Administration for full five years in New Delhi. In all these training assignments I met and interacted with hundreds of officers in a whole range of governmental and semi governmental organisations. It was a substantial contribution to human resources development in administration.

Public Administration – An Opportunity for Serving the Nation

From the beginning of my administrative career, I had looked upon it not as means of earning a living but as an opportunity to serve the nation. This is what I had told the ICS head of the Union Public Several Commission who had interviewed me and this was what I adhered to till the end of my administrative career. I found that this posture of mine was never appreciated. The Chairman of the UPSC himself was skeptical about it and felt that this was purely said to please the interviewing panel and getting selected though I was quite earnest. Slowly I realized that to be earnest was itself suspect in the cynical world of public administration under the shadow of self-serving politicians. That is why a cynical administrative superior asked me "Have you still retained your conscience?" I was taken aback but did not tell him that I could not live and work without a conscience.

Later on I added one more dimension to my posture as a civil servant when I was taken up by the definition of a civil servant as a "social scientist in action". This definition implied that the civil servant should go about his work in a scientific manner—trying to understand the deeper background of a problem or a situation in an objective manner, reflect upon it, read the relevant literature and then try to tackle it. So a civil servant should not only be dedicated and an idealist but also be a thinking administrator. This was a different approach than merely being a "professional". The latter is a more limited concept—a purely technocratic concept without any ideological connotation which I have always considered as inadequate for an administrator. The professional's starting point is a given objective or job which he should perform with competence. The administrator should constantly examine his objectives and job content to see whether they fulfill the larger social good.

I also believed that it was for the politicians in power to make proper use of talents and experience of a civil servant and not for the civil servants to curry favour with the politicians to secure coveted postings.

Price of Idealism

This posture of mine was bound to put me at odds and put me in uneasy relationships though often without my realizing it. Though I understood that I had to work in a hierarchical system, and be accountable to administrative and political authorities above me, I never considered that I was working for them. I was working for larger good—for the nation as a whole. I therefore could not serve the "higher authorities" in a blind manner doing whatever was necessary to please them or fulfill their desires or objectives no matter if they were not consistent with the higher objectives of administration. I could never adopt wrong methods with utter cynicism. There is often an idea prevalent that civil servants are mere mercenaries paid to do what they are asked to do. I could never accept such an idea. The public servant is not there to please his superiors—he is there to do a public duty. That is the difference between employees in a private enterprises and a public servant. For the former idealism in work may have no place. For the latter it is everything. That is why when a Revenue Minister of a supposedly socialist hue asked me to follow the "revenue" departments methods. (i.e. clever tricks) I got upset because I could never adopt either revenue methods or police methods (coercion).

I could never look myself as a servant of politicians in power to do their biddings or currying favour of my administrative superiors. My loyalty was not to them but to the nation. As I advanced in my career I slowly came to realize that the system would not take it well but I did not fully realize it till I found that as a result of my attitude my promotion to the post of Secretary to Govt. was being blocked.

At the same time I must say that despite my posture, I never came in open conflict with any politician or a politician minister. Only I could not become any body's favourite or a "blue-eyed boy". As more and more years passed the objective and impartial character of administration slowly changed and personal and partisan factors became more prominent. Administration became politicized. There emerged groups of civil servants attached to Ministers. Ministers would look for those civil servants who they felt were loyal to them despite the fact that such civil servants had no hesitation in changing their loyalties. Their loyalties were to their own career. Unfortunately such self-serving and clever civil servants always managed to be on the right side.

Politicisation of Civil Service

This phenomenon of civil servants giving up the traditional doctrine of political neutrality and aligning themselves with politicians and forming aligned groups—recently on caste basis—has been called "politicization" of civil service and has been the bane of the Indian Civil Service and has led to people losing their faith and confidence in the impartiality and objectivity of the civil service. I personally strongly believed in the sharp distinction Woodrow Wilson the scholar President of the US made between administration and politics. Dr. Rajendra Prasad the first President of free India put this distinction aptly when he said that "it is the business of politics to represent all interests and it is the business of administration to eliminate all interests" Sardar Patel the creator of IAS also believed in this independent role of the civil service. He told his Secretaries to give their independent advice without fear or favour. It was then for him (the minister) to take the final decision. Unfortunately Jawaharlal Nehru did not quite subscribe to these views and expressed his reservations regarding the neutrality of the civil service. But he did not mean to question neutrality in relation to politics; rather what he decried was neutrality in relation to the interest of the nation. But what is national interest? When his daughter, Indira Gandhi became Prime Minister she decided that national interest was what she perceived it to be and civil servants could not differ. Those who dare to differ would have to pay the price and they did. She unhesitatingly laid down the doctrine of a committed civil service. I wrote an article on "Committed Civil Service" which was published in *IJPA*. In retrospect I believe that I too had to pay the price for this open expression of views though only in an academic manner.

I do not mean to say that all politicians were crooks (politicians of the earlier generations were indeed the people of high standing) and all civil servants angels. Many believe that it is the civil servants who teach the politicians the wrong ways and later become active collaborators in their wrong doings. Politicians cannot succeed in their evil designs without the collaboration of evil civil servants. The upright ones either oppose and go down or remain neutral and look the other way.

Positive Role of Political Administrators

I never took upon myself the role of checkmating the politicians. That is not the role of the civil servants and they cannot succeed if they attempt to play the role because the ultimate power belongs to politicians and they know it. I came to realize that when it comes to crunch, politicians are effective while the civil servants are not and if convinced the politician administrator would do the right thing. When I got my first promotion from the level of Assistant Commissioner to that of Deputy Commissioner and when that was held up because of the protests of the officers of the Mysore Civil Service, I went to the Chief Secretary Ramanathiah who sharply told me not to be emotional but it was Finance Minister Mariyappa (who had held back the promotion order at the instance of Mysore Civil Service officers) who understood the strength of my emotions and allowed the promotion order to stand. When I was transferred as Under Secretary, Defense Ministry in GOI a post which was not to my liking (I thought I would have to work for and with Majors and Colonels rather than the common people), I approached Rebello the Chief Secretary who with cigarette in his mouth expressed his inability to do anything despite the pleading of my immediate boss Latif Razvi to retain me. When later I met Shri B.D. Jatti the Chief Minister at his residence Balabrooie, he appreciated my position and created a special position to enable me to stay on. When in the last phase of my career some crafty civil servants ganged up to cheat me of my legitimate claim to the ultimate elevation to the position of Secretary to Government of India, it was Shri Shankar Rao Chavan, the Education Minister, the then Chairman of the Executive Council of IIPA who sought an appointment with Indira Gandhi, the PM, got it, pleaded for my legitimate case and got the elevation cleared after all the senior civil servants whom I had earlier approached—Shri Krishnaswami Rao Saheb, the Cabinet Secretary, P.C. Alexander, the Principal Secretary to Prime Minister, T.N. Chaturvedi, the Home Secretary, and Shri K.V. Ramanathan the Secretary, Planning Commission, all left me down, not keeping their word. No wonder people attach greater credibility to the word of the politicians than that of the civil servants.

Development of Expertise

During all these years I consciously tried to develop expertise in every area in which I was called upon to work. When I entered into the administrative career,, I believed that Indian Administrative Service should consciously attempt to change the ICS generalist tradition and move to specialism since the scope of state activity would be widening and a generalist may not be able to deal with a wide range of subjects each one of which would require in depth knowledge and insight. There should be a conscious attempt towards career development. I wrote, early in my career, a comprehensive article on Indian administration after independence which was published in Calcutta's "*Modern Review*"—a journal which had gained considerable credibility. The article was republished, as Prof. Dixit from Dharwad told me later, in *Asian Survey*. In that article I had advocated the idea of "career development". But we in India developed a tendency to distort everything. That happened to the idea of career development as well. What the ambitious IAS officers soon discovered was that some posts provided possibilities of visits abroad and special perquisites. They became prize postings. Thus posts in Economic Affairs and other economic ministries and Commerce became coveted jobs and thus ambitious and cunning civil servants brought to bear influence to secure postings in these Ministries, leaving the straight forward non-influential civil servants to settle for other less prestigious ministries no matter how important they would be for nation building. Such maneuvering officers got into these prize posting without any sound knowledge of economics. The failure to match knowledge and experience with specialization brought down the standard of administration and brought bad name to IAS trying to throw about their weight in prestigious postings without requisite knowledge. I had a grievance that I had a first class first master's degree in economics, got very high marks (150 out of 200) in economic theory paper for IAS entrance examination, got a postgraduate qualification in economic administration of London School of Economics and yet was denied a career in economic administration because of the maneuvering ways of Indian administrators.

The specialization approach took a bizarre turn in the report of the study team of Administrative Reforms Commission. It argued that central services like Revenue Service, Audit & Accounts service, or Postal service had areas carved out for them. Similarly. IAS should also have an area carved out for them, *viz.* "land revenue". This was an attempt to downgrade IAS by jealous officers of other services. I did not agree with the approach and wrote an article on the subject which was published in the Indian Journal of Public Administration. But more practical and wily officers in the department of Personnel saw to it that the report was buried in the files of government without any further action. No open intellectual debate, only maneuvering. That became the way of IAS and Indian administration.

In my quest for specialization, I was not taken up by ambition of careerism—though in retrospect I feel I could have given greater attention to the latter! Whatever is good for the people was something which interested me greatly. The large majority of our people live in rural areas and it is their welfare which interested me greatly. My assignments came that way and gave me plenty of opportunities to serve in rural areas—first as SDO in two subdivisions and then as Deputy Commissioner—Director in a district and at a more senior stage as Divisional Commissioner and Administrator of Malaprabha and Ghataprabha projects. In all these field assignments I dealt with every single scheme and area of rural development—community development, extension services, cooperation, panchayati raj, small farmer and marginal farmers development programmes, poverty alleviation programmes, command area development, block and district level planning, and rural credit programmes of commercial banks and regional rural banks. My field work in various schemes of rural development was reinforced by policy making work as Deputy Secretary and Secretary in the State and Joint Secretary and Additional Secretary at the Center. But what was out of ordinary was contribution to thinking on these programmes through writing of large number of papers which were published in various journals devoted to rural development like *Kurukshetra, Indian Cooperative Reviews* and *Cooperator*, and *Indian Journal of Public Administration.* I also delivered innumerable addresses on theses programmes at a number of training programmes conducted by Lal Bahadur Shastri Academy of Administration, Mussorie, Indian Institute of Public Administration, Delhi, several state academies of administration, Vaikunth Mehta National Institute of Cooperative Management and state level cooperative training institutions. I headed or participated in committees relating to rural development like a team on Panchayat Raj and co-operation for Ashok Mehta Committee, on constitutional changes for strengthening Panchayat Raj, a committee on District Planning etc. I published a number of papers on Rural Development which were brought together in a book under the caption "Rural Development Administration" in the year 1970 as well as the book under the caption, "Policy and Performance"—agricultural and rural development in post independence India" brought out by the Sage Publication. My book "Principles and Philosophy of cooperation" was used in universities as also by training institutions abroad. Yet government. did not think of using my expertise by appointing me as Secretary, Rural Development or Secretary Agriculture. It only showed the scant importance that was attached to specialisation in government appointments. No wonder government work tended to be unprofessional and chinks in the knowledge of Secretaries became apparent. Dr Manmohan Singh once candidly told me that my talents were underutilized but did nothing to use them even when he was in a position to do so.

As the dependence of bureaucrats on the whims of politicians to secure appointments became apparent, they looked like sycophants and tended to lose prestige as professionals. The press started taking liberties with them by addressing them all the time as "Babus"—no better than mere clerks albeit in elevated positions. This kind of image of higher civil servants did great damage to the standing of administration in the country. My position was always different. I could not accept subservience and attitude of servility. Civil servants may be accountable to politicians holding positions in government. but they should not be servile. When serving in Secretariat, they should look upon themselves independent professional advisors—giving advice on the basis of their expertise and experience and not working to their bidding or serving their interests. They should not forget that Secretary is Secretary to Government. and not to Minister in a personal capacity. While in the field, the civil servants should act as independent administrators and not as hirelings of the party in power. But by acting according to these principles, I did not become a favourite of politicians in power and had to pay the price in getting overlooked in appointment to coveted positions in government.

Attitude to Common People

Civil servants tend to be servile to their superiors but high handed towards their subordinates and the common people who approach them – people who have no influential and powerful politicians to support. My attitude was just the opposite. I was invariably kind towards my subordinates and considerate and caring for the common people. *Nirbal Ke Balaram* – administrator is the power of the powerless was how I looked at me as an Administrator. My doors were always open to them. I never kept restricted hours for people to meet me. I was always aware that people were coming from distances and restricted hours could limit their access and thus inconvenience them. Administrators should always be accessible if they have to serve the people. This may be an interruption to the work on hand and inconvenience to the civil servants. But civil servants have facilities which common people do not have and should bear with inconvenience. My accessibility created wide satisfaction amongst common people and minimized public dissatisfaction. Whenever I served, I could see that strife and conflict arising out of dissatisfaction were avoided. Law and order depends not on the use of the coercive powers of the police but ever-vigilant people oriented administration.

Issue of Corruption

I always believed that it is right of the people to be served by the civil servants and the duty of the civil servants to serve them without expecting any illegal gratification. Administration should be clean without being tainted by corruption. Nowadays it is believed that administration is steeped in corruption – from top to bottom. The US secretary of Treasury in his recent visit to India openly stated that it is corruption which has made foreign investors reluctant to invest in India – corruption is a major deterrent to economic progress apart from polluting the society. Many reports have gone into causes of corruption – one of which is the low salaries of civil servants. After the fifth Pay Commission salaries of civil servants were steeply raised breaking the back of the public exchequer But has this brought down corruption? Corruption is not so much related to level of compensation as to the values upheld by administration and the society as a whole. Talking for myself, throughout my forty years of pubic service (thirty five years in IAS and five years as VC) I took no illegal gratification not because I rejected it but because it was never offered! What could account for it? Did it mean that throughout my service I held no post where there were no opportunities for corruption? That was not quite so. In my very first posting as Deputy Commissioner, Raichur, I had to hold excise sales which my excise officer had assured me was a gold mine for making a fortune. But no excise contractor approached me for underhand dealing. I was Secretary PWD & E albeit for a short while but no contractor approached me for any corrupt dealing. As Establishment Officer and in many other administrative assignments I had to deal with appointments and postings. Nowadays it is believed that corrupt money is offered in such cases but none was ever offered to me. I would therefore say that despite the talk of pervasive corruption, an honest officer can remain honest if he wishes to be He can work without any fear because honesty would be his shield. An honest officer may not be given any "prize" posting but that should not matter in the ultimate analysis. The reputation for honesty is enough to keep the corrupt at bay. Reputation for incorruptibility of a civil servant is a greater deterrent to corruption than a formal anti-corruption machinery.

Satisfaction of a Civil Service Career

As I look back at my career in the civil service, can I look back with satisfaction? I cannot say "Yes" It is undoubtedly true that in every assignment I had, I poured my heart and soul in it. There was no assignment I had which could be called sinecure. Indeed in most public assignments one had opportunities to serve the public I did justice to every assignment. I achieved results. I served the people or the "client group" with all the devotion I could bestow I contributed to the great process of development of the nation which under Nehru's leadership had become the main purpose of Indian administration.

Yet before my eyes, was the larger phenomenon of deteriorating standards of Indian administration. I must say that this was in the ultimate analysis the result of falling standards of Indian politics. If all the administrators had been honest and persons of integrity, the fall in the standard of administration could have been halted.

But that was too much to expect.

A career in civil service left me profoundly unhappy because ultimately one had to serve the politicians most of whom were lesser people. All the time one was required to be anonymous. (Civil servants, nowadays, do not choose to be so) One was restricted and inhibited by the government. servant's conduct rules. This creates a suffocating atmosphere. As is rightly said, if one is not allowed to express, ultimately one would left with nothing to express!

The civil servant is often described it as a horse which the politician rides. I never came to terms with such a view of a civil servant. Another civil servant had described the civil servant as a driver, not the owner of the vehicle. The civil servant has to drive in the direction the owner wishes to go. This view too was not to my liking. Should the civil servant be a mindless person with nothing to say about the direction in which the country should go? The essentially subordinate role of a civil servant can be damaging to the full flowering of the personality of the civil servant and can be profoundly unsatisfactory.

A career diplomat Shri B.K. Nehru had titled his autobiography—"Good guys finish second". This despite the prize assignments he got. After all he bore the magical "Nehru" name and higher echelons were his birthright. If he laments that he finished "second" what would others do who do not bear "Nehru" name and could not wangle the favour of politicians? They finish, third, fourth or even last!

But there are the rewards of the upright. Unlike in many other careers, a civil servant is not the servant of some "private" master. He serves the public. The public is his master. There cannot be greater reward than serving public interest. One would like to serve the public because this is reward in itself. The salary and perquisites are additional benefits! So one cannot regret a career in public service—whether one finishes "second" or last!